angles on

second edition

psychology

Julia Russell

Matt Jarvis

Phil Gorman

Text © Matt Jarvis, Julia Russell and Phil Gorman 2004

Original illustrations © Nelson Thornes Ltd 2004

Published in 2004 by:

Nelson Thornes Ltd
Delta Place
27 Bath Road
CHELTENHAM
GL53 7TH
United Kingdom

04 05 06 07 08/ 10 9 8 7 6 5 4 3 2 1

A catalogue record for this book is available from the British Library

ISBN 0 7487 8032 7

Illustrations by Ian Fraser Jackson and Oxford Designers and Illustrators
Page make-up by Pantek Arts Ltd, Maidstone, Kent
Printed and bound in Spain by Graficas Estella

contents

introduction

There are a number of reasons why we decided to write a second edition to the highly successful *Angles on Psychology*, first published in 2000. First, we wanted to make the text more useful to students taking Edexcel AS-level psychology – our main market. These examinations have been held for several years and it is now much clearer exactly what information students need to have at their fingertips. We have thus beefed-up sections dealing with key assumptions and research methods, and have made our discussion and 'for and against' sections more substantial. The 'research methods' chapter is more closely linked to coursework requirements. We have also added a new chapter, written by Edexcel Chief Examiner Phil Gorman, dealing with the question of how to approach the exams. (Edexcel officially endorses the second edition of *Angles*.)

The second reason for writing a new edition was to bring you the advantages of some of the latest developments in our understanding of learning. We want you to do well and we believe that a good textbook can make a difference. Our philosophy is that student achievement is based not on intelligence (there is almost no relationship between IQ and academic success) but on good study habits, motivation and thinking skills. A textbook like this can help you with all of these, especially if used in conjunction with a study guide. In our new introductory chapter we explain what psychology is but we also provide some useful information about how to go about studying it independently, locating sources of information and evaluating them critically. This is important because success is associated with taking an active role in your learning rather than just doing as your teachers say. Most importantly, we introduce you to critical thinking and provide you with a set of tools with which to evaluate the theories and studies that you will encounter in this book and elsewhere.

Psychology is interesting! This sounds obvious but an interest in a subject has a powerful effect on motivation to study, which will probably be the most important factor affecting your success. Time and time again we have seen AS-level students fall in love with psychology and work hard and independently, achieving grades their GCSE teachers wouldn't have believed possible. We have made *Angles* as interesting as possible by focusing on studies that are up-to-date and relevant to real life. We have also introduced elements of popular culture whenever possible. You will thus have the opportunity to look at the hidden meaning in pop lyrics, what makes people watch *Buffy* and why David Beckham is such a good role model for boys. People who are new to psychology or any other subject often find that they become lost in the sheer volume of new information they are learning. We have tried to use headings in such a way as to make the text as easy to follow as possible. However, if you find that you are losing your direction a useful tip is to return to the **what's ahead ?** at the start of the chapter or the *Conclusions* section at the end. This reminds you where you are and helps to organise your thoughts.

One development in the second edition is a major beefing-up of interactive features. These aim to develop thinking skills by helping you to engage with the material that you are studying. Our **media watch** features encourage you to apply psychological theory and research to real-life events as they are reported in the media. **interactive angles** aim to encourage you to step back for a moment and think about what you are learning. This might involve applying theory or research to a real-life situation or considering a problem from a different angle. **angling with the net** aims to develop Internet skills, either by guiding you to useful sites or giving you search tasks.

for Edexcel AS-level students

Angles on Psychology provides almost everything you need to prepare for your AS-level. The only other things you will need will be a specification (or a breakdown of it) and practice exam questions. The Edexcel specification is highly structured and it may be helpful to have a look at just how it breaks down.

Like all AS-levels, psychology is examined in three units. Units 1 and 2 are concerned with approaches to psychology and unit 3 is coursework, consisting of a psychological study designed, carried out and written up by you. Units 1 and 2 contain three approaches each.

unit 1	unit 2
The social approach	The learning approach
The cognitive approach	The psychodynamic approach
The cognitive-developmental approach	The physiological approach

You are required to know the following key aspects of each approach:

◆ key assumptions of the approach;

◆ key research methods that are particularly important in the approach;

◆ an in-depth area of study from the approach;

◆ at least two studies in detail from the approach (of your choice);

◆ a key application of the approach (specified);

◆ a contemporary issue in psychology (of your choice) that can be explained using ideas and research from the approach.

To help you follow the Edexcel specification, here is a table of terms (in *Angles on Psychology* we prefer to use some rather more user-friendly titles):

edexcel term	*angles* term
Key assumptions	What's it about?
Study in detail	Classic research (old) Research now (new)
Key application	Real lives
Contemporary issue	Talking points

Psychology is probably new to you and it might take it little time for it all to 'click'. Remember that motivation, good study habits and the development of critical thinking skills are the things that will secure you the grades you want. Spend plenty of time reading, both *Angles* and other sources of information, and practise your evaluation skills on every theory and study you find. Enjoy!

acknowledgements

The authors and publisher are grateful to the following for permission to reproduce material:

◆ Kevin Toolis (p.54)

◆ Oliver James (p.157)

◆ Phil Revell and the *Times Educational Supplement* (p.80)

◆ *The Guardian* (p.49, p.137)

◆ *The Independent* (p.15)

◆ *The Observer* (p.27, p.38, p.122)

◆ *The People* (p.104)

◆ *Times Educational Supplement* (p.119)

Every effort has been made to contact copyright holders and we apologise if anyone has been overlooked.

photo credits:
Alamy Images/A Woolfitt: pp.40–41; Alamy Images/ Pedro Luz Cunha: pp.2–3, pp.100–101, pp.134–135; Albert Bandura: p.121; Alexandra Milgram: p.12 (bottom); Ardea/Chris Harvey: p.118 (bottom); Art Directors & Trip Photo Library: p.7, p.24, p.68–69, pp.164–165, p.175 (top), p.193; Associated Press: p.20, p.106 (top); BBC Photo Library: p.33 (top); B F Skinner Foundation: p.110; Corbis Images: p.84, p.102; Corel 145 (NT): p.18; Corel 184 (NT): p.52; Corel 712 (NT): p.148 (bottom); Davidson Films: p.83; Digital Stock 12 (NT): p.173; Dumbleton Photographers, Cambridge, UK: p.87; Education Photos/John Walmsley: p.118 (top), pp.242–243; Hulton Archive: p.59 (top); Illustrated London News V1 (NT): p.37 p.136; Image 100 37 (NT): p.95, p.131; John Birdsall Photography: p.116; JORVIK: p.53; Kobal: p.106 (bottom), p.128, p.153; Kobal/Paramount Pictures: p.78; Nat Photos/Digital Vision AF (NT): p.184; Offside Sports Photography: pp.10–11, p.32; Photofusion: p.33 (bottom), p.89; Photofusion/Robert Brook: p.125, p.185; Rex Features Ltd: p.15, p.59 (bottom), p.61, p.104, p.112, p.122, p.137, p.139; Rubberball WW (NT): p.194; Sally & Richard Greenhill: pp.202–203; Science Photo Library: p.47, p.70, p.167, p.168, p.174, p.175 (bottom); Slumber Bedtime Milk/Red Kite Farms: p.181; Stephen Frink/Digital Vision AF (NT): p.138; Stockpix 4 (NT): p.148 (top); Topham Picturepoint: p.12 (top), p.119; Topham Picturepoint/ UPPA: p.27; Vin Mag Archive: p.159 (both); Wellcome Trust Medical Picture Library: p.103.

Picture research by Sue Sharp

what's ahead?

In this introductory chapter we look briefly at some of the things you should know a little about before continuing to study psychology. We define psychology and explain why it comprises so many approaches. We also explain the differences between the key terms 'theory', 'study' and 'research method'. Crucially, we introduce you to ways to evaluate psychological material and we try to prepare you to think critically about the theories, studies and research methods that you will encounter throughout this book. Finally, we explain our ideas about the place of a book like this in the study of psychology, and we offer some advice on where else to look for information about psychology.

what is psychology?

Psychology is often defined as the 'science of mind and behaviour'. By this we mean that it is the study of how people (and sometimes animals) behave and how their minds work. The subject matter of psychology is extremely wide-ranging, covering everything from what makes David Beckham such a good role model (chapter 5) to why so many people watch *Buffy the Vampire Slayer!* (chapter 6). One thing to which you need to get used to immediately if you are going to study psychology is the range of different approaches we can bring to bear on it. Chapters 2 to 7 introduce you to six particularly important approaches to psychology. Table 1.1 summarises them briefly.

approach	description	examples of real-life applications
Social	Concerned with how people interact and how individuals, groups and society and culture at large influence us.	Understanding and reducing prejudice.
Cognitive	Concerned with the workings of mental processes such as thinking and memory, which we use to make sense of information.	Understanding and improving the accuracy of eyewitness testimony.
Cognitive-developmental	Concerned with how mental processes develop with age – for example how thinking changes from infancy through childhood to adulthood.	Understanding and improving the education system.
Learning	Concerned with how we learn behaviours, for example by associating different events and observing others.	Altering behaviour to make it more desirable.
Psychodynamic	Concerned with the influence of the unconscious mind – mental processes of which we are not normally aware.	Understanding the influence of early experiences on mental health.
Physiological	Concerned with the relationship between biological processes, in particular the workings of the brain, and psychological functions.	Understanding and reducing the impact of factors like jet lag and shift work, which disrupt brain function and hence have psychological effects.

table 1.1 Six major approaches to psychology

Some psychologists work very much within a framework of one particular approach. Thus social psychologists may think very much in social terms and bring social-psychological theory and research to bear on a range of problems. Others draw freely on a range of approaches and are said to be *eclectic*.

theories, studies and research methods

There are many technical terms to learn as you study psychology. Before you go any further it is worth being absolutely clear about three terms in particular. As examiners we have seen many knowledgeable students fail to achieve their potential because, in the examination, they wrote about a theory when the question asked for a study, or a study when the question required a research method. All psychology will make more sense when you are clear about the distinction between theories, studies and research methods.

what is a theory?

A theory is an *explanation* for a psychological phenomenon. Some theories (for example Freud's theory, see p. 136) are very ambitious, aiming to explain almost everything about human nature. Others are much narrower, seeking to explain something very specific. For example, the multi-store model of memory (p. 43) just aims to show that human memory involves more than one system.

It is important to remember that, although there are usually several different theories concerned with a phenomenon, our task is *not* to choose the correct theory and discard the others. Often, different theories are concerned with different aspects of the same broad area. For example, in chapter 2 we look at two theories of obedience. Milgram's agency theory is an attempt to explain why people have a general tendency to obey the orders of people in authority. Charismatic leadership on the other hand is concerned with explaining why some people seem to be particularly successful in obtaining obedience. These theories are complementary rather than rivals because each explains a different aspect of obedience.

what is a study?

A study is any exercise where data (information) are gathered and analysed. This is quite a different idea from a theory. There are many different studies, and you will encounter more studies than anything else as you learn about psychology. Some studies aim to test a theory. Others just gather information about a psychological phenomenon. A classic example of a study is Hofling et al.'s investigation of nurses' obedience to doctors (p. 14). This involved gathering two types of data from nurses. First, they were asked how they thought they would behave if ordered by a doctor to do something that would harm a patient. Secondly, they were actually put in that position and their behaviour recorded. Studies should tell us something useful. For example, Hofling et al.'s study showed how nurses tended to follow doctors' orders unquestioningly and that this obedience could sometimes pose a danger to patients.

what is a research method?

Studies make use of one or more research methods – techniques for gathering and/or analysing data. These methods are discussed in detail in chapters 2–7. You will come across a range of research methods in this book, some being particularly associated with particular approaches to psychology. For example surveys and field experiments are particularly associated with social psychology. This is not to say that they are only used in social psychology, or that social psychologists rely on them alone; just that they have a particular role in that area.

interactive
angles

Look up each of the following and identify them as a theory, a study or a research method.

◆ Milgram's idea of agency (p. 16).

◆ Case studies of brain-damaged patients (p. 45).

◆ Naughty Teddy (p. 76).

◆ Field experiments (p. 14).

◆ Little Albert (p. 107).

◆ Erikson's psychosocial development (p. 150).

learning to think critically about psychological material

Assessments in psychology (such as examinations) test two main abilities. First, you have to be able to describe psychological material, such as theories and studies, clearly, accurately and in sufficient detail. This is quite a straightforward task if you have learnt the material and you understand the question. However, there is another more difficult skill to develop: the *evaluation* of psychological material. This means being able to identify its strengths and weaknesses and to identify any other issues attached to it. If you are studying A-level then you need to be aware that evaluation is worth 40% of AS-level marks and 60% of A2 marks. The ability to evaluate is what really distinguishes students who achieve grades A, C and E.

evaluating theories

Although we help you in this book with discussion sections and 'for and against' summary boxes, try to avoid simply learning these evaluations parrot fashion. Try, instead, to ask yourself the following questions every time you encounter a theory:

◆ **On what sort of evidence is this theory based?** A theory might not apply to everybody equally well if it is derived from a few unrepresentative cases. If it is based on laboratory studies then it might not explain people's behaviour in real-life situations.

◆ **Is this theory testable?** If it is difficult to test then this is a weakness.

◆ **Is there supporting evidence?** Have you found studies that could be used to support the theory or does it seem to be based just on speculation?

◆ **Is there conflicting evidence?** Are there studies that suggest that the theory is incorrect or at least limited in what it can explain?

◆ **Is the theory useful?** Does it have applications for understanding or intervening in a real-life situation?

◆ **Is the theory socially sensitive?** By this we mean, is the theory likely to offend people, perhaps because it places blame on someone for a psychological phenomenon, or because it identifies something undesirable about human nature?

◆ **Is there something important that this theory cannot explain?** A common limitation of theories is the inability to explain all aspects of the phenomenon – for example why people vary so much individually.

interactive
angles

Turn to Milgram's agency theory (p. 16). Consider the theory in terms of each of the seven questions. Some will be more applicable than others but by going through them all you should be able to compile quite a detailed evaluation.

figure 1.1
The Thinker

interactive
angles

Turn to Milgram's famous study of destructive obedience (p. 12). Consider each of the seven questions with regard to Milgram's study. Again, some will be more important than others but see how far you can build a detailed evaluation.

evaluating studies

There are so many studies in a book like this that it is impossible to evaluate all of them. However, you can acquire the habit of asking yourself the following questions whenever you encounter a study:

◆ **Has this study been conducted ethically?** Have participants been put at risk, been taken advantage of, had their privacy invaded or in some other way had their rights violated? See p. 223 for a detailed account of the British Psychological Society code of ethics.

◆ **Are the findings socially sensitive?** Do the findings of the study risk offence to people because they place blame on particular people or justify discrimination against a vulnerable group?

◆ **Has the study involved a representative group of people?** If, as is often the case, researchers have used their own students as participants, how representative are students of the population? Have men and women and people of a good range of ages participated?

◆ **Has it been carried out in an artificial environment or a natural one?** If the study was carried out in a laboratory can we be sure that participants behaved as they would in their own surroundings?

◆ **Are the tasks given to participants like the tasks they would encounter in real life?** A common limitation of research is putting participants in situations or giving them things to do that bear little resemblance to their real lives.

◆ **How good are the measures used to record the results?** For example if the study used a questionnaire, was it a standard one widely accepted by psychologists or did the researchers make it up for the study? If it is a standard measure this is an advantage.

◆ **Do the findings of this study conflict with those of other studies?** If so, think about how the findings are different and try to explain why they differ. You might be able to suggest which study was better designed and to which results we should accord more importance.

Of course in some cases there are specific criticisms you might want to make about a theory or study. For example, you might wish to quote what another psychologist has said about it. That is fine, but don't try to learn specific criticisms for every theory and study – there is too much information.

other sources of information about psychology

Although we have put this book together with a lot of care, the last thing you should do is accept everything we say. That might sound a little odd! However, it is important to realise that different writers in psychology see things in slightly different ways. When we cover a theory like Piaget's (p. 70) or Freud's (p. 136) we summarise a few key ideas out of several decades of work. It is inevitable that every writer will select slightly different material and present it slightly differently. Ultimately this means that if you study psychology to a high level you should read the original material rather than relying on textbooks like this. If you are studying at a relatively introductory level then that is a little harsh and you will need to rely on people like us to give you a fair picture of the field. However, it is *always* worth reading a range of books rather than just one. Apart from anything else, it is valuable to see how different writers have different opinions about psychology. There are many good general psychology texts available. We can advise you on a few other good sources of information.

journals

New research is published in a huge variety of journals. Most of these are very advanced and difficult to read but a few are well worth considering even if you are new to psychology. *Psychology Review* is aimed specifically at pre-degree level students and carries articles by leading experts that are pitched at people who are fairly new to psychology. *The Psychologist* is rather more advanced but, unlike most journals, is pitched at those without a detailed knowledge of specialist areas in psychology and it can therefore be fairly readable for students new to the subject. The British Psychological Society also publishes *Psych-Talk*, a newsletter put together by student members. This contains articles by university students and interviews with experts. Like *Psychology Review* it should be relatively easy to read.

the Internet

There is a huge range of material on psychology available online. Beware of some pitfalls however. Much of the material on the Web is generated by amateurs and contains serious inaccuracies. Even some of the material on sites designated .ac.uk (British universities and colleges) or .edu (American universities) has been posted by students and can be unreliable. We would advise using the Internet in three main ways:

◆ When you see a news story that interests you because it relates to some psychology you have studied, try putting key words into a general search engine like *Google*. Some newspapers and broadcasters have their own search engines to locate material they have publicised, and these can also be searched. The *BBC*, the *Guardian* and the *Times Educational Supplement* all have such search facilities.

◆ There are organisations that have good Web pages and have links to other good sources of information. The *British Psychological Society* and the *American Psychological Association* are perhaps the best general sources of information and links but, of course, there are sites devoted to areas within psychology. There are for example institutions devoted to key figures such as Freud and Piaget (see for example *The Freud Museum*, the *British Psychoanalytic Society* and the *Jean Piaget Society* Web sites). You can easily locate all these by means of a Google search.

◆ There are some online databases that give access to summaries of the latest psychological research. The best known of these are PsycINFO and MEDLINE. Unfortunately you are unlikely to gain access to these without a password, which is difficult and expensive to obtain. However, try to find PUBMED. This is a medical database that is not password protected, and it gives access to some good psychological material.

angling
with the net

Try some Internet searching now. Take Stanley Milgram, who is best known for studying obedience.

◆ Locate and look at the Stanley Milgram Web site.

◆ Locate the *Guardian* and BBC Web sites and search there for recent articles mentioning obedience.

◆ Locate the British Psychological Society Web site and see what Milgram or obedience-related links you can find.

◆ Locate PUBMED and input 'obedience' as a search term.

conclusions

There are several things you should know about psychology before starting to study it. Be aware that there are different approaches to the subject and that each treats it as something slightly different. Know your key terms. In particular be clear about the difference between a theory, a study and a research method. Rather than learning criticisms of every theory and study parrot fashion, develop your skills of critical thinking and learn to evaluate all psychological material whenever you encounter it. Finally, seek information from a variety of sources and don't worry when they present the same idea differently, or when different writers have different opinions on a topic. In particular learn how to use the Internet effectively.

what's it about ?

key assumptions

The social approach is based on the following ideas:

◆ Other individuals influence our behaviour. There are numerous ways in which we are subject constantly to the influence of other people. In this chapter we explore the example of obedience. Research has found that we are remarkably obedient to individuals whom we perceive as figures of authority. In addition, some individuals are particularly skilled at gaining our obedience.

◆ Groups also affect us in many ways. For example, we respond differently to people according to the nature of the groups to which they belong and we tend to display favouritism towards members of groups to which we also belong.

◆ Other people's influence on us is not limited to the individuals and groups we encounter directly. Our culture exerts more subtle influences of which we might not normally be aware. One way in which culture influences us is through *discourse* – the way we use language. In this chapter we explore discourse as an explanation for prejudice.

◆ Social-psychological research is highly varied in nature, ranging from the use of laboratory and field experiments, surveys and discourse analysis.

what's ahead?

This chapter is about social psychology and the social approach to psychology. Social psychology is the study of the ways in which people affect one another. A social approach to psychology is any approach that emphasizes the influence of human society or social situations on human behaviour as opposed to the influence of genes, learning, information processing or early relationships. In this chapter we will look at two classic areas of social psychology: obedience and prejudice. In our *real lives* section we can look at ways in which we can apply psychological theory and research to tackle the problem of prejudice and in *talking points* we can look from a social-psychological perspective at two topics of current interest: genocide and the growing use of the Internet.

obedience

Obedience means the following of orders. When we obey an order we do as we are told. Technically, obedience is distinct from *compliance*, which means going along with suggestions or instructions, and *conformity*, which means adopting the attitudes and behaviours of those around us. Although we like to think of ourselves as free and independent, most of the time a degree of obedience is probably a good thing. If we did not usually obey road signs and traffic lights there would be carnage every time we took to the streets, and if students didn't do what their teachers say (some of the time anyway) they would probably make little headway with their studies. However, there is a downside to our tendency to obey; when we are ordered to do something immoral we frequently obey, even if this causes us distress and we bitterly regret doing so later. This phenomenon is known as *destructive obedience*.

figure 2.1
Sixty years after the Holocaust the world remains shocked at scenes like this

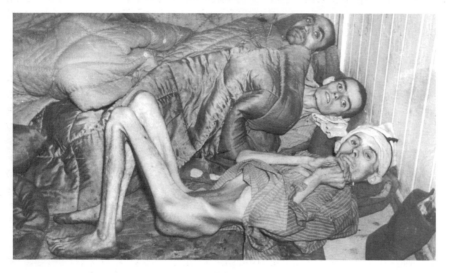

The attention of psychologists turned to destructive obedience following the Holocaust of the 1940s, in which the Nazis and their collaborators obeyed unquestioningly when ordered to perform monstrous acts, including the extermination of several million Jews, Romanies, communists and trade unionists. Stanley Milgram was one of an international network of researchers committed to investigating the psychology underlying the Holocaust with the intention of preventing anything like it happening again. Early attempts to explain the Holocaust focused on the idea that there was something distinctive about German culture that had allowed the Holocaust to take place. Milgram initially set out to test the idea that the German people were unusual in their response to orders from authority figures but he quickly found that people in general are surprisingly obedient to people in authority.

the Milgram studies

Milgram (1963) set out to investigate how obedient people would be in a situation where following orders would mean breaking participants' moral codes and harming another person. In his original study, Milgram advertised for male volunteers to take part in a memory experiment for a fee of $4. When the 40 participants arrived at the university, they were told they would be either a teacher or a learner. They were then introduced to 'Mr Wallace', a mild-mannered and pleasant middle-aged man as a fellow participant (in fact he was an actor working for Milgram). By fiddling an apparently random procedure, Milgram ensured that the participant was always the teacher and 'Mr Wallace' was always the learner.

figure 2.2
Milgram's study

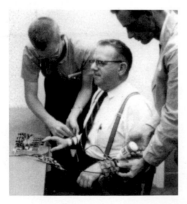

Mr Wallace was then strapped into a chair and given a memory task involving remembering pairs of words. Every time Wallace made a mistake Milgram ordered the participant to give him an electric shock. Of course there were no real shocks but there was no way for the participant to realise this. Following each mistake the level of the 'shock' appeared to increase. The shock levels on the machine were labelled from 0 to 450 volts and also had signs saying 'danger – severe shock' and, at 450 volts, 'XXX'. Milgram ordered participants to continue giving increased shocks whilst the learner shouted and screamed in pain then appeared to collapse. When participants protested Milgram told them 'the experiment requires that you continue'.

To Milgram's great surprise, all the participants gave Mr Wallace at least 300 volts (more than you would receive from the mains supply in Britain), and 65% went the distance, giving the full 450 volts to an apparently dead Mr Wallace! Most of the participants protested and some wept and begged in their distress, obviously believing that they had killed Mr Wallace. However most people did not feel that they could stop when ordered to continue by Milgram. The minority of participants who defied Milgram showed particular signs of stress as they agonised over their decision; however this disappeared once they had made their decision to disobey. This dramatic study demonstrates the power of authority over our behaviour. What is particularly remarkable about the results is that participants were clearly very upset by what they had to do but *saw no alternative except to obey*.

variations on the original procedure

In a series of variations on the original experiment, Milgram found that the circumstances affected the percentage of people who would follow orders to the point of killing. When the setting was moved from a prestigious university to a run-down office block the number of people willing to give 450-volt shocks declined to 47.5%. When Milgram gave orders by telephone from another room the percentage dropped to 20.5%. When the teacher was required to force Mr Wallace's hand down on to an electrode, the percentage willing to go to 450 volts was 30%. We can see, then, that the situation is important in determining how obedient we are to authority.

⟳ discussion

Milgram's studies were of great value to the world as they showed, contrary to most people's expectations, that most of us have a tendency towards destructive obedience. This has helped us understand historical events, such as the Holocaust, in which large numbers of people obeyed orders that required them to breach the moral codes by which they normally lived. Nonetheless, some psychologists criticised Milgram on the basis of the ethics of his studies. Participants were deceived, denied the right to withdraw from the study and subjected to distress. In response to these concerns Milgram was briefly suspended from the American Psychological Association. However, he was reinstated after an investigation, which concluded that he had taken care to check the welfare of each participant following the procedure and that his work was sufficiently important to justify his methods.

There have also been methodological criticisms of Milgram's work. He carried out his studies under laboratory conditions and gave participants a task that they do not normally come across in everyday life. Thus the situation in which participants found themselves was in some ways quite artificial. However, many features of the experiment reproduced quite accurately the features of destructive obedience in real life. As a scientist running an experiment, Milgram was in a position of legitimate authority and, dressed as scientist and based in a university laboratory, he had the trappings of authority. In some ways this made him comparable to a military commander with a title and uniform.

In some ways, however, there is no doubt that some features of Milgram's procedure differed from the situations in which destructive obedience takes place in real life. For example, Milgram assured participants that, although the shocks were painful, Mr Wallace would come to no real harm. That is very different from, say, the position of a Nazi concentration camp guard who could have no doubt that his charges would die as a result of his actions.

later studies of obedience

Other studies, including those carried out in real-life settings, have confirmed that people have a remarkable tendency to obey those in authority. One real-life setting where a degree of obedience is necessary for smooth running is in medicine. In a classic field experiment, Hofling et al. (1966) demonstrated that nurses would obey doctors even when doing so would be likely to endanger patients.

angling with the net

Why not visit the Milgram Web site, currently **www.stanleymilgram.com**? See what further details of his experiments you can add to your notes.

the social approach

classic research
studies in detail

playing doctors and nurses

Hofling, K. C., Brotzman, E., Dalrymple, S., Graves, N. and Pierce, C. M. (1966)
An experimental study in the nurse-physician relationship. *Journal of Nervous and Mental Disorders*, **143**, 171–180.

Aim: researchers were interested in whether nurses would obey a doctor when doing so would breach hospital regulations and endanger the lives of patients.

Procedure: boxes of capsules labelled 'Astrofen' were placed with other medicines in 22 wards in American hospitals. In the capsules was glucose, harmless to most patients, however the label identified the maximum safe daily dose as 10 mg. A researcher calling himself 'Dr Smith from the psychiatric department' telephoned nurses on duty on each ward and instructed them to give a patient, Mr Jones, 20 mg of Astrofen. Although written authorization was normally required before nurses were allowed give drugs, Dr Smith said that he was running late and would come and sign the necessary authorization shortly. Meanwhile 22 other nurses not involved in the field experiment were interviewed and asked whether, if a doctor telephoned when they were on duty and instructed them to administer more than the maximum safe dose, they would do so.

Findings: 21 of the 22 nurses interviewed said that they would not obey the doctor's instructions, yet 21 of the 22 nurses told by telephone to give a large dose of Astrofen did so. When questioned later, 11 of these nurses said that they had not noticed the discrepancy between the maximum dose and the dose they were told to give. The other 10 did notice it but judged that it must be safe if the doctor ordered them to give it.

Conclusion: although the nurses believed that they would not obey a doctor unquestioningly if they were ordered to do something that breached regulations and endangered patients, in fact they did just that.

research methods

field experiments

The Hofling et al. study is a classic example of a field experiment, a research method commonly used in social psychology. Like all experiments, field experiments involve the manipulation of an independent variable to test its effect on the dependent variable. What distinguishes the field experiment is that this all takes place in the participants' natural environment. This is particularly important when studying social behaviour because social behaviour varies according to the situation. By testing nurses' obedience in a hospital rather than in a laboratory Hofling et al. were able to capture their real-life behaviour. This is obviously an advantage of field experiments, but they also have their drawbacks.

◆ Field experiments interfere with participants' everyday lives and may have unforeseen consequences. For example, what if a nurse, distracted by the researcher's unexpected order, made an error with another patient?

◆ Participants do not generally have the opportunity to give their permission to take part in a field experiment.

◆ It is hard to control all the conditions when experiments are carried out outside the laboratory. This means that other variables may creep in and affect results.

More recent research has continued to demonstrate our tendency to obey. Influenced by early studies such as that of Hofling et al., some research still focuses on the doctor-nurse relationship. Krackow and Blass (1995) gave 68 American nurses a questionnaire asking them about the last time they had disagreed with a doctor's order. Two factors emerged as influencing the nurses' decision whether to obey or disobey. The most important factor was the authority of the doctor: most nurses obeyed the order because they recognized the doctor as a legitimate authority with a right to make the decision. However, their responses were also influenced by the seriousness of the consequences to the patient. Where these were serious the nurses were more likely to take responsibility for the decision themselves and challenge the order.

Another area where obedience research has important implications is in accident prevention. Tarnow (2000) has suggested that many accidents occur when the people in a crisis situation with the best information on which to base decisions follow orders from those in authority who have less information on which to base their orders. Tarnow analysed the records from 37 plane crashes and suggested that 25% of them were the direct result of pilots following orders from the ground in spite of their being aware that the orders were a mistake. In *media watch* we can look at a real-life example of this.

media watch

Russian pilot obeyed wrong instructions

By Barrie Clement, *Independent*, 9 July 2002

The Russian pilot involved in a mid-air crash last week that killed 71 people was given conflicting orders by Swiss air traffic control and his automatic warning system, German investigators said yesterday.

Ground staff told the pilot to dive to avoid an oncoming cargo plane, but the TCAS on-board crash-avoidance device ordered the plane to climb. The pilot of the Tupolev 154 airliner, Alexander Gross, obeyed the second command from controllers to descend and 30 seconds later crashed into a Boeing 757 freight jet.

Voice recorders recovered from fragments of the two planes scattered across the Swiss-German border showed that the on-board system on the Boeing had told its pilot to climb. The systems are designed to communicate so that aircraft are sent in opposite directions to avoid a collision.

If the Russian pilot had obeyed the machine rather then the air traffic controller, the disaster might have been avoided.

figure 2.3
Up to 25% of plane crashes may result from pilots mistakenly obeying orders

questions

Based on the studies you have read so far, suggest why the Russian pilot might have obeyed the air traffic controller and not his instruments.

explanations for obedience

We can look at two very different explanations for the phenomenon of obedience. Milgram (1974) has proposed a broad theory for our general tendency to obey people whom we identify as being in positions of authority. An alternative angle on explaining obedience comes from studies of *charismatic leaders* – people who seem to have exceptional abilities to command obedience in others.

Milgram's agency theory

Milgram (1974) proposed that our general tendency to obey those whom we perceive to be in authority is a mechanism for maintaining a stable society. For us to exist in complex societies we need social rules, and keeping to these rules requires that we give up a degree of our free will – at least some of the time. Milgram proposed that, in order to accomplish this, we have evolved two social states. In the *autonomous state* we are free to act as we wish, including how our conscience dictates. However in our *agentic state* we surrender our free will and conscience in order to serve the interests of the wider group. When we are in an agentic state we see ourselves as primarily the agents of those in authority and only secondarily as individuals.

We are socialised into developing the capacity for the agentic state during childhood. In school, we learn to put aside our individual wishes in favour of maintaining order, putting the good of the class as a whole first. Milgram believed that, like children in the classroom, we are all constantly subordinating our own needs and wishes to those of society. We can see this tendency in our job-related behaviour. In theory, most people would say that they work for their own benefit and would not go out of their way for their employers. In reality however, once people are in a job and they identify themselves as part of an organisation, they have a tendency to put the needs of their employers above their own.

The strategies we use to deal with *moral strain* are an important aspect of the agentic state. Moral strain results when we have to do something we believe to be immoral in order to function as an agent of authority, and so benefit society. Milgram suggested that we use defence mechanisms (see chapter 6) to avoid the distress of having to perform acts we would normally find abhorrent. *Denial* was found to be particularly common in participants in the Milgram studies, and in the Holocaust as perpetrators refused to confront what they were doing.

for+against

agency theory

+ The idea that obedience serves the function of allowing complex human societies to develop makes sense. It has *face validity*. It also neatly explains a range of real-life situations in which people obey orders, and it explains the results of studies like those of Milgram and Hofling.

+ There is direct support for agency theory from studies such as Blass (1996), which show that people do not see those obeying orders as responsible for their actions.

− The idea of an identifiable agentic state has proved very difficult to pin down. Simply saying that people are in an agentic state because they obey and that they obey because they are in an agentic state is circular logic.

− Agency theory does not explain individual differences in obedience, for example why some people did not obey Milgram. Nor does it explain easily why some people carrying no more authority are so skilled at commanding obedience.

➋ discussion

Agency theory explains a wide range of social behaviours, ranging from how we act at work to the way in which peaceful people can go to war and, of course, how 'normal' people become involved in atrocities such as the Holocaust. The idea of moral strain explains Milgram's finding that the minority of dissenters in his studies showed signs of stress while deciding whether to obey, but not after making the decision to disobey.

Agency theory is also supported by studies showing that we attribute less responsibility to actors following orders than people acting of their own free will. In one study, Blass (1996) showed students an edited film of Milgram's study and questioned them about the relative responsibility of Milgram and his participants in administering shocks. Participants identified Milgram in the role of authority figure and attributed responsibility for the treatment of Mr Wallace to him rather than themselves. This supports agency theory because the participants were seen as in an agentic state and therefore not to blame for their actions.

A limitation of agency theory is that it does not easily explain individual differences in obedience or in the ability of leaders to command obedience from subordinates. Remember that a significant minority of Milgram's participants held their ground and did not obey him. Bear in mind, too, that some leaders, known as *charismatic* or *transformational* leaders seem to have a remarkable ability to persuade people to obey their wishes.

media watch

do as you're told

By Nicci Gerrard, *Observer Review*, 12 October 1997

You wouldn't attach electrodes to her. Or dip her in boiling water. Or hold a gun to her head and pull the trigger. No, not you . . . What would you do for £1m? Would you bully someone, or cheat them? Hurt them a little? Hurt them a lot? If you were out of the room, and administering pain by remote control, would that make it easier? What would you do for £100 000? Or £1000? What would you do just because someone in authority told you to?

CP Snow wrote that 'more hideous crimes have been committed in the name of obedience than have ever been committed in the name of rebellion.'

In the early hours of 13 July 1942, the 500 men of the German Reserve Police Force Battalion 101 – middle-aged family men, too old for the army, barely trained and stationed in Poland – were addressed by their leader, Commander Trapp. In a voice shaky with distress he told them of their next assignment: to seek out and kill the 1800 women and children in the nearby village of Jozefow. Then, astonishingly, Trapp told them he knew what a repugnant task some might find it, and that anyone could stand out with no punishment and no reprisals. Out of 500, only 12 men stood out.

During that terrible day, a further 10–20% managed to evade their duty; many more became distressed but continued to carry out the orders. Quite a few exhibited no signs of distress. A few seemed to enjoy themselves.

We are necessarily bred into obedience the moment we are born. How else does a society operate? Politeness and embarrassment are important factors, as is the unwillingness to let someone down. The absorption in the technical aspects of the task makes us lose our sense of what we are doing. We easily fool ourselves that we are not to blame – divesting ourselves of authority and attributing it to a legitimate authority, so that we become a simple agent: 'I was just doing my job'.

questions

1 What parallels can you see between the responses of the men of Battalion 101 and those of Milgram's participants?

2 Explain the events of 13 July 1942 using Milgram's agency theory.

charismatic leadership

House et al. (1991) define charisma as 'the ability of a leader to exercise diffuse and intensive influence over the beliefs, values, behaviour and performance of others' (1991, p. 366). It appears that some leaders can induce especially high levels of obedience. This extraordinary obedience can have positive or negative consequences according to the situation. On the downside, charisma enhances people's tendency towards destructive obedience and it seems likely that Hitler's charisma may have contributed to obedience in Nazi Germany, permitting the Holocaust. Historically, many of the national leaders that we associate with particularly violent or immoral actions – including Hitler, Stalin and Thatcher – were charismatic leaders. However, we should remember that charismatic leadership can also bring about positive change, as evinced by the achievements of Ghandi and Martin Luther King.

We can understand charisma both in terms of the characteristics of leaders and the relationship they have with their followers. House et al. (1991) identified charismatic leaders as having excellent communication skills, a high level of concern for the needs of their followers and a mastery of impression management (the skill of making others see us as we wish them to). These attributes all help in obtaining obedience. However, personal characteristics seem to be only part of the story and most contemporary social psychologists place more weight on the *processes* by which charismatic leaders obtain obedience from others. Such leaders tend to establish a clear vision of what they are trying to achieve and how they intend to achieve it. This enhances the motivation of followers to obey their instructions. Charismatic leaders also tend to frame their orders in terms of achieving their goal, so that there are clear reasons to obey them. Charismatic leaders also tend to use emotive language that fires up followers to the extent that they tend to obey instructions without pausing to reflect on them.

◔ discussion

Studies have supported House's idea that charisma is associated with vision and particular social skills. Berson et al. (2001) assessed charisma in 141 community leaders and videotaped them speaking to their communities. A strong correlation emerged between charisma and the strength of their 'vision'. Another recent study by Cherulnik et al. (2001) demonstrated the importance of facial expression in arousing a response from followers – see *research now*.

research now
studies in detail

you've either got it or you haven't!

Cherulnik, P. D., Donley, K. A., Wiewel, T. S. R. and Miller, S. (2001) Charisma is contagious: the effect of leaders' charisma on observers' affect. *Journal of Applied Social Psychology*, **31**, 2149–2159.

Aim: to test the idea that the skills of non-verbal communication associated with charisma, including smiling and visual attention, lead to an emotional response in listeners.

Procedure: two studies were performed. In the first, 84 students gave speeches intended to simulate political campaign speeches. The duration and intensity of their smiles were recorded, as was the time spent directing their gaze to the audience. The emotional responses of their audience were also recorded. In the second study, 22 students watched excerpts of former American presidents George Bush Senior and Bill Clinton engaged in a public debate. The smiling and visual attention of Bush and Clinton and the emotional responses of the student audience were recorded.

Findings: the two studies showed very much the same thing; emotional responses in audiences were associated with both duration and intensity of smiling and with time spent directing gaze towards the audience. Clinton displayed these skills more effectively than did Bush.

Conclusions: charisma, as measured by facial expression during public speaking, was associated with emotional responses in listeners. This suggests that the key to charisma is the ability to arouse such responses.

figure 2.4
Bill Clinton was a charismatic leader

Charisma does not belong to political leaders exclusively. Business benefits from using charismatic leaders to boost productivity. In a recent study Geyer and Speyrer (1997) measured the charisma of managers in 116 Austrian banks, using reports from a total of 1456 employees, and found a strong relationship between charisma and the productivity of the bank. It thus appears that introducing a charismatic manager is an extremely effective way of increasing productivity in a workforce.

It is important to understand the relationship between charisma and obedience because many of those who demand our obedience – such as politicians – use charisma to obtain our obedience. However, charisma is clearly not a complete explanation for obedience. The classic studies of obedience have shown that in general we obey regardless of the charisma of the person giving the orders provided the person giving the orders is identifiable as being in a position of authority. In Hofling's study for example, nurses obeyed simple telephone instructions and had no basis on which to judge and respond to the doctor's charisma.

where to now?

The following are good sources of further information about research and theory regarding obedience.

▶ **Gross, R.** (1998) *Key Studies in Psychology*, 3rd edn. Hodder & Stoughton, London. Excellent detailed coverage of the Milgram studies and later research on obedience.

▶ **Milgram, S.** (1997) *Obedience to Authority: An Experimental View*. Pinter & Martin, Boston. Nothing like hearing it from the expert!

prejudice

The word *prejudice* can be broken down to *pre* (meaning before) and *judice* (meaning judgement). You can see, therefore, that to be prejudiced means to pre-judge someone – in other words, to form a judgement about them before finding out anything about them as individuals. A prejudice is an extreme attitude towards a group that causes us to pre-judge individuals based only on their membership of that group. Like all attitudes, prejudices consist of three elements:

◆ **The cognitive element**: this involves the beliefs held about the group. These beliefs will be in the form of *stereotypes*, common but oversimple views of what particular groups of people are like.

◆ **The affective element**: this involves the feelings experienced in response to the group. If we are prejudiced against a group we may experience anger, fear, hate or disgust when we encounter a member of that group.

◆ **The behavioural element**: this consists of our actions towards the object of our prejudice. Behaving differently towards people based on their membership of a group is called *discrimination*. Our actions against members of a group against which we hold a prejudice can range from avoidance and verbal criticism to mass extermination.

We can illustrate these three elements with the example of prejudice against university students. Stereotyped views of students might include that they are lazy and spoilt, that they make inconsiderate neighbours and that they are heavy drinkers. People who subscribe to those stereotypes are likely to feel angry (and perhaps jealous!) in response to students. The resulting behaviour will probably include verbally criticising students and avoiding places where students congregate. In a minority of people with strong anti-student views, behaviour extends to physical violence.

figure 2.5
What stereotyped views might you hold about these students?

19

interactive
angles

Complete the following table by identifying the cognitive, affective and behavioural components of prejudice against the following groups. This should help you understand the different forms prejudice can take towards different groups.

	stereotypes	emotional responses	nature of discrimination
Goths			
Blonde women			
Trekkies (*Star Trek* fans)			

table 2.1 Prejudice against various groups

the targets of prejudice

Prejudice is universal. However much value we might place personally on being tolerant of human diversity, we are bound to have stereotyped views about some groups and to prefer the company of some groups over others. If your politics are left wing then you are probably a bit wary about Tory voters (and vice versa). If you are a full-time student of psychology then you probably have a preference for other psychology students over sociology students and perhaps for social science students in general over mathematicians. Although prejudice is universal, and perhaps to some extent inevitable, it is important not to lose sight of the terrible harm it causes. Racism in 1940s Germany led to the Holocaust and incidents of 'ethnic cleansing' still take place today. Currently AIDS patients in America receive less attention from health professionals than do other patients (Hunter and Ross, 1991); 20% of black men in Britain hold managerial positions as opposed to 36% of white men (Skellington, 1995), and sponsorship deals for female athletes go almost exclusively to conventionally attractive heterosexual women (Krane, 1998). Three forms of prejudice have been extensively studied by psychologists: racism, sexism and homophobia.

figure 2.6
There is still much overt racism in Britain today

racism

The most extensively studied prejudice is racism. Racism exists in a range of cultures and situations, including between Tamils and Sinhalese in Sri Lanka, Catholics and Protestants in Northern Ireland and Albanians and Serbs in the former Yugoslavia. A Gallup poll in Britain (reported in Skellington, 1995) aimed to discover the extent to which racist attitudes are held by a sample of 959 white British people. Questions aimed at discovering whether participants held racist views about matters such as whether they would object to living next door to a non-white person, their views on the law in relation to race (such as whether anti-racist laws should be strengthened or abolished) and their perception of race relations in Britain. Results showed a very wide spectrum of views about issues of race and attitudes towards minority ethnic groups: 75% of participants rated race relations in 1990s Britain as 'fair' or 'poor'. Only 25% believed that race relations were good. A sizeable minority of participants expressed openly racist views: 25% of people questioned said they would object to a non-white person living next door and 10% of people wanted anti-racism laws to be abolished, although 40% of participants wanted anti-racism laws strengthened.

sexism

Worldwide, women are probably the group that suffers the most discrimination. Sexism takes a range of forms. At its most extreme there are still societies in which adultery by women (although not by men) is punishable by death and in which women cannot travel alone, own property or vote. In Europe and the United States sexism is likely to be more subtle. For example, women are likely to experience *benevolent sexism*, a patronising attitude in which men are not hostile towards women but treat them as incapable of independence or performing tasks. Women are also likely to encounter the 'glass ceiling' in their careers. This means that women, like minority ethnic groups, are much less likely to be promoted beyond a certain level at work.

homophobia

One of the most extreme examples of prejudice is that directed against lesbians and gay men. Homophobia is of particular concern for two reasons. Firstly, unlike racism and sexism, homophobia is a largely socially acceptable prejudice. By this we mean that whereas most people holding racist and sexist views are wary of voicing them in public, people have no such qualms about making anti-gay comments. Secondly, gay people are particularly likely to suffer extreme forms of discrimination including hate crimes, commonly in the form of violence. A recent study by Ellis and Fox (2001) serves to demonstrate how ordinary people discriminate against lesbians and gay men.

sorry, I would help . . . but you're gay

Ellis, J. and Fox, P. (2001) The effect of self-identified sexual orientation on helping behaviour in a British sample: are lesbians and gay men treated differently? *Journal of Applied Social Psychology*, **31**, 1238–1247.

Aim: the aim of the study was to see whether people would be equally inclined to help a person in mild difficulty if they were aware that that person was gay.

Procedure: a field experiment was carried out in which 232 British men and women were telephoned at home. The caller said that they had dialled a wrong number and that they had no more change. They then requested that the participant relay a message to the caller's partner. In the experimental condition the partner was identified as the same sex as the caller, and in the control condition they were identified as the opposite sex.

Findings: overall, both gay men and lesbians were less likely to receive help than heterosexuals. Women were also more likely to receive help than men, thus the same percentage of lesbians were assisted as heterosexual men. Male participants were less likely to offer help to gay men than to lesbians, but women were no less likely to offer help to lesbians.

Conclusions: people are less likely to offer help to a gay person in difficulty. Men are less helpful than women and gay men are the least likely to receive help.

explanations for prejudice

Psychological approaches to explaining prejudice fall into two broad areas. *Social approaches* centre on the social factors that contribute to prejudice in general, whereas *individual differences approaches* centre on what factors make some people particularly prone to prejudice. To understand prejudice fully we need to take into account social and individual factors. First let us look at social factors. Perhaps the most-researched social theory of prejudice is social identity theory, proposed by Tajfel and Turner (1979).

the social approach

social identity theory

Social identity theory is one of a group of theories that share the assumption that prejudice can be explained by our tendency to identify ourselves as part of a group and to classify other people as either within or outside that group. This means that we tend to make sharp judgements of people as either one of 'us or them'. The exact nature of the groups we see ourselves as belonging to varies widely according to our individual experience and the culture we live in. However our tendency to think of ourselves as belonging to one or more groups is a fundamental part of human nature. Tajfel and Turner's theory was based on a series of laboratory experiments called the minimal group studies. One such study is reported in *classic research*.

is just being part of a group sufficient to lead to prejudice?

Tajfel, H. (1970) Experiments in intergroup discrimination. *Scientific American*, **223**, 96–102.

Aim: previous studies have established clearly that two groups in competition would show prejudice towards one another. The aim of this study was to see whether members of two clearly identifiable groups, which were not in competition, would still favour their own group over the other.

Procedure: two experiments were set up, using 14- to 15-year-old British schoolboys as participants. The first is reported here. Sixty-four participants were told that the researchers were investigating vision. They were shown clusters of dots on a screen and asked to estimate the number of dots. They were divided into two groups (underestimators and overestimators), supposedly on the basis of their number estimates. In fact they were randomly divided into two groups. The boys were then given the task of allocating points to each other, choosing which one of a pair of boys should receive points for their estimates of the numbers of dots. They were told that points could later be

converted into money. The participants did not know which individuals they were allotting the money to but they *did* know which group each boy was in. In one condition, the choice was between two boys in the in-group, in the second condition the choice was between two boys in the out-group and in the third group it was between one boy from the in-group and one from the out-group.

Findings: the boys overwhelmingly chose to allocate points to boys who had been identified as in the same group as themselves, either overestimators or underestimators. This occurred irrespective of the accuracy of the boys' estimates.

Conclusion: despite the fact that there was no direct competition between the two groups, participants consistently displayed favouritism towards those who were identified as being in the same group as themselves and against those identified as in a different group.

Based on the minimal group experiments, Tajfel and Turner (1979) proposed that there are three cognitive processes involved in evaluating others as either one of 'us or them'. *Social categorisation* takes place when we categorise other people as members of particular social groups. Categories we all tend to subscribe to involve gender, race and social class. Others are more relevant to some people than others – for example to football supporters or cat lovers. We tend to adopt the identity of the group to which we have categorised ourselves as belonging. This is called *social identification* and it is the feature that distinguishes social identity theory from other theories of in-group favouritism. There is an emotional significance to identification with a group, and one's self-esteem becomes bound up with group membership. If our self-esteem is to be maintained our group needs to compare well against other groups. This is assessed in a process of *social comparison*. Hostility between groups is thus not only a matter of competing for resources like jobs, but also the result of competing identities.

⊘ discussion

Social identity theory explains a whole host of social phenomena, ranging from racism and class conflict to the sense of togetherness we experience from following a football club or band. Significantly, social identity theory provides at least a partial explanation for the tendency for people to discriminate in favour of people from their own country and against those from other countries. We can look at one study of this phenomenon in detail.

what do Europeans think of each other?

Poppe, E. and Linssen, H. (1999) In-group favouritism and the reflection of realistic dimensions of difference between national states in Central and Eastern European nationality stereotypes. *British Journal of Social Psychology*, **38**, 85–102.

Aim: the aim was to establish what views young people in Eastern Europe held with regard to the characteristics of people in their own country, neighbouring countries and Western European countries.

Procedure: 1143 15- to 18-year-old students from Russia, Bulgaria, Hungary, Poland, Belaruss and Czechoslovakia answered a questionnaire that examined beliefs about the characteristics of people from European countries including all those from which participants were taken plus Italy, Germany and England. The questionnaires required participants to rate each nationality according its competence and its morality. *Counterbalancing* was employed – in other words, the questionnaires given to different participants listed the various nationalities in different order. This ensured that the participants were not influenced by the order in which the nationalities were presented. The responses were analysed to see whether people tended to favour their own nationality over others or whether general national stereotypes (such as German efficiency) proved a more important factor in judgements.

Findings: the Eastern Europeans tended to favour their own nationality over those of other Eastern Europeans but not over Western Europeans. Overall, national stereotypes were upheld, and participants consistently rated Germans as the most competent (though least moral) and the English as the most moral people.

Conclusion: social identity theory correctly predicted that the Eastern European countries would show in-group favouritism in relation to other East European countries. Interestingly, people did not blindly favour their own nationality, and economic and historical factors proved important in creating national stereotypes.

research methods

surveys

Surveys like that carried out by Poppe and Linssen are an important way of gathering information about people's attitudes, beliefs and intentions. Surveys can involve questionnaires as in the Poppe and Linssen study, or interviews. The best way to find out about people's attitudes, beliefs and intentions is to survey them rather than judge attitudes from people's behaviour. This is because people's behaviour can be entirely unrelated to their attitudes; for instance someone might express racist attitudes but treat individuals they know from minority ethnic groups with kindness and fairness. Surveys also have the advantage that, compared to other research methods, they are quick and easy, and can involve very large numbers of people. They do however have some limitations.

◆ Surveys rely on the accuracy of what respondents say. This can be affected by many factors. People may be inclined to give socially acceptable answers or those they believe the researcher wants to hear. If the respondents meet the researchers face to face and find them attractive then this can be a particular problem!

◆ Because there is little correspondence between people's attitudes and their behaviour, surveys are not effective in predicting how people would behave in a given situation.

Early minimal group studies suggested that the categorisation of people into groups and comparison of these groups was always sufficient to create in-group favouritism. However, recent studies have challenged this. Dobbs and Crano (2001) conducted a minimal group study with different conditions, some of which involved having to explain why fewer points were allocated to out-group members. In the condition where the person allocating the points was in the majority group and had to justify their decision, there was much less in-group favouritism than in the control condition. However, when the allocator was in the minority and had to justify discriminating against the majority out-group, in-group favouritism increased. This suggests that in-group favouritism is actually a more complex business than indicated by the original studies.

A closer look at the minimal group studies also tells us that individual participants differed considerably in the extent to which they favoured the in-group over the out-group. Platow et al. (1990) assessed individual differences in responses to the minimal group situation and concluded that participants assessed as highly competitive showed greater in-group favouritism than those assessed as highly cooperative. The latter tended to favour fair distribution of resources rather than the interests of the in-group. Although social identity theory has proved useful in understanding relations between groups, studies like Platow's show clearly that social identity alone is not sufficient to explain prejudice in its entirety.

for+against

social identity theory

+ There is clear evidence from the minimal group studies, for example Tajfel, that being part of a group is sufficient to lead to prejudice against people not within that group. This suggests that social identity rather than competition between groups is responsible for prejudice.

+ Social identity explains a wide range of real-life phenomena, ranging from support for football teams to racism, and can be applied to a wide range of social situations.

– Some contemporary minimal group studies, for example Dobbs and Crano (2001), show that under some circumstances people show much less in-group favouritism than was suggested by early studies like that of Tajfel (1970).

– Social identity theory does not neatly explain individual differences in prejudice. A closer look at the results of the minimal group studies shows wide variations in the degree to which people discriminate against the out-group.

the authoritarian personality

We have already established that social explanations of prejudice like social identity theory have the limitation that they do not easily explain why some people are so much more prone to prejudice than others. To understand this aspect of prejudice we need to turn to individual difference approaches to prejudice. The most influential individual differences theory of prejudice concerns the *authoritarian personality*. Adorno et al. (1950) proposed that individual differences in prejudice could be explained by the idea of authoritarianism. Authoritarianism is characterised by political conservatism, hostility, rigid morality, strong racial in-group favouritism (ethnocentrism) and intolerance of challenges to authority or deviations from conventional behaviour (totalitarianism). Like Milgram, Adorno was interested in the characteristics of the Nazis.

Adorno and his colleagues devised tests to measure ethnocentrism, anti-Semitism (anti-Jewish prejudice), political conservatism and totalitarianism. As expected, the same people tended to score highly on all these characteristics, indicating that there are indeed people with an authoritarian personality. The four scales were collectively called the F-Scale (F stands for *fascism*). The items in Adorno's original F-Scale were very much tied up with the social and political situation in the 1940s and 1950s, and the scale in its original form is probably not of much use today. However, Ray (1972) has produced an updated version that relies less on current affairs. Some items from Ray's scale are shown in Table 2.2.

Having established a test of authoritarianism, Adorno and his colleagues went on to interview individuals who had been identified as authoritarian, in order to obtain an idea of what factors might have led to their developing this type of personality. It emerged strongly from these interviews that authoritarians tended to have had a distinctive style of upbringing. They were generally from cold, unloving homes with a hostile atmosphere. Parents of authoritarians tended to be aloof and controlling and they typically insisted on high levels of achievement and self-discipline in their children. The primary strategy for ensuring that children complied with their wishes was

figure 2.7
Cold, harsh parenting may be linked to the development of highly prejudiced individuals

	strongly agree	agree	don't know	disagree	strongly disagree
If everybody would talk less and work more everybody would be better off.					
Disobedience to the government is sometimes justified.					
Young people sometimes get rebellious ideas but as they grow up they should get over them and settle down.					
Obedience and respect for authority are the most important virtues a child can learn.					

table 2.2 Items from Ray's updated F-Scale

the withdrawal of affection. Adorno and his colleagues suggested that, to cope with this parenting, children repressed their anger at their treatment and identified strongly with the parent.

Adorno et al. proposed that this power-oriented, authoritarian pattern established in childhood spills over into other aspects of the children's lives, leaving them cold and conventional and carrying unexpressed anger that needs to be taken out on a convenient group. The child who has learned to respect only uncompromising strength will have a tendency in adulthood to orient themselves towards institutions like extreme right-wing political groups, which extol the virtues of strength and are themselves uncompromising.

ᗒ discussion

We need to remember two things when evaluating Adorno's theory. Firstly, he did not propose that authoritarian upbringing led directly to prejudice – just that it could lead to a personality type that was liable to acquire prejudices. Because of this we would expect research to show only a moderate correspondence between those who had authoritarian upbringings and those who displayed high levels of prejudice. A large body of research has supported such a relationship (McKnight and Sutton, 1994). Secondly, the idea of the authoritarian personality is not intended as a complete explanation of the phenomenon of prejudice, just as an explanation of which individuals are most likely to acquire prejudices. Clearly there are social-psychological factors such as social identity that affect prejudice, along with historical, political and economic realities, as we saw in the Poppe and Linssen study. Theories of the prejudiced personality, based just on the psychological development of the individual, cannot easily explain large-scale conflict between groups such as we have recently seen between Serbs and Kosovo Albanians in the former Yugoslavia.

In spite of these limitations, authoritarianism remains an extremely important concept in understanding prejudice. Numerous studies have supported Adorno et al.'s findings about the characteristics of authoritarians – for example their conservatism. Rubinstein (1995) measured the relationship between authoritarianism, religiosity and gender attitudes in 165 Jewish students. Those high in authoritarianism tended to be more religious and have more traditional attitudes to gender than did those lower in authoritarianism. The idea that authoritarians show greater prejudice than others is also well supported by modern studies. Whitley and Lee (2000) assessed attitudes to homosexuality in 216 American students along with a number of personality variables, including authoritarianism. Authoritarianism proved to be the personality variable most strongly associated with homophobic attitudes.

the discursive approach to prejudice

The discursive approach takes a very different approach to prejudice from social identity theory or prejudiced personality theory. Discursive psychologists study the ways in which our perceptions of the social world are shaped by *discourse*. The term 'discourse' refers to the nature of the language we use when we speak, write or sing about a topic. The central idea behind the discursive approach to prejudice is that the language we use to discuss issues like race, gender, age and sexual orientation promotes and even creates negative or stereotyped views of the groups involved.

for+against

the authoritarian personality

+ There is substantial evidence from modern studies to support the existence of the authoritarian personality. There is also evidence that authoritarianism is associated with particular child-rearing practices.

+ There is clear evidence (for example, from Whitley and Lee, 2000) that authoritarians tend to be more prone to prejudice than other people.

— Although authoritarianism helps us understand individual differences in prejudice, this is not in itself a complete explanation of why prejudice exists. For a more complete understanding of prejudice we also need to draw on social psychological theories like social identity theory and the social constructionist view. These theories explain the social processes underlying prejudice.

socially constructed categories of person

To begin with, let us take the word 'race'. We use the term race rather like we do the word species to mean a distinct group but, unlike species, which has a precise scientific definition, the term race is scientifically meaningless. There is far more variation between the members of any 'race' than there is between any two 'races' and to classify people as different on the basis of their 'race' is scientifically just as arbitrary as dividing the world into people with blue and brown eyes, or short and tall people. By using the term 'race' we are *socially constructing* an artificial way of classifying people. Other socially constructed categories of people include 'asylum seekers' and 'immigrants'. There is no reason why those seeking political asylum should share any personal characteristics other than the misfortune to be fleeing political persecution. However, following intensive political debate and media coverage, we have come to think of asylum seekers as a very distinct group.

other linguistic devices that foster prejudice

◆ **Classifying people using nouns rather than adjectives.** Whenever we speak of groups, naming them according to their defining characteristic, we position them as in some way separate and different from the rest of humanity. For example, we might speak of 'blacks' or 'gays'. However, when we speak of 'black people' or 'gay men' it is much clearer that we are speaking about human beings rather than some out-group, and this may dispose a listener or reader to respond more favourably towards the group in question. Disability campaigners have gone a step further and said that to speak of 'disabled people' is still unacceptable because this places too much emphasis on the disability. The term 'person with a disability' is thus preferable.

◆ **Using terms associated with minority groups as negative terms.** Whenever we use terms like 'black hearted' or 'the black sheep of the family' we are promoting the idea that there is something inherently bad about being black. When we accuse someone behaving cautiously as 'an old woman' we are effectively saying that there is something wrong with being older or a woman. Similarly, if we use words like 'gay' as general insults, then we are similarly implying that to actually *be* gay must be a bad thing.

◆ **Juxtapositioning minority groups with negative terms.** To juxtaposition something is to place it next to something. If we consistently refer to a minority group in relation to something generally considered to be a bad thing then we inevitably come to associate the group with that thing. Condor (1988) gave an example of this in analysing the 1987 Conservative Party manifesto, in which under a general heading of 'freedom, law and responsibility' there was a subheading 'race' along with 'the fight against crime' and 'tackling drug abuse'. This clearly links minority ethnic groups with drugs and crime.

◆ **Unnecessary use of loaded terms.** If we are discussing a topic supposedly from a neutral position then we can prejudice a reader or listener by introducing negative terms used as if they were in fact neutral. Jarvis (2000) gives an example of this in a discussion of prejudice against Freudian ideas in psychology. One leading American text used the following clause to sum up current attitudes to Freud: 'his notoriety still colours people's perceptions of psychology . . .' The term 'notoriety' is used simply as if it just means 'fame'. However, whereas 'fame' has positive connotations, 'notoriety' conveys a very negative impression, predisposing the reader to think negatively about Freud.

media watch

MPs under fire for race riots

By Martin Bright, *Observer*, 1 July 2001.

British politicians are stoking racial hatred with inflammatory comments on asylum and immigration, according to an independent report to be put to the United Nations tomorrow.

As new trouble flared in the north of England yesterday, with an Asian family of seven being forced to flee their house which was petrol bombed as they slept, Amnesty International and other human rights groups said comments by Labour and Tory politicians had led to violence against asylum seekers.

In a damning report to the UN Human Rights Committee, 11 organisations, led by Liberty, the civil rights group, and including the Law Society and the Bar Human Rights Committee, say 'politicians and media alike have been encouraging racist hostility in their public attitudes towards asylum seekers.'

They say 'such negative presentation of asylum seekers has not only led to direct attacks on asylum seekers, but also an underlying greater hostility towards all those from ethnic minority communities, and heightened racial tensions.'

questions

1 Using your understanding of the social construction of prejudice, explain how media coverage of asylum seekers might lead to racism.

2 Locate some tabloid articles on asylum seekers. You can do this online using the British Library Web site, currently found at bl.org.uk. Try to unpack as many linguistic devices as possible that might transmit prejudice.

figure 2.8
The band, Aqua

discourse analysis

The major research method in discursive psychology is called *discourse analysis*. Discourse analysts 'unpack' as much hidden meaning as possible from the language we use in relation to an issue. A discourse analysis from Burns (1998) shows how the lyrics of popular music help construct stereotypes of how men and women conduct themselves in relationships. Burns unpacked the lyrics to Aqua's *Barbie Girl*, which reached No. 1 in the UK Charts in 1997. Verses 2, 3 and 4 are shown below.

> (Barbie) *I'm a blonde bimbo girl*
> *In a fantasy world*
> *Dress me up*
> *Make it tight*
> *I'm your dolly.*

(Ken) You're my doll
Rock'n'roll
Feel the glamour and pain
Kiss me there
Touch me there
Hanky panky

(Barbie) You can touch
You can play
If you say
I'm always yours   (Reproduced by permission of MCA Records Ltd.)

angling with the net

◆ Locate some more lyrics, using the Internet. There are various Web sites you can use for this. Try for example **www.lyrics.com or www.songfile.com.**

◆ Have a go at deconstructing some songs to see what hidden messages are there.

◆ To what extent do you think people are affected by lyrics?

You may remember the song as irritating but light-hearted, happy and extremely harmless. However Burns has revealed how some worrying beliefs about male-female relationships are expressed in these lyrics. Firstly, here is a discourse in which love, sex and ownership are closely linked together, suggesting that in fact ownership is a feature of sexual relationships. Barbie is constructed as a self-confessed blonde bimbo who describes herself as 'your dolly', thus reducing herself to something less than a person ('dolly') and as the property of Ken ('your'). She offers herself as a sexual plaything ('you can touch, you can play'), on the condition that Ken gives a lasting commitment to her ('if you say I'm always yours'). Ken on the other hand is constructed as relatively unemotional. He makes no declarations of love, but instead demands sexual services ('kiss me there, touch me there'). Here is a representation of relationships in which women want love and men want sex and, worse, in which men swap love for sex and women give sex in exchange for love.

You can see that a very unhealthily stereotypical and sad account of human relationships is being played out here. You might say 'So what, it's just a song?' However, to a discursive psychologist people construct their perceptions of relationships from the discourse of relationships they encounter. This means that songs like *Barbie Girl* may perpetuate unhealthy stereotypes of what men and women want from relationships.

We can see such stereotyped representations of what is normal or acceptable all around us. In a recent but already classic discourse analysis Ian Parker has demonstrated that deconstructing something as innocuous as a toothpaste packet reveals sinister hidden messages about cultural assumptions of normality and reality.

research now

studies in detail

you can unpack a lot from a toothpaste packet!

Parker, I. (1999) Tracing therapeutic discourse in material culture. *British Journal of Medical Psychology*, **72**, 577–589.

Aim: the aim of the study was to demonstrate how discourse as apparently trivial as the packaging on an American children's toothpaste, marketed through health-food shops, contains what Parker calls 'the regime of truth', cultural assumptions about how people do and should live.

The discourse: the packaging contained a message for parents, a message for children and a warning that children under six should be supervised in their use of toothpaste. The message for adults read as follows:

The story of our children's natural toothpaste

Dear parent,
We think the time is right to make a natural toothpaste just for children. For over 20 years we have committed ourselves to natural oral and body care products. Many adults have come to trust our natural toothpastes made without saccharin or synthetic flavours, preservatives, dyes or animal ingredients.

We now offer a delicious and effective natural toothpaste with sensible ingredients and natural fruit flavours created with your child's taste in mind. It contains none of the stripes and 'sparkles', neon colours and sweet bubble gum flavour you see in other brands. Our gentle formulation is low in abrasivity and contains fluoride to help prevent dental decay.

The message for children read as follows:

JUST foR KiDS by Luke Chappell (age 8¾)

About animals – Do you like animals? At home we have a dog Hershey, a bird Eli, and a hamster named Carol. At Tom's of Maine my Mom and Dad make sure our products are safe without testing them on animals. If you have a favourite animal, draw a picture and send it to me.

About recycling – At home we recycle cans, bottles, newspaper and plastic. Tom's of Maine gave our town green bins so each family can separate and store their recycled things until a special truck picks

them up every week. If you do recycling at home, let me know. I'm trying to get recycling news from all the states.

The analysis: looking closely at the messages aimed at parents and children it is apparent that the text aims to construct this product as natural, gentle and healthy, and being given in friendship from one family to another. There is reference to 'our town'. This suggests that using this commercial product is part of being in a community, and that a community consists of families of a particular structure – mom, dad, the child and the pets. A particular vision of the relationship between private enterprise and the community is also constructed in which the former exists to look after the latter. The term 'each family' positions the family as the basic unit of humanity. The term 'natural' refers directly to the toothpaste but is linked indirectly with the nature of the family, the community and the relationship between the private sector and the public.

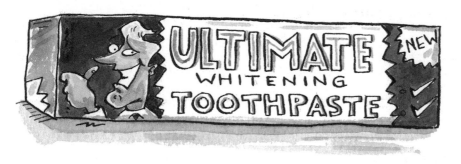

figure 2.9
The most innocent pieces of writing contain assumptions about what is 'real' and 'normal'

There is no suggestion in Parker's study that this discourse is aimed towards creating prejudice. However, it does show how the most innocent writing we encounter contains subtle messages about what is 'real' and 'normal'. By setting up what is normal, discourse like this implies that deviations from the world as portrayed in this way are abnormal. For example, those who do not live in two-parent heterosexual families with children or who do not see private enterprise as benevolent can be viewed as abnormal. This may foster prejudice against gay people, single people, childless people and those who choose not to patronise private health producers.

discussion

There have been numerous studies performed on discourse as diverse as political speeches and manifestos, popular lyrics, psychology books and even toothpaste packets! It is quite clear from these that we are constantly bombarded by language containing stereotyped ideas about what is normal, and in some cases by overt prejudice towards minority groups. What is much more difficult to ascertain is the extent to which our attitudes are a product of such discourse. This is largely impossible to test directly as this would mean having to control all the numerous sources of discourse to which we are exposed. In any case, discursive psychologists generally do not favour research methods that test cause and effect. What we can do is look for associations between the generation of particular discourses and prejudice in the public. Looking at the increase in racial violence following the politicisation of the asylum issue, it certainly seems that there may be a link, however we can't be sure of this as the upsurge in racial violence might have been affected by numerous other factors.

for+against

discursive theory

+ Studies (for example, Burns, 1998; Parker, 1999) have clearly shown that language can be used in ways that construct a particular view of reality.

+ Understanding how use of language affects people's view of the world has practical applications, for example in developing 'politically correct' language, designed to minimize the construction of prejudiced views.

− Because discourse is all around us and exerts a constant influence, it is not possible to isolate people exposed only to certain discourse and demonstrate that their own view of the world is shaped by it. This means that it is hard to know just how important discourse is in creating prejudice.

where to now?

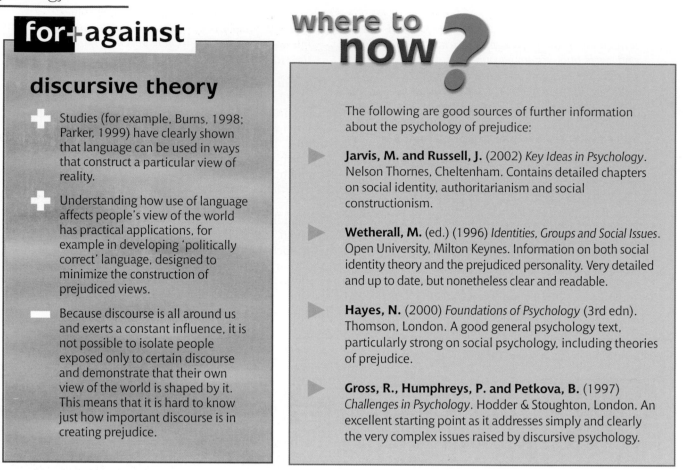

The following are good sources of further information about the psychology of prejudice:

▶ **Jarvis, M. and Russell, J.** (2002) *Key Ideas in Psychology*. Nelson Thornes, Cheltenham. Contains detailed chapters on social identity, authoritarianism and social constructionism.

▶ **Wetherall, M.** (ed.) (1996) *Identities, Groups and Social Issues*. Open University, Milton Keynes. Information on both social identity theory and the prejudiced personality. Very detailed and up to date, but nonetheless clear and readable.

▶ **Hayes, N.** (2000) *Foundations of Psychology* (3rd edn). Thomson, London. A good general psychology text, particularly strong on social psychology, including theories of prejudice.

▶ **Gross, R., Humphreys, P. and Petkova, B.** (1997) *Challenges in Psychology*. Hodder & Stoughton, London. An excellent starting point as it addresses simply and clearly the very complex issues raised by discursive psychology.

real lives

key application

tackling the problem of prejudice

We have already said that prejudice is universal and probably to some extent inevitable. This does not mean, however, that we should adopt an attitude of helplessness towards it. Psychologists have been involved in many attempts to reduce prejudice. We can look briefly here at two ways in which prejudice can be tackled.

intergroup contact

If we accept that the negative stereotypes held by different groups towards one another are inaccurate, and that hostility towards out-groups is irrational, then common sense would suggest that increasing the contact these groups have with each other should allow people to see for themselves the inaccuracy of their stereotypes and so to get on better. Research has shown that in real life the situation is a little more complicated. Deutsch and Collins (1951) surveyed white Americans who lived in housing projects that were either racially segregated or mixed and found that people in the mixed projects had significantly more positive attitudes towards black people. In this instance it appeared that intergroup contact succeeded in breaking down boundaries.

At around the same time, in 1954, the law was changed in America to make racially segregated schooling illegal. It was expected that this would have a similar effect to the mixed housing projects but unfortunately this was not the case and prejudice between groups of children actually increased. This piece of history tells us that simply increasing intergroup contact is not always sufficient to reduce prejudice. Aronson, Wilson and Akert (1994) identified six conditions that need to be met before contact will reduce prejudice. The groups must depend on each other. They must share common goals and have equal status. Members of the groups must be able to interact informally and on a one-to-one basis. They must also have multiple contacts with different members of the other group(s). Finally, a social norm of tolerance of differences between groups must be established.

⊘ discussion

Research supports the idea that, under the right circumstances, contact can reduce prejudice. Bowen and Bourgeois (2001) surveyed 109 American university students about their personal comfort in the presence of gay men, lesbians and bisexuals. Interestingly, attitudes were associated with location so that particular buildings and corridors were associated with positive or negative attitudes towards gay people. The locations associated with the most positive attitudes were those in which a gay student lived, suggesting that contact with gay people led to reduced homophobia. Interaction in this situation tends to meet Aronson's six criteria. However, when we deliberately bring groups into contact in order to reduce prejudice between them this is somewhat harder to achieve. There are programmes in Israel for bringing Israeli and Palestinian children and adults into contact in order to reduce prejudice. Maoz (2002) observed a number of planned contact sessions and calculated that overall actual one-to-one informal and equal status contact took place only 65% of the time. In programmes involving primary school children the number of such contacts was somewhat lower and so was likely to prove ineffective.

for+against

contact

+ Groups that have regular contact in real-life situations often do seem to get on better. This has been demonstrated in mixed-race communities, and can be applied as a deliberate strategy to reduce prejudice between hostile groups; see, for example, Maoz (2002).

+ Studies have shown that people who have regular contact with minority groups express more positive attitudes towards them. For example, Latane and Bourgeois showed that people who had regular contact with gay people were more comfortable with them.

— In practice several conditions need to be met before contact becomes effective. This can be difficult to achieve. For example, where one group has traditionally oppressed another, equal status contact can be hard to create.

the common in-group identity model: cooperation reduces conflict

A more sophisticated approach to prejudice reduction than the simple 'increased contact' hypothesis comes from Gaertner et al. (1989). This was particularly concerned with reducing racism. The rationale of Gaertner's approach is that we should be able to reduce prejudice by stopping people from classifying each other as part of an in-group or out-group. In terms of social identity theory, this means that there will be no need for in-group favouritism to protect the esteem of the in-group. According to Gaertner, weakening the 'us-and-them' boundaries should initiate a process where more positive attitudes lead to an increase in contact between groups. From there prejudice should naturally reduce.

So how do we get people to redraw their boundaries so that members of different groups will be perceived as one group? According to Gaertner, one way is to establish *cooperative interaction* between different groups. In practice this means getting groups to work together towards achieving the same goal. In one experiment, Gaertner et al. (1990) demonstrated that cooperative interaction leads people to redraw in-group and out-group boundaries. The researchers established two groups of three people. In the experimental condition the two groups were brought into contact so that they could work together. In the control condition the two groups were brought into contact but did not work together. When the groups were later surveyed about their perceptions of who was in the group, the groups who had worked together identified themselves as one group of six, whereas the groups who had not worked together identified themselves as two groups of three.

discussion

A problem with laboratory experiments like the one above is that they lack *ecological validity* – they are not representative of real-world situations. There is a difference between groups thrown together for an experiment and naturally occurring cultural groups who have identified themselves as distinct groups for their whole lives and who may have experienced conflict with other groups. Nonetheless there are real-life situations where people are forced to reclassify themselves and cooperate. Take, for example, what happens when athletes come together from regional teams to form an international team. Footballers from Manchester United, Leeds and Arsenal see each other from week to week as rival out-groups, yet when they come together to play for England they cooperate under a common umbrella. This suggests that forming a common in-group through cooperation to achieve a goal (no pun intended!) does reduce prejudice.

figure 2.10 When international sports teams come together they have to develop a common in-group identity and forget that they are rivals most of the time

for+against

cooperation

+ Gaertner has devised a strategy based on intergroup cooperation to increase contact. Studies have shown that at least under certain circumstances this can reduce prejudice.

− Gaertner's approach relies on the members of different groups being prepared to cooperate. This may not be practical when groups have already fallen out.

+ There are real-life scenarios in which people do reclassify themselves into common in-groups through cooperation, and this appears to be effective in reducing prejudice. This is what happens when Premier League football players from different teams cooperate as the England team.

− In some cases other group dynamics interfere with effective cooperation, for example where some group members wish to cooperate and others don't. This was demonstrated in the series *Castaway*.

figure 2.11
Forcing two groups to cooperate in *Castaway* failed to create a single, harmonious group

Where practical, Gaertner's approach can be an effective way to tackle prejudice. However, there are many factors that can scupper effective cooperation, as was shown dramatically on the BBC television programme *Castaway*, in which the successful members of two groups of applicants were thrown together to live on a remote Scottish island. Their progress was followed up by Scottish psychologists McVey et al. (2003). Although the groups were forced to cooperate, some members did so much more enthusiastically than others. This meant that rather than the two groups coming together, splits occurred within each and a third group of 'cooperators' emerged.

collective action

Whereas strategies to increase intergroup contact are aimed at reducing prejudice in individuals and targeted communities, collective action has a more ambitious purpose – to reform the attitudes of society as a whole and prevent discrimination on a national or world level. Collective action takes place whenever an individual acts as a representative of a group and their action is directed towards improving conditions for that group (Wright, 1990). Collective action takes the form of political movements, and may use strategies ranging from generating literature through public protest (such as marches and demonstrations) to violence. Whenever people perceive that they are disadvantaged because of their membership of a group rather than because of individual circumstances (this is called *relative deprivation*), collective action becomes likely.

In the light of our understanding of social identity theory, it is interesting to see that collective action operates in the opposite way to intergroup contact and cooperation. Rather than blurring boundaries between groups, collective action strengthens the group identity of members of the disadvantaged group, and asserts the rights of that group for equal status. This serves to increase both the self-esteem of group members and the social power of the minority group relative to that of the majority. A good example of collective action comes from the feminist movement. Research into the beliefs and feelings of feminist activists has supported the idea that both relative deprivation and social identity are important psychological factors underlying collective action. Kelly and Breinlinger (1996) interviewed a sample of feminist activists in order to try to understand what factors influenced their political activism. They found that most of the activists interviewed reported that their initial reason for taking action was their perception of women as a group suffering discrimination (relative deprivation). Once they were politically active, however, and had formed links with other activists, it seemed that social identity was the most important single factor maintaining their activism. Not standing up to be counted would be incompatible with feminists' social identity as both feminists and as women.

Kelly and Breinlinger (1996) have suggested that, in contemporary British culture, the majority of people frown upon collective action. Thus, whilst in principle most people would support equal rights for women, perceptions of feminists *as* individuals seem to be largely unrelated to the aims of the feminist movement and are surprisingly negative. Our tendency to see activists as an out-group irrespective of their aims is exploited by politicians.

figure 2.12
Collective action on the part of students in the 1980s and 1990s failed to stop the abolition of the student grant

⟁ discussion

So what does history tell us about the success of collective action as a strategy to reduce discrimination? Student grants have been abolished, so clearly collective action is not always effective. However, anti-discrimination laws protecting the rights of women and minority ethnic groups have been passed following collective action (although of course these laws have not been entirely effective at eliminating discrimination), and there has been a gradual shift in public opinion away from traditional racist and sexist views. In general, then, it seems that, although the effects of collective action are long term rather than immediate, and although there are no guarantees of success, it *is* a valid strategy for effecting social change and reducing prejudice.

for+against

collective action

➕ Because collective action tends to emerge in response to relative deprivation, it provides a way of identifying and addressing social inequality.

➖ In Britain we tend to have negative stereotypical views of political activists. This means that we tend not to take activists seriously, reducing the effectiveness of collective action.

➕ Collective action has led to anti-discriminatory laws and a gradual shift in public attitudes. For example the feminist and disability movements have been effective in pressing for anti-discriminatory legislation.

➖ Anti-discrimination laws have failed to eliminate discrimination and even more so prejudice. It may therefore be the case that collective action is more effective in tackling the law than people's attitudes and behaviour.

where to now?

The following are good sources of further information on the reduction of prejudice:

▶ **Aronson, E., Wilson, T. D. and Akert, R. M.** (1994) *Social Psychology, the Heart and the Mind*. HarperCollins, New York. A very well-written American social psychology text, featuring particularly good information on intergroup contact.

▶ **Eysenck, M.** (ed.) (1998) *Psychology, an Integrated Approach*. Longman, Harlow. This has a particularly detailed and up-to-date social psychology section, and features some excellent material on collective action.

▶ **Crisp, R. J.** (2002) Social categorisation: blurring the boundaries. *The Psychologist*, **15**, 612–615. A state-of-the-art review of the contact and common in-group approaches to prejudice reduction.

talking point

contemporary issues

internet interaction

background

At the turn of the millennium the usage and importance of the Internet is growing rapidly. Internet use has implications for society as a whole and the social psychology of the individual. Social interaction on the Internet is now highly sophisticated and many people have 'virtual lives' that rival their 'real lives' in importance. Friendships and even romantic relationships in cyberspace are now common and highly cohesive groups form among people who may never meet in 'real life'. Research has begun into these social-psychological aspects of Internet use and fascinating results are emerging, including in some of the areas we have looked at in this chapter.

applying social-psychological ideas to understanding Internet interaction

Psychologists have applied a range of social psychological assumptions, concepts and theories to understanding Internet interaction. We can look, here, at three examples that highlight the potential of the Internet for both negative and positive action. On the downside, in-group favouritism is rife on the Internet and inexperienced users are likely to find themselves excluded by highly cohesive in-groups. On a more positive note, the Internet allows equal status contact between members of different groups and can serve as a medium for collective action.

social identity and in-group favouritism in Internet groups

Groups of Internet users develop powerful group identities. The usual visual cues for group membership, for example those allowing us to judge age, ethnicity, gender and so on, are not easily available during Internet interaction. However, in-groups tend to use different criteria for distinguishing themselves from out-groups and excluding out-siders. One such strategy is *expertism*. Insiders such as members of newsgroups taunt would-be group members by demonstrating their expertise in whatever topic has brought the newsgroup together. They may lay traps to humiliate outsiders. This is called *trolling*, and an example comes from Wallace (1999). In a *Star Trek* discussion group a troll was set by pointing out that light does not travel in space, hence the shadows shown on the hull of the Enterprise were a technical error. Of course this is nonsense – light does travel in space, but unsuspecting outsiders who point this out are immediately identified and humiliated by their lack of understanding of the troll.

An interesting question about social identity and the Internet concerns the extent to which Internet users are themselves an in-group. Katz (1997) tested this idea in a major survey of Internet users. Katz identified a hard core of regular and expert 'digital citizens' who were surprisingly similar in their characteristics. Digital citizens emerged in the Katz survey as well informed, outspoken and proud of the culture of the Internet. This does support the idea of at least some Internet users as an in-group. However, although this is a relatively recent study, use of the Internet has changed beyond recognition since 1997 and it is likely that, if such a survey were carried out today, Internet users would emerge as a much more diverse group.

the Internet as a medium for equal status contact

One of the most positive aspects of interacting with other people on the Internet is that we need only give away whatever information we choose to about ourselves. This means that some of the usual highly visible characteristics we use to form judgements about people need not be factors in Internet interaction. Although e-mail addresses may give away gender and the signature file may reveal occupation, information about age and race are not automatically available as they are in face-to-face interaction. Although in social interactions on the Internet, people do sometimes ask the age of people with whom they are communicating, enquiries about race are rare (Wallace, 1999).

Studies have also shown that differences between the status of individuals do not produce the same barriers to communication in Internet discussions as they do in face-to-face discussions. In one of the earliest studies of Internet communication, Kiesler et al. (1984) compared three-way conversations under two conditions, face-to-face and by e-mail. They found that face-to-face conversations tended to be dominated by the individual with the highest status but that this phenomenon was much reduced when communication took place by e-mail. You may recall that when we looked at intergroup contact we said that equal status contact was a necessary condition for reducing prejudice. This means that the Internet may be an effective

medium for tackling prejudice. As Wallace (1999) puts it, if you are a rich lawyer who dabbles in Internet interaction as a hobby, and you find that one of your 'cyber-companions' is an unemployed youth, you might reappraise your stereotypes of unemployed people.

the Internet and collective action

The Internet is also an effective facilitator for collective action. Eng (1995) has reported that in response to California's new anti-immigration laws of the mid-1990s, the Internet was the means by which information was quickly disseminated and protests organised. No other medium would have allowed such an efficiently organised response by protesters. Other protests, including the Tiananmen Square pro-democracy demonstration of 1989, have been coordinated by use of the Internet.

thinking critically

Internet use is changing rapidly, and some of the 'facts' that have been established about Internet use may cease to hold true. As more people use the Internet the idea that there is a distinct group of 'digital citizens' is fast becoming obsolete. Similarly, with the growth of Web cam use, the assumption that Internet interaction fosters equal status contact may soon be out of date and Internet users may be able to obtain all the visual cues we use to categorise people in face-to-face contact. What is certain is that the Internet will become an increasingly important medium for social interaction and a focus of study for social psychologists.

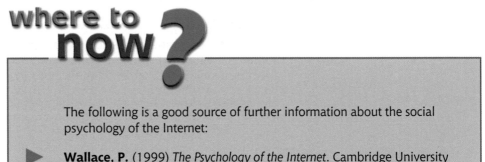

The following is a good source of further information about the social psychology of the Internet:

▶ **Wallace, P.** (1999) *The Psychology of the Internet*. Cambridge University Press, Cambridge. A very readable general introduction to the ways in which basic psychology has been applied to understanding Internet use.

talking
point
contemporary issues

why do people participate in genocide?

background

Genocide is defined as a systematic effort to wipe out a group of people. Stop for a moment and consider what a staggering thought that is – people will make the decision and follow it through to devote their time, energy and resources to purging another group of human beings from the planet. The classic incident of genocide was the Holocaust, and this inspired much of the research we have looked at in this chapter concerning both obedience and prejudice. However, be in no doubt that genocide still takes place. In the 1990s genocide took place in Rwanda, Iraq and the former Yugoslavia. One of the most important questions social psychologists can address is why do ordinary people willingly take part in genocide?

applying social-psychological ideas to understanding genocide

figure 2.13
Hitler possessed a vision of Germany and successfully put it across to his followers

Although genocide is incomprehensible to the lay person, having studied some social psychology you may begin to understand the phenomenon. Just to take some relatively simple examples of social-psychological concepts, we can show how obedience and agency, charisma, in-group favouritism and authoritarianism can all contribute to genocide.

obedience and agency

The research of Milgram and others has clearly shown that people have a remarkable tendency to follow orders, even when doing so breaches their personal moral beliefs. Looking in particular at Milgram's research, we should face the uncomfortable truth that if ordered by someone we accepted to be in a position of authority to commit an atrocity, we would probably do it. Agency probably also contributes to genocide. Interviews with Nazis and participants in more recent instances of genocide (for example, Peters and Richards, 1998) reveal that people believe that they are serving the interests of their community or society, and that even if they find their tasks repulsive they believe that they must carry them out.

charisma

Modern research has revealed that charisma is not so much a set of personality traits, as was once believed, but rather a set of social skills, for example the ability to convey a vision to followers. Leaders such as Hitler undoubtedly had this skill in abundance and this may have contributed to the mass obedience of his orders.

in-group favouritism and social identity

Perhaps the first process that needs to take place before genocide can take place is the categorization of people into 'them and us'. Whenever we can identify someone as a member of a different group from our own we tend to exhibit in-group favouritism – we favour members of our own group. According to social identity theory we do this to protect our self-esteem, which is tied up with the status of our group relative to others. Although in-group favouritism does not normally lead to genocide it is perhaps a necessary condition for it to take place.

authoritarianism

It is clear from research into authoritarianism that a certain personality type, associated with a particular pattern of child rearing, is particularly prone to obedience to authority and prejudice. Adorno, like Milgram, was investigating possible factors involved in the Holocaust, and he suggested that one such influence was the high incidence of authoritarianism in Germany in the 1940s. It is clear from other social-psychological research that we are all prone to both prejudice and destructive obedience. However it is likely that authoritarians are particularly prone to these behaviours and so their influence, though not necessary or sufficient for genocide, probably feeds into the situation and makes matters worse.

thinking critically

It is clear that obedience, agency, charisma, in-group favouritism and authoritarianism are potential influences on genocide. However, there is a lot we do not know. Which of these factors are the most important? Is there one particular factor that is always necessary for genocide to occur? Given the tendency for destructive obedience and in-group favouritism in all of us, is there any need to consider individual differences in authoritarianism or charisma? These things remain unclear. In any case, thinking more broadly for a moment, are psychological factors the most important ones in genocide? Historians, political scientists and economists have a range of alternative ways to explain genocide that do not involve social-psychological factors at all. Although it is always important to think critically and consider these questions, it does seem likely that social psychology will remain very important in understanding genocide.

media watch

revealed: why evil lurks in us all

Martin Bright, *Observer*, 17 December 2000

Psychologists have struggled for decades to explain why ordinary people participate in atrocities such as the Nazi Holocaust or the Stalinist purges.

Now experiments carried out in Britain reveal that most people obey authority unquestioningly and would also walk past an injured stranger who did not come from their ethnic or social group. The findings will shake the long-held British belief that this country is immune from the kinds of tyranny found in other parts of the world.

Research carried out at Lancaster University among football supporters found that they failed consistently to come to the aid of an injured supporter from a rival team. Secret cameras filmed individual Manchester United fans as they ignored a Liverpool fan played by an actor as he writhed on the floor. When the actor wore a Manchester United shirt the supporters helped him in 80% of cases.

A separate experiment – again filmed with a secret camera – shows the majority of people on a train complying with a stranger's order to give up their seat. When the stranger is accompanied by a man in a uniform not a single passenger chooses to disobey.

Dr Mark Levine, the psychologist who developed the football fan experiment, said: 'these are ordinary people. If you ask people whether they would help a stranger in distress, they say they would. But in reality, they just don't do it.'

Colonel Bob Stewart, former commander of UN forces in Bosnia, said his experiences in the Balkans left him in no doubt that, given the right circumstances, similar human rights atrocities could be committed in Britain. 'What makes a man go for a drink with his neighbour one moment and shoot him the next? We still don't understand what causes normally good people to go over the edge. Until we do, there is the possibility that it will happen.'

questions

1 Do the experiments reported in this article fit in with the previous research you have studied?

2 To what extent do you agree with Colonel Stewart that we do not yet fully understand the psychological processes involved in genocide?

conclusions

Social psychology is a wide field, concerned with how and why humans interact with and influence one another. We have looked in particular at two aspects of social interaction: obedience and prejudice. A feature of human social behaviour is our tendency to obey authority. Milgram has explained this in his agency theory as an innate tendency, which helps us form stable societies. Some individuals – charismatic leaders – appear to have a particular ability to obtain obedience from their followers.

Prejudice is another important feature of human interaction. Social identity theory provides us with a good basis from which to study and understand prejudice, although it does not neatly explain individual differences in prejudice. This is addressed by a complementary approach, authoritarian personality theory. There has been much recent interest in the social constructionist approach to prejudice, and it appears that prejudice is encouraged by our use of language. Psychologists have been involved in a variety of strategies designed to reduce prejudice. Whereas the common in-group approach aims to blur the boundaries between groups, collective action strengthens the social identity of groups and encourages them to assert their rights. We can also use social-psychological concepts to understand a wide range of real-life situations. We have looked at two very different social situations of great contemporary interest to psychologists, Internet interaction and genocide. Our understanding of both these phenomena has been enhanced by ideas such as in-group favouritism and social identity.

what do you know ?

1 Describe one key study from the social approach to psychology. (5)

2 Outline one assumption of the social approach. (3)

3 (a) Describe one research method used in the social approach. (4)
   (b) Evaluate the method you described in (a). (4)

4 (a) Describe one theory of human obedience. (5)
   (b) Evaluate the theory you described in (a). (5)

5 Discuss one way in which psychologists have attempted to reduce prejudice. (10)

6 Discuss one contemporary issue in social psychology. (12)

The cognitive approach is based on the following ideas:

◆ In contrast to social psychology, which focuses on the external influences of our social and cultural environment on our behaviour, cognitive psychologists are concerned with the internal operations of the mind. Cognitive (mental) processes include *perception* – the ways in which we take in information via the senses and make sense of it; *memory* – the processes of storing and retrieving information; and *thinking* – the mental manipulation of information that allows us to have ideas, hold opinions and decide on courses of action.

◆ It stresses the importance of understanding how the human mind processes information. Cognitive psychologists think of the mind as a system for handling information. We constantly receive information from the external environment, interpret it in the light of existing information in our memory and think about it. We then respond to the information, for example with an opinion, an emotional response or sometimes with action.

◆ Many cognitive psychologists find it helpful to think of the mind as operating in a similar way to a computer. In some ways the mind handles information like a computer: it has an input of information from the senses; throughput of information in the form of memory, thinking and language; and an output in the form of decisions, speech and action. In some ways, of course, the mind is not like a computer. We are much more fallible and slower at searching for information. On the other hand we are much better at using mental shortcuts to locate information. Despite these differences, the workings of a computer can serve as an *analogy* to understand the human mind. We can thus think of ourselves as having hardware (the nervous system), and of acquiring programming through experience.

what's ahead?

In this chapter we look at the cognitive approach to psychology. Cognitive psychology focuses on mental processes such as perception, memory, language and thinking. Here we are particularly concerned with memory. We look at some of the classic theories of how our memory operates and of how we forget information. In the *real lives* section we apply these theories to help understand the usefulness but also the pitfalls of eyewitness testimony. In *talking points* we examine two issues of great importance to psychologists, namely the controversy over recovered memories and flashbulb memory, and explain them using cognitive concepts.

memory

Memory is absolutely fundamental to our lives. In the course of a day we have to store vast amounts of new information and retrieve even more that we have already stored. We have to recall who we are, recognise the faces of everyone we meet and retrieve all the relevant information about them, and remember how to move and communicate. We also have to refer back to information from our past experiences and recall technical information such as psychological theories! In this chapter we look at a number of case studies of people who, through accident or illness, have lost one or more aspects of their memory. To lose just one aspect of memory, such as the ability to store new memories of events, can be severely disabling, yet storing new events is only a fraction of what we are constantly doing with our memory. In this chapter we are concerned with two main theoretical issues. First, how does memory operate? Second, how and why do we forget things?

theories of memory

the multi-store model

The multi-store approach to memory is concerned with identifying different memory stores. Atkinson and Shiffrin (1968) proposed an influential multi-store model, which suggested that there are three types of information store. Initially, information is stored for a fraction of a second at the sensory organs in a *sensory register*. Information that is attended to whilst in the sensory register passes on to short-term memory (STM), which holds a few items and lasts a few seconds. Material that is rehearsed in short-term memory is subsequently passed on to long-term memory (LTM). The processes of sensory registration, short-term and long-term memory can be shown in Fig. 3.1.

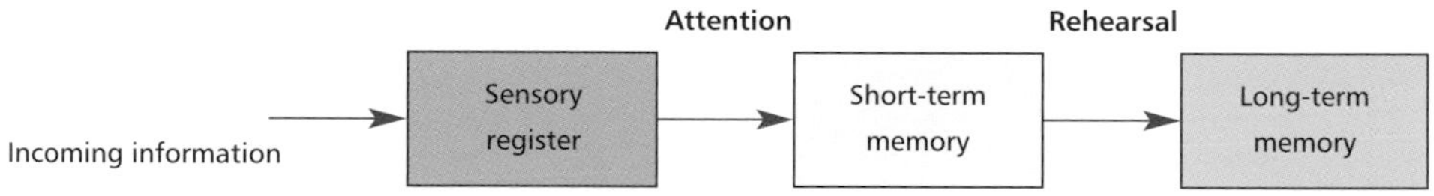

figure 3.1
Atkinson and Shiffrin's model

short-term memory

Material that we attend to is held for a few seconds in short-term memory. At this stage it is kept in acoustic form (the *sound* of words is stored). The capacity of short-term memory is small, approximately seven items. Material that is *rehearsed* – repeated back – remains in short-term memory long enough to be transferred to long-term memory. Otherwise it is lost when new information comes in and displaces it. Words that are not rehearsed are lost on the first-in-first-out (FIFO) principle.

long-term memory

Long-term memory is rather different from short-term memory. It has an unlimited capacity and information may last a lifetime, although some things are forgotten relatively quickly. Information is held in semantic rather than acoustic form. This means that what is stored is the *meaning* rather than the sound of items. Long-term memory is a single store: facts, skills and events are stored together and items are stored in the order they have been learnt.

➋ discussion

The multi-store model has been of enormous use in understanding memory, and most psychologists support the existence of separate short- and long-term memory. However, we now know rather more about the way both short- and long-term memory work, and it appears that both systems are more complex than those proposed by Atkinson and Shiffrin.

evidence for separate STM and LTM

There are two types of evidence for the existence of separate short- and long-term memory systems. First there are laboratory experiments. Glanzer and Cunitz (1966) carried out a study on recall of words from the beginning, middle and end of a list. They found that people recalled more words from the beginning (the primacy effect) and the end of the list (the recency effect), and fewest words from the middle. This suggests that the early words in the list had been transferred to long-term memory, while those late in the list were still in short-term memory. We would expect that words in the middle would be least likely to be available because they were in the middle of being transferred from STM to LTM. The primacy-recency effect disappeared if recall of the list was delayed by 30 seconds, meaning that all the words that were going to be transferred to long-term memory had already been transferred.

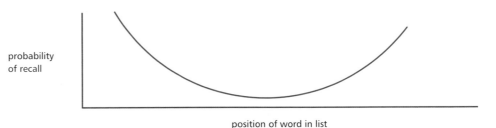

probability of recall

position of word in list

figure 3.2
The primacy-recency effect

Additional evidence for separate short- and long-term stores comes from cases of brain-damaged patients who have sustained damage to either short- or long-term memory but in whom the other system remains intact. We can look at one classic case – that of 'HM' – in detail. Note that we use initials to describe cases of this sort in order to preserve the privacy of the patient.

classic research
studies in detail

the case of HM

Scoville, W. B. and Milner, B. (1957) The loss of recent memory after bilateral hippocampal lesions. *Journal of Neurology, Neurosurgery and Psychiatry*, **20**, 11–21. Wicklegren, W. A. (1968) Sparing of short-term memory in an amnesic patient: implications for strength theory of memory. *Neuropsychologia*, **6**, 235–244.

Background: HM was a male patient suffering severe epilepsy. In 1953, at the age of 27, he had major surgery in an attempt to relieve the epilepsy. The temporal lobes on both side of his brain were removed. This had a profound effect on his memory.

Case history: since the day of the operation HM has been virtually unable to form new memories for facts or events, although he can still learn new motor skills. He shows only mild difficulty in recalling events for 11 years prior to the operation and no difficulty in recalling

events from before the age of 16. Most interestingly, in spite of his severe difficulty in forming new long-term memories, his short-term memory is relatively normal. He was found to be able to retain the normal seven items in short-term memory, although unlike most of us he could not extend this by rehearsal.

Interpretation: HM has a severely damaged long-term memory but a largely intact short-term memory. This is powerful evidence to suggest that short- and long-term memory are in fact separate systems.

the nature of short-term memory

Although there is considerable support for the idea of the existence of separate short- and long-term memory systems, it appears that the way Atkinson and Shiffrin thought of short-term memory is flawed. Gelkopf and Zakai (1991) tested whether information is lost from short-term memory on a first-in-first-out basis as Atkinson and Shiffrin suggested. A total of 120 students were presented with a list of 28 words and given 3 minutes to rehearse and recall them. If words were lost from STM on a FIFO basis we would expect that words from the beginning of the list would be poorly recalled but this was not the case, showing that words are not in fact displaced in this way. There is also some question as to whether words in short-term memory are in fact encoded in semantic as well as acoustic form (their meaning is processed as well as the sound). This is demonstrated by the case of FK.

The case of FK

Forde, E. M. E. and Humphreys, G. W. (2002) The role of semantic knowledge in short-term memory. *Neurocase*, **8**, 13–27.

Background: FK is a male patient who suffered brain damage from carbon monoxide poisoning at the age of 29. He has suffered damage to long-term memory and has difficulty in recalling facts although he has a relatively normal ability to recall events.

Case history: FK has particular difficulty remembering the meanings of particular words, though not all. A list of 'known' words, the meaning of which he did understand, was established along with a list of 'unknown' words, the meaning of which he did not understand. He was then tested on reading tasks involving the known and unknown words. He made many errors in pronunciation of the unknown words but not of the known words.

Interpretation: reading involves short-term memory. If there were no semantic processing of words in short-term memory we would expect no difference in FK's ability to pronounce known and unknown words. In fact FK has considerable difficulty pronouncing words, the meaning of which he does not know. This strongly suggests that information in short-term memory is processed semantically.

case studies of brain-damaged patients

Cases such as HM and FK are classic examples of cognitive problems suffered by people with brain damage. The study of such cases is part of a particular branch of cognitive psychology known as *cognitive neuropsychology*. Cognitive neuropsychologists are concerned with studying cognitive processes as they occur in the brain. Often, the best way to achieve this is to compare the information-processing abilities of brain-damaged patients with non-damaged participants.

People suffer brain damage for a variety of reasons, including head trauma, stroke, poisoning and as a side effect of surgery. When particular areas of the brain are damaged, specific cognitive problems tend to result. As well as giving us general information about which areas of the brain are responsible for particular mental functions, this gives us clues about how cognitive functions work. For example, in HM's case the fact that his long-term memory was severely damaged while his short-term memory remains almost normal is strong evidence for separate systems of STM and LTM. Although case studies of brain-damaged patients are extremely useful to cognitive psychologists they have limitations:

◆ Each case is unique and we simply do not know how far we can generalize the effects of damage to one patient.

◆ It is unusual for only one part of the brain to be damaged or for only one cognitive ability to be impaired following stroke, accident and so forth. This means that it can be difficult to disentangle which particular impairments are due to particular areas of damage.

There appears to be more than one system of short-term memory responsible for handling different types of information. If STM were a single system, as suggested by Atkinson and Shiffrin, we would expect that introducing a new task involving visual information would disrupt the ability of STM to handle verbal information and vice versa. However if there are separate visual and verbal systems we would expect an additional visual task to have little impact on verbal STM. Seitz and Schumann-Hengsteler (2000) tested this. Twelve students were given multiplication tasks to perform while either listening to irrelevant speech (verbal disruption) or tapping items on a map (visuo-spatial disruption). Listening to irrelevant speech but not the visuo-spatial task spoiled performance on the sums. This suggests that there are separate short-term memory systems to handle visual and verbal information.

the nature of long-term memory

Recall the cases of HM and FK: HM has had impaired memory for events and facts encountered since his operation but no problem learning new motor skills; FK has difficulty in recalling some factual information such as word meanings but no problem recalling events. These cases suggest that there are at least three different storage systems in long-term memory, and indeed most cognitive psychologists support the existence of three separate long-term memory systems. *Semantic* memory is the system responsible for memory of facts. *Episodic* memory contains our memory for events and *procedural* memory deals with our motor skills – memory of how to do things. There is strong evidence from numerous cases like HM and FK that in fact semantic, episodic and procedural memories are separate long-term memory systems.

the levels-of-processing (LOP) approach

Craik and Lockhart (1972) put forward a radical alternative to the multi-store approach. Rather than looking at memory as a series of different stores they focused on the different ways information can be processed and the effect these can have on how well information is remembered. Memory is thus a by-product of the general

for+against

the multi-store model

+ There is clear evidence both from experiments (such as Glanzer and Cunitz, 1966) and case studies of brain-damaged patients (for example HM) that there are separate systems of short- and long-term memory.

— It is now widely believed that there is more than one short-term system designed to handle different types of information. This is shown by studies such as that of Seitz and Schumann-Hengsteler in which verbal information but not a motor task interfered with the ability to do sums.

— There is also evidence, for example from the case of FK, to suggest that material in short-term memory is analysed for meaning and not just for sound.

— There is strong evidence, for example from the cases of HM and FK, to suggest that there are several separate stores of long-term memory, for example for facts, events and skills.

processing of information in the mind. Information that is deeply processed (thought about deeply) is likely to be remembered. Craik and Lockhart suggested three levels at which information is processed:

◆ structural processing (processing information about what things look like);

◆ phonetic processing (processing information about what something sounds like);

◆ semantic processing (processing information about what something means).

Semantic processing is the deepest form of information processing – it involves the most cognitive work. Material that is semantically processed is likely to be the best remembered. Structural processing is the shallowest form of information processing and is likely to result in the least material being remembered. This was demonstrated in a classic study by Craik and Tulving (1975).

classic research
studies in detail

deepest processed best remembered

Craik, F. I. M. and Tulving, E. (1975) Depth of processing and retention of words in episodic memory. *Journal of Experimental Psychology*, **104**, 268–294.

Aim: to test whether words that were processed for their meaning would be better remembered than words that were processed for information about their appearance or sound.

Procedure: students were given four tasks that involved reading word lists and analysing the words for either their appearance, sound or meaning. For example, in one experiment participants were asked whether each word was written in capitals (structural), whether it rhymed with another word (phonetic) or whether it was part of a category (semantic). At this point they were unaware that the experiment was concerned with memory, so were not expecting to be tested. Later they were given tests for their memory of the words.

Findings: in all four experiments participants best remembered the words that they had processed semantically. For example, they recognized 70% of words that been processed for whether they had been members of categories. Memory was worst for words that had been processed structurally. For example, participants only recognized 15% of words after they had been processed for capital letters.

Conclusion: the extent to which words are remembered depends on how deeply they are processed. Semantic processing – thinking about the meaning of the words – leads to them being remembered best.

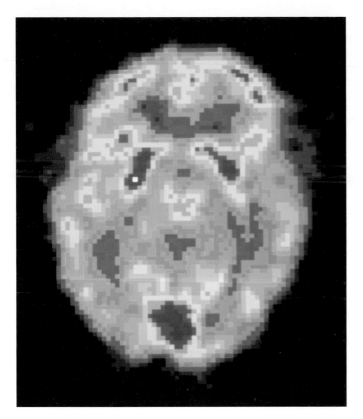

figure 3.3 The brain is more active when material is being deeply processed

The levels-of-processing approach has accomplished its aim, which was to make us realise that there is more to memory than transferring information from one store to another and that we should think of memory not in isolation but as part of the whole information-processing system of the mind. There is some support from cognitive neuropsychology for the idea that processing information semantically does involve more cognitive work than other forms of processing. Nyberg (2002) examined brain-scanning studies looking at information processing and memory. He concluded that activity in the frontal and temporal lobes of the brain is greater when information is semantically processed. This suggests that these regions are doing 'more work' when information is processed for meaning. The LOP model also has practical applications in helping people to remember information better by processing it more deeply. For example it is important for advertisers to make sure that adverts are processed semantically if watchers are to remember the product (Nordhielm, 1994). In education, it is widely believed that 'deep learning' helps students learn material better than does 'shallow learning' (Riding and Rayner, 1998).

inter**active** angles

Compare the multi-store and levels-of-processing approaches. Think about what each theory emphasizes and how each explains what material is best remembered. Compare the evidence for each.

Although the levels-of-processing approach has proved very useful in helping us understand memory, the model, in its classic form, has limitations. One problem is that factors other than how deeply words are processed affect how well they are remembered. Information that is particularly unusual or carries a lot of emotional significance also tends to be remembered well. Reber et al. (1994) carried out an experiment with secondary school and university students, in which words high or low in emotional content were presented in ways that led to their being processed in either a deep or shallow way. Words without emotional significance were recalled best when they were processed semantically, but the way in which the

for+against

the levels-of-processing approach

+ The idea of levels of processing is helpful in reminding us that memory is part of a wider system of information processing and not simply a matter of stores. It thus enhances our general understanding of cognitive processes.

+ There is experimental support (Craik and Tulving, 1975) for the idea that semantically processed information is better remembered than structurally or phonetically processed material.

+ There is also evidence from brain-scanning studies, such as Nyberg (2002), to show that when material is semantically processed, there is more brain activity than when it is processed in a more shallow way. This extra brain activity may equate to deeper processing.

− Other factors also affect how well material is remembered, independent of depth of processing. For example, Reber et al. (1994) showed that emotional content of words affected recall independent of depth of processing.

words were presented had no effect on the emotional words, which were recalled as well as the semantically processed non-emotional words. This suggests that the emotional content of information acts as an influence on how well it is remembered independently of the level of processing.

the reconstructive memory approach

This is another very different way to understand memory. In contrast with levels-of-processing theory, which emphasises what happens when memories are encoded and stored, the reconstructive memory approach is more concerned with what happens when information is stored and retrieved from memory. To the lay person, memory operates in much the same way as a video recorder; we keep a complete, sequential record of everything that has happened to us. When we remember something we are locating the right piece of videotape and playing it back. However, Bartlett (1932) suggested that memory was more of 'an imaginative reconstruction' of past events; influenced by our attitudes and our responses to those events at the time they occurred (1932, p. 213). Retrieval of stored memories thus involves an active process of *reconstruction*. Whenever we try to recall an event, we actively piece it together using a range of information.

Bartlett developed the *serial reproduction* method of studying reconstructive memory. This is rather like the children's game of 'Chinese whispers'. One person tells another a story, and this person tells it to a third one, and so on. This replicates under laboratory conditions the process in which information is passed from one person to another in real life. Bartlett famously used the Native American story, *The War of the Ghosts*, in serial reproduction studies because it was unfamiliar and different in cultural origins to the participants.

an edited version of *The War of the Ghosts*

One night two men from Edulac went down the river to hunt seals, and while they were there it became foggy and calm. Then they heard war cries, and they thought; 'maybe this is a war-party'. They escaped to the shore, and hid behind a log. Now canoes came up. They heard the noise of paddles and saw one canoe coming up to them. There were five men in the canoe and they said: 'What do you think? We wish to take you along. We are going up the river to make war on the people.' . . . So one of the young men went and the other returned home . . . the young man went ashore to his house and made a fire. And he told everybody and said: 'behold I accompanied the ghosts and went to fight. Many of our fellows were killed and many of those who attacked us were killed.' . . . When the sun rose he fell down. Something black came out of his mouth. His face became contorted. The people jumped up and cried. He was dead.

Bartlett found that once it had been reproduced through six people the story changed in particular ways. It was shorter – typically around half its original length. The details that were left out tended to be those specific to Native American culture, so the story became more like an English story. Bartlett also used stories like *The War of the Ghosts* in his *repeated reproduction* procedure. In repeated reproduction the same participant retells the story on a number of occasions. The results were the same. After a number of retellings the story became shorter and more Anglicised.

schemas and stereotyping

Bartlett (1932) proposed that the reason for the changes in stories like *The War of the Ghosts* during serial and repeated reproduction was the fact that remembering involves looking at units of memory called *schemas*. We each have a schema for every aspect of the world, consisting of all the information we have that is related to it. When we reconstruct memories we activate the relevant schemas and make use of the information in them. For example, when trying to recall *The War of the Ghosts* we might make use of our ghost schema, war schema and death schema. When Bartlett's participants remembered the story, they scanned all the relevant schemas for more information and eliminated information that did not fit into their understanding of ghosts, war and so forth.

One way of thinking about the effect of reproduction on *The War of the Ghosts* is to say that the story became increasingly *stereotyped*. In other words it increasingly fitted in with the participants' preconceived ideas about what a story involving ghosts and war should be like. This may be much the same process that operates when we stereotype people. In a classic study of stereotyping, Allport and Postman (1947) showed white participants a picture in which a scruffy white man armed with a cut-throat razor was arguing with a black man in a suit. Descriptions of the scene were passed on to other participants through serial reproduction. After a few reproductions the descriptions changed so that the black man was usually described as holding the razor. Presumably the participants accessed their 'black-schema' and 'white-schema' and the information they found there required that they distort the scene to make it logical to them.

media watch

no thanks for the memory . . . it was only a TV advert

By Tim Radford, *Guardian*, 5 September 2001

Future generations of Britons will wistfully recall their wholemeal Hovis childhoods, that first Werther's original toffee from cuddly Grandpa, and those festive meals around a Bisto gravy Sunday roast – even though they might never have experienced them.

Elizabeth Loftus, a psychologist from the University of Washington, told the [British] Association [of Science] yesterday that commercial advertisers could be unwittingly implanting false memories in unsuspecting viewers.

She and colleagues had studied a Walt Disney TV advertising campaign called 'Remember the magic'. This used imagery that evoked family outings and what seemed to be home movies of people shaking hands with Mickey Mouse. She wondered if these ads had triggered 'memories' in viewers who might never have been to Disneyland or shaken hands with Mickey Mouse.

So she tested volunteers with her own 'Disneyland advert' in which someone shook hands with an impossible character – Bugs Bunny, created by Warner Brothers [*not* Disney]. She found she was right – some of the volunteers who saw her film were more likely to believe they had in fact met Bugs Bunny at Disneyland.

She found that Ovaltine, Alka Seltzer and Maxwell House had begun to dig into their vaults for nostalgic film of 40 years ago. In one study, US adults 'remembered' drinking Stewart's root beer from bottles in their youth, although the bottles had only been in production for 10 years.

questions

1 Explain this phenomenon using the idea of reconstructive memory.

2 Think of some other adverts that have made use of 'retro' imagery. Can you accurately remember whether the scenes they portrayed really existed?

the cognitive approach

discussion

The idea that memory involves reconstruction is widely accepted in psychology. There is a wealth of evidence to show that we both interpret new information and reconstruct past information in the light of our schemas. One way of testing the role of schemas is to see whether memory is distorted in such a way as to make it more stereotyped. In one study by Carli (1999), 135 undergraduates read a story and were asked to reproduce it. In one condition the story ended abruptly without a conclusion and in the other it ended with a rape scene. In the second condition, participants tended to distort the story more they did in the first. These distortions tended to be consistent with the theme of rape, thus the rapist was described in threatening terms prior to the rape.

for+against

reconstructive memory

+ Our memory is certainly inaccurate, in particular when we have a relevant existing schema. This strongly suggests that memory involves a process of reconstruction using all available information.

+ There is clear evidence (for example, from Carli, 1999) that memories become more stereotyped following reproduction – as we would expect if retrieval involves accessing schemas. This supports the idea that memory is reconstructive.

– Reconstruction is a retrieval process, and there are other important aspects of memory that are not explained by the reconstructive memory approach. For example, the approach does not address the range of memory systems, as does the multistore approach, nor the effect of the form in which information is taken in, as does the levels-of-processing approach.

Further support for the role of schemas in retrieval comes from the fact that memory does not appear to be distorted when we have a new experience. This is because there are no existing schemas containing information to distort the memory. This was demonstrated by Wynn and Logie (1998) in a repeated reproduction task in which undergraduate students were asked to recall their first week at university. There was no decline in the accuracy of their recollections – as we would expect as they had no pre-existing schemas containing stereotyped accounts of starting university.

Although reconstruction probably does occur, this approach to memory is primarily concerned with the retrieval of information and tells us little about how memories are stored. It is therefore not mutually exclusive with the multi-store model, which emphasises different storage systems or the levels of processing model, which emphasises the different ways in which information can be processed prior to storage.

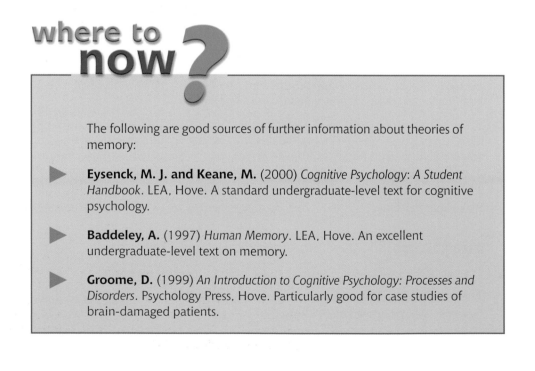

where to now?

The following are good sources of further information about theories of memory:

▶ **Eysenck, M. J. and Keane, M.** (2000) *Cognitive Psychology: A Student Handbook*. LEA, Hove. A standard undergraduate-level text for cognitive psychology.

▶ **Baddeley, A.** (1997) *Human Memory*. LEA, Hove. An excellent undergraduate-level text on memory.

▶ **Groome, D.** (1999) *An Introduction to Cognitive Psychology: Processes and Disorders*. Psychology Press, Hove. Particularly good for case studies of brain-damaged patients.

comparing the approaches

The multi-store, levels-of-processing and reconstructive approaches to memory are very different and may seem quite difficult to reconcile with one another. However, there is plenty of support for the basic principles of each approach. Rather than choose which is the 'best' approach, it is more useful to reflect on what each has taught us. From the multi-store approach we have learnt that memory involves a number of separate processes, some of which fall under the heading of 'short-term memory' and others under the umbrella of 'long-term memory'. The levels-of-processing approach reminds us that memory is only one aspect of the mind's processing of information, and that we store information while we are doing other things with it. The reconstructive memory approach has taught us much about the accuracy of retrieval and the relationship between memory for events and our existing knowledge.

forgetting

We have all had the experience of not being able to remember a fact or event. One of the basic questions cognitive psychologists have to answer is why we forget information. Several theories have been put forward to explain forgetting. Some theories propose that memories are forgotten because they have been permanently lost from the brain. These are called *availability theories*. The simplest availability theory is trace decay, the idea that the physical trace left in the brain of a memory disappears over time. Other approaches (collectively known as *accessibility theories*) work on the basis that memories still exist, but that we have trouble retrieving them. With regard to long-term memory, accessibility theories have rather more credibility than availability theories. We can look here at two accessibility theories of forgetting, cue dependency (also called retrieval failure) and repression.

cue dependency

This is probably the most common reason why we forget things (Eysenck, 1998). We have all experienced the 'tip-of-the-tongue' phenomenon, in which we know we know something but are temporarily unable to retrieve it. Endel Tulving (1972) proposed that forgetting takes place when we have the information we are seeking in our memory but we lack the necessary *cues* to access it. Cues are additional pieces of information that guide us to the information we are seeking, rather like the contents page of a book.

In a classic experiment, Tulving and Pearlstone (1966) demonstrated that we can remember more words if we have access to the categories from which the words are taken. Participants were read lists of words that fell into categories, for example dogs. The category names, for example 'dog', were included as well as a few examples of each category. In one condition the participants recalled the words without cues (free recall) and in the other they were given the category titles as cues (cued recall). In the cued condition the participants remembered more words. The category titles are a form of *semantic cue*. The word 'semantic' refers to the meaning of words, thus a semantic cue is one which works because its *meaning* triggers recall.

state and context cues

It is well known that if you return to a place to which you haven't been for a while (such as your old school) the familiar sights, sounds and smells will bring a flood of memories rushing back. This is because this distinctive sensory information serves as a cue to retrieve old memories that have been dormant for years. This type of cued retrieval is known as *context dependent* – it depends on cues from the external environment (context). Context-dependent recall was demonstrated in a fascinating study by Godden and Baddeley (1975).

the cognitive approach

figure 3.4
Divers recall information learnt
underwater better when
underwater again

Physiological cues – the state we are in when we learn something – can work in much the same way. Recall is said to be *state dependent* if it requires a physiological cue for recall. When we are in a particular state at the time of learning information then that physiological state can act as a cue to help us retrieve that information. Emotional states can act as state cues; thus if we are excited or afraid when we encode information we find it easier to retrieve that information if we are in the same mood.

discussion

The effects of state and context have been demonstrated in many studies. Duka et al. (2001) had 48 participants perform a range of memory tasks with or without alcohol at learning and retrieval. Overall the alcohol had no effect on the accuracy of retrieval; however those who had drunk alcohol in the encoding tasks remembered better when they had drunk alcohol again at retrieval stage, whereas those who had learnt having drunk a placebo remembered better without alcohol. Another study by Aggleton and Waskett (1999) made use of the real-life situation in which people visited a museum characterised by distinctive smells.

classic research
studies in detail

like a diver out of water!

Godden, D. R. and Baddeley, A. D. (1975) Context-dependent memory in two natural environments: on land and underwater. *British Journal of Psychology*, **66**, 325–331.

Aim: the aim of the study was to see whether words would be remembered better when recalled in the same environment than in a very different environment. In this case the two environments were a beach and under the sea.

Procedure: 18 divers were given word lists to learn. These were presented either on the beach or 15 feet under the sea. The divers were then asked to recall the words. In one condition the participants were in the same location as they were when they learnt the words, and in another condition they were in the other location. To control for the possibility that any decline in accuracy of recall was due to the disruptive change from land to sea or vice versa, participants were also given a recognition test on the words.

Findings: overall, whether words were presented on land or under water did not affect the accuracy of recall. However, lists learned under water were recalled considerably better when recalled under water and those learnt on the beach were similarly better recalled on the beach. In fact, 40% more words were forgotten if recall took place in a different environment. In the recognition test, changing environment had no effect.

Conclusion: recall was considerably better if the context was the same as when information was learned. This suggests that context cues enhanced recall. The fact that recognition was unaffected by a change in environment suggests that the change itself was not responsible for the decline in accuracy of recall.

the smelly museum study

Aggleton, J. P. and Waskett, L. (1999) The ability of odours to serve as state-dependent cues for real-world memories: can Viking smells aid the recall of Viking memories? *British Journal of Psychology*, **90**, 1–7.

Aim: the aim of the study was to find out whether memory of a visit to a museum characterized by distinctive smells would be improved by the presence of the same smells at recall.

Procedure: participants were 45 volunteers who had visited the Jorvik Viking Centre in York, on average between 6 and 7 years prior to the study. The experience of visiting the Jorvik Centre is characterized by a set of distinctive smells specially manufactured by a Blackpool company. They include 'burnt wood', 'rubbish acrid' and 'fish market'.

Participants were allocated to three groups, each of which completed a questionnaire about the museum exhibits twice. In one condition the first questionnaire was accompanied by a selection of the bottled smells from the museum. In the second condition the smells accompanied the second questionnaire and in the control condition no smells were given.

Findings: the group who received the museum smells with the first presentation of the questionnaire recalled most detail about the museum. The second group showed a sharp increase in accuracy of recall in the second questionnaire, which was accompanied by the smells.

Conclusion: the distinctive smells of the museum acted as cues, which aided recall of information about the museum.

figure 3.5
The Jorvik Viking Centre

The phenomenon of cue dependency has important practical applications. Jerabek and Standing (1992) found that students taking examinations in a different room from the one that they studied in could enhance their recall in the examinations by imagining their classroom. This is called *context reinstatement*. We consider context reinstatement further in our discussion of eyewitness testimony (p. 56). State dependency also has clinical applications. In a fascinating recent study, Mystkowski et al. (2003) gave participants caffeine or a placebo while they were being treated for a phobia of spiders. A week later they were shown spiders, either with or without receiving caffeine. Those who had the caffeine during the treatment were much more likely to be afraid if they had no caffeine in their system when later shown the spider. It appears that they only remembered that they weren't afraid of spiders any more if they had the state cue of caffeine!

media watch

shock tactics

By Kevin Toolis, *Guardian*, 13 November 1999

Gary Meadows does not like the smell of roasting meat. It gives him bad thoughts. He says it gives him flash-backs to his days as a paramedic ambulanceman attending car crashes, seeing smashed skulls, mangled limbs and burning flesh.

truth in the broken mirror

By Gunter Grass, *Guardian*, 27 January 2001

Suddenly I was standing outside the closed bathing station, beside the entrance next to the kiosk, likewise chained and padlocked. And all in a moment I could feel once more the thrill of one of the modest pleasures of my childhood: lemonade crystals tasting of straw-berry, lemon and lily of the valley. But the minute this refreshing drink began to sparkle in my memory it began to stir up stories, deceitful stories, which had been waiting, needing only a single word of recognition to bring them to the surface.

questions

1 Explain how each of the cases described above might be a result of cue-dependent memory.

2 Think of an example where you remembered details of something after you had the correct cues.

for+against

cue dependency

➕ There is a wealth of experimental evidence (for example, Aggleton and Waskett, 1999) to support the importance of cue dependency in forgetting.

➕ Cue dependency explains the very common 'tip-of-the- tongue' experience. It also explains the experience of returning to an old haunt and suddenly recalling events that took place there. It is thus very relevant to understanding our everyday experiences of forgetting.

➕ Cue dependency has many important practical applications, as we can enhance people's recall by introducing context or state cues. For example, students can enhance their recall of work in an exam by imagining their classroom.

➖ Cue dependency is probably not a complete explanation of forgetting. It does not explain for example why some emotionally charged memories remain vivid in the absence of cues and why we generally tend to recall happy material better than unhappy.

Although cue dependency is probably the single most common reason for forgetting, there are instances that it cannot easily explain. For example, we retain a vivid memory for distinctive and emotionally charged events (called flashbulb memories), even though we may encounter relatively few cues after the event (Brown and Kulik, 1977). Neither does cue dependency easily explain why we tend in general to recall happy memories better than unhappy ones.

repression

Sigmund Freud (1894) proposed the idea that we forget facts or events that provoke anxiety or unhappiness, thus protecting ourselves from having to experience these negative emotions (see also p. 139). Freud believed that repressed memories remain active in the mind, although the individual is not aware of them, and that they can trigger symptoms. The tendency to use repression as a defence against negative emotions is acquired in childhood, a response to poor-quality relationships with parents.

Repression can take a range of forms. At its most dramatic, repression involves the complete blanking out of highly traumatic memories. There are numerous recorded cases of people who suffered sexual abuse in childhood, then forgot their abuse throughout adolescence only to have the memory recur in early adulthood. More common is the general tendency to recall happy memories more easily than unhappy ones. On occasion we may recall events but repress the emotion attached to them.

discussion

The idea of repression has proved useful to therapists (see p. 138 for a discussion), but rather frustrating to cognitive psychologists because it is so difficult to investigate using the sort of research methods cognitive psychologists favour. To carry out laboratory experiments on repression would mean traumatising participants sufficiently to make them want to forget the experience and, for ethical reasons, we simply are not able to do that sort of thing. There are, of course, numerous case studies from the psychodynamic approach, but cognitive psychologists tend not to accept case studies of this type as real evidence.

Recently, new approaches have been developed to help us investigate repression in ways more acceptable to cognitive psychologists. One approach involves the use of diaries. Walker et al. (1997) had participants keep diaries of pleasant and unpleasant events for a few weeks. When tested later they showed good recall of pleasant events but poor recall of unpleasant events, suggesting that these may have been repressed.

There is also evidence to support Freud's idea that the tendency to use repression as a defence mechanism is learnt in childhood and associated with poor quality relationships with parents. Myers and Brewin (1994) classified women as *repressors* on the basis that they scored low on tests of anxiety but high on tests of defensiveness. Repressors took up to three times as long as others to recall unhappy childhood memories, supporting the validity of the term. Furthermore, when interviewed, the repressors had a strong tendency to report a poor-quality relationship with their fathers.

Studies such as these suggest that repression does take place and that we tend to censor much of our memory. However, there are still controversies surrounding repression. Solid evidence for the complete blocking out of highly traumatic memories remains very difficult to obtain and we don't understand well why some people who suffer traumatic events appear to repress them whereas others tend to have difficulty forgetting them.

for+against

repression

+ Many cases have been documented of people who have forgotten highly traumatic events, temporarily or permanently. Repression is a good explanation because we would normally expect such events to be highly memorable.

− There are other possible explanations for these cases (such as cue dependency) and, in any case, one-off case studies of this type do not constitute strong evidence for cognitive psychologists.

+ There is now solid evidence for the existence of repression, for example from diary studies (Walker et al., 1997) and experimental studies (Myers and Brewin, 1994).

− We know relatively little about how common repression is or what factors determine when it takes place. Nor do we have a good understanding of why some people who undergo highly traumatic experiences have difficulty forgetting them rather than remembering them.

the cognitive approach

where to now?

The following are good sources of further information about theories of forgetting:

▶ **Eysenck, M. J. and Keane, M.** (2000) *Cognitive Psychology: A Student Handbook*. LEA, Hove. A standard undergraduate-level text for cognitive psychology in general.

▶ **Baddeley, A.** (1997) *Human Memory*. LEA, Hove. An excellent undergraduate-level text on memory.

▶ **Groome, D.** (1999) *An Introduction to Cognitive Psychology: Processes and Disorders*. Psychology Press, Hove. Particularly good for case studies of brain damaged patients.

real lives
key application

eyewitness testimony

One of the ways in which cognitive psychology has been put to use in the real world is in understanding the accuracy of eyewitness testimony. The outcome of many criminal trials hinges upon the accounts of crimes provided by witnesses. In the 1970s a series of experiments by American cognitive psychologist Elizabeth Loftus called the accuracy of eyewitness testimony into question. Loftus applied Bartlett's idea of reconstructive memory to show how memory for events can be distorted, in particular by the sort of questions asked of witnesses. Remember that according to the reconstructive memory model, when we remember something we access not only memory itself, but also all the relevant information to which we have access. Following questioning, the information contained in the questions forms part of the information we can access when we try to reconstruct a memory. We can look in detail at one of Loftus's experiments demonstrating the effect of questions on the accuracy of recall.

Loftus and her colleagues conducted a number of related experiments. Loftus and Palmer (1974) showed that changing the nature of the *verbs* embedded in questions can influence the way in which a witness recalls events. Participants were shown footage of a car crash and asked 'How fast were the cars going when they "smashed", "collided", "bumped", "hit" or "contacted"?' These different verbs imply different speeds, and this affected participants' recall. The 'smashed' group estimated 41 miles per hour and the 'contacted' group estimated 32 miles per hour. Loftus and Palmer tested other participants for 'smashed' or 'hit' (with similar results) and another group who were not asked about speed. One week later the participants were asked 'Did you see any broken glass?' and 32% of the 'smashed' group reported seeing broken glass, compared with just 14% of the 'hit' group and 12% of the control group. In fact there was no broken glass in the film.

Loftus and Zanni (1975) again showed participants film of a car crash and tested the effect of using the definite article (*the*) as opposed to the indefinite article (*a*). One group were asked 'Did you see *a* broken headlight?' and another group were instead asked 'Did you see *the* broken headlight?' Of those asked about *a* broken headlight, 7% reported seeing one as opposed to 17% of those asked about *the* broken headlight. These studies all illustrate the impact of *post-event information* on memory. They show that when we reconstruct our memory of an event we draw on information we have encountered since the event. More recently, Loftus and colleagues have shown that post-event information can be used to make people forget events.

dodgy questioning

Loftus E. F. (1975) Leading questions and the eyewitness report. *Cognitive Psychology*, **7**, 560–572.

Aim: the aim was to see whether participants could be influenced by misleading questions to remember false details of a film.

Procedure: 150 student participants were shown a piece of film of a car being involved in a crash. They were then presented with 10 questions about the film. Nine of the questions were given to all participants but one differed. In one condition, the participants received the question 'How fast was the white car going when it passed the barn?' There was in fact no barn. In a control condition in which the equivalent question contained no misleading information, participants instead were asked 'How fast was the car going while travelling along the country road?' One week later the participants were given a further 10 questions about the film, one of which was 'Did you see a barn?'

Findings: participants in the misleading condition, who had seen the question 'How fast was the white car going when it passed the barn?' were more likely to respond a week later by saying that they had seen the barn: 17% reported seeing a barn as opposed to less than 3% of the control group.

Conclusion: the barn introduced in the question was remembered. When the participants later reconstructed their memory of the film, some of them accessed the information about the barn and incorporated it into the memory.

now you see it; now you don't!

Wright D. B., Loftus E. F. and Hall M. (2001)
Now you see it; now you don't: inhibiting recall and recognition of scenes. *Applied Cognitive Psychology*, **15**, 471–482.

Aim: the aim was to see whether post-event information could make people forget events – specifically whether seeing a scene again without a key event would prevent people remembering the event.

Procedure: 268 participants were shown one of a selection of scenes by slides or a video-clip. These included an incident of drunk driving. In an experimental condition they were shown the same scenario then shown it again but without a critical event, and were asked to make up a story about it. In the control condition they saw the scenario twice in its entirety. Participants were then tested both for recall of what took place and recognition of whether particular things happened or not.

Findings: both in tests of recall and recognition, participants in the experimental condition remembered fewer details of the scene than those in the control condition.

Conclusion: these findings suggest that post-event information involving something not happening can prevent people remembering that such an event did in fact take place.

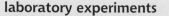

laboratory experiments

The laboratory experiment is the most commonly used research method in cognitive psychology. The experiments carried out by Elizabeth Loftus are classic laboratory experiments. Experimental research is characterized by the comparing of two or more conditions between which only one factor – *the independent variable* – differs. This allows us to see the effect this independent variable has on a dependent variable. Laboratory experiments are carried out under controlled conditions. In Loftus's (1975) study on leading questions, the independent variable was whether questions contained misleading information. In the experimental condition there was a misleading question, whereas in the control condition there was not. The dependent variable was the accuracy of the participants' memories of the event. Conducting experiments in the laboratory rather than in the field means that we have complete control over all the variables; we can be reasonably sure that any difference in the results between conditions is due to those conditions and not to anything else. There are however limitations to laboratory experiments:

◆ The experiment takes place in artificial surroundings and participants know they are taking part in a psychological study. This means that they may not behave naturally.

◆ The tasks given to people in the laboratory are often rather different from the ways in which we use our memory in real life. In Loftus's research for example, people were asked to watch a film. This is a very different experience to witnessing a crime. We are likely to be less aroused and less motivated to remember accurately what we saw.

studies of real-life events

Loftus's work has certainly improved our understanding both of reconstructive memory and of eyewitness testimony. We now understand that we reconstruct memories using post-event information as well as pre-existing schemas. She has also played an important role in changing attitudes towards eyewitness testimony, which has traditionally been thought of in the legal system as extremely powerful evidence. Nonetheless there are limitations to her procedures. The major criticism is that her laboratory-based studies are conducted in very artificial settings that may not effectively recreate the experience of witnessing a real crime. These studies can thus be said to lack *ecological validity*.

We should perhaps be rather cautious about applying the results of laboratory studies such as these to real life. Generally, studies of eyewitness memory for real events have found that witnesses do rather better than is the case in laboratory studies. Yuille and Cutshall (1986) followed up 13 of the 21 witnesses to a shoot-out between an armed robber and a gun shop owner in Vancouver, Canada. Five months later they were interviewed again, the interviews including two misleading questions. They were unfazed by the misleading questions and produced highly detailed and accurate accounts. More recently, Riniolo et al. (2003) studied the eyewitness accounts of 20 survivors of the sinking of the *Titanic* and found that in general they recalled events accurately. The stereotypical scene of a ship sinking is that it slides intact beneath the surface. In fact the *Titanic* broke apart and sank in bits, and 15 of the 20 witnesses clearly recalled this.

On the other hand some studies have shown that memory for real-life events is not accurate. Seven weeks after the terrorist attack on New York on 11 September 2001, Kathy Pezdek (2002) surveyed 690 people, including students from New York, Hawaii and California, firefighters from California and airline staff from United and American Airlines about their recall of the incident. Overall, the New York students and airline staff had the most accurate recall (as we would expect as the event was most directly relevant to them). However, all the groups made errors. For example, when asked how long there was between the plane striking the first tower and its collapse the average estimate was 62 minutes whereas in fact it was 108 minutes.

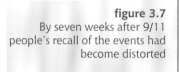

the memory conformity effect

One aspect of eyewitness memory that has been of particular interest recently is the *memory conformity effect*. One important source of post-event information, which we use when reconstructing our memory for an event, is what other witnesses say happened. This means that as witnesses hear each other's stories, their accounts become more similar. Memory conformity was an important aspect of the investigation into the Oklahoma bombing of 1995, in which 168 people were killed when right-wing anti-government terrorists bombed a federal building in Oklahoma City. Memon and Wright (1999) studied what took place following the bombing. In one case a witness reported seeing Timothy McVeigh with a second man renting the truck that was used in the bombing. Although other witnesses had not reported this second man, following the publicity over John Doe 2, as he became known, they later came to believe that they had in fact seen him.

media watch

differing accounts give jury hard task

By Jamie Satterfield, Knews.com

At least half a dozen people saw Jeffrey Martin Reaves shoot Mark Campbell in August 1997, but not one of them can agree on exactly what they witnessed.

Were there four shots fired? Six? Eight? Was Reaves waving empty hands in anger before the shooting or was he lugging an engine valve cover? Was Campbell at his son's side when Reaves opened fire or was he walking on a roadway towards his son?

The reliability of eyewitness accounts, long considered among the best and strongest evidence in any criminal case, is increasingly coming under scrutiny across the nation, defence attorneys and prosecutors say.

Veteran defence attorney Herbert S. Moncier said he believes eyewitness accounts are afforded far more weight by juries than they deserve. He argues that our recall of what we see is always coloured by our psyches.

Moncier has used psychological experts in court to argue against the reliability of eyewitness testimony. But he won't be able to do that any more. Last year the State Supreme Court ruled the use of such experts is not admissible in court.

questions

1 Use your understanding of reconstructive memory to suggest how pre-existing schemas and post-event information could have led to the differing witness accounts in this case.

2 Consider the evidence from laboratory and real-life studies. Do you think that testimony from memory experts should be allowed in court?

figure 3.8
Confusion following the 1995 Oklahoma bombing stimulated research into the memory conformity effect

Memory conformity has also been demonstrated in the laboratory. Wright et al. (2000) attempted to replicate this 'John Doe 2 phenomenon' by setting up an experiment in which pairs of participants looked at a picture story in which a woman stole men's wallets from a pool hall. In each pair, one participant saw pictures in which a man entered the pool hall with the thief. The other saw an identical sequence of pictures except that there was no male accomplice. They were asked to recount the story together then fill in a questionnaire individually. One of the questions asked whether the thief had an accomplice. About half the participants who had not seen pictures showing the accomplice conformed to their partner's account and reported an accomplice.

the cognitive interview

The cognitive interview (Fisher and Geiselman, 1988) is an interview procedure designed by cognitive psychologists in order to maximise the accuracy of witness recall. At the time of writing the procedure is being increasingly used by British police. The interview relies on the principle of cue dependency. Its aim is to maximise the range of retrieval cues available to the interviewee without introducing post-event information that might distort the memory. Semantic, state and context cues are used. Questions such as 'How did you feel then?' are designed to act as state cues, reinstating the same mood as at the time of the witnessed event. Witnesses are asked to imagine as many details as possible of the setting in which the witnessed event took place in order to make use of context cues. They may also be asked to recall events from the beginning, the end and the middle in order to maximise the number of semantic cues available.

Research has generally supported the usefulness of the cognitive interview. Koehnken et al. (1999) performed a meta-analysis on 42 studies of the effectiveness of the cognitive interview, combining the results of the previous studies. They concluded that cognitive interviewing leads to a significant increase in the amount of accurate information recalled in interviews, although only a small increase in the accuracy of recall. Recently, a spin-off benefit of the cognitive interview has been discovered; witnesses appear to be less vulnerable to the distorting effects of post-event information having had a cognitive interview. In one study Holliday (2003) gave children aged 9 to 10 years a cognitive interview or a standard interview about a real-life event, then a written summary of the event containing inaccurate information. Those who had had the cognitive interview were found to be less likely to be influenced by the misleading information. It may be that once we have accurately reconstructed our memory, using cues, we are likely to use this accurate reconstruction as the basis for future recall.

the cognitive approach

Go to the homepage of Gary Wells, currently located at **www.psychology.iastate.edu/ faculty/gwells/homepage.htm**. You can download a range of academic and newspaper articles related to eyewitness testimony, in particular concerned with identifying suspects from line-ups.

for+against

eyewitness testimony

— Numerous laboratory experiments, for example those by Loftus and her colleagues, have found that witness memory can be highly inaccurate, and easily distorted by post-event information.

+ However, laboratory experiments may fail to reproduce the conditions in which people witness real crimes. A smaller body of research using witnesses to real events (for example, the sinking of the *Titanic*) has shown better recall.

— It is well established in both laboratory experiments and real-life events that witnesses are influenced by each other's accounts. This means that witnesses who have heard news accounts of the events they witnessed or have compared accounts with other witnesses are likely to be unreliable.

+ The cognitive interview is reasonably successful at retrieving accurate accounts of events and appears to help witnesses avoid the distorting effects of post-event information.

where to now**?**

▶ **Dwyer, D.** (2001) *Angles on Criminal Psychology*. Nelson Thornes, Cheltenham. This contains a chapter giving rather more detail on eyewitness testimony.

▶ **Vrij, A.** (1998) Psychological factors in eyewitness testimony. In Memon, A., Vrij, A. and Bull, R. (eds) *Psychology and Law, Truthfulness, Accuracy and Credibility*. McGraw-Hill, London. An excellent chapter summarizing some recent research findings on eyewitness testimony.

▶ **Gross, R.** (2003) *Key Studies in Psychology* (4th edn). Hodder & Stoughton, London. Contains a detailed account of the work of Elizabeth Loftus, and reviews some more up-to-date studies.

the accuracy of recovered memories

The experience of recovered memory takes place when an event comes to mind that we have not been able to recall for some time. Obviously this is a common enough experience. However, some people have had the experience of recovering their memory of events that are so dramatic it is hard to understand how they could have been forgotten in the first place. Recovered memories came to public attention in the early 1990s when a number of patients in therapy 'recovered' memories of events including childhood sexual abuse and witnessing their parents committing murder that were demonstrated to be false. The term *false memory syndrome* describes this 'remembering' of events that did not in fact take place. An example of a dramatic and high-profile case was that of Beth Rutherford. In 1992 she remembered, during therapy, that she had been repeatedly raped by her father over a period of seven years, and had twice become pregnant and been forced to abort the foetus. Examination revealed that in fact she was a virgin, and she subsequently successfully sued her therapist.

A fierce debate has taken place throughout the last decade concerning the accuracy of recovered memories. At one extreme, many therapists questioned the existence of false memory syndrome and suggested that all recovered memories should be regarded as being genuine. At the other extreme, some memory researchers denied the possibility that any recovered memories were real, and explained all recovered memories in terms of false memory syndrome. Nowadays we have a better understanding of the processes of recovered memory and it is widely acknowledged that recovered memories can be genuine or false.

applying cognitive psychology to understanding recovered memories

We can apply theories of memory and of forgetting to understand how it is possible to forget important events and later remember them, and how it is possible to 'recover' completely false memories. We look here at how repression and cue dependency can explain the loss and later recovery of genuine memories and how reconstructive memory can explain false memory syndrome.

repression and the forgetting of trauma

Perhaps the most obvious explanation for forgetting traumatic memories is Freud's idea of repression. Repression is a psychological defence mechanism in which we forget an event in order to shield ourselves from the unpleasant emotions associated with it. It is widely believed amongst therapists that traumatic events such as childhood sexual abuse are often repressed in order to shield the victim from the pain and shame of the memory. So how does repression explain the recovery of traumatic memories? According to Freud, repression requires an expenditure of effort, and one reason therapy is helpful is that it removes the defence and thus saves us the mental effort of keeping a memory repressed. The fact that so many memories are recovered in therapy as defences are broken down suggests that repression is at the root of at least some recovered memories.

cue dependency; an alternative explanation

Jarvis (2003) has pointed out that although repression is the most obvious explanation for forgetting traumatic events it is not, in fact, the only one and that it may be a mistake to link too closely the debate over recovered memories and that over repression. Another possible explanation for forgetting trauma is cue dependency. If we suffer an experience and then do not experience it again then, over time we may not have the necessary cues to continue to recall it. When memories are recovered in therapy it may be that the therapist unintentionally provides cues that reinstate the context of memories in much the same way as interviewers do when conducting cognitive interviews. This would explain why so many memories are recovered during therapy. Cue dependency also explains why recall can be triggered by related adult events. For example many memories of childhood sexual abuse are recovered in adolescence and early adulthood when young people are starting to have sexual relationships. It is possible that the experience of adult consensual sex serves as a memory cue and allows the recall of childhood sexual abuse.

reconstructive memory and false memory syndrome

Although repression and cue dependency explain the recovery of genuine memories they cannot account for false ones such as those experienced by Beth Rutherford. Reconstructive memory explains how memories can become wildly distorted as we interpret them in the light of both our pre-existing schemas and post-event information. Elizabeth Loftus has demonstrated in a series of studies how easy it is to implant a false memory. In one study Loftus and Pickrell (1995) attempted to implant false memories in 24 adult participants. Using information from relatives, they made up, for each participant, a booklet containing short stories about three real events from the life of each participant, and one false story about being lost in a shopping mall at the age of 5 years. Participants were then asked to write what they remembered about the events described in the booklet. Seven of the 24 'remembered' the false event, sometimes in vivid detail. Loftus and many other memory researchers suggest that false memories are generated during therapy in much the same way, as therapists unintentionally provide post-event information in their questioning of patients. Thus a therapist who suspects sexual abuse might use leading questions and actually create a false memory of the abuse.

thinking critically

Using the concepts of repression, cue dependency and reconstructive memory we can see how both genuine and false recovered memories can occur. The British Psychological Society issued guidelines for psychologists dealing with recovered memories. Their position is as follows:

> there can be little doubt that at least some recovered memories of CSA [childhood sexual abuse] are recollections of historical events. However there is a genuine cause for concern that some interventions may foster in clients false beliefs concerning CSA or can lead them to develop illusory memories. (BPS, 1999)

In other words the current 'official position' of psychologists is to support the existence of both false memory syndrome and genuine recovered memories. In the absence of other supportive evidence it is difficult to know whether a recovered memory of, say, childhood abuse is true or false. In general, in such cases, it is probably unsafe to accept that the recovered memory is true if:

◆ people claim that they can, as a result of therapy, now remember abuse they suffered in the first year or two of their lives;

◆ the therapist used hypnosis, drugs or guided imagery to help the patient remember the abuse;

◆ the memories of the abuse become more detailed and bizarre over time.

angling
with the net

Access the two following Web sites: **www.jimhopper. com/memory/#de** and **http.faculty.washington.edu/eloftus/**. One provides a strong case for the accuracy of recovered memories and the other the argument against it. Working in two groups, access one site each and, based on the arguments put forward there, hold a student conference on the status of recovered memories.

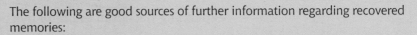

The following are good sources of further information regarding recovered memories:

▶ **Memon, A.** (1998) Recovered memories: psychological issues and legal questions. In Memon, A., Vrij, A. and Bull, R. (eds) *Psychology and Law, Truthfulness, Accuracy and Credibility*. McGraw-Hill, London. A very balanced account of the evidence for and against recovered memory.

▶ **Conway, M. A.** (ed.) (1997) *Recovered Memories and False Memories*. Oxford, Oxford University Press. This brings together the positions of therapists and memory researchers. Rather than a single, balanced account, you will find here both sides of the debate over the status of recovered memories.

talking
point
Contemporary issues

flashbulb memory

Every day we have numerous minor experiences and encounter a huge amount of information. Under normal circumstances we simply forget most of this, just remembering the relatively small number of facts and events that are important to us. However, occasionally we witness an event of such historical importance that we remember it with exceptional clarity. Under these circumstances people appear to be able to recall the most trivial details of things they were doing at the time. This ability to recall trivia alongside the major event is known as *flashbulb memory*. Researchers have looked at people's memory for momentous historical events to see how much peripheral detail they recall. For example Neisser and Harsch (1992) studied people's recall of the explosion of the space shuttle *Challenger* and Conway et al. (1994) have looked at memory for the resignation of Margaret Thatcher.

applying cognitive psychology to understanding flashbulb memory

There are two related research questions concerning flashbulb memory. First, is there some special process in forming a flashbulb memory, or can we in fact explain the apparent existence of flashbulb memories by the normal processes of memory? Second, do we really recall more peripheral details of great historical moments or do we just believe we can?

special mechanisms theory

Brown and Kulik (1977) proposed that flashbulb memories are a unique type of memory that is immune from the usual processes of decay and distortion. Memory traces for particularly emotional, shocking and personally relevant events are stored in a different way from other memories. This is an evolutionary mechanism for ensuring that we do not forget details of catastrophic events – clearly this may be information directly relevant to our survival. Brown and Kulik tested their hypothesis by asking 80 participants what they were doing when they heard of President Kennedy's assassination. They found that all but one person recalled quite well what they were doing.

Some, although by no means all, later studies have supported this idea that dramatic news events are so well remembered that minor peripheral details are clear. Cohen et al. (1994) asked young and older adults to recall as many details as possible about how they learned of Margaret Thatcher's resignation in 1991. They were first questioned 2 weeks after the event then again 11 months later. The finding was that 90% of young adults and 42% of older adults met the criteria for a true flashbulb memory – there was little or no decline in the accuracy of their recall of what they were doing when they heard the news between the two occasions.

explaining flashbulb memory by conventional theories

It is quite possible to explain the experience of flashbulb memories without proposing any special mechanisms. We can for example apply the multi-store model of memory. Remember that, according to Atkinson and Shiffrin, the main factor affecting how well things are recalled is how many times they are rehearsed. After a momentous event such as Kennedy's assassination or Thatcher's resignation it is likely that we talk to several people on several occasions about the event. This means that all aspects of the event will be rehearsed many times.

From a levels-of-processing perspective what matters is how deeply we process the information. If an event is deeply important to us then it is likely that we process it deeply. Events such as Kennedy's assassination and Thatcher's fall from power, being of great importance, are probably thought about in great depth and so are processed very deeply.

Of course the peripheral details of what we were doing when we heard about great historical events may not be rehearsed extensively during later conversations and may not be processed particularly deeply. To explain why such details may be so well remembered Groome (1999) has suggested that such minor details require extensive cues to be recalled and that the dramatic events stored as flashbulb memories provide such cues.

thinking critically

Of course flashbulb memories only require explanation if peripheral details are *really* better remembered than ordinary events. Although Brown and Kulik, and Cohen et al. did report such dramatic recall other studies have not. Neisser and Harsch (1992) questioned participants about what they were doing when they heard about the *Challenger* disaster the following day and again three years later. They found that about half the peripheral details were changed between the two occasions. Schmolck et al. (2000) asked students how they had heard the verdict of the O. J. Simpson trial three days after the event then 15 and 32 months later. After 15 months answers were fairly close to what they said after 3 days and only 11% contained major inaccuracies. However, after 32 months a lot more detail was forgotten. Only 29% of people recalled details accurately. Results like these call into question the whole existence of flashbulb memories.

angling with

Go to **http://cc6.cumber.edu/ psych/c/fmq.htm** and read the information on flashbulb memory. Download the flashbulb memory questionnaire, which concerns the events of 11 September 2001. *Check that no one you are with lost any family or friends in the attack*. If they did not, then individually complete the questionnaire and discuss the level of detail in your responses. Based on this, do you think there is something special about flashbulb memories?

where to now?

The following is a good source of further information about flashbulb memory:

▶ **Eysenck, M. W. and Keane, M**. (2000) *Cognitive Psychology; A Student Handbook*. Psychology Press, Hove. Contains a detailed section on flashbulb memories.

conclusion

Cognitive psychology regards the human mind as an information processing system, rather like a computer. Here we have looked at memory as an example of a cognitive function. There are a number of different ways of thinking about memory. Some think in terms of separate systems of short- and long-term memory. By contrast others explain memory in terms of levels of information processing. A third approach is to focus on the reconstructive nature of memory. How we forget information is of crucial importance to understanding memory. Repression is a defence mechanism in which memories associated with strong negative emotions are pushed out of consciousness to prevent the unpleasant experience of recalling them. The most common reason for forgetting is probably cue dependency. We experience this when we require a cue that was present when the fact or event was stored before we can recall it.

There are many practical applications of memory research. One such application is in eyewitness testimony. There is some debate as to how accurate witnesses' memories of crime are. Most laboratory experiments have found considerable memory distortion, but some studies of real-life events have found rather better recall. Based on cue dependency, psychologists have developed the cognitive interview, a technique for improving the accuracy of eyewitness memory. Two issues of considerable current importance are recovered memories and flashbulb memories. Both of these are highly controversial phenomena and psychologists are divided as to whether they really exist.

what do you know?

1 Outline two key assumptions of the cognitive approach to psychology. *(6)*

2 (a) Describe the multi-store model of memory. *(4)*
   (b) Evaluate the multi-store model. *(4)*
   (c) Compare and contrast the multi-store and levels-of-
       processing approaches. *(6)*

3 (a) Describe one study from the cognitive approach. *(5)*
   (b) Evaluate the study you described in (a). *(5)*

4 (a) Describe one study into the accuracy of eyewitness testimony. *(4)*
   (b) Using psychological theory, explain how eyewitness memory can
       become inaccurate. *(6)*

5 Discuss one contemporary issue in psychology and explain it using
   concepts from the cognitive approach. *(12)*

The cognitive-developmental approach is based on the following ideas:

◆ As for any cognitive approach, in cognitive-developmental psychology, mental processes such as thinking are seen as being of primary importance in understanding people. This contrasts with the emphasis on behaviour in learning theory (chapter 5) or emotion in psychodynamic theory (chapter 6).

◆ Cognitive processes change with age. Different cognitive-developmental theories emphasise different reasons for these changes. To Piaget, children are scientists who discover the world, moving from a simple understanding to an increasingly advanced one as they build successive layers of understanding. Vygotsky placed his emphasis on the role of others in instructing children's development, whereas most modular theorists see mental abilities as being activated as the brain matures.

4 the cognitive-developmental approach

what's ahead?

If you have read chapter 3 you will know that cognitive psychology involves the study of *cognitive* or mental processes, including perception, memory and thinking. Cognitive-developmental psychology is concerned with how these cognitive processes develop throughout the lifespan. In this chapter we are most concerned with the development of thinking and reasoning. We look at the classic theories of Jean Piaget and Lev Vygotsky. We also look at the modern and exciting modular approach to cognitive development. In our *real lives* section we see how these three approaches have been applied in education. In *talking points* we apply a range of theories to understand the use of computers in education and how children learn to understand the thoughts and feelings of other people.

the work of Jean Piaget

The best-known and most influential theory of cognitive development is that of the Swiss psychologist, Jean Piaget. Piaget researched and wrote on the subject of children's cognitive development from the 1920s until the 1980s. Piaget's great contribution to psychology was his understanding that the ways in which children think are not simply less sophisticated than those of adults simply because they have less knowledge; rather, they think in an entirely different way. Piaget was interested in both how children learnt and how they thought. From this starting point Piaget went on to contribute three main areas of theory:

◆ the way in which children acquire knowledge;

◆ the logical flaws in children's thinking;

◆ stages of cognitive development through which children pass.

In this chapter we will examine each of these areas separately, although you will see that they are all closely interrelated.

how children learn

agency

Perhaps the most distinctive aspect of Piaget's view of cognitive development as opposed to other more recent theories is the idea of *agency*. Take care not to confuse this with Stanley Milgram's very different use of the same word (p. 16). To Piaget 'agency' is our motivation to actively pursue knowledge. In other words we are agents of our own cognitive development. Piaget noted that even very young children are very inquisitive about their own abilities and about the details of the world. Cognitive development is thus an active process in which we explore the world and construct a mental representation of reality based on what we discover in our explorations. The sophistication of our mental representation of the world increases with age as we explore in a more sophisticated manner, building on our existing understandings to create more advanced mental representations.

schemas and equilibration

Schemas are mental structures, each of which contains all the information the individual has relating to one aspect of the world. We have schemas for people, objects,

figure 4.1
Piaget

actions and more abstract concepts, such as ideas you have studied in psychology. Piaget believed that we are born with a few innate schemas that enable us to interact with others. During the first year of life we construct other schemas. When our existing schemas are capable of explaining what we can perceive around us, we are said to be in a state of *equilibrium*. However, whenever we meet a new situation that cannot be explained by our existing schemas, we experience the unpleasant sensation of disequilibrium. We are instinctively driven to gain an understanding of the world and so escape disequilibrium. Piaget identified two processes by which equilibration takes place, *assimilation* and *accommodation*. Collectively these are known as adaptation.

◆ Assimilation takes place when a new experience can be understood by adding information to an existing schema. For example, when a child whose family has canaries and who is familiar with watching sparrows in the garden first encounters more exotic but recognisable birds, these are assimilated into the child's understanding of birds.

◆ Accommodation takes place in response to more radically new experiences, as the child has to accommodate the existence of something new into their understanding of the world. For example, a child who encounters aggressive birds such as a gaggle of geese has to accommodate to this characteristic by learning to keep out of their way. This can involve radical alteration of a schema or the creation of a new one.

Assimilation and accommodation are not mutually exclusive. A child who encounters geese for the first time and is hissed at or chased by them will both assimilate their existence *and* accommodate to the fact that they are potentially dangerous.

operations

As well as knowledge of things we will encounter in the world, we also need to understand the rules by which the world operates. Piaget called these rules *operations* and, very importantly, he suggested that the reason that children think in different ways at different stages of their development is because the operations of which we are capable change with age. Piaget believed that, while schemas develop with experience, operations develop as the child's brain matures. Very young children do not have operations at all, and they are thus said to be *pre-operational*. The first operations to appear are *concrete*. This means that children can understand the rules governing something provided they can see it. Later, rules governing abstract concepts are understood. The rest of Piaget's theory largely depends on this idea of operations. The errors of logic that Piaget identified in children's thinking take place because of the limited operations available to them.

∂ discussion

Children are certainly curious from a young age and can thus be described as agents of their own learning. The idea of the schema as the basic unit of knowledge is widely accepted by psychologists, although there is little direct evidence of assimilation and accommodation as two separate processes. However, studies have shown that the motivation to learn increases once we have some understanding of a subject (Andreani, 1995). This does not fit neatly with Piaget's idea of agency, which suggests that we are motivated to learn by our discomfort at not understanding something. A further problem with Piaget's view is that it sees children acquiring knowledge in isolation. In reality, other people can be important agents of our learning and Piaget probably underemphasised their importance. For example we imitate other people's actions and they may instruct us in a skill.

logical flaws in children's thinking

Piaget conducted a number of studies of children's ability to carry out tasks of logic. His earliest studies were observations of children playing. Piaget noted that different children of the same age tended to make the same mistakes and he suggested that this was because children of the same age tended to commit the same errors in logic. From these observations the idea was born that children do not just know less but think differently from adults. Piaget went on to conduct experimental studies, initially on his own children but later on large numbers of children at a psychology laboratory. He also interviewed children (at least those who were old enough) to try to get an idea of how they were thinking when they committed errors in logic. We can look now at some of Piaget's major areas of research into children's thinking.

object permanence

Piaget was interested in children's intellectual development from birth until adolescence. His best-known work on very young children concerned their understanding of *object permanence*. Object permanence refers to the understanding that objects exist permanently even when they are no longer visible. Piaget observed the behaviour of infants who were looking at an attractive object when it was removed from their sight. Until about 8 months, children would immediately switch their attention away from the object once it was out of sight. However, from around 8 months they would search for the object actively. If, for example, it were placed behind a screen within their reach the child would simply push the screen aside. Piaget concluded from this that, prior to about 8 months of age, children do not understand that objects continue to exist once they are out of sight. Support for Piaget's idea comes from a variation in his procedure in which a sheet covers the hidden object so that the object's shape is clearly visible to the child. Children still did not respond to the object, suggesting they really did not understand that the object continued to exist.

It seems that even when young children have grasped the fact that objects still exist after they cannot be seen, for a time they continue to have difficulty with locating hidden objects. In a variation on his object permanence procedure, Piaget noted that when children become accustomed to looking behind a particular screen for the concealed object, they will sometimes continue to look behind the same screen even when they have seen the experimenter hide the object elsewhere. This showed that, although grasping object permanence was a significant milestone in the child's development, there are further steps to be taken in the child's understanding of the properties of objects.

figure 4.2
This 9 month old has no difficulty in locating his teddy bear behind a screen!

Some later researchers have questioned the validity of Piaget's research on object permanence and his assertion that children do not begin to understand object permanence until 8 months. In one study Baillargeon and DeVos (1991) set up a screen with a window in the top half in front of 3-month-old babies. Long and short carrots were passed behind the screen held vertically. In a 'possible' condition, long carrots could be seen passing by the window and the short carrots could not be seen until they emerged at the edge of the screen. In an 'impossible' condition the long and short carrots were passed behind the screen, but neither were visible in the window, although they emerged as expected at the edge of the screen. The babies looked for significantly longer at the long carrots that had not appeared in the window during the 'impossible' condition once they had reappeared at the edge of the screen. This suggests that they recognised that there was something unusual about this condition

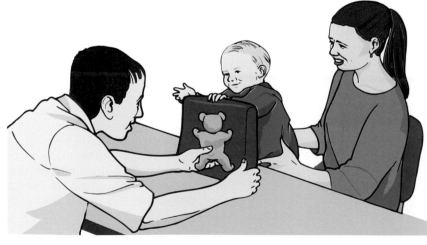

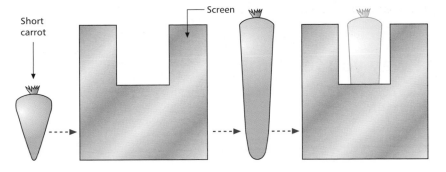

Screen

figure 4.3
The apparatus used by
Baillargeon and DeVos (1991)

and hence that they had some under-standing of object permanence. In a recent follow-up Aquiar and Baillargeon (1999) carried out a similar experiment using a toy mouse passing behind a screen. They found that 10-week-old infants did not differentiate between the possible and impossible condition, and hence that they did not have the same understanding of object perma-nence. This suggests that 3 months is a critical turning point.

egocentrism

Egocentrism is the tendency to see the world entirely from our own perspective, and to have great difficulty in seeing the world from the viewpoint of others. Unlike difficulty with object impermanence, which is associated with specific ages, egocentrism declines gradually throughout childhood. Piaget saw egocentrism as applying to both abstract and concrete concepts. A classic study by Piaget and Inhelder (1956) illus-trated egocentrism in the physical environment.

In Piaget and Inhelder's famous 'three mountains experiment' each model mountain had a different marker on the top: a cross, a house or a covering of snow. A doll was positioned to the side of the three mountains. Children were sat in front of the scene and shown pictures of the scene from different viewpoints. Their task was to select the picture that best matched what the doll could 'see'. Piaget and Inhelder noted that children aged under 7 had difficulty with this task, and tended to choose the picture of the scene from their own point of view. You can witness egocentrism for yourself by watching the television news with a young child, and asking them what the news-reader can see. Young children will often believe that the newsreader can see them.

Although children undoubtedly do become less egocentric with age, some studies have suggested that they can successfully perform tasks assessing egocentrism from a much younger age. Hughes (1975) conducted such a study.

figure 4.4
Piaget and Inhelder's 'three mountains' experiment

classic research

studies in detail

it's the way you tell 'em!

Hughes, M. (1975) *Egocentrism in Preschool Children*. PhD thesis, Edinburgh University.

Aim: the aim was to create a task similar to Piaget's three mountains experiment but with the crucial difference that the situation makes more sense to the child. It was hypothesized that if this could be achieved then children would succeed in an egocentrism task earlier than was suggested by Piaget.

Procedure: 30 children aged between $3\frac{1}{2}$ and 5 years took part in the experiment. They were individually shown a scene on a table in which two walls crossed in the middle, creating four areas. The scene is shown in Figure 4.5. A toy policeman was positioned at the end of one of the walls, from where he could 'see' two of the four areas created by the walls. A boy doll was placed in each of the four areas and the child was

asked each time whether the policeman could see him. Then the policeman was moved and the child was asked to position the boy where he could not be seen. A second policeman was introduced and the child was asked to place the boy where neither could see him.

Findings: 90% of the children (including 88% of the 10 aged $3\frac{1}{2}$ years to 4 years) succeeded in placing the boy where neither policeman could see him.

Conclusion: children as young as $3\frac{1}{2}$ years could shift perspective and understand what the policeman could and could not see. This suggests that the results of Piaget's three mountains task were not due to egocentrism but to the children's difficulty in making sense of the situation and the task required of them.

figure 4.5 Hughes's apparatus

There is, of course, a difference between tasks like the three mountains one and Hughes' policemen on the one hand and the inability to understand someone else's view in the abstract, for example during an argument. The former is known in modern psychology as a *mental rotation task* and the latter as a *perspective taking task*. To Piaget, cognitive development was a single process, therefore the ability to mentally rotate an object and to understand someone else's perspective were simply different aspects of the same wider ability. However, many psychologists nowadays disagree. Evidence that mental rotation and perspective taking are different abilities comes from a study by Inagaki et al. (2002). They tested young, middle-aged and older adults on tasks assessing both abilities and found that the same people were not necessarily successful at the two tasks, and that perspective taking but not mental rotation abilities declined in older adults. This suggests that Piaget's belief that all tasks involving shifting perspective measure the same ability – egocentrism – was incorrect.

animism

Piaget (1973) reported that children aged 2 to 4 years typically attribute lifelike characteristics to inanimate objects. They may for example worry about hurting or offending their toys, or indeed they may punish their toys when they are 'naughty'. This phenomenon of *animism* is closely related to egocentrism because it takes place when children judge all objects to have the same feelings and motives as themselves. By about 4 years Piaget believed that children have a clear understanding of which objects around them are alive and which are not. There has been considerable modern research into animism in children and adults, and in general this supports the idea of animistic beliefs in children. In a recent review, Subbotsky (2000) concluded that children up to 6 years old tended to hold animistic beliefs.

the cognitive-developmental approach

the use of observation and clinical interviews

Piaget often used the technique of watching children playing or trying to perform a task, then questioning them on what they were doing and why. This combination of observing and clinical interviewing is illustrated by his work on animism. By observing children's behaviour it is possible to gain an insight into their thinking – for example if a child calls a toy 'naughty' and punishes it this gives a clue that the child must think of the toy as in some way alive and capable of understanding them. This can then be tested further by asking the child questions. The main feature of the *clinical interview* used by Piaget is that questions are formulated based on what the child is doing and later questions are based on the answers to early ones. Thus not all children are asked the same questions. Although observation and clinical interviews are useful they do have their limitations:

◆ If children are playing, it can be difficult to distinguish pretend play from behaviour that illustrates their real beliefs. For example, just because a teddy bear is being punished this does not conclusively demonstrate that the child believes in animism – the child may simply be playing.

◆ All interview techniques rely on the understanding of the interviewee, their honesty and the social pressures of the situation. We have already seen from Martin Hughes's work on egocentrism how easy it is for children to fail to understand the situation and so give misleading answers.

◆ As clinical interviews do not involve standard questions, it is very difficult to compare children, for example of different ages, based on their answers.

figure 4.6
Piaget's demonstration of number conservation

Children at the pre-operational stage say that the two rows contain the same number of pennies...

...but also that there are more pennies in the more spread-out, second row

conservation

Conservation refers to the understanding that objects remain the same in quantity even when their appearance changes. Piaget (1952) reported that young children had difficulty with conservation tasks. He demonstrated this in a number of situations, two of which are particularly well known.

◆ *Number conservation.* Piaget found that if two rows of counters are laid out side by side, with the same number of counters spaced apart at the same distance, children correctly spotted that there were the same number of counters in each row. If you want to try this at home Smarties make ideal counters (but as the child will probably eat them, check with the parents first!). If, however, the counters in one of the rows were pushed closer together, young children typically thought that there were now fewer counters in that row.

◆ *Liquid conservation.* Piaget found that if children saw two glasses together with liquid coming up to the same height in each, they could correctly spot the fact that they contain the same amount of liquid. If, however, liquid was poured from a short, wide glass to a taller, thinner container, young children typically believed there was now more liquid in the taller container.

figure 4.7
Piaget's demonstration of liquid conservation

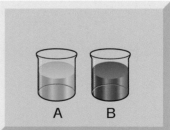

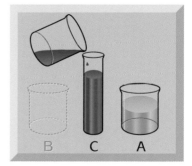

There have been challenges to Piaget's ideas concerning when children become capable of this sort of task. McGarrigle and Donaldson (1974) suggested that the children did understand that there were still the same number of counters but that the cognitive-developmental approach

they had assumed that Piaget had wanted them to say that there were now fewer counters, otherwise why would he ask the question? They tested this idea by creating a condition in which the length of the row appeared to change accidentally rather than deliberately.

classic research studies in detail

the one with Naughty Teddy

McGarrigle, J. and Donaldson, M. (1974) Conservation accidents. *Cognition*, **3**, 341–350.

Aim: to recreate Piaget's task of number conservation but with a condition in which the counters appeared to move accidentally rather than be moved deliberately by the experimenter. It was hypothesized that in this 'accidental' condition children would be more likely to give the correct answer.

Procedure: 80 participants aged 4 to 6 years took part in both conditions. In the control condition, they were subjected to the standard Piagetian task in which the experimenter presented them with the two rows of counters, asked them whether there were the same number in each row, then pushed the counters in one row closer and asked them again. In the experimental condition, once the children had been asked whether there were the same number in each row, a 'naughty teddy' ran across the table and, apparently accidentally,

pushed the counters in one row closer together. The children were then asked whether there were the same number of counters in each row.

Findings: there was a large difference between children's apparent ability to conserve in the two conditions. In the Piaget condition only 13 of the 80 children (16%) correctly said that there was the same number of counters in the two rows. However, in the experimental condition 50 of the children (62%) answered correctly.

Conclusion: children acquire their understanding of number conservation at an earlier age than was believed by Piaget. Piaget's results were not due to difficulty in understanding conservation but rather due to difficulty in understanding what the experimenter wanted them to say.

It is worth noting that numerous researchers have attempted to replicate this study, and that not all have confirmed the results of McGarrigle and Donaldson. We are thus not entirely sure how important the questions asked of children are or at what age children can really conserve. Modern studies of conservation using Piaget-type procedures continue to show that the ability to conserve increases with age, although they also reveal other interesting facts. Li et al. (1999) conducted the standard Piaget liquid conservation test on 486 Chinese children, and found, as expected, that success in the task increased with age. Although this is in line with Piagetian theory, it is interesting to note that there were considerable variations in the success of children from different schools. This suggests an important role for education in cognitive development, something underestimated by Piaget.

class inclusion

One important operation that children need to understand is *class inclusion*. This is the understanding that some classes of object fall within others. For example, cats are animals. Animals are the larger or *superordinate* class and cats are the smaller or *subordinate* class. Piaget found that pre-operational children found it hard to think clearly about the two classes at the same time.

formal reasoning

Piaget believed that from about 11 years of age, children became capable of formal reasoning. The term *formal* indicates that children capable of this type of reasoning can focus on the *form* of an argument and not be distracted by its content. For example if a child capable of formal reasoning is presented with the following syllogism: 'All green birds have two heads. I have a green bird called Charlie. How many heads does

Charlie have?' They should be able to answer 'two' (Smith et al., 1998). Before children become capable of this type of reasoning they would be more likely to become distracted by the content and point out that birds do not really have two heads. At this stage children can also reason about abstract concepts. Thus ideas like peace and justice become meaningful. This idea that children become capable of understanding philosophical issues at a certain age has proved useful to those writing television scripts aimed at young people – see *media watch*.

Once children can reason formally they become capable of scientific reasoning. Inhelder and Piaget (1958) gave Swiss schoolchildren some science questions and gave them the task of devising hypotheses and carrying out experiments to test these. One such task was to investigate the pendulum problem. Children were given pendulums of different weights and string of different lengths. Their task was to determine whether the speed of the pendulum depends on its weight or the length of the string. It was found that most 11 to 15 year olds were capable of setting up and carrying out this and similar tasks.

Piaget believed that we all achieve formal reasoning eventually, although there is some variation in age and some only achieve formal thinking by the age of 20. However a number of studies have concluded that many people are not capable of formal thinking. In a longitudinal study (one in which participants are followed up over a long period), Bradmetz (1999) studied the cognitive development of 62 children from the age of 7 until they were 15 years old, regularly giving them a battery of tests, including the Inhelder and Piaget science task, designed to measure formal thinking. Only one of the 62 young people proved capable of formal thinking – less than 2%. Of course, if they were tested again at the age of 20 many more may demonstrate formal operational thinking, but Bradmetz's results do at least show that formal thinking tends to develop later than Piaget believed.

research methods

longitudinal studies

The Bradmetz study is a good example of a longitudinal study, a method often employed by cognitive-developmental researchers. Longitudinal studies take place over a long period as they involve tracking the same individuals through a period of development. In Bradmetz's study, children were tracked and assessed for 8 years. Studies concerned with lifespan cognitive development can run over much longer periods. The alternative to the longitudinal method is to compare different people of different ages, for example some pre-operational children and some concrete operational children. This is called a cross-sectional design. Longitudinal studies have the major advantage that, because the same children are taking part throughout, results cannot be distorted by individual differences in the cognitive abilities of the children. However, longitudinal studies do have some disadvantages:

◆ Participants are administered the same type of tasks several times over the course of the study. Improvements in performance may be due to practice as well as cognitive development.

◆ The procedure takes considerable time, and some participants may die, leave the area or refuse to continue before the end of the study.

for+against

Piaget's research

+ From his early observational studies Piaget developed highly original and quite effective experimental procedures such as the three mountains experiment and conservation tasks. These have been useful in understanding children's thinking.

– Later research has uncovered limitations with some of Piaget's procedures, in particular that they do not make 'human sense' to young children. Researchers such as Hughes and Donaldson have shown that young children can carry out tasks similar to those that Piaget thought were only possible for older children if they are designed to make human sense.

+ Piaget's basic finding that the sophistication of children's reasoning increases with age is generally supported by later research.

– There have been challenges to Piaget's ideas about the ages at which children develop different abilities. Most contemporary psychologists believe that children achieve object permanence and conservation at an earlier age than was suggested by Piaget but that abstract reasoning is achieved later, if at all.

⊘ discussion

Remember that Piaget researched cognitive development over several decades, and that we have just touched on a few key areas. However we have shown that Piaget was a brilliant and original thinker and researcher. Some of his methods, such as liquid conservation, are still extensively used in modern research. That said, more recent research has shown up some limitations in his approach. In particular Margaret Donaldson and her team, including Martin Hughes, have shown that if children are presented with tasks that are clear and comprehensible they are capable of rather more advanced reasoning than Piaget believed. Donaldson (1978) suggests that some of Piaget's tasks do not make 'human sense' to children.

stages of development

Based on the types of logical error Piaget identified as typical of children of different ages, he proposed a stage theory of development. Piaget identified four stages of development:

◆ *sensorimotor* stage – 0–2 years;

◆ *pre-operational* stage – 2–7 years;

◆ *concrete operational* stage – 7–11 years;

◆ *formal operational* stage – 11 years +.

Piaget believed that we all pass through all four stages in the same order, hence he referred to them as *invariant*. However, we vary considerably in the age at which we arrive at each stage, and the ages given above for each stage are intended only as broad averages. We reach each stage when we have constructed a new and more sophisticated mental representation of the world. Let us look briefly at the type of thinking that takes place at each stage.

the sensorimotor stage

This lasts for approximately the first two years of life. Piaget believed that our main focus at this point is on physical sensation and on learning to co-ordinate our bodies. We learn by trial and error that certain actions have certain effects. Infants are fascinated when they realise that they can move parts of their body and eventually other

media watch

holo, goodbye

By Paul Simpson and Ruth Thomas, from *SFX Magazine*, June 2001.

In a discussion of the current lack of popularity of *Star Trek*, Robert Picardo [the actor who plays the holographic doctor in *Star Trek Voyager*] has a theory. '*Star Wars* is back. They appeal to young people in a way our show does not – our show is much more cerebral and much less cartoony.'

So, in the competition for the all-important young male audience, *Star Trek* gets a late start. 'A very intellectual 6 or 7 year old might be interested, but we really hook people at 9, 10, 11 and 12, because there are certain broad themes and philosophical issues that you're just not going to get if you're a child. Children can watch *Star Wars*, the story is so elemental and there's so much campy action that I think they can watch it just as a live cartoon and have a great time.'

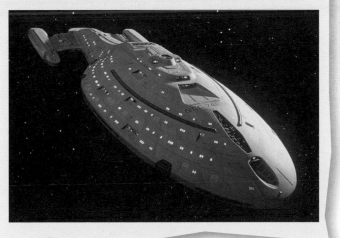

figure 4.8 TV script writers take account of the developmental stage of their audience when planning story lines

questions

1 What Piagetian stage does Picardo see *Star Trek* plot lines aimed at?

2 Based on modern studies of formal reasoning, what advice would you give *Star Trek* writers?

objects. At around 8 months the child develops an understanding of object permanence. By the second year of life infants are quite mobile and so are well equipped to explore their environment actively. They are extremely curious and often experiment with actions to discover their effects. For most of the sensorimotor stage children are profoundly egocentric; they do not see the perspective of others and they do not recognise the boundaries between themselves and others. Thus other people are experienced as extensions of the infant's body. By the end of the sensorimotor stage the infant is aware of other people as separate beings, has a grasp of language and can think, using symbols such as words.

the pre-operational stage

By the end of the second year the child has sufficient grasp of language for its thinking to be based around symbolic thought rather than physical sensation. However the child has not developed sufficiently to grasp logical rules or operations (hence the term *pre-operational*) and it deals with the world very much as it appears rather than as it is. The child can thus be said to be *semi-logical*. Pre-operational children display centration – in other words, they can focus only on one aspect of a situation at a time. This means that they are very egocentric and animistic and have difficulty with conservation tasks.

the concrete operational stage

The child's mind is now mature enough to use logical thought or operations, although children can only apply logic to objects and situations that are present and physical (hence *concrete* operational). Thus they lose their tendency for animism at this stage. They become rather less egocentric (although they do not lose the tendency altogether) and can succeed at conservation tasks. However, concrete operational children have great difficulty carrying out logical tasks without the physical objects in front of them. Think back for a moment to the tasks we looked at when we examined formal reasoning earlier in this chapter, such as syllogisms. Children in the concrete operational stage find syllogisms very difficult.

media watch

swot shop

By Phil Revell, *Times Educational Supplement*, 7 December 2001.

A footballing analogy to make Piaget's stages make sense.

Young minds, he said, develop sequentially through stages of cognitive ability whereby each step is a prerequisite for the next. The first stage is the sensory-motor period, from birth to about 18 months. Children make reflex responses and solve practical problems, but are egocentric in that others are but dimly perceived – a sort of Paul Gascoigne stage.

In the pre-operational stage they get to grips with the physical world and handle objects with confidence, but will make errors about volume. For example they'd see three pints as different amounts in different sized glasses – a sort of George Best period. This is followed by the Vinny Jones [concrete operational] period, in which complex ideas can be grasped, but only if physical connections are made. Example: Vinny is told that three players are going for goal; Kevin is a better player than Michael but not as good as Frank. Who does Vinny mark? On the pitch this would be no problem, but 10-year-olds often find such verbal sequencing hard.

In the formal operations stage – from puberty to adulthood – Piaget argued that adults could think in the abstract without concrete representation.

Some adults never become formal operational thinkers. Alex Ferguson for example seems to have a problem seeing other people's point of view.

the formal operational stage

In the formal operational stage children become capable of formal reasoning. Formal operational thinkers can respond to the form of syllogisms, think about abstract concepts and devise and test hypotheses. Piaget took this to mean that children had entered a new stage of adult logic, where abstract reasoning was possible. As well as systematic abstract reasoning, formal operational thinking permits the development of a system of values and ideals, and an appreciation of philosophical issues.

☯ discussion

Piaget's stages have proved extremely useful for anyone who has to explain ideas to children of different ages. One area where this is clearly important is education, and we will spend some time later in this chapter looking at how Piaget's ideas have been applied to teaching and designing programmes of study. There are however other important applications. We have already seen the way television writers plan programmes appealing to young people around what concepts children of different ages appreciate (*media watch*, p. 79). Another important application of Piaget's stages is in paediatric medicine and nursing. Hurley and Whelan (1988) noted the behaviour and comments of children of different ages in severe pain, and concluded that their understanding of their pain corresponded closely to their Piagetian stage.

piagetian stage	perception of pain
Pre-operational	Pain is primarily a physical experience. Children think about the magical disappearance of pain. They are not able to distinguish between cause and effect of pain. Pain is often perceived as a punishment for a wrongdoing or bad thought (Gildea and Quirk, 1977), particularly if the child did something he or she was told not to immediately before the pain started. Children's egocentricity means that they hold someone else responsible for their pain and, therefore, are likely to strike out verbally or physically when they have pain. Children may tell a nurse who gave them an injection 'You are mean' (McCaffery, 1972).
Concrete operational	Relate to pain physically. Able to specify location in terms of body parts. Increased awareness of the body and internal organs means that fear of bodily harm is a strong influence in their perceptions of painful events. Fear of total annihilation (bodily destruction and death) enters their thinking (Alex and Ritchie, 1991; Schultz, 1971).
Transitional; formal	Have a perception of pain that is not quite as sophisticated as formal operational children. Their perception of pain is not as literal as would be expected in children who are in the concrete operational stage of development. Children in the transitional stage are beginning to understand the concept of 'if-then' propositions.
Formal operational	Begin to solve problems. Do not always have required coping mechanisms to facilitate consistent mature responses. Imagine the sinister implications of pain (Muller et al., 1986).

table 4.1 how children perceive the cause and effect of pain (Hurley and Whelan, 1988)

However, there have been challenges to Piaget's stages. Although there is strong support for the distinction between concrete and formal operations, findings like those of Hughes (1975) and McGarrigle and Donaldson (1974) call the existence of a pre-operational stage into question. This is because the children Piaget called pre-operational appear to be able to perform tasks of conservation under the right conditions. However a recent study by Wilberg (2002) provides support for the distinction between pre-operational and concrete operational thinking.

is there really a pre-operational stage?

Wilberg, S. (2002) Preschooler's cognitive representations of their homeland. *British Journal of Developmental Psychology*, **20**, 157–170.

Aim: the aim of the study was to see whether children classed as concrete operational would have a different perception of their homeland from those classed as pre-operational.

Procedure: participants were 106 German children (52 boys and 54 girls) aged between 4 years 8 months and 5 years 9 months. They were classed as either pre-operational or concrete operational by means of six class inclusion questions. They were then asked a series of questions about Germany and being German, ranging from 'Can you tell me in which country you live?' to 'Have you ever heard the word foreigner? Can you tell me what it means?'

Findings: the children were classified as pre-operational (none of the six class inclusion tasks correct), transitional (one or two tasks correct) or concrete operational (three or more correct). In line with Piaget's theory concrete operational children were more likely to answer questions about their homeland correctly. There was no relationship between age and responses to questions.

Conclusion: children classified as concrete operational had a more accurate and sophisticated understanding of their homeland and nationality than did pre-operational children. Age did not affect the results. This supports Piaget's distinction between pre-operational and concrete operational thinking.

for+against

Piaget's stages

+ The idea that children become capable of more advanced logic as they get older is uncontroversial. This is the basic idea behind Piaget's stages.

− However the Piagetian idea that development takes place in distinct stages is controversial. It may be that children simply learn to tackle more complex logical tasks with more experience or education and with greater brain maturation.

− Although there is strong support for the idea of concrete operational logic the pre-operational stage is more controversial. Much post-Piagetian research has cast doubt on Piaget's findings concerning children's inability to conserve and perform egocentrism tasks.

+ Some recent studies, for example Wilberg (2002), support the distinction between pre-operational and concrete operational thinking, showing that performance on concrete operational tasks but not age predicted the sophistication of children's understanding of nationality.

− Numerous studies, for example that of Bradmetz (1999), have found that most teenagers do not reach Piaget's formal operational stage. This suggests that Piaget was wrong to suggest that formal reasoning was the natural end-point of cognitive development.

angling with the net

There is a huge volume of material on the Web concerning Piaget. Try the following to read further and supplement your notes.

www.time.com/time100/scientist/profile/piaget.html
http://chiron.valdosta.edu/whuitt/col/cogsys/piaget.html
http://facultyweb.cortland.edu/andersmd/PIAGET/sms.HTML

where to now?

The following are further sources of good information regarding Piaget's work:

▶ **Phillips, J. L.** (1975) *The Origins of Intellect: Piaget's Theory*. Freeman, San Francisco. Quite old, but still perhaps the best review of Piaget's work. In-depth coverage of the issues we have discussed here, although of course without the newer research findings.

▶ **Smith, P. K., Cowie, H. and Blades, M.** (2003) *Understanding Children's Development*. Blackwell, Oxford. An excellent general child development text with a large chunk devoted to the work of Piaget.

▶ **Lee, V. and Das Gupta, P.** (1995) *Children's Cognitive and Language Development*. Blackwell, Oxford. The first chapter gives a good, detailed but quite easy-to-follow account of Piaget's major contributions.

Vygotsky's theory of cognitive development

figure 4.9
Lev Vygotsky

Lev Vygotsky was a contemporary of Piaget in Piaget's early days, although Vygotsky died young in 1934. His work was first published in the West in the 1960s. Since then it has grown hugely in influence, especially in the last 15 years (Wertsch and Tulviste, 1996). Vygotsky agreed with Piaget on many key points – for example that cognitive development takes place in stages characterised by different styles of thinking. He disagreed, however, with Piaget's view of the child as exploring the world alone and instead placed a strong emphasis on social interaction during learning and the culture in which the child grows up.

the importance of culture and social interaction

Vygotsky placed far more emphasis than did Piaget on the role played by culture in the child's development. Vygotsky saw children as being born with basic mental functions such as the ability to perceive the outside world and to focus attention on particular objects. However, children lack higher mental functions such as thinking and problem solving. These higher mental functions are seen as 'tools' of the culture in which the individual lives, and are cultural in origin. Tools are transmitted to children by older members of the culture in guided learning experiences (such as lessons in school), and include the ability to use language, art and mathematics. Experiences with other people gradually become internalised and form the child's internal representation of the world. Thus the way each child thinks and sees the world is shared with other members of the child's culture. What this means is that people in different cultures will have quite different sets of tools, hence different ways of thinking.

the zone of proximal development

In contrast to Piaget, who emphasised how much children can learn by exploring their environment, Vygotsky emphasised the fact that children can develop their understanding far more quickly whilst interacting with other people, such as adults or more experienced peers. Children, according to Vygotsky, could never develop formal operational thinking without the help of others. The difference between what a child can understand on its own and what it can potentially understand through interaction with others is called the *zone of proximal development* (ZPD). Whereas Piaget believed that the limiting factor in what a child could learn at any time was its stage of development, Vygotsky believed that the crucial factor was the availability of other 'experts' who could instruct the child. Unlike Piaget, Vygotsky emphasised instruction from others in how to do things in order for the child to achieve its potential. As the child progresses through a zone of proximal development or *learning cycle*, the amount of instruction (or scaffolding) from experts will reduce. At first, explicit and detailed instructions are needed, but later on prompts are sufficient to help the child progress. An example of the transition through the ZPD comes from Wood et al. (1991), shown in Table 4.2. In this example a mother is helping a 4-year-old put together wooden blocks.

level of help	nature of prompt	example
5	Demonstration	Mother assembles two blocks
4	Preparation for child	Mother positions blocks for child to push together
3	Indication of materials	Mother points to blocks
2	Specific verbal instructions	Mother says 'get four big blocks'
1	General prompts	Mother says 'now you make something'

table 4.2 An example of crossing the ZPD. Adapted from Wood et al. (1991)

figure 4.10

the role of language

Vygotsky placed far more emphasis on the importance of language in cognitive development than did Piaget. For Piaget, language simply appeared when the child had reached a sufficiently advanced stage of development. The child's grasp of language depended on its current level of cognitive development. For Vygotsky, however, language developed from social interactions with others and was a very important cultural tool. At first the sole function of language is communication, and language and thought develop separately. Later, the child internalises language and learns to use it as a tool of thinking. In the pre-operational stage, as children learn to use language to solve problems, they speak aloud while solving problems (you can often hear children doing this). Once they are in the concrete operational stage this inner speech becomes silent.

⮌ discussion

Vygotsky appears to have been correct in saying that Piaget underestimated the importance of social interaction with more experienced people during learning. Many studies have demonstrated that children receiving help from other people pick up skills that they probably could not have mastered alone. In one such study, Roazzi and Bryant (1998) gave children aged 4 and 5 years the task of working out how many sweets there were in a box on a set of weighing scales. In one condition children worked alone and in another they had the help of an older child who was not allowed to tell them the solution explicitly. In the assisted condition the older children clearly went through the process of giving successively less explicit prompts until the younger children worked out how to perform the task. Most children in this condition mastered

does reading aloud help children understand?

Prior, S. M. and Welling, K. A. (2001) 'Read in your head.' A Vygotskian analysis of the transition from oral to silent reading. *Reading Psychology*, **22**, 1–15.

Aim: the aim was to test Vygotsky's idea that pre-operational stage children think aloud as they master language as a tool of thinking. Vygotsky's approach would predict that pre-operational children (under 7 years) would understand material better having read it aloud but that concrete operational children (7+) would not.

Procedure: 73 Canadian children aged 5 to 8 years were given passages to read. Teacher ratings of their reading competence were collected so that results were not affected by individual differences in reading ability. In one condition the participants read silently and in another they read aloud. After reading they were tested on their understanding of what they had just read.

Findings: in the younger children (5 to 6 years) there was no difference in the comprehension of the passage following reading silently or aloud. By contrast, older (concrete operational) children performed better on the comprehension test if they read aloud.

Conclusion: the results did not support Vygotsky, whose theory predicts that pre-operational children should benefit from reading aloud whilst concrete operational children should not.

the task whereas those working alone did not. This supports strongly the existence of the ZPD. The fact that children tend to learn during social interaction has been put to use in education in collective group work and peer tutoring (see p. 90 for a discussion). Vygotsky's idea that children use speech as an aid to thinking is more controversial. A recent study by Prior and Welling suggests that Vygotsky's idea that children initially think aloud then internalise speech and use it to think silently may not be entirely correct.

A more controversial aspect of Vygotsky's theory was the idea that, because tools are specific to different cultures, cultures that do not have formal schooling do not develop the ability for abstract thinking. Effectively this is saying that some cultures are better at thinking than others. Contemporary psychologists influenced by Vygotsky see different cultures as having different 'toolkits' (Wertsch, 1991) – qualitatively different sets of tools – rather than some having more tools than others. There is some research to support the existence of different cultural toolkits. In a comparison of American and Native American children's performance on the Wechsler test of IQ, Salois (1999) found that Native American children came out worse in verbal ability but better in visuo-spatial ability. The two cultures displayed different mental abilities, as would be predicted by Vygotsky's theory.

angling
with

Like Piaget, Vygotsky is well represented on the Web, but there is lots of rubbish about! These are a couple of the more useful sites.

http://www.funderstanding.com/vygotsky.cfm

http://www.kolar.org/vygotsky/

for+against

Vygotsky's theory

+ Vygotsky was probably correct to criticize Piaget for underestimating the importance of social interaction in learning. He has certainly enhanced our understanding of cognitive development by emphasizing the importance of other people, culture and language.

+ There is considerable support for the idea that children develop quicker with some instruction (for example, Roazzi and Bryant, 1998). This demonstrates the existence of the ZPD.

– Vygotsky's view of cultural differences in thinking is, by modern standards, ethnocentric because he believed that cultures that use formal schooling to transmit the tools of the culture – as happens in Europe – produce children capable of more advanced thinking than cultures which do not have formal schooling.

+ Modern Vygotskians have tackled this problem by seeing the tools of different cultures as qualitatively different rather than superior or inferior to one another. There is some support for these qualitative differences in mental abilities in different cultures.

– Vygotsky's emphasis on the importance of thinking aloud remains controversial. It is challenged by studies such as that of Prior and Welling (2001), which show that reading aloud is more helpful to older than younger children.

where to now?

The following are good sources of information on the work of Vygotsky:

▶ **Faulkner, D., Littleton, K. and Woodhead, M.** (1998) *Learning Relationships in the Classroom*. Routledge, London. A collection of papers from some contemporary researchers that focus on Vygotsky's view of learning.

▶ **Lee, V. and Das Gupta, P.** (1995) *Children's Cognitive and Language Development*. Blackwell, Oxford. The first chapter gives a good and detailed account of Vygotsky's major contributions, which is easy to follow.

▶ **Cohen, D.** (2002) *How the Child's Mind Develops*. Routledge, London. A superb up-to-date but extremely readable book covering Vygotsky, Piaget and so forth.

the modular approach to cognitive development

One thing that the theories of Piaget and Vygotsky have in common is that they are *domain-general* approaches. This means that they see all the changes in mental abilities that take place during a child's cognitive development as happening because of the same underlying developmental process. A domain is an aspect of cognitive development, such as language (particularly important to Vygotsky) or physical understanding of the world (particularly important to Piaget). Thus, for Piaget, children's increasing ability to conserve, their declining egocentrism and their loss of animism are all results of a general increase in cognitive ability that comes as the child builds successive layers of understanding through exploration of the world.

In recent years, however, another approach has been gaining in popularity. This is the *domain-specific* approach, which sees different mental abilities as developing independently of one another. Each domain of cognitive development is accounted for by a *module*. A module is a structure in the brain designed to handle particular types of information. Thus, for example, there is a module for language. According to modular theorists, language develops independent of other cognitive functions. Some modular theorists, such as Jerry Fodor (1983), have suggested that cognitive development can be accounted for entirely by the maturation of different modules. According to Fodor we are all born with modules adapted to processing the kind if information that has proved necessary in our evolutionary past. There is thus little or no role in cognitive

figure 4.11
Annette Karmiloff-Smith

development for curiosity, as emphasised by Piaget, or social interaction, as emphasised by Vygotsky. This is not to suggest that children do not need experiences for cognitive development. Clearly, children will not learn a language if they have never heard it! However it does suggest that what a child can learn at any particular time is limited by the maturity of the relevant modules rather than by variations in the child's environment.

discussion

Fodor's theory has the advantage that it neatly explains why some people can be so advanced in some aspects of cognitive development and not in others. Domain-general theorists such as Piaget and Vygotsky would find it difficult to explain, for example, why some autistic children can have very good development in certain skills, for example mathematics, but very poor development of language and social skills. There is also a less well-known condition called *Williams syndrome*, characterised by low general IQ but very rich language and social skills. To modular theorists these conditions are much easier to explain – autism is associated with poor development of the modules responsible for language and social interaction, whilst Williams syndrome is associated with good development of these modules and poor development of others.

There are, however, limitations to Fodor's theory, in that it does not easily explain the effects of experience on individual cognitive development. Karmiloff-Smith (1996) has suggested a less rigid theory of cognitive development known as the *progressive modularisation* approach. To Karmiloff-Smith the child is born with domain-relevant biases in the brain that preferentially (although not exclusively) respond to certain types of information. Here she differs from Fodor's domain-specific approach as well as from Piaget's domain-general approach. These biases give the child a good start in processing different stimuli in the world. However, children then modify their initial understanding by building successively more complex understandings of the world through experience – much as Piaget suggested. In a sense, Karmiloff-Smith's account of cognitive development can be seen as a compromise between the ideas of Fodor and Piaget. Because Karmiloff-Smith believes that modules are progressively formed over developmental time, with domain specifity emerging as a function of both the initial biases and experience, her theory can explain the dramatic individual differences in particular mental abilities shown by both particular clinical groups such children with autism or with Williams syndrome, and by non-clinical individuals. This explanation of normal variations in different mental abilities has important applications in education where it is now widely acknowledged that students have a range of learning styles based on strengths in particular mental abilities (see p. 92 for a discussion of learning styles).

At the time of writing there are exciting debates between developmental psychologists who favour domain-specific and domain-general theories. Essentially, both approaches can be used to explain any finding in cognitive development (Goswami, 1998), although some facts are more neatly explained by one or other approach. Moreover, as Goswami explains, domain-general and domain-specific development approaches are not actually mutually exclusive. It is entirely possible that there is a domain-general process of development as Piaget and Vygotsky said but that certain specific abilities do develop independently as particular modules mature.

for+against

the modular approach

+ Modular theories explain neatly the existence of conditions such as autism and Williams syndrome, in which some mental abilities are affected but not others.

+ Modular theories also explain normal variations in learning style, as many students have particular strengths in one cognitive domain (such as language) but not in another.

− Early modular theories were rigid and played down the role of the environment in cognitive development. This meant that they could not explain the role of other people as emphasized by Vygotsky.

+ There are now modular theories (for example, by Karmiloff-Smith) that are more flexible and account for the role of experience.

the cognitive-developmental approach

applying theories of cognitive development to education

Since the 1960s education has been influenced by cognitive-developmental theory. Initially this involved using the ideas of Piaget, but more recently elements of Vygotsky's theory and the modular approach have also been incorporated into teaching.

the Plowden report

You may have heard about, or seen, film of the ways in which people used to be taught in primary schools. Pupils typically sat in rows, copying material from the board as it was explained (chalk-and-talk) and learnt material by rote – in other words they repeated it in unison until they knew it by heart. Children not able to keep up with the pace at which the majority learnt were often punished. In the 1960s, however, the Plowden committee was set up in order to examine ways of improving primary education. They investigated the work of Piaget and incorporated his ideas into their report. The final report, published in 1967, recommended a shift away from traditional teaching towards *child-centred teaching* – teaching based on the abilities and wishes of children. We can pick out three main messages from the Plowden report:

◆ Children need to be given individual attention and cannot all be treated in the same way.

◆ Children should not be taught things until they are developed enough intellectually to cope with them.

◆ Children mature intellectually, physically and emotionally at different rates. Teachers should be aware of the stage of development each child has reached and should treat them accordingly.

implications of Piagetian theory for education

Piaget's research was generally not aimed at education, although in one of his later publications (Piaget, 1970), he made clear his support for the new child-centred methods. Following the Plowden report and Piaget's book, teachers began to put Piaget's ideas into practice in the classroom. Two of the main ways we can apply Piaget's ideas to education are by adapting to children's understanding of the world and by facilitating discovery learning.

adapting to the child's understanding of the world

As children think in different and less logical ways than adults, teachers need to adapt to these ways of thinking rather than expecting children to adapt to adult ways of thinking. For example, teachers should expect a degree of egocentrism in younger children.

In the case opposite, the teacher failed to appreciate the child's egocentrism – to him the word 'present' meant a gift, not a time, and he was unable to decentre and think about what she might have meant. Such misunderstandings are inevitable if teachers do not understand how children see the world.

It is also important to create tasks and situations that are appropriate for children at each particular age. The National Curriculum reflects Piaget's stages, one of its key aims being that children should encounter ideas when they are ready to cope with them. We would not, for example, give children still in the concrete operational stage tasks that require skills of abstract reasoning. Such tasks would become appropriate only after the child achieves formal operations. This means that the primary curriculum, which ends with Piaget's concrete operational stage at age 11, should contain no material that requires formal reasoning. Key Stage 3, covering ages 11 to 14, also contains little or no formal reasoning, reflecting research showing that Piaget was optimistic and that few children achieve formal reasoning before their mid-teens.

facilitating discovery learning

According to Piaget, children need to construct their understanding of the world. This is an active process, and could not be achieved in the traditional classroom situation where children sat passively receiving information. Children learn best by *discovery*. The role of the teacher is thus to facilitate learning situations in which children can find things out for themselves. This does not, of course, simply mean leaving children to their own

figure 4.12
Primary classrooms often feature sand and water so that children can discover their physical properties

devices. In effective child-centred learning the teacher presents children with tasks specifically designed to lead them to discover things for themselves. A wide variety of such tasks need to be given, in order for children to construct their knowledge of all necessary aspects of the world. In nursery and primary school, materials such as water, sand, bricks and crayons all help children build physical and hence mental constructions. Later, projects and practical science exercises help children explore the nature of their world.

The aim of education is to develop children's thinking rather than just to increase their level of knowledge. This means that, when children try to work things out, what is important is their *reasoning* rather than the answer. It is therefore important that teachers encourage children for producing answers that are technically wrong but well thought out.

⌕ discussion

Some of the ways in which Piagetian ideas have influenced education are fairly uncontroversial. Common sense tells us that teachers need to give children appropriate tasks for their age and explain them in terms that the children will understand. However, a large body of research conducted in the 1970s, when Piagetian education had taken hold in British primary schools, comparing the effectiveness of traditional teaching and individual discovery learning, has found little advantage for either approach.

applying Piagetian principles to education

+ The principle that children are not passive receivers of knowledge but need somehow to construct their own knowledge is widely accepted in educational circles.

— There is, however, considerable disagreement over whether discovery learning best achieves this. Modern 'chalk-and-talk' teaching is much more interactive than the pre-Piaget 'traditional' styles and may be at least as effective.

— Whereas Piaget believed that learning is an individual process, and individual learning is encouraged in some schools, modern research shows clearly that children learn faster when working in groups and with the intervention of adults. We will look at some such research later in this section.

+ Piaget has given us a good base for developing the curriculum (for example, focusing on concrete tasks in primary education), although modern curricula take account of our current belief that Piaget tended to underestimate the abilities of younger children and overestimate the abilities of older children.

implications of Vygotsky's theory for education

To a much greater extent than Piaget, Vygotsky was interested in applying his ideas to education. Vygotsky's central idea is that learning is linked closely to social interaction. The key to learning from a Vygotskian point of view is thus to maximise the opportunities for meaningful interaction during learning experiences. This can involve an adult working individually with children to move them through the ZPD or by cooperative group learning or peer tutoring.

scaffolding

Vygotsky proposed a more important role for adults in children's learning than did Piaget. Like Piaget, however, he proposed that children should be actively involved in learning rather than behaving as passive receivers of knowledge. What this means in practice is that teachers should actively assist children who are engaged in learning tasks. In theoretical terms this means that children are working within their ZPD and teachers provide the *scaffolding* to enable children to move through the ZPD. A classic Vygotskian lesson would have pupils working on a task with a teacher or other expert assisting them, providing each child or small group with assistance tailored to their level of understanding.

working together

From a Vygotskian perspective, peers as well as teachers can be important influences on cognitive development. *Cooperative group work* as opposed to individual discovery learning appears to speed up children's development. An extension of the idea of cooperative group work is peer tutoring, where one child instructs another who is slightly less advanced. Foot et al. (1990) have explained the success of peer tutoring using Vygotsky's theory. One child can be effective in guiding another through the ZPD because, having only recently made that advance, the child is in a good position to see the difficulties faced by the other child and provide appropriate scaffolding.

⊘ discussion

There is a large body of research showing that children working with assistance, in the form of adult tutoring, cooperative group work or peer tutoring, learn more than those engaged in individual discovery learning or chalk-and-talk teaching. Peer tutoring has proved extremely beneficial, both to mainstream students and those with special educational needs. One recent study shows how useful peer tutoring is in studying psychology.

how to improve your psychology grades!

Oley, N. (2002) Extra credit and peer tutoring: impact on the quality of writing in introductory psychology in an open admissions college. In *Handbook for Teaching Introductory Psychology*, vol. 3 (ed. Griggs, R. A.). LEA, Mahwah NJ.

Aim: to test the idea that peer tutoring leads to better marks in a psychology essay. Both voluntary and forced peer tutoring were tested.

Procedure: 65 students aged 17 or over from an American open admissions college took part in the study. They were each given a five-page essay that had to be extensively researched. All were given instruction on how to use the library. Peer tutoring from more experienced students was then made available. In one condition participants were forced to seek peer tutor-

ing. The completed essays were graded on a four-point scale.

Findings: participants who made use of peer tutoring scored significantly higher grades than those who worked alone. This was irrespective of whether the decision to use tutors was voluntary or forced. There was a positive correlation between the number of consultations with a peer tutor and final grade.

Conclusion: peer tutoring is a helpful strategy in challenging and unfamiliar tasks such as researched essays.

for+against

applying Vygotsky's theory to education

+ Research has shown clearly that children learn more effectively together and that adults and peers can effectively provide scaffolding. This has been demonstrated in psychology students by Nancy Oley.

+ The idea of scaffolding has provided teachers with a way of intervening actively in children's learning without resorting to traditional teaching. A limitation of Piagetian discovery learning was the limited role for teachers, and using Vygotskian ideas has helped overcome this.

− There is some evidence to suggest that a minority of children do not benefit from group work. This is difficult to explain from a Vygotskian perspective.

− There are practical problems with the use of cooperative group work. There are more opportunities for children to be off-task in group work, and there are 'free riders' who do not contribute to the work of the group.

implications of the modular approach for education

The modular approach has rather different implications for education than do the theories of Piaget and Vygotsky. If we see the mind as comprising different modules, each of which processes a different type of information, then we see cognitive abilities as developing independently of one another. This means that, rather than looking at a child's educational progress as a single process, we should instead look separately at every developing ability – linguistic, mathematical and so on. This leads us to a different way of judging children's abilities and an understanding that different individuals will have different learning styles, based on which modules are well developed and which are less so.

thinking about student ability

One of the important ways teachers think about their students concerns their 'intelligence'. Like Piaget, many teachers think of intelligence as a general characteristic; thus students can be thought about as 'strong' or 'weak', 'bright' or 'dull', and so forth. The *self-fulfilling prophecy* occurs when pupils have been labelled as high or low in intelligence and they conform to the expectations resulting from these labels. From the modular perspective this sort of labelling is misleading because everyone has a range of mental abilities that develop independently of one another. Rather than labelling a child as high or low ability in general terms, the modular approach allows us to think of students' individual strengths and weaknesses. This in turn allows us to encourage students' strengths and identify and tackle specific weaknesses – a healthier attitude perhaps than thinking of generally 'strong' and 'weak' students.

learning styles

If different modules develop independently of one another it is likely that some will develop better than others. Different modular theories differ in how they explain these differences but are in agreement that we all have an individual profile of cognitive abilities. In practice this means that, when we come to understand and learn material, different ways of studying suit different people. There are a number of ways of classifying learning styles. One popular approach comes from the work of Gardner (1993). Gardner has proposed a theory of *multiple intelligences*, which include linguistic (verbal ability), logical (including mathematical ability), musical, spatial (including artistic ability), bodily (including grace and sporting ability), interpersonal (social) and intrapersonal (self-awareness). Our preferred learning styles depend on which of these intelligences (modules) we are strongest in. Thus we have verbal learners, who flourish through reading, visual learners, who make particular use of diagrams, flow charts, mind maps and so forth and kinaesthetic learners, who learn by physically doing things rather than learning in the abstract. Once students and teachers are aware of students' learning styles it is possible to tailor teaching methods to their needs.

⟳ discussion

A modular understanding of cognitive development is currently making its way into educational practice and there is currently considerable discussion of learning styles and their applications. There is strong evidence that there are indeed a range of learning styles, although it is also widely believed that the current classifications of learning styles are all oversimplifications and that preferences for different learning styles are a much more complex business than any one theory currently explains. Learning styles may also go a long way towards explaining why so many people do not succeed in the school system, although they flourish in the workplace. Snyder (2000) assessed learning style in 128 American high school (secondary school) students, and found that the overwhelming majority (81%) were kinaesthetic learners. Such individuals favour practical hands-on situations, and these are difficult to provide in the conventional school environment. Students with particular learning styles may also orientate towards particular careers, thus James-Gordon and Bal (2001) looked at 42 engineers and found an overwhelming preference for visual learning.

The modular way of thinking is making inroads into education and an increasing number of teachers are thinking in terms of learning styles and independent cognitive abilities but there are some practical limitations with the approach. Existing curricula are by definition academic and simply do not lend themselves to certain learning styles. Of course this may change with the advent of vocational GCSEs. Moreover, teachers also have learning styles, and certain teaching methods will always come more naturally to them than others. The mismatch between teacher and student learning styles is a major obstacle to learning (Mahlios, 2001) and this cannot easily be tackled.

angling with

Go to
http://worksearch.gc.ca/ english/index.pl?&tid=134& sid=BfBGLF3siXRXYL.
You can assess your own learning style online. This questionnaire is based on Gardner's classification of learning styles.

interactive angles

Think about your own education. Can you identify lessons or courses that have used the ideas of Piaget or Vygotsky? For example you might think of a particularly worthwhile piece of discovery learning or scaffolding.

where to now?

We recommend the following as good sources of information about cognitive development and education:

▶ **Jarvis, M.** (in press) *The Psychology of Learning and Teaching*. Nelson Thornes, Cheltenham. A very up-to-date review of research in education. Includes chapters on learning style and cognitive-developmental theory.

▶ **Hartley, J.** (1998) *Learning and Studying*. Routledge, London. This does not focus particularly on a cognitive-developmental approach to education but is useful in drawing together different psychological approaches and showing how each has influenced educational practice.

▶ **Daniels, H.** (2001) *Vygotsky and Pedagogy*. Routledge/Falmer, London. A detailed look at the application of Vygotsky's ideas to education.

talking point

contemporary issues

do computers help people learn?

If you are or have recently been a student, the chances are that you have encountered computers at some point in your education. *Computer-assisted learning* (CAL) is currently a tremendous growth area and a large body of research is being generated about its effectiveness. Think for a moment about the variety of ways in which you have used computers in the course of your studies. You have probably word-processed assignments. You may have used statistical programs to analyse the results of research. You may also have taken part in or administered studies that present tasks to participants by computer. Packages are available that guide students through sequences of tasks that allow one to master a skill or a topic. Revision tests are also available via computer, and there are now even computer packages available that will mark your essays! You may have had the opportunity to program computers in the course of your study. The usefulness of computers in teaching and learning is interesting in its own right. In this chapter, however, we are interested specifically in understanding the processes of computer-aided learning using ideas from cognitive-developmental psychology.

applying cognitive-developmental theory to understanding computer-assisted learning

Computer-assisted learning can be used to provide scaffolding, both from the use of the computer itself and the social interaction stimulated by computers. When children use educational software the computer provides detailed help or prompts as required according to the child's position in the ZPD. Certain children in the class are inevitably more skilled in the use of computers and so take on the role of peer tutors. With pupils working on computers, the teacher is free to target individuals who require help and target appropriate scaffolding to each child. We will return to look in more detail at the effectiveness of computer-assisted learning later in this chapter.

Piagetian theory

From a Piagetian perspective, computers are highly versatile tools for individual discovery learning. If you have ever used CD-ROMS or the Internet to research a topic on your own, you have experienced computer-aided discovery. Computers also offer a way to develop thinking skills. Papert (1980) suggested that children can acquire new thinking skills when they learn to program computers. Papert was one of a team that developed the child-friendly programming language, Logo. An example of a child-friendly feature of Logo is a turtle graphic that can be directed to draw lines by typed commands. For example the command FORWARD 50, LEFT 90 would direct the turtle graphic to draw a 50 mm straight line then turn 90° to the left. Papert believes that using Logo helped children's thinking by developing their ability to use formal operational reasoning as opposed to concrete operational thought.

Vygotskian theory

From a Vygotskian perspective computers offer a way of crossing the zone of proximal development. This can be achieved by interaction with peers or by onscreen scaffolding. Vygotsky would predict that students working together on computers achieve more than those working alone. Mevarech et al. (1991) tested the effectiveness of pair work by seeing whether students working sharing a computer do better than students working alone. Twelve year olds worked on computer-based arithmetic tasks for 5 months. Half the students had their own computer and the other half shared a computer and worked in pairs. The latter group did significantly better when tested later on their arithmetic ability. Lou et al. (2001) carried out a meta-analysis of 122 studies comparing cooperative group learning on computers to individual learning. Overall group work came out ahead, leading to higher average achievement and satisfaction. However, it also emerged that some people benefit much more than others and that a minority of learners may learn better alone.

Whenever we use educational software there are a series of onscreen prompts that help us progress through the task at hand. Crook (1994) has suggested that these prompts constitute a form of scaffolding that serves to move learners through a zone of proximal development. There are normally choices that learners can make as to how much detail they require from prompts. This means that, just as teachers will reduce the amount of help they give as the learner moves through the ZPD, the computer-aided learner can select a declining level of detail in their on-screen prompts. There are now educational programmes designed on this principle. Bornas and Llabres (2001) developed interactive software for teaching maths and reading. This had options for three levels of scaffolding throughout. After 10 weeks (15 hours), children working on this programme were assessed for achievement and style of reasoning in the subjects. Although the group using the interactive programme showed no more achievement than controls they were significantly more advanced in their thinking strategies. This is very supportive of Vygotsky as it illustrates the transmission of tools of thinking.

modularity and learning styles

Learning styles help us understand why some students do better than others using computers. Note, for example, that in the Lou et al. (2001) meta-analysis (above) a minority of students did not benefit from cooperative learning. This can be understood in terms of Gardner's theory as being a result of these students having a low interpersonal intelligence, which means that interaction with other people is their least preferred method of study.

There is some evidence, for example, to suggest that using computers is most beneficial to students with a visual learning style. Smith and Woody (2000) assessed learning styles in a college and followed up a psychology class using a predominantly computer-based approach and a control class receiving conventional teaching for one term. They found that, at first, the class using computers did worse but by the end of the term it exceeded the achievements of the conventional group. Interestingly, the students that benefited most from the use of computer-based learning were those with a visual learning style. This makes sense as looking at a computer screen is a very visual experience.

thinking critically

It is highly likely that the use of computers in education will increase in the future. The studies we have looked at here show the potential of computers to enhance learning, in terms of discovery, developing thinking skills, cooperative learning and accommodating those with a visual learning style. Based on learning styles, we are also beginning to understand why some people appear to benefit less than others from learning technology. For example, those with visual learning as their least preferred learning style might not enjoy sitting in front of a screen under any circumstances.

Currently, however, our understanding of computer-aided learning is still in its infancy. Many attempts to give computers a greater role in education have floundered because they did not take enough account of how people learn. Computer-aided learning also raises other concerns, for example the risk of reducing interaction with teachers. Onscreen scaffolding may be helpful but it is probably not equivalent to being able to ask a good teacher a difficult question.

for+against

computer-aided learning

+ Computers can provide opportunities for both discovery learning and cooperative learning. They also provide opportunities for both developing individual thinking skills and scaffolding the development of skills. This means that computer-assisted learning is compatible with both the Piagetian view of education and the Vygotsky-Bruner model.

— It has been suggested that the excessive use of computers in the classroom may lead to social isolation and the breakdown of the essential teacher-learner relationship.

+ However, if the majority of learners are receiving onscreen scaffolding, this frees the teacher to spend more time with each learner. Provided computer-assisted learning does not lead to the phasing out of teachers, it appears that it will probably not lead to social problems.

+ Computer-based learning is highly beneficial to students with a visual learning style (demonstrated by Smith and Woody) as using a computer screen is such a visual experience.

where to now?

The following are good sources of further information about computer-aided learning:

▶ **Bancroft, D. and Carr, R.** (ed.) (1995) *Influencing Children's Development*. Open University, Milton Keynes. This contains an excellent chapter by Karen Littleton on various aspects of computer-assisted learning.

▶ **Messer, D. and Millar, S.** (ed.) (1999) *Exploring Developmental Psychology*. Arnold, London. Contains a good chapter by Charles Crook, one of the leading researchers in the area of computer-aided learning.

talking point

contemporary issues

the development of children's theory of mind

Theory of mind is not a theory. It means the understanding we have of other people's thoughts, motives and feelings. In other words it refers to the personal theories we all have of what is going on in the minds of others. The ability to interpret what another person is thinking or feeling is sometimes called *mind reading*. Theory of mind is currently an extremely important area of cognitive development.

A classic demonstration of the sudden development of theory of mind comes from Wimmer and Perner (1983). They presented children with a story in which a boy called Maxi had left his chocolate in a green container in the kitchen. Maxi's mother had taken some of the chocolate for cooking and put the rest in a blue container. The child's task was to say which container Maxi would look in when he returned. Of course the correct answer is the green container, because Maxi would not know that his mother had moved it. However this task requires an understanding of the concept of other people's minds, and Wimmer and Perner found that very few 3 year olds gave the correct answer, although the majority of 4 year olds did so.

applying cognitive-developmental theory to understanding theory of mind

Although Piaget and Vygotsky died before the term *theory of mind* was invented, it is quite possible to explain the development of theory of mind using their theories. Indeed, important current research takes their theories as a starting point. However, most research into theory of mind has come from a modular perspective. We can look here at how all three approaches explain how children acquire an understanding of other people's minds.

Piagetian theory

Recall that Piaget saw cognitive development as a single, generalised process. To a Piagetian, therefore, theory of mind develops when a certain level of understanding of the world has been achieved. The fact that children can perform false belief tasks from around the age of 4 years simply means that by that age their understanding of their environment is sufficiently sophisticated for them to do so. Perner et al. (2002) have suggested that, if other unrelated cognitive abilities also appear at around the same time as theory of mind, this points towards cognitive development being a general process. They tested this by giving 48 children aged between 2.8 and 4.9 years a false belief task similar to that used by Wimmer and Perner, tasks of synonyms – identifying words with the same meaning – and a Piaget-style class inclusion task. It was found that success in the false belief task was very closely associated with success in the other two tasks. This provides strong support for the Piagetian idea that theory of mind simply develops along with a host of other mental abilities in a general process of cognitive development.

Vygotskian theory

Like Piaget, Vygotsky saw cognitive development as a domain-general process. However his emphasis was on the role of interaction with other people as opposed to individual curiosity (agency). Astington (1998) has suggested that children internalise a theory of mind during their early interactions with other people, in particular the primary carer. This idea predicts that performance on theory of mind tasks will be superior in children who have secure attachments and whose primary carers display high levels of sensitivity. This is because these children have had a history of good quality interactions with others. Symons and Clark (2000) measured both maternal sensitivity and security of attachment in 2-year-old children and followed them up until they were 5 years old, when they were tested on false belief tasks like that used by Wimmer and Perner (1983). It was found that the children assessed as securely attached and those whose mothers were rated as the most sensitive when the children were aged 2 years (these were usually but not always the same children) generally had a superior theory of mind at 5 years. This suggests that a Vygotskian perspective on theory of mind is helpful.

modular theory

Leslie (1994) has suggested that the most obvious explanation for the sudden development of the ability to perform false belief tasks in 4 year olds is that a particular module of the brain becomes active at that age. This module is responsible for theory of mind. Much of the research on theory of mind has taken place with autistic children. Autism is a genetic condition that becomes evident in early childhood and is characterised by difficulty in communication, repetitive movements and lack of inter-est and skill in social interaction and emotional attachment. Baron-Cohen (1995) has suggested that autism is associated with impaired theory of mind. Certainly autistic children generally fail the Wimmer and Perner test. The study of autistic children who never develop a theory of mind, although they may go on to develop some mental abilities to very high levels, is important because it provides powerful evidence that cognitive development is modular rather than generalised as suggested by Piaget.

thinking critically

There is no controversy over the existence or the importance of theory of mind. What is slightly troubling is that it can be explained equally neatly from the perspective of Piaget, Vygotsky or the modular approach. Moreover each theoretical approach can produce sound evidence in its favour. One way to explain this is to suggest that all three approaches have something to offer. It is conceivable that theory of mind does develop in line with general cognitive development (Piaget), that this general devel-opment is enhanced by good quality early interaction (Vygotsky), and that the activation of a module at around 4 years enhances theory of mind abilities and allows the sudden appearance of the ability to complete false belief tasks.

where to now?

The following are good sources of further information about theory of mind:

▶ **Bryant, P.** (1998) Cognitive development. In Eysenck, M. (1998) (ed.) *Psychology, an Integrated Approach*. Longman, Harlow. This contains an excellent chapter on cognitive development, including a detailed but very clear account of theory of mind research.

▶ **Baron-Cohen, S., Tager-Flusberg, H. and Cohen, D. J.** (2000) *Understanding Other Minds*. Oxford University Press, Oxford. An extremely detailed account of research into theory of mind.

▶ **Jarvis, M.** (2001) *Angles on Child Psychology*. Nelson Thornes, Cheltenham. A slightly more detailed account of theory of mind research than is possible here.

conclusions

The cognitive-developmental approach to psychology has centred around the develop-ment of children's thinking. The most famous theory, that of Piaget, emphasised children's innate motivation to explore and learn from their environment and the gradual acquisition of logical thought. Vygotsky placed much greater emphasis on the importance of other people in learning. Both these theories are domain general in nature – they see all aspects of cognitive development as taking place together, controlled by the same underlying processes. A newer approach is to look at domain-specific development – the separate development of different cognitive abilities.

The major application of the cognitive-developmental approach has been in education. The approaches of Piaget and Vygotsky point towards an active role for children as discoverers of knowledge rather than passive receivers. However, Vygotsky proposed a more active role for teachers than have followers of Piaget. The modular approach has also aided our understanding of education, for example in terms of understanding individual differences in learning style. The use of computers in education provides opportunities for enhanced learning. Piagetians emphasise the opportunities provided by computers for discovery learning and the development of thinking, whereas followers of Vygotsky place more emphasis on the opportunities for scaffolding and cooperative learning provided by computers. Research has also shown the importance of learning styles – visual learners appear to derive particular benefit from the visual experience of working at a computer screen.

what do you know?

1 (a) Describe in detail *two* studies from the cognitive-developmental approach. (8)
   (b) Evaluate one of these studies. (4)

2 Outline two differences between the approach of Piaget and *one* alternative theory. (6)

3 Describe *two* ways in which *one* cognitive-developmental theory *other than that of Piaget* has been applied in education. (6)

4 Discuss how the cognitive-developmental approach has helped us understand *one* contemporary issue of your choice in psychology. *(10)*

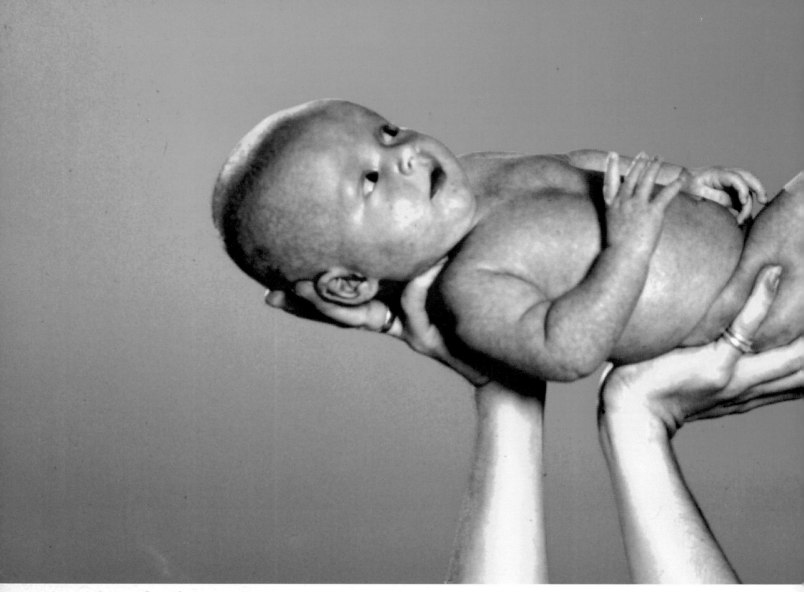

The learning theory approach is based on the following ideas:

◆ The environment influences behaviour. In contrast to the physiological approach, which emphasises the influence of genes, and the psychodynamic approach, which emphasises the role of instinct and family dynamics, the learning approach focuses on the ways in which people's behaviour is directly affected by their environment. In all the mechanisms of learning, the environment is central, although each explanation for learning suggests that the environment affects the individual in a different way.

◆ We can best understand the ways in which the environment influences behaviour by the concept of *learning*, which can be defined as 'a relatively permanent change in behavioural potential which accompanies experience' (Kimble, 1961). Learning can occur in a range of different ways. Classical conditioning relies on associations between stimuli (we learn that two things happen together). In operant conditioning behaviours are determined by their consequences, whilst in social learning individuals learn by imitating others. In each of these routes to learning, the environment is central, providing stimuli, consequences (rewards or punishments), or models for behaviour.

◆ Although there are different models of learning, some general processes of learning are common to all of these. These include responding with the same behaviour in similar situations (generalisation); distinguishing between situations and responding differently to them (discrimination); and ceasing to respond in the absence of positive effects (extinction).

◆ Animals differ from humans only in the complexity of their behaviour. The ways in which their behaviour is determined by the environment are exactly the same as those in humans. This means that we can study learning in animals and apply the results to understanding human behaviour.

what's ahead?

This chapter introduces the learning theory approach to psychology, sometimes called *behavioural psychology* or *behaviour analysis*. This approach is based on the study of learning in non-human animals, which, being generally less complex in their behaviour than humans, are easier to study. We will look at three particularly important types of learning: classical conditioning, operant conditioning and social learning. In our *real lives* section we discuss behaviour therapy, an example of how learning theory can help us to alter people's behaviour deliberately in order to reduce maladaptive behaviour. In *talking points* we apply the learning approach to two current issues in psychology: the risk of addiction to the Internet and media violence.

classical conditioning

Ivan Pavlov

figure 5.1
Ivan Pavlov

Ivan Petrivitch Pavlov was born in Russia in 1849. He trained as a medical doctor and conducted research on the nervous system and digestion, for which he won the Nobel Prize in 1904. When Pavlov was appointed Director of the Department of Physiology at the Russian Institute of Medicine, he established the world's first clinic and operating theatre to be used exclusively for animals. He always took the same care in his operations on dogs as was taken with people. As he insisted on complete cleanliness, his dogs almost always made a complete recovery. Furthermore, he recognised that he could not expect to gain reliable results from his experiments if the animals were suffering pain, discomfort or fear. For tests on digestion, however, anaesthesia was impossible so Pavlov aimed to reduce the stress his subjects experienced by ensuring that each one received excellent care. He could not depend on his laboratory assistants for this so his took the animals home to be looked after. The importance of the wellbeing of research animals to the validity of experimental outcomes is only just beginning to resurface as a concern in modern psychology.

As a physiologist Pavlov was interested in digestion. He noticed that his experimental dogs salivated to the sound of his footsteps, ahead of the arrival of their food. Pavlov realised that the dogs' responses were in anticipation of their dinner! The work on learning, for which Pavlov is now best remembered, explains how this type of association is established.

the mechanism of classical conditioning

The mechanism of classical conditioning relies upon building an association between a *neutral stimulus* – some aspect of the environment that does not elicit a response – and an existing *unconditioned stimulus*, which does. These two stimuli are presented to the animal until the previously neutral stimulus acquires the same effect as the unconditioned stimulus, the ability to elicit a response. Note that a new behaviour is not learned. Rather, an existing behaviour now takes place in response to a new stimulus. This behaviour is now called a *conditioned response* and the trigger a *conditioned stimulus*. In the case of Pavlov's dogs the sound of footsteps was initially a neutral stimulus; however, when the sound was associated with food it became a conditioned stimulus and the salivation a conditioned response.

Pavlov (1927) went on to demonstrate classical conditioning in his dogs using the sound of a metronome as the neutral stimulus (NS) and a bowl of meat powder as the

prior to conditioning	sound of metronome	→	no salivation
	neutral stimulus	→	*no response*
	meat powder	→	salivation
	unconditioned stimulus	→	*unconditioned response*
during conditioning	sound of metronome + meat powder	→	salivation
	neutral stimulus + unconditioned stimulus	→	*unconditioned response*
after conditioning	sound of metronome	→	salivation
	conditioned stimulus	→	*conditioned response*

table 5.1 The process of classical conditioning in Pavlov's dogs

unconditioned stimulus (UCS). Prior to the experiment, the dogs would salivate in response to the meat powder (the unconditioned response, UCR) but not to the sound. During the conditioning phase the meat powder was presented at the same time as the metronome. Repeated pairings of meat and metronome resulted in *conditioning*; the animal would subsequently salivate to the sound alone. As a result of the pairings, the NS (the sound) had become a conditioned stimulus (CS) capable of producing the behaviour (salivation) in a new situation. This behaviour, triggered by the CS, is called a conditioned response (CR). Acquiring a conditioned response often takes many, or at least several, pairings of the UCS and CS. For example, Pavlov (1955) describes a conditioning procedure used by Krestinokov in which dog learned to salivate when food was associated with an object being rotated in front of it – this took five pairings.

classical conditioning in humans

Just like Pavlov's dogs, you may have been classically conditioned to salivate. Visual stimuli such as chocolate wrappers (the NS) do not initially cause salivation, although eating chocolate (the UCS) will do so. As we open the wrapper before we eat the chocolate, we tend to have it in sight so it can become a conditioned stimulus. After eating many bars of chocolate the NS and UCS have had multiple pairings so salivation (the CR) becomes conditioned to the wrapper (the CS).

figure 5.2
Pavlov's apparatus enabled him to control the exposure of the dog to different stimuli and to measure the response accurately, in this case salivation

Our attitudes, as well as our behaviour, can be affected by classical conditioning. Olson and Fazio (2001) showed participants hundreds of words and images in pairs, one of which was a neutral stimulus (it did not elicit emotional responses) and the other designed to elicit a positive or negative emotional response (an unconditioned stimulus). In a surprise task, in which participants were asked to rate how positively they felt about the words or images, those that had been paired with positive UCSs were found to be rated more positively than those paired with negative items. This shows that the participants' attitudes had been classically conditioned. This is precisely what advertisements aim to do – alter our perception of products such as food, films or phones so that we feel more positively about them and are more likely to want them.

In the same way, classical conditioning can explain some of our sexual responses. In a recent animal study, Kippin (2000) classically conditioned rats to ejaculate to the smell of lemon or almond. The male rats were allowed to copulate with females bearing one of the two odours. The males initially showed no preference for females with a particular smell but, after conditioning, they preferred to mate again with those bearing the smell that they had come to associate with ejaculation. It is believed that humans can acquire sexual preferences by classical conditioning in much the same way. An amusing example is shown in *media watch*.

media
watch the Barry White experiment

Dr Vernon Coleman's Casebook, *The People*, 16th January 2000

Q My boyfriend and I tried an experiment that I'd like to tell you about. For two months, we made love every night with Barry White on continuous play on our CD player. Now, whenever either of us hears that music we become sexually aroused.

A A long-dead foreigner called Pavlov did much the same sort of experiment but used dogs, bells and food. Your research project sounds far more interesting and I suggest that you apply for a grant to help you continue with your studies. You might like to see if your boyfriend's enthusiasm can be triggered by constant exposure to the sound of the Abergwili Male Voice Choir airing their tonsils.

Alternatively, try Seth Pitt and Eva Legova singing *Tonight's the Night*. Meanwhile, a warning. You could find yourself in a tricky situation if a Barry White track is played when you're in your local pub.

figure 5.3 Barry White

questions

1 Explain this couple's experience in terms of classical conditioning.

2 Give an example of how a more serious sexual fetish might be acquired by classical conditioning.

higher order conditioning

As Pavlov demonstrated, for a strong CS (that is, one producing a strong CR) there appears to be little difference between the UCR and CR; they are the same response to different stimuli. Pavlov (1927) demonstrated that after a dog had learned to respond to one stimulus, this CS could be used to condition the same response to another neutral stimulus as shown below. This is *higher order conditioning*. The only way in which the new response differs is that it is weaker.

---

higher order conditioning

during conditioning:

meat powder	+ metronome beat	→ salivation
UCS	+ CS1	→ UCR

after conditioning:

metronome beat	→ salivation
CS1	→ CR

during second order conditioning:

metronome beat	+ black square	→ salivation
CS1	+ UCS	→ CR

after second order conditioning:

black square	→ salivation
CS2	→ CR

does timing matter?

It is usually assumed that the UCS and CS must be presented simultaneously and although this is the most effective arrangement it is not the only one. *Forward or delayed conditioning* appears to 'prepare' the animal for the arrival of the UCS, which follows the CS in time. As a consequence it may be as effective as simultaneous presentation of the CS and UCS. *Trace conditioning* introduces a time delay between the appearance and disappearance of the CS and the arrival of the UCS. As such, the UCS can still be of some use in predicting the CS. In *backward conditioning*, the UCS appears before the CS and this is generally the least effective.

Consider these in terms of using the information provided by an aircraft seatbelt light. A sign (CS) that is illuminated before the flight becomes bumpy (UCS) will be a highly effective warning (equivalent to forward conditioning). Signs that appear a long time before the bumps (trace conditioning) may be of some use but one that only lights up after the bumps (backward conditioning) is of no value; we would learn nothing new about dangers of the journey.

Russell et al. (1984) tested the simultaneous presentation of an odour of fish or sulphur (CS) and the injection of an allergen (UCS) in guinea pigs. The animals were conditioned to produce an allergic reaction (CR) to the associated odours. If you suffer from hay fever and have sneezed at the sight of a combine harvester or a vase of plastic flowers classical conditioning could be the reason!

one-trial learning: is once enough?

In some instances an animal can acquire a new behaviour in a single pairing of the NS and UCS. This is called *one-trial learning*, and it tends to happen when the consequences of failing to learn are fatal. Garcia et al. (1974) demonstrated one trial learning by rats in a *taste aversion* task. Rats tend to taste a little food, wait to see if it makes them ill, then consume more if it doesn't. Their survival therefore depends on being able to remember unwholesome foods they have consumed only once. When tested with poisoned bait, Garcia et al.'s wild rats learned to avoid the food with a single vomit-inducing incident. It seems that consuming excessive alcohol can have a similar effect in humans! If you have ever had the experience of drinking slightly too much of a distinctively flavoured drink such as Pernod or cider and feeling ill, you may be unable to face that taste or smell for some time.

during conditioning:	smell and taste of novel food	+	vomit-inducing substance	→	unpleasantness of sickness
	NS	+	UCS	→	UCR
after conditioning:	smell of novel food		→ unpleasantness (aversion)		
	CS		→ CR		

table 5.2 One-trial learning

Ferguson and Cassaday (1999) have suggested that some of the symptoms of *Gulf War Syndrome* (GWS) can be explained by a similar process. Gulf War syndrome is a set of symptoms including memory, sexual and sleep problems, nausea, headaches, depression, rashes and increased sensitivity to pain. Typically, each individual suffers only some of these symptoms. Medical explanations for GWS, such as exposure to organophosphates or the cocktail of drugs administered to soldiers to protect them cannot easily explain this wide range of symptoms in sufferers. Ferguson and Cassaday have proposed a classical conditioning model, which suggests that a sickness response has been acquired by association with a range of stimuli including oil fire fumes (present

figure 5.4
The symptoms of Gulf War Syndrome may result from classical conditioning

throughout the fighting) and stressful events such as witnessing injuries during the war. Symptoms of GWS such as nausea can be explained as the body's conditioned responses (CRs) to these. After the war, exposure to any of these conditioned stimuli would produce the conditioned sickness response. An example of one case, which can perhaps be best explained by classical conditioning, comes from Ferguson and Cassaday, who described an army mechanic who, following the war, could no longer tolerate the smell of petrol without acute nausea. Presumably, the smell of petrol had become associated with other noxious stimuli from the war.

extinction and spontaneous recovery

What happens if the CS is repeatedly presented in the absence of the UCS? Over time the strength of the CR declines and eventually disappears, an effect called *extinction*. Thus if a dog was conditioned to salivate to a bell, then the bell was rung many times in the absence of food, salivation to the bell would eventually cease. However, if the bell is silent for a while, then subsequently rung again, the response may reappear. This is called *spontaneous recovery*.

inter**active**
■ **angles**

questions

Films use a classically conditioned association to scare us:

1 How do you feel when you hear the music that accompanies this scene?

2 Explain how classical conditioning could lead to elicit a fear response when we hear the *Jaws* music.

generalisation

How do animals respond to stimuli that are similar to the CS? If the stimuli are sufficiently alike, the new stimulus can also trigger the CR; this is called *generalisation*. These responses may, however, be slower to appear after the presentation of the CS, or they may be weaker. For example, a rabbit that has been conditioned to blink to a certain tone may also do so to a tone of a higher frequency but its response may be a fraction of a second slower. Similarly, a dog that has been conditioned to salivate to a particularly shaped stimulus may salivate less to a slightly different shape.

classic research
studies in detail

the case of Little Albert

Watson, J. B. and Rayner, R. (1920) Conditioned emotional responses. *Journal of Experimental Psychology*, **3**(1), 1–14. Details from laboratory notes reported in Watson (1924) *Behaviorism*. Norton, New York.

Aim: to explore whether a fear response to an innocuous stimulus could be classically conditioned.

Procedure: a 9-month-old infant was chosen and assessed for emotional stability. He was unafraid of a range of stimuli, including a white rat. Two months later he was shown the rat again and, when he reached for it, a loud noise was made with a hammer and a steel bar, which scared him. This was repeated five times, one week later.

Findings: whenever the steel bar was struck Albert displayed fear. By the second trial, he was cautious about the rat and leaned away when the rat was presented. A further five days later, Albert cried in response to the rat and various similar objects including a fur coat, cotton wool and a Father Christmas beard, and these responses persisted until the final testing, 7 weeks after the start of the study.

Conclusion: Albert was classically conditioned to be afraid of the rat and, through generalisation, became afraid of other white, furry objects.

discrimination

The process of generalisation can, however, be counteracted. If a UCS (such as food) is repeatedly paired with one NS (such as a low tone) and a similar but slightly different NS (such as a higher tone) is presented alone, the animal will learn to *discriminate* – that is the NS paired with the UCS will become a conditioned stimulus capable of eliciting a conditioned response, but the NS presented alone will not. So, in this case, the low tone would cause salivation, but the higher tone would not. Discrimination has been demonstrated in humans. For example Field (2001) exposed smokers to different CSs with and without cigarettes so their cigarette craving became selectively associated with one stimulus and not the other. Such findings could have practical applications for health.

preparedness: do we learn some responses more easily than others?

In much the same way that evolution has shaped rats to learn taste aversions to foods, people seem to learn some responses more readily than others. *Phobias* are a case in point. There are millions of objects and situations in life that could be the focus of fear, but only about 130 are common enough to have been given a technical term of their own. Furthermore, we are only likely to develop a phobic response to objects and situations that, in our evolutionary history, may have presented a threat. Snakes, spiders, rats, heights, small spaces and the dark are all common targets for fear. Why not trees, electrical sockets, guns, knives or garden strimmers?

figure 5.5
Recent inventions do not usually become associated with a fear response

Thousands of years of human evolution have favoured the survival of individuals with a readiness to become afraid of threats to health and life. Snakes and spiders may be poisonous; rats carry disease; confined spaces are often unsafe; and darkness exposes us to dangers we cannot see. Trees, however, have never posed a threat. In contrast, electricity, whilst being potentially dangerous, is too recent in terms of evolution for any benefit to have accrued from a tendency to fear it. For such benefits to evolve, deaths from these situations would have to limit the survival of those who failed to respect the risks they impose.

The tendency to learn more readily about ancient dangers has been termed *preparedness*. Ohman et al. (1976) provided evidence to support this notion by conditioning student volunteers to fear pictures of snakes and spiders (prepared stimuli) or houses, faces and flowers (unprepared stimuli). The pictures acted as the CS and preceded a brief, painful electric shock (UCS) by 10 seconds; the fear associated with this caused sweating, detected as an decrease in GSR (galvanic skin resistance). This forward conditioning resulted in the acquisition of a CR to all pictures. However, conditioning to the prepared stimuli was quicker, taking only one trial to establish (compared to four or five for the unprepared stimuli) and was more resistant to extinction.

discussion of classical conditioning

We have seen that classical conditioning can explain a variety of human behaviours ranging from phobias and taste aversion to attitudes and sexual fetishes. The existence of this type of learning is not controversial. It is easily demonstrated in the laboratory and seen in real-life situations. Its importance in acquiring the range of complex human behaviours is more contentious. Early behavioural psychologists, such as J. B. Watson, thought that we could explain all human behaviours and characteristics by classical conditioning but that is now known to be untrue. Classical conditioning cannot explain how we learn new behaviours, only how we learn to exhibit existing behaviours in response to different situations. Neither does classical conditioning explain how we learn from the consequences of our actions or from observing others. These are now known to be important learning mechanisms.

for+against

classical conditioning as an explanation of human behaviour

+ It can explain the acquisition of some aspects of behaviour, where a specific response is associated with a particular stimulus – for example, in taste aversion. Some responses that cannot be accounted for by other theories, including some symptoms of Gulf War Syndrome, may be explained through classical conditioning.

+ Classical conditioning has a range of practical applications. Later in this chapter we shall look at how the principles of classical conditioning are used in behavioural therapies.

– It can only account for the appearance of existing behaviours in response to new situations, not the acquisition of entirely new behaviours, so cannot account for complex behaviours.

– It is insufficient as an explanation of all human learning. There are other important mechanisms of learning including operant conditioning, observational learning and processes such as insight through which animals acquire new behaviours without any overt conditioning phase.

operant conditioning

Observe the random behaviour of a cat in a kitchen and it won't be long before it has located a source of food – not by smell but by hanging off cupboard doors and making them swing open or pushing its paw into a swing-top bin. It seems that the cat is not systematically investigating the room but, rather, is experimenting with exploratory behaviours until it chances upon food. Some of the earliest experiments into such behaviours were conducted by E. L. Thorndike. To Thorndike, animals did not work out things like the whereabouts of food by any logical process; they simply engaged in behaviours that, by trial and error, led to the discovery of a useful response. Even then they were not always quick to benefit from the experience, often taking many rewarded repetitions to learn.

Thorndike (1911) studied the acquisition of novel behaviours in kittens using a range of specially built puzzle boxes. A typical experiment involved a kitten confined to a box containing little but a paddle on the floor, with food outside that it could see and smell. When it pushed the paddle this opened the door of the box via a series of pulleys. A hungry kitten would engage in various behaviours – biting, clawing, moving around the box or trying to squeeze out between the bars – before eventually operating the mechanism to open the door by accident, thus leading to the food. Such a procedure differs from Pavlov's classical conditioning because the kitten only received the food as a consequence of performing the appropriate behaviour. After feeding, the kitten was returned to the box and would repeat its array of behaviours, again stumbling by chance on the one resulting in escape. After several repetitions, the kitten performed the response necessary to open the door more quickly. This reduction in *latency* from about 5 minutes to as little as 5 seconds over ten trials indicated that the kitten was learning the puzzle.

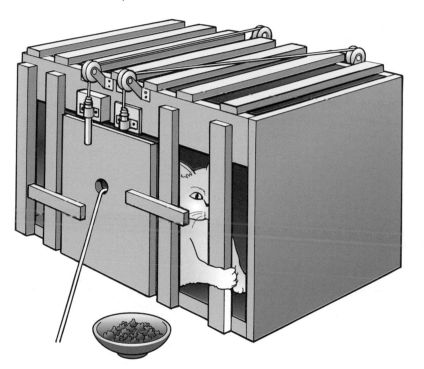

figure 5.6
Thorndike's puzzle box

the law of effect

Thorndike did not assume that the kittens improved their performance because they understood the situation. Instead, he suggested that they solved the problem more quickly because they learnt which behaviour led to the desired effect. The consequence of enhancing such links between the stimulus and the response is expressed by Thorndike (1911) as the *law of effect*: 'of several responses made to the same situation, those which are accompanied or closely followed by satisfaction to the animal will, all other things being equal, be more firmly connected with the situation' (Thorndike, 1911).

In sum, Thorndike demonstrated that an animal learns a response not through reasoning but because favourable consequences increase the probability that the behaviour which immediately precedes them will be repeated.

the work of B. F. Skinner

The kind of learning studied by Thorndike became known as instrumental or *operant conditioning* and was studied in detail by B. F. Skinner (1874–1949). To maximise the objectivity, accuracy and ease of recording behaviour in his experiments, Skinner developed a chamber in which an animal, such as a rat or pigeon, could learn a specific response. The apparatus could present stimuli (called *antecedents*) and allowed responses (called *behaviours*) to be measured and recorded. *Consequences* followed the performance of a particular behaviour. The antecedents (A) included lights and noises, the behaviours (B) were bar presses or pecks directed at a disc and the consequences (C) were food or electric shocks. These chambers, later known as *Skinner boxes*, offered precise control over the animal's experience so that the factors affecting learning could be rigorously investigated. They also allowed automated recording, further reducing external influences on the experimental animals.

the process of operant conditioning

The learning sequence can be represented as:

A	→	B	→	C
bar	→	press	→	food

A elicits B, which results in C

A rat placed in a Skinner box will perform a range of behaviours, the majority of which are irrelevant to the situation. When it chances to strike the bar, perhaps by stretching up against the wall, the mechanism will release a food pellet into the hopper. As this makes a 'click' the rat may investigate and find the food immediately or may only do so later. Each time the rat hits the bar another pellet is released and as it discovers food in the hopper, it checks more often. The rat is thus likely to encounter the food soon after pressing the bar. As food is found only after the bar (A) is pressed and not following any other behaviour, it is this response that is *reinforced* – the frequency of the bar pressing (B) is increased because it immediately precedes the arrival of the food (C). This illustrates Thorndike's law of effect and was expressed by Skinner (1938) as 'behaviour is shaped and maintained by its consequences'.

reinforcement: the effect of rewards

Skinner proposed that the consequences of a behaviour could serve to strengthen or weaken a response. How can this occur? Reinforcement, the process by which an animal is rewarded for a behaviour, can occur in two ways, each of which acts to increase the frequency of the immediately preceding behaviour.

Positive reinforcers are good things that can happen to an animal, such as receiving food, water, the opportunity to play with a companion or access to a mate. When a behaviour is followed by a positive reinforcer, its frequency increases: an animal is more likely to perform a behaviour that has pleasant consequences. A rat will press a bar to receive food, children will tidy their bedrooms for the opportunity to watch television. Koba and Tanida (1999) used operant conditioning to train miniature pigs to recognise their handlers. The piglets were touched and fed raisins as positive reinforcement whenever they approached their handler. Training continued using a Y maze, giving the piglets a choice between their own handler (wearing dark blue overalls) and a non-handler (in white). The handlers also wore different fragrances. The piglets achieved successful discrimination, relying mainly on colour cues. A similar experiment has been conducted with calves.

figure 5.7
A Skinner box

colour-crazy calves

Rybarczyk, P., Rushen, J. and De Passile, A. M. (2003) Recognition of people by dairy calves using colour of clothing. *Applied Animal Behaviour Science,* **81**(4), 307–319.

Aim: to test whether cows can be conditioned operantly to discriminate between people wearing different colour clothing.

Procedure: Holstein calves aged 1 to 2 weeks were tested in a discrimination task in which they had to choose a path through a Y maze at the end of the stall. The choice was always between two individuals wearing different coloured clothing although these colours were varied during the test. One, the 'familiar rewarder', had previously always worn the same colour clothes when giving the calf milk, speaking gently to it and patting it in its individual stall and, in the test, gave a reinforcement of 200 ml of milk. The other, the 'non-rewarder', was unfamiliar and gave the calves nothing in the test if they chose that path. The measure of successful learning was the calf making at least six correct choices in eight trials over two consecutive days of testing.

Findings: the calves were most successful at choosing the path that led to the milk when the familiar rewarder was wearing the same colour clothing as worn during previous encounters and the non-rewarder was in a different colour.

Conclusion: colour cues could be used to help calves to discriminate between people.

Negative reinforcers are things that are good when they stop happening, such as the reduction of pain when an electric shock is switched off or the relief when the sound of a pneumatic drill outside your house stops. When a behaviour is followed by a negative reinforcer, as with a positive reinforcer, its frequency increases because the situation is more pleasant than before. A rat will press a bar to turn an electric current off and I will repeatedly walk across the room to bang the TV to stop it buzzing.

punishment: learning what not to do

Unlike reinforcement, which always has pleasant effects, *punishment* imposes an unpleasant consequence. This may be the arrival of something nasty (such as a shock) or the removal of something nice (such as pocket money). Punishment serves to reduce the frequency of the behaviour that precedes it. If, each time I leave the house it rains and I find this unpleasant, I will be disinclined towards excursions; the effect of the rain is to reduce the likelihood of my going out. In this case rain is a punisher.

interactive angles

Decide whether each of these scenarios is an example of positive reinforcement, negative reinforcement or punishment:

1 A man with toothache visits the dentist and suffers more pain. He does not go back.

2 A girl goes to the dentist with toothache and it is sorted out. She then has regular check-ups.

3 A young man wears deodorant for the first time when clubbing. He pulls and continues to wear deodorant.

4 A student smokes in bed, setting fire to her room and destroying her Buffy video collection. She never smokes in bed again.

5 A boy does his homework for the first time and is praised by his teacher. After this he does his homework every week.

6 A student is allowed to drop a boring subject. Her effort in other subjects improves.

figure 5.8
Squirrels can be taught tricks by offering accessible rewards, then making them successively more difficult to reach, thus shaping their behaviour

shaping: reinforcing successive approximations

Skinner proposed that a particular action could be conditioned by reinforcing behaviours that more closely resembled the desired response on each occasion – that is, *successive approximations*. To make children keep their rooms tidy, parents might initially reward them for picking up their dirty clothes, later for putting their books away as well, and subsequently only when the entire floor is visible. On each occasion the child is only rewarded if its attempts at tidying are better than the last.

uncontrollable reinforcers and learning to be superstitious

When a positive consequence follows a behaviour we will tend to repeat that behaviour even if it was not the cause of the reward. Positive consequences that occur regardless of our behaviour are called *uncontrollable reinforcers* – 'uncontrollable' because they occur regardless of our behaviour and 'reinforcers' because they increase the probability of the behaviour being performed at the time being repeated. The power of uncontrollable reinforcers was first demonstrated by Skinner (1948). The behaviours that arise as a consequence of such reinforcement are called *superstitious* behaviours. We might expect superstition, the belief in a relationship that does not in fact exist, to be uniquely human as we assume that animals do not have beliefs. However, Skinner designed this experiment to demonstrate that superstitious behaviours could be acquired by animals. He proposed that superstitious behaviours simply arise because they are accidentally reinforced by some consequence that is not dependent upon that response.

More recently, Helena Matute has examined the role of uncontrollable reinforcers in

figure 5.9
Our belief in the dangers of ladders is reinforced every time we walk around one

classic research
studies in detail

pigeons are superstitious!

Skinner, B. F. (1948) Superstition in the pigeon. *Journal of Experimental Psychology*, **38**, 168–172.

Aim: to demonstrate that superstitious behaviours could be acquired by animals.

Procedure: eight hungry pigeons were placed in individual Skinner boxes for a few minutes a day and received a food pellet every 15 seconds regardless of their behaviour. After several days of conditioning, two independent observers recorded the birds' behaviour. The time interval between pellets was increased and finally the pigeons were given time for acquired behaviours to extinguish.

Findings: of the eight pigeons, six developed repetitive behaviours that they performed between the arrival of pel-

lets. These included turning anti-clockwise, hopping, head tossing and pendulum swings of the head, none of which were exhibited before the experiment. When the time between reinforcers (food pellets) was extended to one minute the pigeons' behaviour increased until they became frantic. Extinction of these new behaviours was slow.

Conclusion: the pigeons behaved as though they believed that the delivery of food pellets depended upon their response even though it did not, as people do when they hold superstitions. Reinforcement was intermittent so the pigeons' behaviour, like that of superstitious humans, was difficult to extinguish.

human behaviour. In one study, Matute (1996) tested whether a superstitious behaviour can arise because we fail to test the possibility that a positive outcome can occur irrespective of our behaviour. Participants worked on computers, some of which periodically emitted beeps. If the participants had the opportunity to discover that doing nothing led to the beep stopping on its own, they learned to wait. However, when they were instructed to try to stop the beep, the participants acquired superstitious responses. In an attempt to stop the noise they tried pressing particular buttons, and learned (wrongly) that it was this button that made the noise stop.

schedules of reinforcement

Do animals learn better when they are reinforced on every performance of the required behaviour or not? The answer to this question depends on what is meant by *better*. In some respects, frequent, predictable reinforcement is better, in others infrequent, unpredictable reinforcement is more effective. Skinner investigated the effects of different reinforcement regimes using rats and pigeons in Skinner boxes by varying how many responses they had to perform before receiving reinforcement, or the time delay between reinforcement becoming available.

◆ An animal that receives a reward for every performance of a behaviour is on a *continuous reinforcement* schedule. This is like getting a treat every time you go to the dentist. Continuous reinforcement results in a low but steady response rate and the behaviour will extinguish very readily if reinforcement is withheld. All other patterns of reinforcement only offer rewards for some instances of the behaviour. This is called *partial reinforcement*.

◆ On a *fixed ratio* schedule (FR), reinforcement is related to the number of behaviours performed. In general, ratio schedules tend to produce high, steady, response rates, although there may be a post-reinforcement pause (PRP), a gap between receiving reinforcement and resuming performance of the behaviour. For example, a person working on a production line might be paid per 100 items. Immediately after each batch is completed the person might have a break, but work hard again on the next 100. Extinction of behaviours reinforced on FR schedules is quite rapid.

◆ On *variable ratio* schedules animals are reinforced only after several responses have been made, the exact number varying around an average. As with FR, the response rate tends to be high, although in laboratory animals the PRP tends to be absent. A variable ratio of five, for instance, would reward every fifth behaviour *on average*; in reality the first, tenth, thirteenth, seventeenth and twenty-fifth responses may be reinforced. This pattern of reinforcement produces the fastest response rate and the greatest resistance to extinction. Gamblers receive payouts after variable numbers of attempts, thus their gambling behaviour is persistent even in the face of nil returns.

◆ A *fixed interval* schedule provides reinforcement at regular times – for instance receiving pocket money every Saturday if your room has been tidy. This results in an uneven pattern of response; you suddenly start to clear up on Thursdays and Fridays. The response extinguishes quite quickly; you are unlikely to bother cleaning your room at all if no money is forthcoming. In laboratory animals there are more responses as the end of the interval approaches. Once the reinforcement has been received, a PRP may follow. The overall response rate tends to be lower than with ratio schedules as the behaviour only needs to be performed once in each interval in order to receive reinforcement.

◆ Finally, a *variable interval* schedule provides reinforcement at timed intervals but the gap between each reinforcement varies around an average. For example, a variable interval schedule of one minute would provide rewards on average every 60 seconds but these may, in fact, arrive at 20, 80, 90, 40, 30 and 100-second intervals. The response rate is high and steady and extinction occurs only very gradually. As with variable ratio schedules, there is no PRP. You are most likely to keep working hard if you are unsure when an inspector is going to arrive to judge the quality of your output.

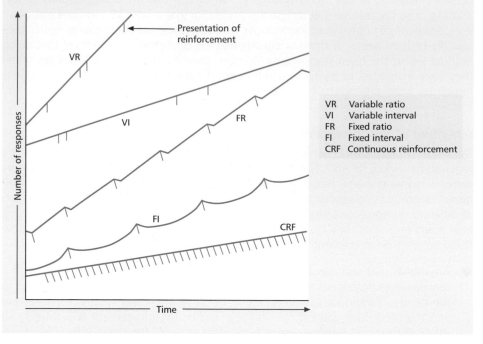

figure 5.10
The different schedules of
reinforcement produce differing
response patterns as indicated
by records of cumulative
reinforcements over time

Partial reinforcement clearly affects both response rate and resistance to extinction. Gambling seems to fulfil the criterion of a variable ratio schedule, producing both high response rates and resistance to extinction, in fact gambling shows many properties of addiction. However, Delfabbro and Winefield (1999) have shown that the response rates of gamblers do not exactly replicate the high, steady response rates predicted for a variable ratio schedule of reinforcement. Rather, the response rate of players on poker machines (the Australian equivalent of fruit machines or slot machines) dipped after a payout. These post-reinforcement pauses depended on the size of the reward and the experience of the players (experienced players taking longer pauses after a big win). These findings suggest that gamblers, unlike rats, are sensitive to machine events.

inter**active** ▪ angles

Partial reinforcement schedules in real life:

1 Sarah is trying to get hold of Kate on the phone but Kate's number is busy. Sarah keeps pressing redial over and over again.

2 Netball is Sally's favourite sport. She really wants to be a credit to her team and hurtles about trying to shoot as often as she can. Just occasionally she succeeds in scoring and basks in the cheers of the crowd.

3 Pete's cooking a lasagne for some friends. After he's put it in the oven he leaves it alone but once it's been in for a while he keeps going to check if it's done – he really wants it to be perfect.

4 Jim works in the post room, which is downstairs in his two-storey office block, so he has to carry packages up one flight of stairs of 32 steps. The packages are heavy and he feels relieved (a positive reinforcer) each time he reaches the top of the stairs. He tends not to stop on the way up, though often has a rest at the top of the stairs.

Each of the examples above represents one of the partial reinforcement schedules. Which is which?

animal learning studies   research methods

Animal learning studies can be conducted in a number of different ways. In most cases, many animals are used in order to demonstrate general effects from which 'laws' of behaviour can be derived. A strict protocol is followed so that the experience of each animal is the same; any differences can then be assumed to be due to the manipulation of the researcher (as in experiments). In order to minimise the effects of human interference, animal learning studies often use mechanised equipment or remote video recording. The Skinner box (see p. 110) is an example of this. Once the food hopper is filled with pellets and the animal (typically a rat or pigeon) has been put into the box, its behaviour can be recorded without the presence of any people and the procedures can be varied (such as the number of bar presses or pecks it must generate to receive a reward).

Mazes are also used to test animal learning. Simple T or Y shaped mazes offer animals a choice between two alleyways (arms) and are used to test discrimination learning – whether the animal can learn to tell two stimuli apart by systematically rewarding the choice of arm that is signalled at the choice point by a particular stimulus (such as a coloured square). More complex mazes are used to investigate spatial learning – that is, whether the animal can remember a route using landmarks or directional cues. These mazes consist either of a complex series of turns and blind alleys and may require the animal (such as a rat) to swim through opaque water (for example, in a Morris milk maze) or a large number of simultaneous choices (in a radial arm maze). This method does, however, have limitations:

◆ laboratory animals may not respond in the same way as humans, or even as animals in their natural habitats, so the results of such studies may not be generalisable;

◆ animals may use cues other than those provided by the researcher – for example, in maze studies rats may use pictures on the wall of the laboratory rather than stimuli within the maze to navigate their way – if so, the experimental results may be invalid;

◆ procedures such as food deprivation, and electric shocks used as punishment or as negative reinforcement, may cause suffering to animals, raising ethical issues.

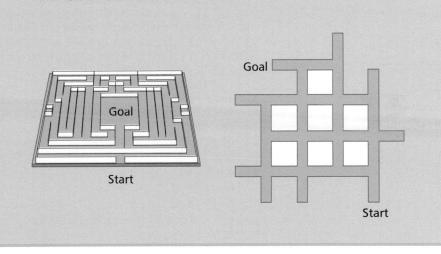

figure 5.11
Two different types of maze

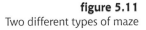

You can try out maze learning for yourselves by building a 'finger maze' in which a participant has to learn a route through a maze with series of turns and dead ends (such as illustrated above). A maze like this can be simply constructed by sticking string (textured gardening string is best) to stiff cardboard with glue. The participant closes his eyes and traces his way along the string. Alternatively, you can find mazes in comic books and on the Internet. You could record the number of trials taken to learn the correct route; number of errors made, time taken to complete the maze and differences between groups such as males and females.

figure 5.12
The factually correct 'nice doggy'
is more likely to be reinforced
than the grammatically correct
'that is a nice cat'

operant conditioning and language acquisition

Skinner (1957) proposed that children acquired language through imitation and shaping. Imitation must clearly play a part in language acquisition as our speech resembles the speech of those around us. This can, for instance, account for why we develop a regional accent. The acquisition of speech sounds or phonemes can also be explained by imitation. Infants initially generate an international range of phonemes before limiting their scope to those of the language they hear (Oller, 1981). Deaf babies fail to do this and eventually stop babbling altogether although those exposed to sign language imitate signs on schedule (Pinker, 1994). The learning of whole words also depends on imitation. Children who imitate the most expand their vocabulary the fastest (Masur, 1995).

Shaping also plays a part in language acquisition. A child's first utterances will be met with enthusiasm, a positive reinforcer, and subsequent attempts at words are praised and further reinforced. For infants learning their first words it is easy to see how shaping could operate. A child hears the sound of the word *grandad* and goes *g-g-g* to the delight of the grandparents; his excitement is rewarding. Subsequently the child may be praised for saying *gagad* long before the whole word can be articulated. This progressive reinforcement could shape the child's utterances.

Consider why older children start to swear; they copy words they hear, repeating them to their friends from whom they receive respect, a positive reinforcer. They then say them to their parents and are reprimanded. This may serve as a genuine punisher, reducing the probability of such language being used (at least in the home) or the consequence may act as a positive reinforcer to attract attention or satisfy a sense of revenge.

One might expect the greatest reinforcement to come from being understood; children with accurate speech should be more likely to achieve their aim, to obtain an ice cream for instance. This is not, however, the case; *i-keem*, *i-keem* is very likely to be effective. Adults (and siblings) are expert at deciphering attempts at language, thus reinforcing incorrect speech. Truth and intelligibility are more important than grammatical correctness; parents are likely to reinforce a child who says 'nice brown doggy' to a golden Labrador but not one who says 'that's a nice brown dog' to a white cat (Brown et al., 1969). In fact, attempts to correct speech are usually fruitless. Take this example from Kuczaj (1982):

> Ben: I like these candy. I like they.
> Adult: You like them?
> Ben: Yes, I like they.
> Adult: Say *them*.
> Ben: Them.
> Adult: Say 'I like *them*'
> Ben: I like them.
> Adult: Good.
> Ben: I'm good. These candy good too.
> Adult: Are they good?
> Ben: Yes. I like they. You like they?

This shows that, although children can imitate and are reinforced for doing so, their capacity to extract rules from the language they hear and reapply them is also important. Eventually, however, exceptions to the rules must be learned by example. Nelson (1973) found that correcting grammatical errors may in fact be detrimental. She observed mothers' responses to incorrect speech and found that children who were systematically corrected expanded their vocabulary more slowly than children of more forgiving parents.

The greatest problems for the learning theory approach to language acquisition are, however, the speed at which it is acquired and the systematic nature of children's linguistic understanding. At our peak, we learn words at nine per day (Carey, 1978), too many for each to be individually reinforced. From the speech we hear, we seem to extract and re-apply rules of language (syntax) allowing us enormous linguistic flexibility; even the very young generate novel utterances. As this process is rule governed we cannot be exposed to examples of every combination so imitation and shaping are insufficient as explanations. This approach cannot account for the similarity of the sequence of language learning between individuals and across cultures nor the tendency of children to make *overgeneralisation* errors, such as 'I runned' and 'we goed'.

angling with the net

Use a search engine such as Google to locate sites about Ivan Pavlov and B. H. Skinner. Try to find examples of studies they conducted that are different from the ones described here and determine the UCS, UCR, CS and CR in the case of classical conditioning and the nature of the consequences being used in the case of operant conditioning.

where to now?

We recommend the following as further sources of good information about conditioning:

▶ **Gross, R.** (2003) *Key Studies in Psychology*. Hodder & Stoughton, London. This contains detailed accounts of a number of major studies of learning.

▶ **Clamp, A. and Russell, J.** (1998) *Comparative Psychology*. Hodder & Stoughton, London. A rigorous but user-friendly account of conditioning with an emphasis on animal studies.

▶ **Leslie, J. C. and O'Reilly, M. F.** (1999) *Behaviour Analysis*. Harwood, Amsterdam. A very technical and detailed account of conditioning processes.

social learning theory

learning by example

Social learning, by definition, depends on the presence of other individuals, and the role they play must be more than merely incidental. Being surrounded by others may enhance learning by increasing competition or reducing fear but this is not *social*. For

figure 5.13
We acquire many skills by
observation and imitation

social learning to occur, one individual must acquire a new behaviour by imitating another, the *model*. Models need not be aware of their role, although in tutoring models alter their behaviour to maximise learning opportunities.

Monkeys in the wild are afraid of snakes. An adult monkey encountering a snake will indicate fear with its facial expression, make an alarm call and flee. These reactions are notably absent from the response of a laboratory-reared monkey in the same situation. Mineka and Cook (1988) studied how rhesus monkeys (*Macaca mulatta*) learn this response. When laboratory-reared subjects observed the agitation displayed by a wild reared monkey in response to a snake, they modified their behaviour to match the model. On subsequent exposure to snakes, the previously naïve monkeys displayed fear; they appeared to have learnt to be afraid by watching the behaviour of other individuals.

Observing an unafraid model that failed to respond to a snake appeared to immunise the naïve monkeys against developing a fear. When later exposed to models behaving appropriately, these monkeys failed to learn to be afraid of snakes.

Animals can also learn behaviours for which they have not been 'prepared' by evolution. Herbert and Harsh (1944) found that cats would learn to escape from a box more quickly if they observed the trials of a demonstrator learning to get out of the box. The cats did, however, learn faster if they watched the whole learning process than if they just saw a skilled performer at work.

when will observational learning occur?

According to Bandura (1977) there are four requirements for observational learning to occur. These are:

1   *Attention*: the observer must be paying attention to the model.

2   *Retention*: the observer must be capable of retaining a memory of the observed behaviour.

3   *Reproduction*: the observer must be capable of performing the observed action.

4   *Motivation*: the observer must be motivated to generate the learned behaviour either in return for an external reward or because of some intrinsic motivation generated by the model (hence individuals differ in their power as models).

figure 5.14
Dogs really do become like
their owners!

For humans, we must be watching or listening to the model to attend. As schoolchildren we may remember the plaintive cry of 'Pay attention or you won't learn anything' and even earlier than that we may have heard 'Watch how mummy does it'. Having seen models in action, we must then be able to remember their behaviour. This is sometimes more difficult than it sounds. I may have watched carefully the way the mechanic at the garage assembled my new windscreen wipers and be perfectly capable of the actions myself but completely unable to remember what to do.

Unlike classical or operant conditioning where the animal's learning is indicated immediately by its performance, in social learning an animal may acquire, but not necessarily demonstrate, the new behaviour. A young child may observe his parents in the evening having a 'G and T' or a lager but it is not until he is sitting in the trolley at the supermarket pointing at the goods on the conveyor belt that it becomes apparent that he has learned 'Gin for mummy, beer for daddy'. Such examples do, however,

'look, Spot, look': social learning in pet dogs

Kubinyi, E., Topal, J., Miklosi, A. and Csanyi, V. (2003) Dogs (*Canis familiaris*) learn from their owners via observation in a manipulation task. *Journal of Comparative Psychology*, **117**(2), 156–165.

Aim: to demonstrate social learning in dogs.

Procedure: 87 pet dogs in the experimental condition watched their owners solve a task (by pushing the handle of a box) to release a ball. Each dog observed this 10 times.

Findings: when dogs from the experimental condition and control groups were observed with the apparatus, those that had observed their owners demonstrating the use of the handle to get the ball tended to reproduce this behaviour. In contrast, dogs in the control conditions developed different strategies.

Conclusion: domestic dogs can use social learning to acquire new behaviours from their owners.

serve to illustrate another difference between conditioning and social learning. In the latter there is no requirement for reinforcement, at least not to learn. Reinforcement may, however, play a part in the expression of the behaviour. Children who imitate the

media watch

call to turn off *South Park*

Times Educational Supplement, 11 February 2000.

Parents at a North Yorkshire primary school have been urged to stop their children watching the cult TV cartoon *South Park* after an increase in swearing and bad behaviour in the playground.

Glyn Hopper, head of Sowerby County Primary School, near Thirsk, wrote to parents after children raised the issue in her school council.

questions

1 Explain using social learning theory how the children might have acquired antisocial behaviour from watching South Park.

2 How important do you think the media is as an influence on children's behaviour?

figure 5.15
South Park has been cited as a source of undesirable role models

offensive language of others may learn to demonstrate their behaviour only in situations where it will be rewarded.

Duck (1990) suggests that the extent to which the characteristics of the model are reflected in the observer's characteristics may determine their effectiveness as a model. What features might affect the modelling process? As indicated by the findings of Bandura et al. (1961), same-sex models are more effective than opposite-sex models for increasing aggressive behaviour in children. Other key attributes of effective models include power and likeability, hence popstars and sports personalities as well as parents are potent models. In animals, as well as in people, status affects the likelihood of being copied. Nicol and Pope (1999) exposed chickens to a model demonstrating a new way to obtain food. The observer chickens saw different demonstrators – high-, mid- or low-status hens in their flock or cockerels. The chickens tended to imitate the feeding locations of dominant hens rather than submissive ones or cockerels and, as with humans, same-sex models were imitated more frequently than opposite-sex models.

Pennington (1986) identifies three categories of variable that affect imitation: characteristics of the observer and of the model and the consequences of the behaviour for the model. These features include the age and status of the model and the observer's level of self-esteem. Models who are of similar age and high in status are more likely to be imitated. For example, young people who perceive drug-users as high in status may be drawn into drug taking because the sight of high-status people taking drugs is more influential than the threats of their parents.

classic research
studies in detail

will children copy violent behaviour?

Bandura, A., Ross, D. and Ross, S.A. (1961) Transmission of aggression through imitation of aggressive models. *Journal of Abnormal and Social Psychology*, **63**, 575–582.

Aim: to investigate whether aggression could be acquired through modelling and to see whether children were more likely to imitate same-sex role models.

Procedure: children aged 3 to 6 years (36 boys and 36 girls) were assigned to three groups. Two groups were exposed to adult models who behaved in either aggressive or non-aggressive ways with half seeing a same-sex model, the others an opposite-sex model. A control group did not see any model. In the non-aggressive condition, the model assembled Tinker toys for 10 minutes; in the aggressive condition this lasted only 1 minute after which the model attacked the Bobo doll. The Bobo was lain on its side, sat upon, punched on the nose, picked up and hit on the head with the mallet. This sequence was performed three times over 9 minutes accompanied by aggressive comments such as 'kick him' and 'pow'.

All participants were then deliberately annoyed. They were shown to a room with attractive toys such as a fire engine and a doll with a wardrobe (remember, this is the 1960s) but, after being allowed to play for a short time, the children were told that these toys were for other children and were moved to another room containing a range of toys including a Bobo doll. The children were observed playing here for 20 minutes using a one-way mirror.

Findings: children exposed to violent models imitated their exact behaviours and were significantly more aggressive – both physically and verbally – than those children who did not receive aggressive modelling. This effect was greater for boys than girls although girls were more likely to imitate verbal, and boys physical, aggression. Boys were also more likely to imitate a same-sex model as, to a lesser extent, were girls.

Conclusion: observation and imitation can account for the learning of specific acts without reinforcement of either the model or observer. Observers have a greater tendency to imitate same-sex models.

laboratory experiments

In an experiment, one factor, the independent variable (IV), is systematically varied while the effect on another factor, the dependent variable (DV) is measured. By creating different 'levels' of the IV the experimenter can compare the effects of the variable under investigation by using two or more experimental conditions or by comparing an experimental condition to a control condition (from which the IV is absent). The dependent variable (DV) is the measurable outcome in the experiment. Changes in this variable are caused by (are dependent upon) changes in the IV. Any other factors that might affect the dependent variable should be controlled – in other words, they should be kept constant across different conditions of the independent variable. This ensures that any difference in the dependent variable between conditions is the result of the IV and is not due to other, chance variations.

A *laboratory experiment* is conducted in a laboratory or other contrived setting away from the participants' normal environment. In this situation the researcher can manipulate the levels of the independent variable precisely, and accurately record changes in the dependent variable. Potential confounding variables can also be controlled easily. The findings of experiments can therefore be readily replicated and validated. These are the most significant advantages of laboratory studies over other techniques. Researchers in a laboratory can be more confident than their counterparts in the field that any changes they observe in the DV are attributable to the IV rather than being the consequence of some uncontrolled aspect of the situation. There are, however, some limitations to laboratory experiments:

◆ Because they impose rigorous controls, laboratory experiments may not be representative of real-world situations and can consequently lack ecological validity.

◆ Laboratory experiments are unsuitable for some types of research where contrived situations are inappropriate or unethical.

◆ By focusing on a narrow range of measured variables, other important effects may be overlooked.

◆ Participants may become aware of, and respond to, demand characteristics in the laboratory setting that indicate what the experimenter is expecting to happen and this can confound the results.

figure 5.16 The Bobo doll study

the learning approach

⟲ discussion

Social learning theory can help us to understand how behaviours are acquired without going through a conditioning process and, as a consequence, how we can sometimes demonstrate competence in a behaviour without having practised it at all. It also explains the importance of the behaviour of those around us; we tend to imitate behaviours we see, be they good or bad. Although much research has focused on acquiring negative behaviours, social learning theory also tells us about the influence of positive role models.

media watch

dad, lad, gay icon, player – why Beckham is Britain's model man

Denis Campbell, *Observer*, 2 February 2003

David Beckham has overcome the hostility and endless jokes he inspires to emerge as the most influential man in Britain, according to a new academic study. An analysis of the effects of the England captain's global fame portrays him as a bold crusader who is making the world a better place by single-handedly transforming men's attitudes towards sex, love, babies, nights out with the lads and even homosexuality.

'David Beckham is a hugely important figure in popular culture and now probably the most influential male figure for anyone in Britain aged 5 to 60', said Dr Andrew Parker of Warwick University, co-author of the research. 'By defying expectations in areas such as what clothes men are allowed to wear, he has helped create a complex new concept of masculinity. That has already begun to change male behaviour and has the potential to encourage a whole generation of young men who admire him to act more like him.'

The academics praise Beckham as a trailblazer for subverting male stereotypes by showing an interest in ballet and fashion, publicly confessing his love for his wife Victoria and daring to acknowledge his large gay following. 'He has broken so many strict traditional working-class masculine codes of behaviour that he has the potential to influence lots of boys and young men to do the same, for example accepting homosexuality as part of life.'

questions

1 According to Duck (1990), what characteristics might make Beckham such a powerful role model?

2 Explain using social learning theory the process by which a young man might be influenced by David Beckham.

figure 5.17
The world's most potent role model?

Recent research has shown how social learning in children can be used in positive ways. Although children may learn problem behaviour by imitation in aggressive families (Onyskiw and Hayduk, 2001) observation can also be used to provide examples of pro-social behaviour. Huston and Wright (1998) investigated the effect of pro-social models on television, such as *Sesame Street* and *Lassie*. They found that children who watched this kind of programme (showing behaviours such as kindness, sharing and helping) demonstrated more kind and helpful behaviours themselves compared with children who did not engage in such viewing.

Social learning techniques have been used to help language learning in mainstream children and those with learning disabilities. Horner (2000) investigated how modelling attention to the print when reading affected pre-school children. She found that if a child model asked questions about the print in an alphabet book the children who watched him were also more likely to pay attention to the print themselves. This, in turn, led to an improvement in letter-naming ability. Similar improvements were found by Ezell and Justice (2000) with children who observed adult models in a shared book-reading situation. Keel et al. (2000) investigated the effects of social learning in children with learning disabilities. Where students were able to observe other students writing on the board there was a significant improvement in their reading ability.

for+against

social learning theory as an explanation of human behaviour

+ Social learning can explain the acquisition of behaviours, such as aggression, through observation as shown by Bandura. This has important implications for understanding how patterns of behaviour are passed on from one generation to the next in families and for understanding the possible effects of media violence.

+ Social learning can explain why children may appear to have acquired a new behaviour spontaneously. Social learning can occur without immediate demonstration so these behaviours may appear quickly and error free.

— It can be difficult to measure social learning accurately because the acquisition of a new behaviour can occur without its being performed immediately.

— Social learning cannot account for the acquisition of new behaviours that have not been observed in a model.

real lives
key application

deliberately altering human behaviour

Learning theory can be used in clinical settings to alter people's behaviour deliberately. The clinical application of classical conditioning is called *behaviour therapy* whereas operant conditioning has given rise to *behaviour modification*. In this chapter we shall just be looking at behaviour therapy – the use of classical conditioning principles to alter maladaptive behaviour. Behaviour therapy techniques include treatment of phobias using systematic desensitisation and flooding and the use of aversion therapy to eliminate behaviours.

systematic desensitisation

Systematic desensitisation relies on the therapist being able to induce a state of relaxation in the client. This may be achieved by progressive muscle relaxation, hypnosis or the use of anti-anxiety drugs. This relaxed state is the UCR. During conditioning relaxation is paired with items related to the feared stimulus, working through a graduated sequence called an *anxiety hierarchy*. This is a list of stimuli, agreed between the client and therapist, of increasingly feared items leading to the phobic stimulus itself. During desensitisation the UCR is maintained throughout exposure to the hierarchy of increasingly more frightening CSs. *Reciprocal inhibition* prevents the client from feeling two opposite emotions at once. Thus, as the state of relaxation is maintained, the client cannot become afraid. Each pairing results in the new CS becoming associated with the CR of relaxation rather than fear.

the process of desensitisation

prior to desensitisation:

phobic stimulus	→	fear
relaxation training UCS	→	*relaxation* UCR

during desensitisation:

relaxation training
UCS
+   →   relaxation
phobic stimulus   +
CS   fear

Reciprocal inhibition prevents both of these opposite responses exisiting simultaneously. Through the effects of the therapy, relaxation replaces fear as the dominant emotion

after desensitisation:

phobic stimulus CS	→	*relaxation* CR

Freeling and Shemberg (1970) used systematic desensitisation for exam-nerves in a group of students. They first developed an anxiety hierarchy of 15 items ranging from 'you are sitting in a classroom of 100 students listening to a lecture' to 'the test papers are being handed out'. The students were then taught how to achieve deep muscle relaxation and asked to practise the technique every day at home. During desensitisation sessions, the students relaxed with the help of suggestions from the experimenter and were asked to imagine each scene from the hierarchy in turn. They moved on to the next item only when they felt relaxed with the image, up to four items being introduced during each weekly meeting. After six weeks the students were less anxious as indicated by both questionnaire responses and exam performance.

The following example, from Wolpe (1969), who first developed systematic desensitisation, illustrates an anxiety hierarchy for a phobia of physical deformity. As you can see, it begins with mildly fearful stimuli and ends up in the most severe fear-inducing situation for the client. As desensitisation proceeds, the relaxation associated with one situation may generalise to the next, paving the way for progression through the stages.

1. Ambulances
2. Hospitals
3. Wheelchairs
4. Nurses in uniform
5. Automobile accidents
6. The sight of someone who is seriously ill
7. Someone in pain
8. The sight of physical deformity

In research involving long-term follow-up of clients with phobias, Zinbarg et al. (1992) report that systematic desensitisation is more effective than any other form of therapy for most clients with phobias. It is also effective across a range of phobias as well as post-traumatic stress disorder, sexual dysfunction and asthma attacks (Emmelkamp, 1994).

figure 5.18

Nyctophobics don't go out at night and zoophobics steer clear of pet shops. People with phobias tend to avoid the source of their fear, thus are never in a position to test whether the feared situation is actually as unpleasant as they believe. It could be argued that the reason systematic desensitisation works is because it places clients in a situation where they are forced to test reality. On discovering that the feared situation is not, in fact, as horrific as imagined, the phobia is dispelled.

flooding

In contrast to the progressive approach of systematic desensitisation, *flooding* achieves reality testing in a single step. Clients are placed in safe, supportive environments and confront the feared situation head-on, effectively stepping straight up to the top of their hierarchy. They are immersed in this situation until their fear subsides. As with the final stage of a desensitisation hierarchy, the flooding procedure may be *in vivo*, a 'live' situation, or covert, a described, illustrated or imagined scene. The latter is termed *implosion therapy* as the fear *implodes* – it is destroyed inwardly. Covert procedures tend to be used when it would be impractical to introduce the feared stimulus into the therapist's consulting room; snakes, water, fire or heights for example. Virtual reality simulators can offer very effective covert procedures in these instances.

Studies with animals support the effectiveness of the flooding approach. Rats that have learned a signalled shock-avoidance response to a tone are subjected to repeated tones without receiving a shock. This forces reality testing and exposes the rats to a situation that eliminates their fear of the tone (Baum, 1969). Success with flooding therapy appears to be even better than with systematic desensitisation (Marks, 1987). In work with agoraphobics, who fear being helpless and unaided when they are away from their place of security, flooding has been particularly successful. Agoraphobia, which literally means 'fear of the market place' (the *agora* of ancient Greece), is often triggered in crowded places such as shopping centres where the sufferer feels alone and at risk. Therefore, flooding often requires clients to agree (with great trepidation) to spend a prolonged period of time alone in a busy public place. This may be preceded by exposure to a graphic description of their worst fears, for example being knocked down, trampled on and laughed at. After several hours of horrifying immersion during which nothing terrible happens, clients should find that their anxiety has subsided. The improvement achieved through flooding persists; after four years Emmelkamp and Kuipers (1979) found that 75% of a group of 70 agoraphobics were still benefiting from the effects of their treatment. Similar gains are found with flooding therapy for obsessive-compulsive disorders such as repetitive washing in response to fears of contamination (Marks and Rachman, 1978). Whilst more effective, flooding is, of course, more immediately distressing for the client.

Implosion confronts the phobia directly, as is evident in the following description:

an example of implosion
(from Hogan, 1968)

Close your eyes again. Picture the snake out in front of you. Now make yourself pick it up. Reach down, pick it up, put it in your lap, feel it wiggling around in your lap, leave your hand on it, put your hand out and feel it wiggling around. Kind of explore its body with your fingers and hand. You don't like to do it, make yourself do it. Make yourself do it. Really grab onto the snake. Squeeze it a little bit, feel it. Feel it kind of start to wind around your hand. Let it. Leave your hand there, feel it touching your hand there, feel it touching your hand and winding around it, curling around your wrist.

Okay, now put your finger out towards the snake and feel his head coming up. Its head is towards your finger and it is starting to bite your finger. Let it, let it bite at your finger. Put your finger out, let it bite, let it bite at your finger, feel its fangs go right down into your finger. Ooooh, feel the pain going right up your arm and into your shoulder.

Okay, feel him coiling around your hand again, touching you, slimy. Now he is going up on your shoulder and he crawls there and he is sitting on your chest and he is looking you right in the eye. He is black and he is big and he is ugly and he's coiled up and he is ready to strike and he is looking at you. Picture his face, look at his eyes, look at those long sharp fangs . . . He strikes out at you. (Therapist slaps hand.) Feel him bite at your face. Feel him bite at your face, let him bite; let him bite; just relax and let him bite; let him bite at your face; let him bite; let him bite at your face; feel his fangs go right into your cheeks; and the blood is coming out on your face now . . . feel it biting your eye and it is going to pull your eye right out and down on your cheek. It is kind of gnawing on it and eating it, eating at your eye. Your little eye is down on your cheek and it is gnawing and biting at your eye. Picture it. Now it is crawling into your eye socket and wiggling around in there, feel it wiggling and wiggling up into your head.

aversion therapy

Some behaviours are deemed to be maladaptive or undesirable and, in such cases, aversion therapy may be used in an attempt to eliminate them. For example, smokers and alcoholics may undergo aversion therapy. Through classical conditioning, an unpleasant response (the CR) becomes associated with the stimulus to be avoided (CS). This association causes aversion to the stimulus so clients' behaviours are altered as they learn to avoid the unpleasant response. Aversion therapy has been successfully employed by Duker and Seys (2000) to reduce self-injurious behaviour in children with learning difficulties and with sex offenders to eliminate conditioned responses of sexual arousal (Weinrott et al., 1997). The young sex offenders listened to an audiotaped crime scenario that evoked deviant sexual arousal and were then immediately exposed to a videotaped aversive stimulus – the negative social, emotional, physical and legal consequences of sex offences. Weinrott et al. found a significant improvement in both physiological and self-report measures of arousal following this treatment.

for+against

behavioural therapies

+ These techniques can be extremely effective, for example in treating phobias (for example, Zinbarg et al., 1992).

+ In some cases behavioural techniques can also reduce symptoms in more complex conditions such as agoraphobia.

— In cases where genes (see chapter 7) or family relationships (see chapter 6) have played a role in the development of symptoms behavioural treatments, which just alleviate symptoms, cannot be considered cures.

— Sometimes (as we have seen) behavioural treatments can be, to say the least, traumatic for patients. The benefit of the treatment needs to be balanced against this trauma.

where to now?

The following are good sources of information about behavioural therapies:

▶ **Cave, S.** (1999) *Therapeutic Approaches*. Routledge, London. A simple and user-friendly introduction to therapies including behavioural approaches.

▶ **Bergin, A. E. and Garfield, S. L.** (1994) *Handbook of Psychotherapy and Behaviour Change*. Wiley, New York. A very advanced and detailed text with numerous examples of studies of behavioural therapies and their applications and effectiveness.

talking point

contemporary issues

media violence

Parents, teachers and much of society are concerned about violence in young people. One possible cause for the apparent rise in aggressive behaviour is the effect of media violence – violence in television programmes, videos and computer games. Could these influences really be responsible for changes in children's behaviour?

Children are certainly exposed to a lot of media violence. It is estimated that a child leaving primary school will have watched 8000 murders and more than 100 000 other acts of violence on television and video (Eron, 1995). In a field experiment, Troseth (2003) demonstrated that even 2-year-old children could use information they had seen on a video. For two weeks, the children could watch themselves 'live' on the family television and, when later tested on their ability to find a toy they had seen on video being hidden in another room, they were able to do this – achieving a task that children of this age find very difficult. This suggests that children's behaviour may indeed be affected by what they see on television.

interactive angles

If possible, try to work in a group for this activity. Each individual needs to choose a time and television channel to watch and the group needs to agree definitions for aggressive behaviour. Your aim is to compare aspects of television programmes with regard to violence. You might consider when it is shown; whether the aggression is verbal, physical or both; whether it is perpetrated and/or received by males, females or inanimate objects; whether the perpetrator is a powerful character, and so forth. If you have more than one person viewing the same programmes, you can assess their records for inter-observer reliability.

applying learning theory to understanding the effects of media violence

Assuming that there is a direct connection between viewing violence on television and aggressive behaviour then learning theory is well placed to explain it. In particular, social learning theory looks at the importance of imitation and identification with models.

imitation of role models

When characters on television use violence they are modelling aggression. Recall that, for behaviour to be acquired by social learning, four processes take place; attention, retention, reproduction and reinforcement. Watching television often involves giving it your attention. If the violence witnessed is distinctive and arousing this means it is likely to be retained. If children have been impressed by the violence used then they may reproduce it themselves on a later occasion. This is particularly true if they witness models being rewarded for their actions (vicarious reinforcement) or they receive a reward for their own aggression.

identification with role models

TV heroes are designed to have exactly the characteristics that make them effective models. They have high social status and are powerful and likeable. Take the onscreen persona of Jean-Claude Van Damme or Vin Diesel. These are just the sort of characters that young males aspire to be like, therefore they identify with them. This identification makes imitation more likely.

figure 5.19
As a likeable, high-status and extremely cool character, the onscreen actions of Vin Diesel are likely to be imitated

thinking critically

If we accept that there really is a direct link between media violence and aggressive behaviour then social learning theory provides an extremely neat explanation. However, we need to think critically about whether such a link exists.

the case for

In one recent study (Vidal-Vazquez and Clemente-Diaz, 2000) adolescents were shown videos depicting various levels of violence and their views about media violence were tested before viewing. The findings showed that watching violence caused a more positive assessment of, and greater attraction to, violence, even in participants who had expressed a negative view prior to watching the videos. This suggests that viewing media violence affects judgement of the acceptability of violence and its appeal, and could therefore affect an individual's perception of acceptable social behaviour in the real world.

Are changes in beliefs and feelings reflected in behaviour? Eron et al. (1972) measured the television violence level of programmes that 7 and 8-year-old children watched and the children's aggressiveness. They found a positive correlation between the two. Eron et al. found an even stronger positive correlation of violence viewed and aggressiveness in boys (though not girls) by their teenage years. Even more worrying was the finding that the more violence the boys had watched on television as children, the more likely they were to be violent criminals as adults (Eron and Huesmann, 1986). Of course, these findings are based on data from several decades ago and not all the sample were available for the follow-up work so the results may not be generalisable. This study, being correlational, also illustrates the problem of cause and effect – those individuals who were likely to be aggressive may have also chosen to watch more violence, or some other variable – such as harsh parental punishment – could be responsible for both their aggression and enjoyment of watching violence.

the case against

Milavsky et al. (1982) only found a weak link between aggression and viewing of violent television and concluded that, compared to the family and social environment, the influence of violent television was extremely weak. Similarly, Hagell and Newbury (1994) found that young offenders watched no more violent television than a school control group. The delinquents were also less focused on television viewing, being less able to name favourite programmes or television characters they imitated and were more likely to be on the streets and in trouble than indoors watching television. However, they did tend to come from deprived, unhappy homes, which supports Milavsky et al.

Another line of evidence from Charlton et al. (2000) suggests that media violence does not necessarily lead to aggression. The island of St Helena in the South Atlantic first received satellite television in March 1995. In order to observe the effects of this on the children's behaviour, video cameras were installed in two school playgrounds. Children aged 3 to 8 years were filmed before and after television was introduced. Prior to the introduction, the younger children were considered to be among the best behaved in the world and, even though the violent content of the programmes was slightly higher than in the UK (46% as opposed to 41%), they did not seen to be affected negatively. The amount of hitting, kicking, pushing and pinching stayed the same after the introduction of television and teachers rated the children to be as hard working and co-operative as they had been before (Charlton et al., 2000).

where to now?

We recommend the following as further sources of good information about media violence:

▶ **Gunter, B. and McAleer, J.** (1997) *Children and Television*. Routledge, London. This provides an accessible summary of research investigating the effects of television on a range of children's behaviours.

▶ **Russell, J. and Jarvis, M.** (eds) (2003) *Angles on Applied Psychology*. Nelson Thornes, Cheltenham. Contains a detailed chapter on media violence.

talking
point
contemporary issues

internet addiction disorder

In the 1990s the concept of *Internet addiction* (IA or IAD) was treated as a joke – but is it becoming a reality? Chat rooms and MUDs are developing users who are showing the characteristics of addiction demonstrated by compulsive gamblers (MUD stands for *multi user domain* – also known as a *dungeon*, because MUDs were originally used for playing the game *Dungeons and Dragons*, and means any shared environment in virtual reality). The new psychological disorder of Internet addiction has gained both popular and professional recognition in the last decade. It is defined as 'excessive Internet use' and it is considered to be a behavioural addiction similar to pathological gambling. This can be defended by the similarities in terms of reinforcement schedules and resistance to extinction of the behaviours. The criteria that are now used for diagnosing IAD have been cut and pasted from those for pathological gambling contained in the APA's DSM (Hansen, 2002). The problem of IAD, it seems, is real and at least part of the cause relates to the powerful processes of operant conditioning that are responsible for addictive behaviour.

Young (1998) investigated the habits of Internet users with a questionnaire based on one designed to assess pathological gambling. 'Dependent users' were defined as those participants answering 'yes' to five or more of the questions.

items from Young's test for Internet addiction

◆ Do you feel preoccupied with the Internet (think about previous on-line activity or anticipate the next on-line session)?

◆ Do you feel the need to use the Internet for increasing amounts of time in order to achieve satisfaction?

◆ Have you repeatedly made unsuccessful efforts to control, cut back or stop Internet use?

◆ Do you feel restless, moody, depressed or irritable when attempting to cut down or stop Internet use?

◆ Do you stay on-line longer than originally intended?

◆ Have you jeopardised or risked the loss of a significant relationship, job, educational or career opportunity because of the Internet?

◆ Do you use the Internet as a way of escaping from problems or relieving a dysphoric mood (for example, feelings of helplessness, guilt, anxiety, depression)?

Of approximately 600 respondents, almost two-thirds were rated as dependent. This figure is high but it is unsurprising given the sample taken. A typical dependent user was not, as the stereotype might suggest, a young male but a woman in her forties. The non-dependent users in contrast were males in their twenties.

applying learning theory to understanding IAD

Can learning theory shed any light on how these behaviours develop? Learning theorists see behavioural addiction as a result of operant conditioning. Any behaviour that leads to a reward is repeated with increasing frequency. Addiction results when an individual becomes dependent on that reward. We can explain Internet addiction in more depth by means of the characteristics of operant conditioning.

figure 5.20
Although Internet addicts are likely
to be lonely they are not
necessarily stereotypical young
male computer experts

figure 5.20
Although Internet addicts are likely to be lonely they are not necessarily stereotypical young male computer experts

variable ratio reinforcement schedules

As we saw on p. 113, a variable ratio schedule of reinforcement is one where rewards are infrequent and unpredictable. This is very much the nature of reinforcers encountered on the Internet. If, for example, you are looking for some rare compact discs on an auction site, you might look for some time before you find each one at a price you can afford. You feel very happy each time you locate and successfully bid for one of the discs, but when you find each one is unpredictable, so this process is a powerful variable reinforcement schedule. Internet pornography addicts report the same phenomenon as they infrequently and unpredictably encounter images that they find particularly erotic. Variable reinforcement schedules lead to very quick learning of behaviour and behaviours learnt this way are very hard to extinguish. This is one reason why IAD is such a problem.

According to Wallace (1999), synchronous spaces are one of the most compelling Internet environments in part because they offer the same powerful attractions as gambling. Your 'behaviour', perhaps the message you send to a chat room, may generate an immediate consequence (a reply) or may not. This combination of a short time delay when a reward is forthcoming and its unpredictability creates a powerful variable ratio schedule of positive reinforcement. For a rat in a Skinner box or a gambler at a slot machine there are few possible changes they can make to their behaviour in a search for a more profitable response. On the Internet, however, the personality one portrays can be endlessly varied to test the probability of success. Trial and error has far more scope when there are limitless possibilities.

Game-oriented MUDs and chat rooms also construct variable ratio schedules of reinforcement. In the Trivbot chat room users join a team playing a 'trivial pursuit' style game. The first player to enter a correct answer is congratulated and earns a point for his team; the rewards are immediate if infrequent. Similarly, adventure MUDs provide unpredictable reinforcement when the player slays an opponent. Apart from the intrinsic reward of success, there may be onscreen reinforcement and the respect of lower level players. So there is a significant motive to spend more time engaged in play as this is the only route to higher levels.

negative reinforcement

Of course not all reinforcement is positive, like the experience of finding a rare compact disc online. Negative reinforcement is the removal of something unpleasant. One motive for excessive Internet use is loneliness. Using multi-user domains can alleviate loneliness and provide social support, therefore these negative reinforcers can contribute to IAD. This is supported by a study from Pawlak (2002), who studied ninth- to eleventh-grade students in New York State, recoding variables such as loneliness, social support, personality type and gender as well as rating Internet addiction. Internet use was defined as character games, Usenet, chat rooms, instant messaging, surfing the Web and e-mail. Loneliness and social support correlated with IAD, so school students experiencing high levels of loneliness and low levels of social support may turn to the Internet to alleviate these feelings and, ultimately, may be more likely to become addicted to the Internet.

thinking critically

Although the Young study has been very helpful in understanding excessive Internet use, other studies, with less biased samples, have produced lower estimates of addiction. For example, Bai et al. (2001) used a sample of visitors to a virtual mental health clinic: 15% of the respondents met the criteria for IAD. These individuals were also more likely to suffer substance-use disorders, another instance of addictive behaviour. This suggests that it may be an addictive personality rather than the nature of the Internet that explains IA. In a study investigating the online behaviour of Chinese college students, Xuanhui and Gonggu (2001) found only 9.6% of who fulfilled the criteria for IAD. Furthermore, online time and Internet involvement did not lead to IAD for the majority. Thus, although IAD is a reality, we are unsure about how common it really is and it can be explained in other ways without reliance on learning theory.

where to now?

The following are good sources of further information about Internet addiction:

▶ **Wallace, P.** (1999) *The Psychology of the Internet*. Cambridge University Press, Cambridge. A generally excellent text on all aspects of Internet use.

▶ **Griffiths, M.** (1999) Internet addiction: fact or fiction. *The Psychologist*, **12**, 246–250. A state-of-the-art review of recent research into the phenomenon of Internet addiction.

conclusions

The learning theory approach to psychology is based on the importance of learning behaviour by the processes of classical and operant conditioning and by social learning. Because the learning approach sees humans and other animals as learning by similar processes it is often easier to study animals and then apply the results to humans. We have investigated both human and animal studies of conditioning and social learning. Early behavioural psychologists believed that all behaviour could be accounted for by conditioning, but more recent research has revealed that both humans and other animals seem to be predisposed to learning biologically useful behaviours rather than unhelpful behaviours.

The learning approach has given rise to behavioural therapies, which are designed to help people learn new and healthier behaviours in place of maladaptive behaviours. We have looked, in particular, at behaviour therapy, which is based on classical conditioning and is particularly useful for treating phobias. The principles of conditioning and social learning have also greatly enhanced our understanding of the contemporary issues of media violence and Internet addiction.

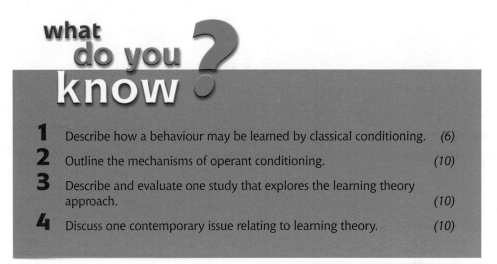

what do you know?

1 Describe how a behaviour may be learned by classical conditioning. *(6)*

2 Outline the mechanisms of operant conditioning. *(10)*

3 Describe and evaluate one study that explores the learning theory approach. *(10)*

4 Discuss one contemporary issue relating to learning theory. *(10)*

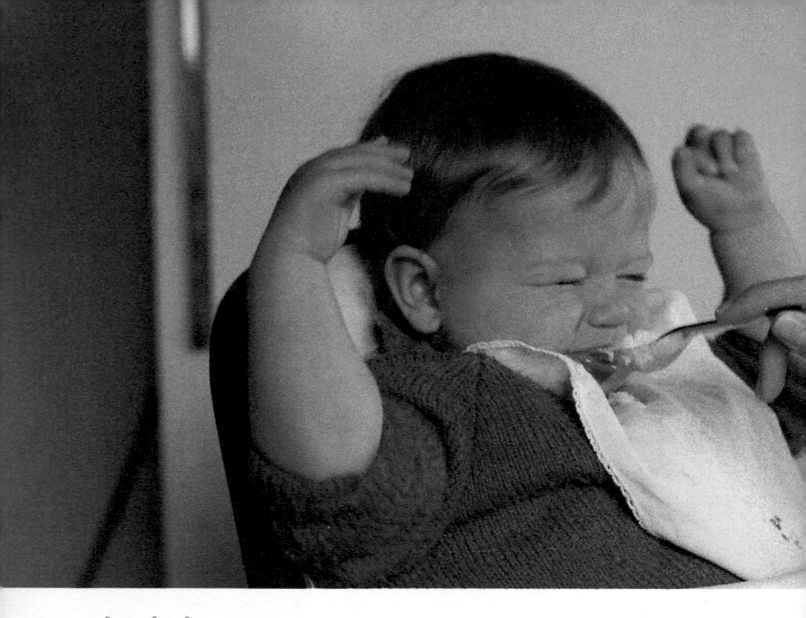

The psychodynamic approach is based on the following ideas:

◆ Our behaviour and feelings as adults (both normal and in the case of psychological problems) are largely rooted in our early childhood experiences. Our early experiences of relationships with other people are of particular importance. Freudian theory emphasizes the role of both parents. Object relations theory places more emphasis on the role of the mother.

◆ Our behaviour, motivation and feelings are influenced by the *unconscious* mind – the mental processes of which we are not consciously aware. Different psychodynamic theories take rather different views of the unconscious. For Freud, for example, we are dominated by powerful sexual and aggressive instincts and early memories. Later theorists have tended to play down the role of sex and aggression. To the object relations school our most important instinct is to form relationships with others.

◆ Psychodynamic psychologists take a broad approach to research and look for information about the functioning of the unconscious mind in dreams, slips of the tongue, symptoms of mental disorder, irrational behaviour and what patients say in therapy.

6 the psychodynamic approach

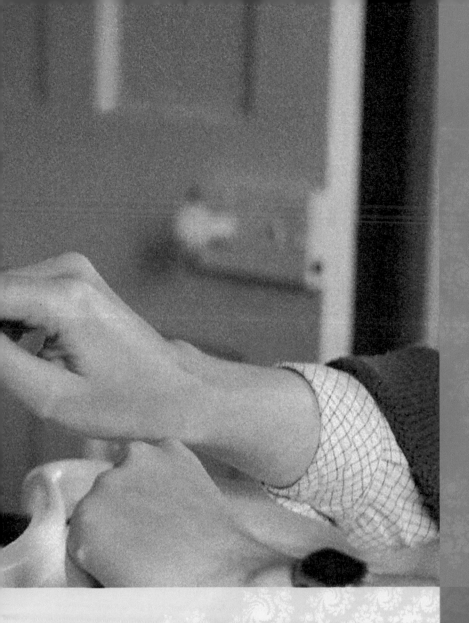

what's ahead?

This chapter concerns the psychodynamic approach to psychology. This is one of the older approaches, dating back to the 1890s. Nowadays psychodynamic approaches still flourish but most commonly outside mainstream psychology. They are more popular in the fields of psychiatry, psychotherapy and counselling. We will look here at three influential psychodynamic theories: those of Sigmund Freud, Erik Erikson and the Object Relations School. In our *real lives* section we will see how we can apply a psychodynamic understanding to mental health issues and in *talking point* we will look at two issues currently being debated in psychology – why we watch *Buffy the Vampire Slayer*, and whether we would all benefit from undergoing *psychoanalysis*, an intensive and long-term psychodynamic therapy.

Freudian theory

figure 6.1
Sigmund Freud

Sigmund Freud, who wrote from the 1890s to the 1930s, remains the best known and the most argued-about psychologist of all time. He developed a collection of ideas, which have formed the basis of the psychodynamic approach to psychology. Freud was a therapist and his ideas are based largely on what his patients told him during therapy, together with reflections on his own life. Freud wrote on a wide variety of topics and developed his ideas throughout the period of his writing. It is not possible to look at all or even most of Freud's ideas in this chapter, but we can examine some of Freud's more important ideas:

◆ the unconscious mind;

◆ Freudian slips;

◆ dreams;

◆ psychological defence mechanisms;

◆ the structure of personality;

◆ psychosexual development.

the unconscious mind

Freud was not the first person to propose that there is an unconscious dimension to the human mind but he was the first to develop a detailed theory of how it operated. Freud distinguished between three levels of consciousness:

◆ The conscious mind consists of the mental processes of which we are fully aware, including memories that can easily be recalled and the more obvious motives underlying behaviour.

◆ The preconscious mind comprises memories of which can be recalled to consciousness under particular circumstances.

◆ The true unconscious involves material that can never be recalled to consciousness, in particular instincts and deeply buried memories. There are two instincts of particular importance. *Libido* is the life instinct that manifests itself as sexuality. *Thanatos* is the death instinct, manifesting itself in aggression and destructiveness.

Freud (1915) suggested a number of ways in which the unconscious mind behaves differently from the conscious. There is no logic, hence opposite feelings such as love and hate can coexist without conflict. The unconscious mind makes no distinction between real events and dreams and fantasies. One object can serve as a symbol for another. Although we are not directly aware of our unconscious mind it exerts a constant influence on us, expressing itself in slips of the tongue, feelings for which we cannot logically account, dreams, irrational behaviour and psychological symptoms. Freud observed that many of our irrational impulses, dreams and symptoms take an aggressive or sexual form, and he explained this in terms of the influence of libido and thanatos.

Freudian slips

Freud (1914) suggested that simple accidents like slips of the tongue could often be accounted for by the influence of the unconscious mind. This influence leads us to substitute an unintended action (such as a word) for an intended one. This phenomenon is known as *parapraxis* or the 'Freudian slip'.

This type of *action slip* is now studied by cognitive psychologists. Reason (2000) has concluded that although there are many causes for action slips, only a minority of them are true Freudian slips, reflecting the influence of the unconscious mind. He suggests that where the substituted word is more commonly used than the intended one it is most likely that the error is a simple cognitive one. However, whenever an uncommon word is substituted for a more common one then it becomes much more likely that it represents a true Freudian slip.

media watch

melons feel the squeeze at Tesco

Libby Brooks, *Guardian*, March 1999

The supermarket psychologists who brought us the theories of trolley daze and aisle alignment, who calculated the relative spend increase induced by the smell of freshly baked bread, have surpassed themselves: they have entered the realm of the psychosexual.

As a consequence Tesco, Britain's biggest supermarket chain, has asked its suppliers to grow smaller melons after focus groups of shoppers revealed that shoppers subconsciously selected fruit according to the trend in breast size.

After investigating a marked drop in melon sales, a retail psychologist's report for Tesco suggested that the modern preference for smaller breasts, as modelled by superwaif Kate Moss, is informing customers' decision to reject larger melons.

The possibility of a subconscious relationship between breast and melon size was first raised by a member of an all-female focus group, set up when Tesco buyers sought to find out why customers consistently picked the smallest fruit from store displays.

The theory was then tested by the retail psychologist, who found that seven out of 10 women questioned agreed that 'breast size was the most likely subconscious factor when selecting size of melon'. Half the women went further, attesting that breast size was a conscious thought when choosing melons.

A Tesco spokesman yesterday said that the findings surprised him, but that the sales spoke for themselves.

'Since we introduced the smaller melons two months ago we have sold more than a million.'

figure 6.2
Every little melon helps!

questions

1 Explain using Freud's ideas about the unconscious mind why the retail psychologist might have found these results.

2 How convincing do you find this study?

situation	intended phrase	substituted phrase
A poor patient who had difficulty swallowing large pills made a request of Freud.	'Please don't give me big pills'	'Please don't give me big **bills**'
A patient was complaining how much harder it was for women to find a suitable partner than men.	'Men just need four straight limbs'	'Men just need **five** straight limbs'

table 6.1 Examples of Freudian slips (from Freud, 1914)

interactive
angles

Looking back at the two examples in Table 6.1, apply Reason's rule. In the context
of that situation which word is more common, the substituted or the intended?
Are these likely to be real Freudian slips?

dreams

Freud (1900) famously called dreams 'the royal road to a knowledge of the activities of the unconscious mind' (Freud, 1900, p. 769). He believed that dreams both perform important functions for the unconscious mind and give us valuable clues to how the unconscious mind operates. Freud suggested that the major function of dreams was the fulfilment of wishes. Freud distinguished between the *manifest content* of a dream – the scenes and 'storyline', that of which the dreamer is aware, and the *latent content* – the underlying wish. The manifest content is often based upon the events of the day. The process whereby the underlying wish is translated into the manifest content is called *dreamwork*. The purpose of dreamwork is to transform the forbidden wish into a non-threatening form, so reducing anxiety and allowing us to sleep in peace.

Some dreams, particularly those of children, express innocent wishes and therefore no dreamwork is required. For example Freud recorded the time when his 19-month-old daughter, after being sick and so not having had dinner, cried out in her sleep 'Anna F'eud, st'awberry, wild st'awberry, omelette Pap!' Presumably there was no need to disguise the child's wish for food. However dreams that express sexual and aggressive impulses do require disguise for their latent content. Otherwise they would be too arousing and prevent us getting a good sleep.

dreamwork

Dreamwork involves three processes, namely displacement, condensation and secondary elaboration. *Displacement* takes place when we change the person or object we are really bothered about into someone or something else. An example of displacement comes from one of Freud's patients, who was extremely resentful of his sister-in-law. He used to refer to her as a dog, and once dreamed of strangling a small white dog. Freud interpreted this as representing his wish to kill his sister-in-law. As you can see, had the patient actually dreamed of killing his sister-in-law, the patient would probably have felt guilty. It appears that the patient's unconscious mind, in transforming her into a dog, protected him from this guilt.

Condensation takes place when we combine different factors into one aspect of the manifest content. Thus a woman who has angry feelings towards her husband and father might dream of punishing a single man, who represents both the father and husband. This man would embody aspects of both the father and husband. *Secondary elaboration* is the final part of dreamwork, and occurs when the unconscious mind strings together wish-fulfilling images into a logical succession of events, further obscuring the latent content. According to Freud this is why the manifest content of dreams can be in the form of plausible chains of events.

universal symbols

In Freud's later work on dreams, he toyed with the possibility of universal symbols in dreams – objects in the manifest content that consistently represent the same latent content for all dreamers. Some of these were sexual in nature, including poles, guns and swords representing penises, and horse-riding and dancing representing intercourse. However, Freud was cautious about these symbols and believed that, in general, symbols were unique to the individual rather than universal, and that one could not interpret what the manifest content of a dream symbolised without knowing about the person's circumstances. 'Dream dictionaries', still popular now, were a source of irritation to Freud. In an amusing example of the limitations of universal symbols, one of Freud's patients dreamed about holding a wriggling fish, and said to him 'that's a Freudian symbol – it must be a penis!' Freud however explored further and it soon turned out that the woman's mother – who was a passionate astrologer and a Pisces – was on the patient's mind because she disapproved of her daughter being in analysis. It seems much

figure 6.3
Freud did not believe that fish were necessarily penis-symbols!

more likely that, as Freud suggested, the fish represented the patient's mother rather than a penis!

⟳ discussion

Since Freud's time there have been a number of alternative psychodynamic explanations for dreaming. To object-relations theorists for example (see pp. 147–149), figures in dreams can represent different aspects of the dreamer's personality. More serious criticisms of Freud's dream theory come from psychologists of other theoretical backgrounds. In Freud's time almost nothing was known about the physiology of sleep and dreaming. Hobson and McCarley (1977) dealt Freudians a blow when they discovered that rapid eye-movement (REM) sleep, the period when the most vivid and best remembered dreams take place, is associated with random firing of cells in the brain stem. This suggested that dreams are a purely physiological process, and that they have no psychological significance.

There is, however, newer evidence from neuroscience (the study of the brain) that suggests that in fact Freud may have been correct to link dreaming and wishing. Solms (2000) points to an area of the brain where the limbic system (associated with emotion and memory processes) links to the cortex, the area associated with higher mental functions such as thinking. Damage to this region of the brain leads to the loss of two mental functions – dreaming and wishing. Although this provides quite strong support for the link between dreaming and wishes, there is little evidence other than isolated case studies to support the idea of dreamwork.

psychological defences

An important aspect of Freudian theory, which has become quite well accepted in mainstream psychology, is the idea of psychological defences. Freud (1894) proposed that we use mental strategies called *defence mechanisms* to protect ourselves from painful, frightening or guilty feelings.

repression

Repression occurs when a memory associated with strong negative emotion, for example a traumatic event, cannot be remembered. We may thus have no conscious recollection of the event, although the memory can still exert a powerful influence on us, sometimes leading to serious symptoms. Bateman and Holmes (1995) give an example of repression in a man who came for therapy for depression. When talking about the death of his mother many years earlier, he suddenly remembered – for the first time as an adult – that his mother had committed suicide. Once he retrieved this memory his symptoms lessened. Repression can also take less dramatic forms, for example finding it harder to recall unhappy memories than happy ones or remembering events accurately but without the strong emotion associated with them.

displacement

Displacement takes place when we redirect emotions away from those who have caused them on to a third party. Displacement is easy to see in everyday life – most of us tend to take out our bad moods on unfortunate colleagues, friends and family, even when they were not the cause of the bad mood. We can also displace positive emotions such as love – this may be why people have so many relationships 'on the rebound' as leftover love from one relationship is displaced on to the new partner.

for+against

Freud's explanation of dreams

+ Freud was probably correct that the content of some of our dreams reflects things that are on our minds. We have all had dreams that reflect our anxieties and wishes. Remember that Freud never believed that all dreams could be interpreted.

– There are almost certainly other reasons for dreaming as well as wish fulfilment. Freud's theory is thus an incomplete explanation.

– There is some evidence from Hobson and McCarley to suggest that dreams are a purely physiological phenomenon and thus have no psychological significance. This is incompatible with Freud's view of dreams as psychological phenomena.

+ There is now evidence from contemporary research (particularly by Mark Solms) to support the idea that dreaming and wishing are closely related processes on a neurological level, as suggested by Freud.

– Other than case studies there is little evidence to support the idea of dreamwork. This is a very difficult concept to investigate.

the psychodynamic approach

defence	description	example
Repression	Forgetting an unpleasant memory or the strong emotion associated with it.	Childhood sexual abuse is frequently forgotten and rediscovered in adulthood.
Denial	Refusal to admit an unpleasant fact.	Patients who learn that they are seriously ill often refuse to accept their diagnosis.
Reaction	Adopting an attitude directly opposed to one's real feelings.	People who are afraid that they might be gay often adopt a homophobic attitude.
Projection	Shifting an undesirable emotion or motive from ourselves on to someone else.	People who envy someone else often claim that in fact that person envies them.
Displacement	Shifting an emotion directed at one person towards another person or other object.	Coming home angry at the boss and snapping at one's partner.
Intellectualisation	Using flawed logic to convince oneself there isn't in fact a problem.	Smokers often argue that there is no proof that smoking is bad for them.
Regression	Using the comforting behaviours typical of an earlier age.	People often cry, eat comfort food and become helpless in response to stress.
Sublimation	Using the energy of negative emotion to achieve something positive.	Artists and musicians often create their best work when desperately unhappy.

table 6.2 Defence mechanisms

figure 6.4
Some of the most creative people, such as Kurt Cobain, have sublimated their unhappiness into music

reaction

Reaction takes place when we go a stage beyond denial and adopt an attitude that is directly opposed to our real feelings. The classic example of reaction is homophobia, in which people who worry that they might be gay deal with the resulting anxiety by adopting a harsh anti-homosexual attitude – this helps convince them of their heterosexuality. There are other examples of reaction; a religious person who suffers a bereavement might adopt a harsh atheist attitude to help deal with the conflict of belief in a benevolent deity and the loss of a loved one.

⊘ discussion

Psychological defences are perhaps the most widely accepted of Freud's ideas nowadays. This is largely because we can easily recognise them from our own experience. Like many Freudian ideas, defence mechanisms have proved fairly tricky to test empirically, but there have been some imaginative attempts. Adams et al. (1996) demonstrated the role of reaction in homophobia by showing homophobic and non-homophobic men heterosexual, lesbian and gay pornography and measuring their sexual arousal. Over 80% of homophobic men were aroused by the gay scenes, as opposed to around 30% of non-homophobic participants. There was no difference in the rates of arousal in response to lesbian and heterosexual scenes. This suggests that homophobic attitudes may indeed be a defence against a fear of being gay.

Of all the defence mechanisms, repression is the most controversial in contemporary psychology, and the issue of repression has become something of a battlefield between psychodynamic practitioners and memory researchers. Memory researchers have pointed out that there is no direct evidence that repression (at least in the form of complete loss of traumatic memories) exists. However, most memory researchers favour *experimental* research. For ethical reasons memory researchers have not been able to recreate the traumatic conditions in which complete repression is alleged to occur. However, there is plenty of support for the general tendency to forget unhappy or anxiety-provoking things. For example, a recent German study shows that threatening words tend to be forgotten – see *research now*. See also chapter 3 for a further review of the evidence for repression.

research now
studies in detail

do we repress threatening words?

Koehler, T., Thiede, G. and Thoens, M. (2002) Long and short-term forgetting of word associations. An experimental study of the Freudian concepts of resistance and repression. *Zeitschrift fuer Klinische Psychologie, Psychiatrie und Psychotherapie*, **50**, 328–333.

Aim: the aim of the study was to test Freud's idea of repression. This was achieved by seeing whether ideas that generated anxiety for participants would be remembered as well as emotionally neutral ideas. Freud's theory would predict that more of the anxiety-provoking ideas would be forgotten.

Procedure: 42 German students aged 21 to 51 years were shown a list of 50 words and asked what was the first thing they associated with each word. As they responded to each word their galvanic skin responses or GSRs (a measure of stress) were recorded. Participants were then tested for their recall of the associations they had produced for each of the words, immediately and again a week later.

Findings: the word associations that produced anxiety in the participants (those which triggered a strong GSR) were much more likely to be forgotten, both immediately and a week later, than those that did not provoke a strong emotional response.

Conclusion: these results fit neatly with the idea of repression, because the word associations that triggered anxiety were more likely to be forgotten, as we would expect if repression occurred in response to anxiety.

for+against

psychological defences

+ Everyday experience tells us that we use psychological defences to make ourselves feel better. The idea of defences thus has good *face validity*.

+ Some of the defence mechanisms have strong supporting evidence, such as the Adams et al. (1996) study of reaction formation and the Koehler et al. (2002) study of repression.

– Defences are tricky to study empirically because they occur in response to threatening or traumatic situations that cannot be replicated artificially. There is thus a fairly small body of supporting evidence.

the structure of personality

Perhaps Freud's most significant idea was that the human personality has more than one aspect. We reveal this when we say things like 'part of me wants to do it, but part of me is afraid to . . .'. Freud (1923) tried to explain this type of experience by

figure 6.5

'dissecting' (as he put it) the personality into three parts, 'I' 'it' and 'above-I'. Each of these parts represents a different aspect of the person and plays a different role in deciding on a course of action. *It* represents the instinctive aspect of the personality, present from birth. *It* operates on the pleasure principle – *it* wants to be satisfied, and *it* does not willingly tolerate delay or denial of its wishes. *I* is the aspect of the person that is aware of both the demands of *it* and the outside world, and which makes decisions. *I* can thus be said to operate on the reality principle. *I* develops through experience of dealing with the world, and has the capacity to think logically. *Above-I* is the aspect of the personality formed from the experience with authority figures such as the parent, which poses restrictions on what actions are allowed. These restrictions represent the rules of society. Your *Above-I* can reward you with pride and punish you with guilt according to whether you go along with its restrictions. It can thus be said to operate according to a morality principle. These three aspects of the personality are commonly called the *id* (it), the *ego* (I) and the *superego* (above-I). The three aspects of the personality interact.

Freud's term	it	I	above-I
Common name	id	ego	superego
Aspect of personality	instinct	logic	society's rules
Operating principle	pleasure principle	reality principle	morality principle

table 6.3 Freud's structural model of the personality

⊘ discussion

Freud (1933) suggested that his model of personality had two major strengths. Firstly, it provided an explanation for the experience of being pulled in different directions by different aspects of the self when making decisions, especially decisions with moral implications. *Phenomenology* is the study of human experience. From a phenomenological perspective, whether or not we can literally divide the mind into id, ego and superego, it is still valid to think of the mind in this way if it helps us understand human experience. Secondly, the idea of the *above-I* aspect of personality is useful in showing how relationships with others affect our personality. Someone with a harsh and punitive upbringing is thus likely to feel guilty a lot of the time because the *above-I* aspect of that person's personality is powerful and punitive.

Jarvis (2003) has commented that the structural model is perhaps the most *complete* theory of personality achieved to date. This is because it shows the three major influences on human nature and on individual differences in our behaviour: instinct, logic and society. Modern evolutionary psychology tells us about the possible influence of instinct, cognitive psychology tells us about logic and social and developmental psychology tell us about the influence of other people. No approach other than Freud's however suggests so neatly how instinct, logic *and* society all affect us. Of course psychology has come a long way since Freud's time in terms of how we see the influence of instinct, logic and society. Thus the Freudian view of instinct, logic and social influence seem rather oversimple to modern psychologists.

the structure of personality

+ Freud has successfully described the experience of being pulled in different directions when making decisions. It can thus be said to be helpful as a phenomenological model.

+ Freud produced a very complete model of human experience, building in the three influences of instinct, logic and society on human nature and individual differences.

— Ideas like id and ego, and even instinct, are rather abstract and very difficult to study. Many psychologists are uncomfortable with concepts like this.

psychosexual development

Freud (1905) proposed that psychological development in childhood takes place in a series of fixed stages. These are called *psychosexual stages* because each stage represents the fixation of libido on a different area of the body. If this sounds slightly odd, it is important to realise that Freud's use of the word 'sexual' was quite broad in meaning, and he did not mean that the child experiences these instincts as 'sexual' in the adult sense. Libido is manifested in childhood as *organ pleasure*, centred on a different organ in each of the first three stages of development.

the oral stage (0–1 year)

In the *oral stage* (the first year of life), while the child is breast feeding and being weaned, the focus of organ pleasure is the mouth. As well as taking nourishment through the mouth, children in the oral stage are taking comfort and their knowledge of the world via the mouth. We take away from the oral stage a number of 'oral characteristics', collectively known as *orality*. Oral characteristics can include an enjoyment of food and drink and attitudes of dependence, helplessness and acceptance. These attitudes represent, on an unconscious level, the relationship a baby has with the world.

We all take away a degree of orality from our first year – without this we would not take an adult enjoyment in food and drink or in being dependent on the people with whom we have relationships. However if the person experiences a trauma in the first year, for example a prolonged separation from the primary carer or a feeding difficulty, that individual can become fixated in the oral stage and the adult personality can become dominated by orality.

the anal stage (2–3 years)

In the *anal stage* (years 2–3), the focus of organ pleasure now shifts to the anus. The child is now fully aware that it is a person in its own right and that its wishes can bring it into conflict with the demands of the outside world. Freud believed that this type of conflict tends to come to a head in potty training, in which adults impose restrictions, for the first time in the child's experience, on when and where the child can defecate. Successful negotiation of the anal stage is what gives us the qualities of assertiveness and order. However, early or harsh potty training can lead to fixation in the anal stage, leading to an adult personality dominated by the three anal personality characteristics of stubbornness, orderliness and lack of generosity.

the phallic stage (3–6 years)

By the start of the *phallic stage* (years 3–6), the focus of organ pleasure has shifted to the genitals, as the child becomes fully aware of its gender. This coincides with a growing awareness of the child's exclusion from some aspects of its parents' lives, such as sleeping in the same room. The resulting three-way relationship is known as the *Oedipus complex*, named after Oedipus, who, in a Greek legend, killed his father and married his mother (not realising who they were). In the Oedipus complex, a rivalry relationship develops between the child and the same-sex parent for the affection of the opposite-sex parent. Freud believed that, on an *unconscious level*, the child is expressing instinctive wishes to have sex with his mother and kill his father. This is not to suggest that children possess a conscious awareness of sexual intercourse or death in the adult sense. One of Freud's case studies, Little Hans (Freud, 1909), illustrates Freud's ideas about the Oedipus complex.

interactive
angles

The following questions are from the *Farber Scale of Anality*. Test yourself if you like, but don't take your score too seriously! This test was developed in the 1950s, and is much less sophisticated than modern personality tests. Score one anality point per yes answer.

	yes	no
1 In general I like to spend my money carefully.	[ ]	[ ]
2 I get irritated by people who can't seem to make their minds up.	[ ]	[ ]
3 It bothers me a great deal when I lose or break something of value.	[ ]	[ ]
4 I usually feel annoyed when things around me are not neat and tidy.	[ ]	[ ]
5 I pride myself in always trying to be on time.	[ ]	[ ]

table 6.4 Questions from the Farber Scale of Anality

questions

1   There are three anal personality characteristics; stubbornness, orderliness and stinginess. Suggest which of these each statement relates to.

2   What are the likely problems with a scale like this?

classic research
studies in detail

a case of the Oedipus complex?

Freud, S. (1909) Analysis of a phobia in a five-year old boy. *Collected Papers* vol. III, 149–295.

Background: Little Hans, a 5-year-old boy, was taken to Freud suffering from a phobia of horses. Freud's therapeutic input in this case was minimal. Accounts vary as to how many times Freud saw Hans but it was probably only once or twice. Most of his information came from weekly reports by Hans's father.

Case history: from the age of 3, Hans had developed such an interest in his own penis that at age 5 his mother had threatened to cut it off if he didn't stop playing with it. At about the same time Hans developed a morbid fear that a white horse would bite him. Hans's father reported that his fear seemed to be related to the horse's large penis. At the time Hans's phobia developed his father began to object to Hans's habit of getting into bed with his parents in the morning. Over a period of weeks Hans's phobia got worse and he feared going out of the house in case he encountered a horse. He also suffered attacks of more generalised anxiety.

Over the next few weeks Hans's phobia gradually began to improve. His fear became limited to horses with black harnesses over their noses. Hans's father interpreted this as related to his own black moustache. The end of Hans's phobia of horses was accompanied by two significant fantasies, which he told to his father. In the first, Hans had several imaginary children. When asked who their mother was, Hans replied 'Why, mummy, and you're their Grandaddy' (p. 238). In the second fantasy, which occurred the next day, Hans imagined that a plumber had come and fitted him with a bigger penis. These fantasies marked the end of Hans's phobia.

Interpretation: Freud saw Hans's phobia as an expression of the Oedipus complex. Horses, particularly horses with black harnesses, symbolised his father. Horses were particularly appropriate father symbols because of their large penises. The fear began as an Oedipal conflict was developing around Hans being allowed in the parents' bed. Freud saw the Oedipus complex happily resolved as Hans fantasised himself with a big penis like his father's and married to his mother with his father present in the role of grandfather.

case studies of patients in therapy

Case studies of patients in therapy have been the most common research method used in the psychodynamic approach. They involve listening in depth as patients with psychological problems talk about their past and their current problems, and offering interpretations of the links between early relationships and traumas and current symptoms. Case studies of this kind are useful because they illustrate how psychological functioning can be understood as related to family dynamics and trauma. However, psychologists feel that case studies have limitations as evidence for ideas such as the Oedipus complex:

◆ Cases can be one offs and do not necessarily tell us much about the influences on everyone's development. For example, even if we accepted that Little Hans really had a fully-fledged Oedipus complex that does not tell us how common the phenomenon is or who else might be affected.

◆ Patients in therapy are not representative of the population at large, because most people do not have therapy. This leaves us with the problem of generalising ideas from people in psychological distress and choosing to deal with it by psychodynamic therapy on the entire population.

◆ Therapists influenced by a particular theory may selectively attend to things the patient says that fit in with that theory and ignore other important information. This exaggerates the extent to which the case really supports the theory. For example Freud focused on Hans's relationship with his father and ignored other important facts – for example the sight of a horse dying in the street had recently upset Hans.

The case of Little Hans does provide limited support for the Oedipus complex. However, there are serious limitations with the case, above and beyond those always associated with clinical case studies. Hans's father, who provided Freud with most of his evidence, was already familiar with the Oedipus complex and interpreted the case in the light of this. It is also possible, therefore, that he supplied Hans with clues that led to his fantasies of marriage to his mother and his new large penis.

discussion

Because it operates unconsciously, psychosexuality is extremely difficult to study empirically. However (bizarrely, you might think!) there is considerable support for the idea of anality. Numerous studies have found that the three anal personality characteristics cluster together in the same people (Jarvis, 2003). O'Neill et al. (1992) have gone a stage further and investigated whether the 'anal' personality type would respond differently to 'anal issues'. Forty women were assessed for the three anal characteristics and their responses to 'lavatorial' jokes. A positive correlation between anality and enjoyment of toilet humour emerged, suggesting that there is indeed something truly 'anal' about the anal personality! Anality is associated with other characteristics, for example right-wing politics. Maltby and Price (1999) assessed anality and political conservatism in 238 university students. There was a strong tendency for highly anal students to be politically conservative, suggesting that conservative politics might be the result of dodgy parenting in toddlerhood. It may be that the orderliness of conservative politics appeals to the anal personality.

One idea that has been firmly rejected by modern psychology is the overriding importance of the Oedipus complex. Remember that Freud believed that this is the most important aspect of psychological development. One way of assessing the Oedipus complex is to compare the development of children from single and same-sex parent families, who have no opportunity for Oedipal conflict, with that of children from two-parent heterosexual families. In a major review Golombok (2000) has concluded that there is no evidence of any deficit in the development of children who have not had the chance for Oedipal conflict because of their family structure. This clearly shows that it does not occupy the central place in psychological development proposed by Freud.

Brown and Pedder (1991) have suggested a useful way of thinking about Freud's stages of development. They suggest that Freud's labels of oral, anal and phallic were too narrow to describe what occurs in these stages. They suggested that we should think of the oral stage as a stage of complete dependency on the caregiver(s), the anal stage as a period of separation from the caregiver and the phallic stage as a time of passionate emotions in which rivalry may form between the child and the same-sex parent for the affection of the opposite-sex parent. The concepts of dependency, separation and rivalry are extremely useful in understanding the developing relationship between a child and its parents.

for+against

Freud's stages of child development

+ Freud was correct to say that our early years and our early relationships with our families are extremely important in affecting our development. He is also probably correct that the themes of dependency, separation and rivalry can be important aspects of the child's development.

− Freud probably overemphasised the importance of body-parts, libido and the 'sexual' nature of children's development. Thus, although his general ideas have validity, some of the specifics of his theory probably do not.

+ There is fairly strong support for the existence of the anal personality in that the three anal characteristics do tend to cluster in the same people and are associated with attitudes to body elimination and political views.

− Freud appears to have overemphasised the importance of the Oedipus complex. Modern research suggests that, even though three-way family dynamics of this sort do occur, they are not strongly associated with later psychological development.

general discussion of Freud's work

Nobody doubts the historical importance of Freud's work, but evaluations of its value to psychology 100 years later vary widely, ranging from complete acceptance to total rejection. Freud's ideas have won more favour amongst therapists than in academic psychology. Although there are a number of 'schools' of therapy (and some of these reject Freud's ideas) many therapists have found an understanding of unconscious desires, defences, actions slips and dreams invaluable to understanding what is going on in the minds of their patients.

The major criticism levelled against Freud concerns the scientific status of his work. Freud, being a practising doctor and medical researcher, was trained in the methods of science. In those days this really meant a heavy reliance on the experimental method. However, despite agonising over his slackness as a scientist (Jones, 1951), Freud rejected experimental research as simply too clumsy to tackle the issues that interested him. How, for example, would you perform a laboratory experiment to see whether a particular dream really represented wish fulfilment? The result of Freud's rejection of empirical research is that many of his ideas are untestable. This is a source of great annoyance to psychologists although, as we have seen, some ideas such as reaction and anality have been successfully researched. A further difficulty with many of Freud's ideas is that they are derived from looking at very small groups of people (his patients). Furthermore, as a group Freud's patients were quite unrepresentative of the population at large, being in the main highly neurotic middle-class Austrians from a historical period characterised by sexual repression. This means that even if we accept Freud's observations as regards his patients there are problems in applying his ideas to people in general.

angling with the net

There are innumerable sources of information regarding Freud on the Internet, but many are extremely dodgy. Try the Freud Museum in Vienna (**http://freud.t0.at/e/index. html**) for a good set of links. This should help you access a range of good information about Freud.

where to now?

The following are further sources of good information regarding Freud's work:

▶ **Jarvis, M.** (2003) *Psychodynamic Psychology: Classic Theory and Contemporary Research*. Thomson, London. Perhaps the most comprehensive but easy-to-read general text on psychodynamics.

▶ **Jacobs, M.** (1992) *Sigmund Freud*. Sage, London. A detailed but readable account of the life and work of Freud. Includes lots of good material on criticisms of Freud and arguments that can be made in his defence.

▶ **Gay, P.** (1989) *The Freud Reader*. Norton, New York. Introduces the reader to some manageable chunks of Freud's writing. Be prepared for the 100-year-old style of writing, but there is nothing like going back to original sources to really understand what the writer was trying to say.

object relations theory

The greatest influence on modern psychodynamic thinking in Britain is not the work of Freud, but rather that of a group of British psychoanalysts collectively called the *Object Relations School*. The word *object* in psychoanalysis means person, so *object relations theory* (or ORT) literally means a theory of relations with others. The key figures in the Object Relations School are Melanie Klein, Ronald Fairbairn, Donald Winnicott, Harry Guntrip and John Bowlby. Object relations theory evolved gradually from Freud's ideas (this development is still going on) but there are some key points that distinguish the approach from Freud's ideas:

◆ We are born with a powerful instinct to form relationships with other people. This is known as the *object-seeking tendency*.

◆ We have a mental representation of the world of other people with whom we have had significant relationships. This is known as the *inner* or *internal world*. How we react to new people and the nature of the relationships we form is powerfully influenced by our inner world.

◆ The relationship with our primary caregiver is of particular importance in our psychological development.

the object-seeking tendency

Whereas Freud saw people as being born as 'bundles of id' that are motivated to satisfy biological needs like hunger, Fairbairn (1952) proposed instead that we are born with an intact sense of identity (Freud's 'I'), and are instead dominated by an instinct to seek out relationships with other people (known as *objects* in psychodynamic theory). Babies are thus *object seeking* rather than *pleasure seeking*.

the inner world

Object relations theory sees the most important aspect of the unconscious as the inner world. We all carry around with us a mental representation of the world. To the OR theorists the most important aspect of this representation of the world involves our relationships with others. The inner world is populated by mental representations of ourselves and all the people with whom we have – or have had –

the psychodynamic approach

significant relationships. These representations of significant people are called *internal objects*. Our internal objects serve as templates for future relationships. Thus, if we have experienced abusive relationships and so have abusive internal objects, the likelihood is that we will fall into further abusive relationships. If however our experiences of relationships have been generally positive we have a much better chance of forming further successful relationships.

the first relationship

In ORT, the first relationship is crucial for the healthy development of the child. The overriding factor in the development of the child's identity is the quality of mothering – how well the primary caregiver picks up and responds to the baby's needs.

figure 6.6
Object relations theory suggests that the happy relationship between this mother and baby will benefit the child's psychological development

Winnicott (1965) called the mother who can adjust to the baby's needs the *good enough mother*. Winnicott suggested that if the mother fails to respond to the infant's needs and instead makes the infant fit in with her demands, healthy ego development does not occur and instead the child develops a *false self*. This is a kind of smoke-screen behind which the child and later the adult hides because it has failed to develop a true sense of identity. The false self is dominated by a tendency for compliance as it has developed through serving the emotional needs of someone else and denying its own needs. The adult with a strong false self and weak ego continues to comply with the wishes of others and fails to assert his or her own wishes.

transitional objects

figure 6.7
According to object relations theory cuddly toys serve an important psychological purpose

Winnicott's (1965) contributed further to object relations theory with the idea of *transitional objects*. Winnicott believed that, when children do not have access to their primary carer, they need to retain a mental image of them in order to feel secure. However, young children are not sufficiently cognitively developed to hold on to such an image for long periods. To get around this, children use *transitional objects* as surrogate attachment figures. Transitional objects are inanimate objects that can temporarily represent the primary carer in the mind of the child. They are called 'transitional' because they are half-way between a real parent and a mental image, so they represent the transition between having a parent present and just having a mental image of them. Teddy bears and other soft toys make good transitional objects and this is, according to Winnicott, why children like soft toys so much.

discussion

There is considerable support from psychological research for many of the major aspects of object relations theory. The idea that a successful first relationship advantages a child in its psychological development has received massive support. For example children who display secure attachments to their primary carer are less likely to suffer mental health problems in adulthood (Horowitz, 1996), and more likely to have successful relationships (McCarthy, 1999) and be skilled parents themselves (Fonagy et al., 1993).

There have been important challenges to object relations theory. Some feminists have suggested that because ORT places so much emphasis on the importance of the first relationship, usually with a woman, it sets up women to take the blame for anything that goes wrong with later development. Moreover, some studies have shown that although the first relationship is important, it is not necessarily the most important single factor affecting development. For example, Massie and Szeinberg (2002) followed up a group of 76 children from birth until they were aged 30. Quality of parenting and quality of relationship with the mother were recorded in infancy, then

teddy bears are important!

Steier, A. J. and Lehman, E. B. (2000) An observational measure of children's attachments to soft objects. *Child Study Journal*, **30**, 253–271.

Aim: to study the way children's preferences for toys varied according to the stress of the situation. According to ORT, soft toys play a role in helping children regulate their emotions when parents are not present.

Procedure: 50 toddlers aged 15 months to 31 months were observed playing with a selection of familiar and unfamiliar soft toys. Their mothers were questioned about which were their favourite toys and their attachment to each soft toy was classified as mild, moderate or strong. The situation in which the toddlers played was varied so as to increase levels of stress. At all times however the children had access to their mothers. Their choice of toys was noted in relation to each level of stress.

Findings: as the stress of the situation increased so did the children's preference for familiar soft toys over unfamiliar ones. They also showed a greater tendency to opt for toys classified during the interviews with mothers as those to which they had a strong attachment.

Conclusion: these findings provide strong support for Winnicott's idea that soft toys play an important role in helping children to regulate their emotions.

traumatic events throughout childhood, adolescence and early adulthood were noted. The quality of parenting and the first relationship were important predictors of mental health at 30, but were less significant than traumatic experiences in later childhood. Object relations theory can thus be said to be *reductionist*, focusing on one factor in development and ignoring others.

for + against

object relations theory

➕ Many aspects of ORT have support from psychological research, in particular the importance of the first relationship for later psychological development.

➖ Some key concepts such as the internal world have proved difficult to study empirically. This is frustrating to psychologists and detracts from the credibility of the theory.

➕ ORT has enhanced our understanding of people's patterns of relationships and the link between mental health and early experience.

➖ ORT is reductionist in that it places huge emphasis on mental representation of early relationships and ignores the numerous other factors that affect child development and mental health. Some research suggests that other factors such as trauma in later childhood are more important than the primary relationship in affecting psychological development.

where to now?

The following are good sources of further information about object relations theory:

▶ **Bateman, A. and Holmes, J.** (1995) *Introduction to Psychoanalysis*. Routledge, London. A detailed but relatively clear account of a variety of psychoanalytic theories, including their links to mental health and therapy.

▶ **Gomez, L.** (1997) *An Introduction to Object Relations*. Free Associations Books, London. A detailed account of the work of each of the major OR theorists.

▶ **Jarvis, M.** (2003) *Psychodynamic Psychology: Classic Theory and Contemporary Research*. Thomson, London. Contains a detailed chapter on different theories of object relations.

Erikson's theory of lifespan development

While the object relations theorists were examining the importance of very early life, Erikson developed psychodynamic theory in the opposite direction and looked at development throughout the entire lifespan. Freud believed that the individual personality was largely established by the age of 6 years, and the object relations theorists saw the first year as being of primary importance. Erikson, by contrast, saw the personality as developing throughout life. Erikson (1959) identified a number of *psychosocial stages* to the human life, each of which is characterised by a particular conflict that must be overcome if the individual's ego is to develop.

age	psychosocial stage	developmental task
0–1	basic trust vs mistrust	to gain a basic sense of trust in the world
1–3	autonomy vs shame and doubt	to establish an independent identity
4–6	initiative vs guilt	to feel free to explore the world
7–12	industry vs inferiority	to be busy in order to learn to achieve
12–18	identity vs identity-diffusion	to develop an adult social and sexual identity
19–25	intimacy vs self-absorbtion	to establish healthy adult relationships
26–40s	generativity vs stagnation	to surrender youth and focus on the next generation
40s+	integrity vs despair	to accept one's own life and impending death

table 6.5 Erikson's psychosocial stages of development

basic trust versus mistrust

The child's focus in its first year is its relationship with its primary carer. It is this first relationship that gives a child a sense of security or *basic trust* in the world and in other people. If the primary carer manages to create a secure, reliable and comfortable environment the child will trust that person and transfer this trust to its dealings with the rest of the world. Inconsistent, neglectful or abusive care on the other hand will leave the child with a sense of mistrust that will affect its later development.

autonomy versus shame and doubt

The child is now aware of its identity as a separate person. This brings the challenge for it to assert its own wishes and to 'do its own thing' – in other words, to have *autonomy* whilst maintaining a close relationship with its parents. Freud saw this period as the anal stage, dominated by the conflict of potty training. Erikson agreed that potty training was important but saw the stage in slightly broader terms. The child is developing its own identity at this point and this risks being crushed by heavy-handed or overly critical parenting. Accidents, for example in toilet training, can be a source of shame to the child and it is essential that this shame does not overwhelm the child's developing sense of self. Firm but gentle parenting is needed to get the child past this period.

the psychodynamic approach

initiative versus guilt

At this point the child is developing physically and intellectually very rapidly and is generally keen to explore the world and the child's own abilities. Having established in the previous stage that it is a person the child now needs to find out what sort of person it is. The child is thus very inquisitive and starts to show curiosity about sex. The child also indulges in considerable fantasy play at this stage as a way of exploring its place in the world. This fantasy typically includes imagining taking the place of the same-sex parent in the relationship with the opposite-sex parent – Freud's Oedipus complex. However, whilst Erikson believed in the Oedipus complex he did not afford it the same importance as did Freud. If parents respond to the child's curiosity and fantasy with embarrassment or treat the child as a nuisance then the child can develop a sense of guilt. If, however, the child is encouraged in these activities it will develop a sense of initiative, which will continue into adulthood.

industry versus inferiority

At this stage the child is focusing on what it can learn about the world. Erikson believed that all cultures have the equivalent of school where the child can learn the practical and technological skills emphasised by the particular culture. The word 'technological' in this context means anything from weapons through manual tools to computers, depending on the culture. Relationships with others outside the family start to assume greater importance at this stage. If the child succeeds in forming relationships outside the family, and in its mastery of technology, it develops a sense of industry – the capacity to be busy. Failure to achieve these goals however leaves the child with a sense of inferiority.

identity versus identity-diffusion

This is adolescence, a time of rapid change for the individual on a physical, psychological and social level. Erikson believed that the developmental task of adolescence is to maintain a stable identity in the face of these changes. At the physical level young people experience rapid and dramatic changes in their body – this requires a period of adjustment. On a social level adolescence is a *moratorium* – a period where we delay responsibilities such as work and marriage in order to give the adolescent time to adjust. However, this moratorium can cause as much difficulty as it prevents; young people are expected to act in an adult manner and to make adult career decisions yet they are excluded from the benefits of adulthood.

Matters are not helped by the fact that different adult agencies do not agree on when we become adults. You can, for example, have to pay full fare on the buses at 16, and you may be required to work full time, yet you are not allowed to participate in adult privileges such as voting or drinking for a further two years. The adolescent who overcomes all these difficulties develops a stable adult identity, however there is a risk of *identity diffusion* in which, during the struggle for identity, some adolescents identify with labels such as 'delinquent' or extreme youth cultures such as violent gangs.

intimacy versus self-absorption

The developmental task at this age is to develop successful platonic, romantic and erotic relationships. Erikson believed that this could only be achieved if the individual had successfully achieved an identity during adolescence. While Erikson emphasised the importance of sexual relationships, he applied the same principles to the establishment of adult friendships and adult relationships to other family members. The developmental conflict of early adulthood is to achieve intimacy in relationships while retaining one's autonomy. Unsuccessful outcomes of this conflict include isolation and loneliness (or superficial, meaningless relationships) at one extreme and, at the other end of the spectrum, submerging one's individuality in a relationship and becoming 'under the thumb' of another person. Erikson considered the capacity for *distantation* very important. Distantation refers to the ability to distance oneself from and to oppose others and what they represent, when necessary even going to war.

generativity versus stagnation (26–40 years)

Generativity refers to the capacity to maintain interest in the next generation. This is manifested in an interest in work, family and the world as a whole, but particularly in one's children and in that which will affect future generations of humanity. A failure in generativity or *stagnation* may lead to loss of the will to work or in impoverished interpersonal relationships. Erikson (1959) observed that many parents he saw in his child guidance work had been unable to maintain an appropriate interest in their children because of their own parenting. Erikson believed that those who did not have children but who channelled their energies into creative or altruistic work were still displaying generativity and could successfully negotiate this stage of development.

measuring generativity

These statements are from the Loyola Generativity Scale (McAdams and St Aubin, 1992), a psychometric test commonly used to assess generativity. Items are rated on a scale of 0 to 3 where 0 means the statement never applies and 3 where it always applies.

◆ I try to pass along the knowledge I have gained through my experiences.

◆ I do not feel that other people need me.

◆ I think I would like to do the work of a teacher.

◆ I feel as though I have made a difference to many people.

◆ I do not volunteer to work for a charity.

ego integrity versus despair and disgust (41 years +)

As one enters the second half of one's life and most of what one is going to achieve has been achieved, and as one's physical and cognitive abilities begin to decline, the psychosocial conflict that must be overcome is between *ego integrity*, as one looks back at one's achievements with contentment, and *despair and disgust* as the unsatisfied individual looks back with regret. Despair results from the awareness that life is too short to start again. Despairing individuals may also feel disgust at their own lack of achievement. This feeling of disgust is commonly projected onto others, thus the individual may appear to be angry, critical and contemptuous of others. Erikson believed that the main determinant of whether a state of integrity or despair and disgust results in the individual is whether generativity has been achieved in the previous stage. If one has thrown oneself wholeheartedly into the development of the next generation one is more likely to sit back and watch contentedly as they take their turn in achievement.

⟁ discussion

Erikson's ideas have found wide popularity and his is perhaps the most widely accepted psychodynamic theory within mainstream psychology. One reason for the greater acceptance of Erikson's ideas is that he has minimised the importance of issues like infant sexuality, which tend to make us uncomfortable (Jarvis, 2003). Another is that some of his ideas are a little more easily testable and have a body of supporting research. For example we can measure generativity using a psychometric test called the Loyola Generativity Scale. McAdams et al. (1997) interviewed adults classified as high and low in generativity by the Loyola Generativity Scale, and performed a content analysis of their life stories. The highly generative adults were characterised by prosocial and moral values and by a belief that negative events can be transformed into positives. This suggests that the Loyola Generativity Scale is a valid test of generativity.

media watch

midlife crisis? We can work it out

Phil Hogan, *Observer Review*, June 2001

What's a poor chap to do when he wakes in a panic on the wrong side of 39? (Having sex with your secretary is not the answer.)

Of course midlife crisis doesn't inevitably lead to a lewd sex act in a public place with someone else you've just met, however compelling that idea may seem as a short-term measure. No, what may start as a sense of loss and unfulfilled ambition can result in something positive and liberating, like climbing the Matterhorn without oxygen or walking backwards to Tunisia.

The point is, there are impulses here that cannot be ignored. Who among us can fail willingly to embrace the following sentiments: 'A man has dreams of walking with giants/to carve his niche in the edifice of time.'

So it's a common theme, and one witnessed nowhere more prominently than in those who choose to pursue their new enthusiasms in the public arena; who tread their chosen path for years and the suddenly take a left or right for no apparent reason. Look at Prince Charles: one minute happy to play polo and wait for the Queen to give him his turn at being king, the next trying to arrest the march of time with his irascible comments on modern buildings.

question

Explain the phenomenon of the midlife crisis using the final stage of Erikson's theory.

Similarly there are psychometric tests to assess identity and intimacy and they allow us to research how these change with age. In one longitudinal study (a study conducted on the same participants over a long period of time) Whitbourne et al. (1992) demonstrated that people's sense of identity and intimate relationships do indeed become stronger in middle adulthood after a shaky adolescence and early adulthood.

figure 6.8
The hit film *American Beauty* captured for many the essence of midlife crisis

classic research
studies in detail

the psychodynamic approach

do identity and intimacy really change with age?

Whitbourne, S. K., Zuschlag, M. K., Elliot, L. B. and Waterman, A. S. (1992) Psychosocial development in adulthood: a 22 year sequential study. *Journal of Personality and Social Psychology*, **63**, 260–271.

Aim: to look at changes in people's sense of identity and the intimacy of their relationships with age. Participants were followed over a 22-year period in order to assess changes in their identity and intimacy.

Procedure: 20-year-old college students were recruited in 1966 and assessed using psychometric tests measuring their sense of identity and the intimacy of their close relationships. In 1977 this first cohort was reassessed using the same psychometric tests and a further cohort of 20-year-old students was also assessed. In 1988 a third cohort of 20-year-old students was assessed and the first two cohorts were assessed again. Scores for identity and intimacy were thus available for the first cohort at ages 20, 31 and 42, for the second cohort at ages 20 and 31, and for the third cohort at age 20.

Findings: for both intimacy and identity, scores for all three cohorts were relatively low at age 20. For cohorts 1 and 2 there was a substantial increase in scores on the identity scale between 20 and 31, and for cohort 1 there was a further increase between 31 and 42. For scores of intimacy, the same pattern was seen except that in cohort 1 intimacy remained stable rather than increasing between 31 and 42 years. Interestingly the scores for each age varied very little between the three cohorts (they were virtually the same for identity).

Conclusion: the results strongly supported Erikson's ideas about identity and intimacy. As his theory would predict people's sense of identity and intimacy were relatively weak at the transition of adolescence and early adulthood and they picked up by the 30s. Most significantly, the massive social changes that took place between 1966 and 1988 had little impact on scores of either identity or intimacy, particularly identity. This suggests that, as Erikson believed, these aspects of development are more dependent on age than external factors.

for+against

Erikson's theory

+ Erikson extended the psychodynamic approach to the study of adulthood, and has given us an understanding of personality development in adults. This is an advantage over other psychodynamic theories that are limited to explaining childhood development.

+ Erikson based his ideas on the study of different cultures and his theory is less culture-bound than other psychoanalytic theories.

+ There is sound research supporting some of Erikson's ideas. The Whitbourne et al. (1992) study is a good example, showing that identity and intimacy do indeed increase during early adulthood.

− Erikson's stages, like those of other stage theories, are rather rigid and underplay the importance of individual differences in lifespan development. For example, significant events such as bereavement at a particular age may be more important for people's development than any predetermined conflicts associated with their stage of development.

where to now?

The following are good sources of further information on Erikson's theory of development:

▶ **Erikson, E. H.** (1959) *Identity and the Life-cycle*. Norton, New York. Erikson's writing is quite easy to follow and, as always, it is ultimately best to read the original material in order to see what the author really meant to say.

▶ **Schaie, K. W. and Willis, S L.** (1996) *Adult Development and Ageing*. HarperCollins, New York. An excellent account of research into adulthood, largely based on Erikson's theory.

▶ **Jarvis, M.** (2003) *Psychodynamic Psychology: Classic Theory and Contemporary Research*. Thomson, London. Contains a detailed chapter on Erikson's theory.

applying the psychodynamic approach to mental health

Psychodynamic ideas are most influential in the mental health professions, although they are more popular amongst psychiatrists and psychotherapists than amongst psychologists. Psychodynamic theory has contributed to our understanding of mental health by showing how experience and relationships in our early life can affect our later mental health, and in some cases how symptoms of mental disorder can represent unconscious conflicts.

early relationships and mental health

Central to psychodynamic psychology is the assumption that the child's developing personality is determined largely by its relationships with its parents. Later mental disorder can represent a failure in normal personality development or the lasting effects of unhappy childhood memories, often a direct consequence of the nature of the parental relationship. The poet Philip Larkin expressed this well when he said:

> They f**k you up, your mum and dad.
> They may not mean to but they do.
> They fill you with all the faults they had.
> And add some extra just for you.

Lemma-Wright (1995) has provided us with an example of a woman called Alex who experienced a panic attack, and explained this in terms of unconscious conflicts dating back to Alex's childhood.

case example

Alex (Lemma-Wright, 1995)

Alex was the older of two sisters. One weekend Alex organised a sea boat trip to celebrate her sister's birthday. The trip went well, but Alex suffered a panic attack on the boat. Alex had always loved her sister dearly, but she had also resented her a little, believing that her family had always doted on her while ignoring Alex. On one occasion as a child, Alex had become so angry with her sister for being the centre of attention that she dragged her into the sea, frightening her badly. As an adult, Alex frequently felt obliged to organise her sister's life and to help her out of financial difficulties. She had no idea why she suffered the panic attack until a few days later when she had a dream in which she had a fight with a friend (who reminded her of her sister) and wished her dead. It then became apparent to Alex that the boat trip, in which Alex had once again taken her sister into the sea, had stirred up guilty memories of the time she had dragged her into the sea.

Looking at the case of Alex we can see that long-buried childhood memories seem to have returned to produce anxiety in the form of a panic attack. This case illustrates well the usefulness of a psychodynamic understanding of mental health, but also its limitations. On one hand, it is likely that Alex's panic attack was the result of a rush of guilt triggered by the boat trip with her sister. You can imagine that, if this were the case, understanding it could be invaluable in helping Alex overcome her symptoms. On the other hand, what evidence do we have that Alex's panic attack, her dream and her childhood experiences are really linked in this way? Psychologists, who in the main think of themselves as hard-nosed scientists, tend to have reservations about accepting this style of linking apparently unrelated events together.

Despite this difficulty, there is a strong body of evidence linking dysfunctional relationships in early childhood to later mental health problems. Fonagy et al. (1996) carried out a study of mixed adult psychiatric in-patients, assessing them for *attachment type*,

the psychodynamic approach

a measure of the quality of the first relationship. They found that the majority of patients suffering depression, anxiety disorder, eating disorders and substance abuse disorders were classified as *unresolved*. This classification is known to be associated with a very dysfunctional first relationship.

early trauma and mental health

There is a large body of research linking susceptibility to mental disorder in adulthood to traumatic experiences in childhood. It seems for example that depression may be linked to early experiences of loss. Freud (1917) proposed that, while some cases of depression were biological in origin, others were linked to early experiences of loss, in which the sense of loss is so powerful that it affects the developing personality and manifests in later childhood or adulthood as depression. A classic study from Brown and Harris (1978) supports this idea.

are early experiences associated with later depression?

Brown, G. W. and Harris, T. O. (1978) *The Social Origins of Depression: A Study of Psychiatric Disorder in Women*. Tavistock, London.

Aim: Brown and Harris (1978) aimed to investigate the link between depression and both current and past stress in the lives of sufferers. They focused on working-class women, as women tend to experience more stress than men, and working-class people tend to experience more stress than the middle classes.

Procedure: 539 women in Camberwell, London were interviewed using a standard interview called the Life Events Difficulties Scale (LEDS). Interviewers obtained details of what stressful events had occurred in the previous year, along with stressful childhood events. Interviews were then rated by a panel of researchers for how stressful the events reported would be. To avoid bias, these raters had no knowledge of whether the person they were looking at had suffered depression. It was later ascertained which interviewees suffered from depression. The association between depression and a range of events was worked out.

Findings: both recent stress and childhood stress were associated with depression. Three of the four factors that had the strongest associations with depression involved recent stress. These were the lack of an intimate relationship, lack of paid employment and the presence of three or more children in the home. However, childhood events were also important, depression being particularly associated with the death of the woman's mother before she reached the age of 11.

Conclusions: recent and childhood stress were both associated with depression. In particular, loss experiences in childhood, especially of the mother, made women vulnerable to depression. This supports both Freud's idea that depression in adults is linked to loss in childhood and the ORT principle that the relationship with the primary caregiver is of paramount importance for the developing child.

the use of interviews in psychodynamic research

Although the bulk of research in psychodynamic psychology is in the form of case studies, there are occasions when researchers look for more solid evidence of the links between past experience and current psychological functioning. One way of doing this is to interview participants, asking questions about their current functioning and past experiences. There are a number of standard interviews available. For example Brown and Harris used the *LEDS*, and Fonagy et al. (1996) used the *Adult Attachment Interview* (AAI). Interviews of this type are extremely useful in gathering empirical data that can be used to evaluate psychodynamic theory. There is however a limitation to their use. All interviews rely on the accuracy of what participants say, and this is affected by a number of factors. For example, recall of past experience can be distorted by current symptoms, and it may be that depressed patients speak negatively about their relationship with doctors because their depression makes them see everything in a negative light.

Many other studies have supported findings linking specific early experiences to later symptoms. Eley and Stevenson (2000) investigated the origins of depression and anxiety and concluded that there was an association between early frightening experiences and later anxiety disorders, and between early loss experiences and later depression. However, they also found evidence that mental disorder has a genetic component. This is important because it reminds us that we cannot explain mental health problems just in terms of psychodynamic factors.

media
watch

real life issues. The love-seeking only child Paula Yates

Oliver James, *Good Housekeeping*, February 2003

Children who are denied stability and affection in early life can find themselves forever repeating their past, even if they have vowed to do the opposite. The tragic television personality Paula Yates was a mass of contradictions that were brought on by her desire to bring up her children in a completely different way from how her own parents raised her, and her inability to keep from repeating the patterns learned in infancy.

'As a colleague, Paula was liable to be as egomaniacal as a toddler,' says Oliver [James], who first met Yates when she plonked herself on his lap. 'Indeed in many ways she never grew up, and this may have been partly because, according to her own account, her childhood was traumatic. The man she thought was her father, Jess Yates, was a depressive TV presenter, but before Paula died it emerged that her biological father was another TV presenter Hughie Green. Her actress mother was often "absent" and Paula missed her terribly.'

questions

1 Identify the psychodynamic factors that might have led to Paula Yates's adult problems.

2 What are the limitations of case studies like this as evidence for psychodynamic ideas?

② discussion

From what we have seen so far, it is clear that there is an important role for psychodynamic psychology in the field of mental health. Many patients seek help for mental health problems already believing that childhood experiences are at the root of their difficulties and many people in such a position benefit from exploring their early lives. Research firmly supports the idea that trauma and poor childhood relationships are risk factors for later mental health problems.

That said, there are also drawbacks and risks to adopting a purely psychodynamic approach to mental health. There is an increasing body of research showing that genes can also be important in predisposing people to mental disorder (as shown in the Eley and Stevenson study). There are also some conditions, such as phobias, that can be explained by simple faulty learning of behaviours, and do not require an understanding of family dynamics. It is important to remember that psychodynamic factors are thus not the only factors that we need to be aware of in working with mental health.

for+against

the psychodynamic approach to mental health

+ In many cases patients can benefit from an understanding of the links between their early experiences and their later symptoms.

+ There is clear evidence that both dysfunctional family relationships and early trauma are major risk factors for developing mental health problems. There is particularly strong evidence for the link between depression and experiences of loss.

− Adopting a purely psychodynamic approach to mental health can mean ignoring other important risk factors such as genetic predisposition to mental disorder. The approach is thus *reductionist*.

where to now?

We recommend the following as good sources of information on the psychodynamic approach to mental health.

▶ **Power, M. and Champion, L.** (2000) *Adult Psychological Problems.* Taylor & Francis, Hove. An up-to-date and well-balanced discussion of several perspectives on mental health.

▶ **Fancher, R. T.** (1995) *Cultures of Healing.* Freeman, New York. A very critical look at how all the major psychological approaches are applied to mental health. This account is biased against the usefulness of all the major psychological approaches including psychoanalysis but if you are prepared for this it makes an interesting read and provides a good counterpoint to the positive attitude adopted in this chapter.

▶ **Jarvis, M., Putwain, D. and Dwyer, D.** (2002) *Angles on Atypical Psychology.* Nelson Thornes, Cheltenham. Contains a chapter on psychodynamic approaches to mental health.

why do we all watch *Buffy*?

The huge popularity of *Buffy the Vampire Slayer* is a social phenomenon so remarkable that it has attracted the attention of psychologists. Why should millions of people be so fascinated by the improbable adventures of a teenage girl with the power to kill vampires and other monsters? There is now a body of psychodynamic literature seeking to explain the appeal of horror in general and *Buffy* in particular.

Buffy, the plot

At the age of 16, Buffy, a shallow and materialistic cheerleader has, against her will, been granted superhuman powers by the 'Powers That Be' so she can function as a 'Slayer' – to oppose the forces of Darkness. Her hometown, Sunnydale, is sited over a 'Hellmouth'. This means that many supernatural beings, in particular vampires, congregate there. Buffy is accompanied in her struggle against evil by a group of allies known as the 'Slayerettes'. Rupert Giles is a middle-aged English librarian and a member of the Watcher's Council, an ancient secret society dedicated to supporting Slayers. Buffy's best friends are Willow, initially a quiet, academic victim of bullying, but who later becomes a powerful witch, and Xander, a socially awkward youth from a dysfunctional family. Willow's boyfriend (at least until she falls in love with another witch in series four) is Oz, laid-back musician and werewolf. Buffy's lover, Angel, is a vampire whose soul has been restored by a Gypsy curse so that he can be tormented forever by guilt about his depredations.

figure 6.9
Buffy the Vampire Slayer

applying psychodynamic ideas to understanding *Buffy*

It is when dealing with the more irrational aspects of human nature that the psychodynamic approach to psychology comes into its own. Because the entire idea of *Buffy* is so implausible we have to look outside the obvious possible reasons for its popularity. Several commentators (such as Schlozman, 2000; Jarvis, 2003) have suggested that a number of aspects of *Buffy* appeal directly to the unconscious mind. For example, monsters can serve as symbols of displaced fears and the plotlines involving the Slayerettes play out the classic developmental crises of adolescence.

displacement and monsters

Recall Freud's idea of displacement from our earlier discussion of psychological defences (p. 140). Displacement occurs when we deal with an unwelcome feeling by shifting it from one person or object to another. Skal (1993) has suggested that the reason why we enjoy monsters in entertainment is that they symbolise our fears, and we can displace fears on to them. For example, we all fear death, but death itself is not a tangible 'thing' that can be fought and beaten. Vampires however are solid 'slayable' beings on to whom we can displace our anxiety about death. Every time Buffy slays a vampire she can be said to be symbolically defeating death (Iylim, 1998).

the developmental tasks of adolescence

Another way of looking at the appeal of *Buffy* involves Erikson's theory of psychosocial development (p. 150). To Erikson, adolescence is an important period for psychological development because the childhood identity has been discarded but no stable adult identity has been adopted. This means that adolescents are uniquely vulnerable to anxiety over academic, social and sexual issues. Schlozman (2000) has suggested that 'Buffy the vampire slayer offers unique illustrations . . . of the ego strength necessary to negotiate the developmental maze of adolescence' (2000, p. 50). We can go

figure 6.10
From a psychodynamic perspective, vampires may be symbols of death

so far as to interpret particular characters as playing out particular adolescent conflicts. Xander, academically and socially awkward, can be seen as representing the fear of failure. Oz the werewolf, with his facial hair problem, awkward monthly cycle and uncontrollable behaviour, can be seen as representing adolescent anxieties over puberty. Ted, the conformist and authoritarian android, may be a symbol of the adolescent fear of losing identity and becoming a faceless, robotic adult.

---

research methods

the analysis of symbols

A central idea in both research and therapy carried out from a psychodynamic perspective is the analysis of symbols. In their analysis of Buffy, writers like Tylim (1998) and Schlozman (2000) have identified monsters and characters as symbolising something of significance to the unconscious mind. Remember that Freud identified one of the defining features of the unconscious mind as the ability for one object to symbolise another. This is the same phenomenon used in dream analysis, and from a psychodynamic perspective this is a powerful tool for uncovering people's hidden anxieties. However, psychologists from other theoretical backgrounds are often suspicious over the psychodynamic analysis of symbols.

◆ Analysis of symbols is subjective, and different analysts might reach different conclusions about what a particular symbol means, if anything.

◆ There is no objective way to decide whether a symbol has been correctly interpreted.

There are many other aspects of Buffy that can be identified as appealing to the unconscious. The siting of Sunnydale High School, attended by the Slayerettes, directly over the Hellmouth, may particularly resonate with adolescents. As Jarvis (2001) says; 'school is Hell' (2001, p. 257). Buffy's relationship with her watcher, Rupert Giles, also bears interpretation. Erikson placed great emphasis on the role of older adults as sources of stability for adolescents, and this role is brilliantly played out by Giles. Leon (2001) has identified a passage where this is made explicit:

Buffy: Nothing's ever simple anymore . . . it's like the more I know the more confused I get.

Giles: I believe that's called growing up.

thinking critically

A psychodynamic understanding of why so many of us are fascinated with *Buffy* illustrates nicely the strengths and weaknesses of the entire approach. On the positive side, no other approach could explain so elegantly the appeal of the programme. However, we should not lose sight of the limitations of psychodynamic interpretation, whether of dreams, defences, action slips or televisual material. We can never assume that any particular interpretation is correct. However neatly we can explain the appeal of Buffy using psychodynamic theory, this does not mean that our explanation is the right one.

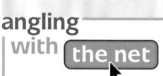

angling with the net

Steven Schlozman's article on the psychology of Buffy, originally published in the journal *Academic Psychiatry*, is available online. Track it down using a search engine such as Google. As a starting point you try to locate *Slayage: the Online Journal of Buffy Studies*, which has a link to the article.

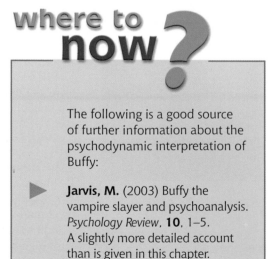

where to now?

The following is a good source of further information about the psychodynamic interpretation of Buffy:

▶ **Jarvis, M.** (2003) Buffy the vampire slayer and psychoanalysis. *Psychology Review*, **10**, 1–5. A slightly more detailed account than is given in this chapter.

should we all be in analysis?

The psychodynamic approach to psychology is mostly applied to provide psychological therapy to help people suffering mental health problems or life difficulties. There are now literally hundreds of 'brand name' psychological therapies available, of which psychodynamic varieties are among the most popular. There are a number of variations on psychodynamic therapy, the most intensive and long-term being *psychoanalysis*. Psychoanalysis involves patients (or *analysands*) free-associating – saying whatever comes into their mind, including childhood memories, dreams, current life situations and feelings towards the analyst. The analyst responds to this with interpretations of the links between past experience, current problems and symptoms and nature of the patient–analyst relationship.

Psychoanalysis occupies a unique place among the psychological therapies because many people undergo it not merely to deal with a particular symptom or problem but as a lifestyle choice. This is particularly the case in the US, where among the rich and famous it is widely considered as important to have an analyst as a flashy car or designer clothes. This culture of psychoanalysis has been criticised as self-indulgent and a waste of time and money. However, there is no doubt that psychoanalysis and the other psychodynamic therapies do alleviate psychological distress and enhance the quality of life for many people. So the question arises; should we all be in analysis?

applying psychodynamic ideas to understanding the benefits of analysis

From a psychodynamic perspective there are several factors that make psychoanalysis and other psychodynamic therapies helpful. What these all have in common is that they involve bringing unconscious influences to the surface, making the unconscious conscious.

early experience and catharsis

From a psychodynamic perspective we are all unconsciously influenced to a greater or lesser extent by the nature of our early experiences, in particular traumatic experiences. One of the key aims of psychodynamic therapies such as psychoanalysis is to loosen the hold these experiences have on us. Trauma can be remembered, re-experienced and worked through in the safety of the therapy room. This process is called *catharsis*. Catharsis is undoubtedly one of the factors that makes all psychological therapies helpful.

early relationships and transference

A key factor affecting our mental health and our ability to relate to other people in adulthood is the quality of our early relationships. In therapy, there is a tendency to play out the nature of our relationships with key people such as parents in our behaviour towards the therapist. This is called *transference*, because feelings towards important figures such as parents are bring *transferred* on to the therapist. By telling patients how their current relationships are distorted by the influence of early relationships the analyst can give them insight into what goes wrong in their relationships. Transference interpretation is arguably the most important technique in classical psychoanalysis.

interpretation of dreams, action slips and defences

Transference is just one thing that can be fed back to patients in analysis to give them insight into the unconscious influences on their feelings and behaviour. Dreams and action slips also give away things that are bothering the patient, and interpretations of these can be fed back to them. Defences are also important because they can profoundly affect the way we interact with other people. The use of defences in therapy sessions gives valuable clues as to the patient's defensive style in everyday life. For example, someone who uses projection a lot is likely to spend a lot of time blaming and arguing with others. Similarly, someone who uses denial a lot is likely to devote much energy to trying not to face problems head on. An analyst can give patients feedback on their use of defences and help them modify their defensive style.

angling with the net

Access the Web sites of the Tavistock Clinic (**www.tavi-port.org**) and the British Psychoanalytical Society (**www.psychoanalysis.org. uk**). You can download what the experts have to say about undertaking psychoanalytic psychotherapy or psychoanalysis. See what you think.

thinking critically

There are two key questions to be asked when evaluating the usefulness of psycho-dynamic therapies like psychoanalysis. First, does it work? Second, what are the downsides?

does analysis work?

Yes. Although early studies (for example, Eysenck, 1952) cast doubt on the effective-ness of psychoanalysis and other varieties of psychodynamic therapy in helping alleviate mental health problems, modern research paints a much more optimistic pic-ture. In a recent Swedish study, Sandell (1999) studied 756 patients receiving psychoanalysis or long-term psychoanalytic psychotherapy. Psychoanalysis was defined as involving four to five sessions per week. Psychotherapy took place once or twice a week. At the end of three years' treatment both the psychotherapy and psy-choanalysis led to a significant reduction in symptoms. At follow-up three years later the psychoanalysis group had significantly fewer symptoms than they had when the analysis ended. It seems that the patients who underwent psychoanalysis continued to improve after the end of their treatment.

are there downsides to being in analysis?

We might all benefit from freeing ourselves from the influence of our more negative early experiences. However, there are also some downsides to being in analysis. This type of therapy is expensive and time-consuming and can prove very disruptive to patients' lives. Existing relationships can break down as the patient develops insight into the unconscious reasons behind their development. It has also been suggested that, for some of us at least, a more effective way of enhancing our quality of life is to focus on the present and future rather than on the past.

media watch

the subversive shrink

Nicci Gerrard, *Observer Review*, 31 October 1999

What is psychoanalysis? Will it heal you, or damage you further by forcing you to dwell upon those sorrows that are part of the human condition? When we feel unbearably sad should we pull up our socks or let down our defences and peer into that raw strange world we call our mind? Can we ever be cured of our-selves: all our fears of risk, of death and love and loss?

'No' says Adam Phillips. 'No we can't.' Phillips, the anti-Freudian Freudian, the psychoanalyst who deftly pulls out the rug from under psychoanalysis, is the nearest thing we have to a philosopher of happiness.

He thinks Freud offers us 'one way of thinking about the things that trouble or perplex us.' He is elo-quently alert to the dangers of analysis. 'It can be a refuge from life.' His task is to turn the people who come to him away from their own interesting unhap-piness back to the extraordinary vitality of the outside world.

'It [psychoanalysis] can be useful for some people with some pre-occupations. But it can be a refuge from poli-tics – by which I mean group life. And it can induce you to be too fascinated by yourself.'

questions

1 What dangers does Phillips see in psychoanalysis?

2 Is he entirely negative in his assessment?

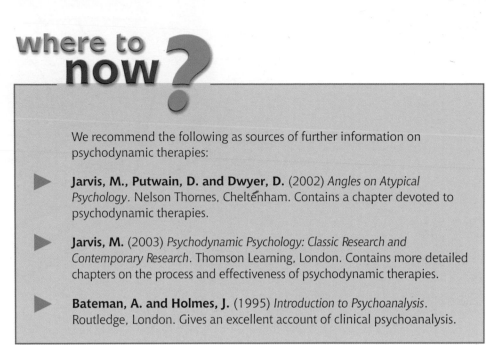

where to now ?

We recommend the following as sources of further information on psychodynamic therapies:

▶ **Jarvis, M., Putwain, D. and Dwyer, D.** (2002) *Angles on Atypical Psychology*. Nelson Thornes, Cheltenham. Contains a chapter devoted to psychodynamic therapies.

▶ **Jarvis, M.** (2003) *Psychodynamic Psychology: Classic Research and Contemporary Research*. Thomson Learning, London. Contains more detailed chapters on the process and effectiveness of psychodynamic therapies.

▶ **Bateman, A. and Holmes, J.** (1995) *Introduction to Psychoanalysis*. Routledge, London. Gives an excellent account of clinical psychoanalysis.

conclusions

The psychodynamic approach to psychology stands apart from the other major approaches in many ways. Its reliance on the subjective interpretation of clinical cases is considered suspect by many psychologists. However, psychodynamic ideas have proved extremely valuable for people seeking to understand what is going on in the mind of the individual, hence they remain popular with therapists. As we have seen, some aspects of psychodynamic theory (such as reaction formation, anality and repression) do have firm empirical support. Psychodynamic theory is at its strongest when applied to understanding irrational behaviour. We can thus use it to understand the symptoms of mental disorder. We can also apply psychodynamic theory to understanding slightly unusual social phenomena such as the popularity of *Buffy the Vampire Slayer*.

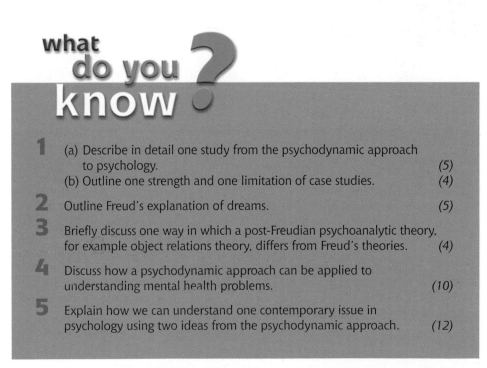

what do you know ?

1 (a) Describe in detail one study from the psychodynamic approach to psychology. *(5)*
(b) Outline one strength and one limitation of case studies. *(4)*

2 Outline Freud's explanation of dreams. *(5)*

3 Briefly discuss one way in which a post-Freudian psychoanalytic theory, for example object relations theory, differs from Freud's theories. *(4)*

4 Discuss how a psychodynamic approach can be applied to understanding mental health problems. *(10)*

5 Explain how we can understand one contemporary issue in psychology using two ideas from the psychodynamic approach. *(12)*

The physiological approach is based on the following ideas:

◆ *Genetic influences.* Our genetic make up, inherited from our parents, is important in determining our individual characteristics, abilities and behaviour. Genes are the messages we inherit that control aspects of our development. They are sections of strands of a chemical called DNA that is found in almost every cell in our bodies. Some individual genes can control specific behaviours, such whether we are able or unable to roll our tongues. However, examples of single genes directly controlling particular behaviours that are of interest to psychology are rare. One example of a single-gene effect is the influence of phenylketonuria on intelligence. More typically, genes interact with one another to produce a behavioural effect. Genes may also interact with environmental factors to determine eventual behavioural outcomes as appears to be the case in schizophrenia.

◆ *The nervous system.* Physiological psychologists are primarily concerned with investigating biological activity. The central biological influence on our thinking, behaviour and feelings (both normal and abnormal) is the activity of our brain and nervous system. The nervous system is built from neurones, cells that are specialized for communication. Neuronal structure is suited to their function. Neurones conveying messages around the body (unlike those in the brain) are long, sending messages along their length. All neurones have highly branched ends enabling them to pass chemical messages on to one or more others. As a consequence of this chemical stage in communication, brain activity can be influenced chemically, such as through the action of drugs. Neurones send electrochemical messages very rapidly along their length (hence we are able to detect brain activity electrically). Neurones also interact with other structures, such as muscles leading to physical behaviours, and glands, leading to the release of hormones (such as in the control of the sleeping–waking cycle). The brain itself is also organised functionally – that is, it has regions devoted to different jobs. For example the hippocampus is important in memory and the suprachiasmatic nucleus is involved in daily rhythms. This is called localisation of function.

In this chapter we will be looking particularly at the importance of two areas of biology. Genetics is the study of inheritance, and neuropsychology is the study of the relationship between psychology and the functioning of the brain. Neuropsychology is a vast area, and in this chapter we will be looking at two related ways in which the workings of the brain affect human psychology, namely bodily rhythms and sleep.

what's ahead?

This chapter concerns the ways in which biological principles can be applied to understanding psychology. This is not a new idea. Before psychology emerged as a distinct discipline about 100 years ago, biologists were investigating the relationship between the brain and human behaviour. The scientific study of biology requires a certain level of technology however and rapid progress is being made in understanding how our psychology is influenced by our biology. We will look here at *behavioural genetics* – the study of the origins of individual differences in human characteristics, abilities and behaviour. We will also examine *neuropsychology* – the study of the role of the brain in determining the way we think, feel and behave. In particular we can focus on the ways we are affected by bodily rhythms and the mechanisms of sleeping and dreaming. In our *real lives* section we examine the effects of shift work and jet lag, and in *talking points*, we will consider two phenomena: lucid dreaming (a state in which dreamers know that they are dreaming), and seasonal affective disorder (a type of depression linked to reduced sunlight in winter).

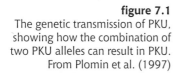
the physiological approach

genetic influences

You may have noticed that, just as some families have a number of very tall or red-headed members, some psychological characteristics also appear to run in families. There are thus families with an unusually large number of highly intelligent or particularly bad-tempered individuals. One possible cause of such patterns is genetics and biological techniques are enabling psychologists to find out more about this influence on behaviour. A questionnaire study by Olson et al. (2001) investigated attitudes to a range of variables including loud music, sweets, taking exercise, receiving the death penalty for murder, crossword puzzles, and the participants' opinions of their own athleticism and attractiveness. Olson et al. found evidence for genetic effects in 26 of the 30 variables they measured, with identical twins being the most similar.

Genes are units of DNA, passed from one generation to the next, which contain the information required to build biological structures. The reason why humans share so many characteristics is that we share 99.9% of our genes. It is relatively easy to understand how a characteristic like eye colour can be under the control of genes because eye colour is obviously physical in nature. The question of how genes might affect psychological characteristics is a more complex one. It appears that genetic differences between individuals produce biological differences between people – which may be very subtle – that, in combination with their environment, lead them to develop into unique individuals.

In general, psychological characteristics that have a genetic component depend on several genes and, in most cases, we do not yet know all the genes involved. However, there are examples of psychological disorders that result from single-gene abnormalities. An example is phenylketonuria (PKU), which causes a form of profound mental retardation. Phenylketonuria is caused by a single gene. The *allele* (meaning a particular form of a gene) for PKU is recessive so PKU will only result if a child inherits the PKU allele from both parents.

If both parents are carriers of the PKU gene, each child has a 25% probability of suffering the disease and a 50% probability of carrying the gene but not developing symptoms. Our understanding of the genetic basis of PKU has allowed us to greatly reduce the number of people suffering mental retardation. The symptoms of PKU result from an inability to break down an amino acid called phenylalanine. A build-up of phenylalanine causes brain damage. We can now simply advise sufferers to avoid foods containing phenylalanine throughout childhood so that they never develop symptoms. Such foods include fizzy drinks sweetened with the artificial sweetener aspartame (NutraSweet).

Behavioural geneticists are interested in genetic and environmental influences on individual differences in people. However, in real life it can be quite difficult to study genes and environment separately because people in the same family tend to share a similar environment as well as a similar set of genes. There are, however, various circumstances under which we can investigate the relative importance of genes and environment, including cases of twins and adoption.

figure 7.1
The genetic transmission of PKU, showing how the combination of two PKU alleles can result in PKU. From Plomin et al. (1997)

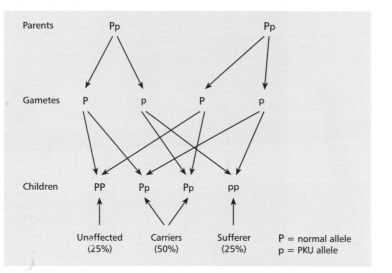

twin studies

We know that identical twins (properly called monozygotic twins or MZs) share 100% of their genes. We also know that fraternal twins (properly called dizygotic twins or

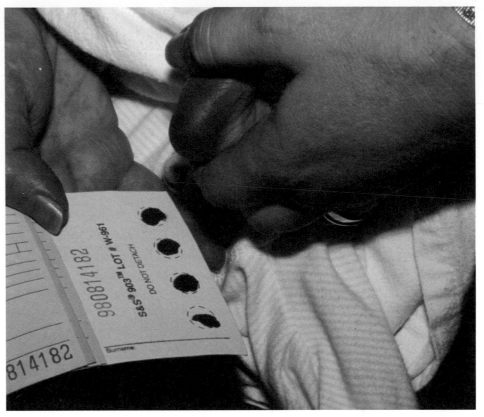

figure 7.2 How do genes and the environment interact to cause PKU?

DZs) only share 50% of their genetic material. These facts give us the basis for two types of *twin study*.

comparing MZ and DZ twins

One design of twin study involves comparing the similarities of MZs and DZs who have been reared together and hence have experienced a similar environment. If MZs, who share all their genes as well as having a similar environment, are more similar than DZs, this is powerful evidence for the importance of genes. An example of such a study comes from Gottesman (1991) who pooled the results of 40 investigations spanning over 60 years to compare the concordance rates of MZs and DZs for schizophrenia. This is a serious mental disorder characterised by hallucinations, delusions and difficulty in thinking coherently. The term concordance refers to the probability of both twins sharing a characteristic like schizophrenia. Gottesman's results are shown in Table 7.1

You can see from Table 7.1 that MZs have a much higher probability of sharing schizophrenia than DZs. This tells us that schizophrenia is at least partially a result of genetic factors. Of course, if schizophrenia were entirely a product of our genes, we would expect that all the identical twins of sufferers would also have the condition. A number

twin type	concordance for schizophrenia (%)
MZs	48
DZs	17

table 7.1 Concordance rates of identical and fraternal twins. Gottesman (1991)

figure 7.3 Identical twins

of environmental risk factors have been suggested, ranging from a dysfunctional family (Tienari et al., 1992) to a difficult birth (Torrey et al., 1994).

separated twins

An alternative approach is to compare the similarity of identical twins who have grown up in the same family or in different environments and see whether those who have grown up together are more alike than those who grew up apart. The fact that MZs reared apart show more differences than those reared together demonstrates the role of the environment but the fact that even separated identical twins tend to be much more alike than two unrelated people demonstrates the importance of genes. Table 7.2 shows the similarity in personality of identical twins who have been reared together and apart. The correlations in the table represent how similar the twins were, with 0 meaning no relationship between the scores of the two twins and 1 being a perfect correlation between them.

correlation twin type	extraversion	neuroticism
MZs reared together	0.51	0.46
MZs reared apart	0.38	0.38

table 7.2 Similarity in personality between identical twins reared together and apart, from Loehlin (1992)

The term *extraversion* refers to how impulsive and sociable the twins were. *Neuroticism* refers to how anxious and moody they were. Looking at Table 7.2, you can see that, although the twins reared apart are distinctly less similar than those reared together, they are still much more similar than we would expect if their genetic similarity were not a factor. Of course, this assumes that personality can be measured with sufficient accuracy to show up differences between different pairs of twins.

correlational techniques

research methods

The technique of comparing two variables is called a *correlation*. It investigates whether the two measurements are related. If genetic factors are important in determining a behaviour then the score for one twin is likely to be close to the score for the other. So, if one twin has a low score, the other one will have a low score too – similarly with high scores. In the case of Loehlin (1992) there were four possible relationships, each of which shared a relationship. The pattern that emerges is called a positive correlation (see p. 233) in which the scores on the two variables (in this case one individual from each pair of twins) are related – one individual's score is expected to be close in value to the other individual's. When such a relationship exists, it can be measured statistically and represented with a correlation coefficient (*r*). For a positive correlation, *r* values are positive numbers between 0 and +1; the higher the value the stronger the correlation, the closer, in general, one twin is to the other on the characteristic being measured. In the case of Loehlin's results, the strongest correlation was 0.51, showing that when reared together, if one twin is extraverted, the other is likely to be an extravert too.

These correlations are measuring naturally occurring variables (such as personality characteristics or the incidence of mental illness) although it is also possible to look for correlations in variables that are actively 'tested', such as reaction time or IQ. In these instances it is particularly important to remember that, in a correlation, we are only looking for existing patterns. Because we are not manipulating a variable (as we would in an experiment) we cannot make judgements about causality – we cannot conclude from a correlational study that one variable *causes the change* in another, simply that they change together. This is relatively easy to see in twin studies – the relatedness between one individual's characteristics and his or her twin's is caused by some other factor. However, in some studies, such as those looking at a relationship between hours of sleep and reaction time, it is tempting to make causal assumptions. If the data are only correlational we cannot conclude that sleeplessness causes an increase in reaction time, only that the two vary together. It may be that – as with twins – the effect is caused by some third factor; perhaps both the reaction time and reduced sleep are the result of illness or age. Nevertheless, correlational studies enable us to investigate patterns that can indicate important variation between individuals.

In summary, correlations look for relationships between two variables. However, because we are not manipulating the variables, we cannot draw conclusions about causality from correlational data; other, unknown factors may be responsible for changes in both of the measured variables.

interactive angles

Fink et al. (2003) found that the risk of smoking in 21 to 40 year olds was higher for MZ twins with a smoking co-twin than for DZ twins with a smoking co-twin. The same was not the case for younger twins (aged 12 to 20 years). What could explain the difference between MZ and DZ twins and why might this only appear in adulthood?

discussion

Twin studies provide a powerful argument for the role of genes in affecting individual differences amongst us with respect to intelligence, personality and mental disorder. However, there are problems with twin studies. In the case of separated identical twins, researchers must rely on data from a small group of people who have been separated at various ages and in a variety of circumstances. Some 'separated' identical twins may have spent considerable time in a similar environment before separation or they might have been 'separated' but have actually lived in very similar environments. They may also been reunited for a considerable time before their personality and intelligence were assessed, so that they had a chance to share an environment for a time and to become more alike. When researchers compare the environments of MZs and DZs reared together, they make the assumption that MZs and DZs grow up in equally similar environments. In fact, because MZs look more alike than DZs, people may treat them in a much more similar manner and hence give them a more similar environment as well as the same genes. This means that when we compare the similarity of MZs and DZs we cannot know to what extent we are seeing the influence of genes and to what extent the effect of environment.

We have considered how underestimation of the similarity of social environments can affect the validity of twin studies. The importance of genetic factors may also have been underestimated because it has been assumed that the biological environment of monozygotic twins during gestation is always identical, but this is not the case. If the developing cells that form MZ twins separate very early (before day four) each will form its own placenta, thus having an independent – and potentially different – blood supply from the mother. If the cell mass separates to form MZ twins after day four the developing embryos will share the same placenta (as the *chorion*, the outer layer of cells that develops into the placenta, has already begun to specialise). This difference may account for some of the variability seen in MZ twins as the placenta provides important functions for development such as supplying nutrition and oxygen and disposal of waste and protection from infection. Davis et al. (1995) investigated differences in concordance for schizophrenia between MZ twins who shared a placenta (monochorionic, MC) and those who did not (dichorionic, DC). They found that twins believed to be monochorionic (based on indicators such as having mirror-image birthmarks and fingerprints) had a concordance rate of 60% whereas in DC twins it was only 10.7%. Thus a previously ignored environmental factor appears to be reducing similarity between some (DC) monozygotic twins. This accounts for the previously surprising finding (Boklage, 1977) that MZ twins who share handedness are also likely to have high concordance for schizophrenia.

for+against

twin study methods

+ Twin studies have generated a very large volume of data, which points towards an important role for both genetic and environmental factors in individual development.

+ Twin studies suggest that genetic components may be involved in a wide range of psychological phenomena. For example, in addition to classic studies of the heritability of intelligence, personality or aspects of mental health, other behaviours may have genetic components. For example, Hettema et al. (2003) found that MZ twins were more similar than DZ twins in their tendency to become classically conditioned to fearful stimuli such as snakes and spiders.

– Separated twins have been separated at a variety of times and in a variety of circumstances and often have not been assessed for similarity until they are reunited. They may also have experienced a similar environment during the period of separation. This means that it is difficult to know if similarities between separated twins are a result of genes or environment.

– Studies showing that MZs reared together are more similar than DZs reared together also have the latter problem. If MZs share a more similar environment than DZs, it may be this as well as the identical genes that lead to the greater similarity between MZs.

– MZ twins do not all share identical uterine environments but most estimates of heritability fail to take account of this.

for+against

adoption studies

+ Adoption studies provide us with the most direct comparison of the influences of genes and environment because they isolate the influences of the environment (due to the effects of the adoptive parents during the adopted individual's childhood).

+ Adoption studies have provided us with useful information concerning the role of genes in individual differences because they isolate the influence of heredity (due to the effect of inherited factors from the biological parents on the development of the adopted child).

– There is an issue of representativeness of samples. Obviously, most people are not adopted, hence by definition people who are adopted are not representative of the whole population.

– Selective placement means that frequently people are placed with families very similar to their biological families. This makes untangling the influences of genes and environment difficult.

adoption studies

The most direct way to isolate the influence of genes and the environment involves adoption. If children are adopted into a different environment from that of their birth family we have a situation in which the children have the genes of the biological parents but the environment is created by the adoptive parents. Any similarity between child and biological parents therefore suggests a role for genes, whilst any similarity between child and the adoptive parents suggests a role for the environment. A classic adoption study conducted by Heston (1966) (described on page 171) demonstrated the importance of genes.

classic research
studies in detail

is there a genetic component to schizophrenia?

Heston, L. L. (1966) Psychiatric disorders in foster home reared children of schizophrenic mothers. *British Journal of Psychiatry*, **112**, 819–825.

Aim: to investigate genetic influences in schizophrenia by comparing adopted children of schizophrenic and non-schizophrenic natural mothers.

Procedure: 47 adults who had been adopted at birth because their mothers were suffering from schizophrenia were matched to 47 adoptees whose mothers were believed to be mentally healthy. This group controlled for the possibility that adoption itself might cause schizophrenia. The adults were interviewed to see whether any had developed schizophrenia themselves.

Findings: of the adults whose mothers suffered from schizophrenia, five had been hospitalized with schizo-phrenia themselves, three of whom were chronically ill. Thus 10% of the adopted children of schizophrenic mothers developed schizophrenia.

Conclusion: genes do appear to play a role in schiz-ophrenia because the percentage of schizophrenic offspring of affected mothers was as predicted, even though they had not been brought up by their biologi-cal mother. None of the control group developed schizophrenia, indicating that the experience of adop-tion was not a factor in schizophrenia. The results also suggested that the environment was not an important factor.

⊘ discussion

Since Heston's research, more sophisticated adoption studies (such as Tienari et al., 1992) have confirmed the importance of genetic factors in the development of schizo-phrenia but, unlike Heston, they have also discovered possible environmental variables that influence the probability of an individual adopted child going on to develop schizophrenia. Adoption studies have also cast light on the role of genes in individual intelligence and personality.

Twin studies, like adoption studies, have their problems. One issue concerns the *representativeness* of adopted children in relation to the population. For example, if we look at the Heston study, clearly not all mothers with schizophrenia have their children adopted. It is thus possible that there was something different about these particular mothers or their babies that led to the adoptions and also contributed to the develop-ment of schizophrenia. A further problem with some adoption studies is *selective placement*. When children are adopted they are frequently placed in a family as similar as possible to their biological family. This means that it is difficult to see whether apparent similarities to the biological family are in fact caused by the influence of the similar adoptive family.

the physiological approach

interactive
angles

Which conclusions go with the design and findings pairs?

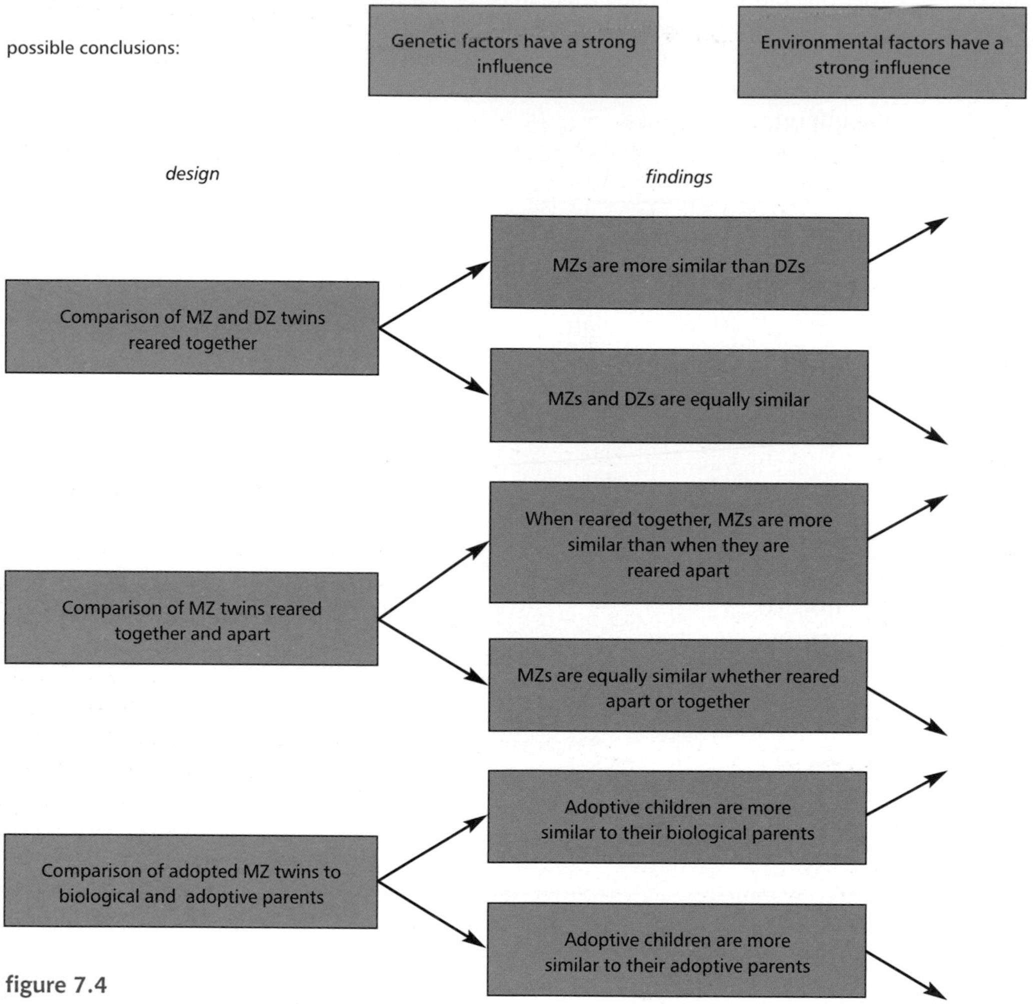

possible conclusions:

| Genetic factors have a strong influence | | Environmental factors have a strong influence |

design | findings

| Comparison of MZ and DZ twins reared together | → | MZs are more similar than DZs | → |
| | → | MZs and DZs are equally similar | → |

| Comparison of MZ twins reared together and apart | → | When reared together, MZs are more similar than when they are reared apart | → |
| | → | MZs are equally similar whether reared apart or together | → |

| Comparison of adopted MZ twins to biological and adoptive parents | → | Adoptive children are more similar to their biological parents | → |
| | → | Adoptive children are more similar to their adoptive parents | → |

figure 7.4

Look back at the section on correlational studies and add examples to the diagram.

where to now?

The following are good sources of further information regarding behavioural genetics:

▶ **Plomin, R., DeFries, J. C., McClearn, G. E. and Rutter, M.** (1997) *Behavioural Genetics*. Freeman, New York. A state-of-the art account of the field of behavioural genetics, including chapters on molecular genetics and genetic influences on intelligence and mental disorder.

▶ **Rose, S., Kamin, L. J. and Lewontin, R. C.** (1984) *Not in our Genes*. Penguin, Harmondsworth. Convincingly states the case against the over-riding importance of genes in behaviour. This is well worth reading as counterpoint to the positive attitude expressed here towards behavioural genetics.

neurophysiology

figure 7.5
MRI scan

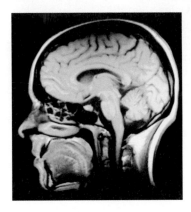

The human brain is a remarkable organ. It is composed of a huge number of interconnected nerve cells or neurones, which send electrochemical messages to each other across gaps called synapses using chemical messengers called neurotransmitters. The brain is responsible for all cognitive processes, and can cope with more information than the most advanced computers (see chapter 3 for a discussion of information processing in the brain).

A detailed discussion of the brain is not within the scope of this chapter. We will, however, look at some of the methods used to study the brain and focus in detail on two ways in which human psychology is powerfully affected by the biological functioning of the brain: bodily rhythms and sleep.

techniques for studying the brain

Single neurones can be studied using microelectrodes inserted into the brain, This, however, is an invasive technique and, as an alternative, much useful information about the brain can be gained from external measures.

electroencephalogram recording

An *electroencephalograph* is a machine that records brain waves – the patterns of electrical activity in the brain. External electrodes are used to detect the activity of groups of neurones, as the output of one cell is too small to measure externally. These recordings are taken from participants using *macroelectrodes* stuck to the scalp with conductive jelly. There may be between 2 and 164 recording electrodes and, when there are many, they are fixed inside a stretchy 'cap' that holds them in place. This is useful as it fixes the electrodes in the international standard pattern – which enables researchers worldwide to make reliable comparisons between their recordings. The wires from each electrode can be held together, forming a pony tail, to enable the participant to sleep. The electrodes are very sensitive, detecting signals of tiny fractions of volts, and a neutral electrode (usually on the earlobe) completes the electrical circuit. The signals are amplified, displayed on a screen and printed out, as an *Electro-Encephalo-Gram* (electric-in-head-writing) or EEG. They may be combined into one signal and transformed mathematically to produce a smoother trace. The recording consists of a rising and falling line from each electrode or group of electrodes, which changes in terms of frequency and amplitude.

figure 7.6
An example of an EEG reading.
Try to remember to use EEG
rather than 'brain waves'

Electroencephalograms have four wave patterns, called alpha, beta, delta and theta waves. Each pattern is characterised by a different wave frequency (how fast the

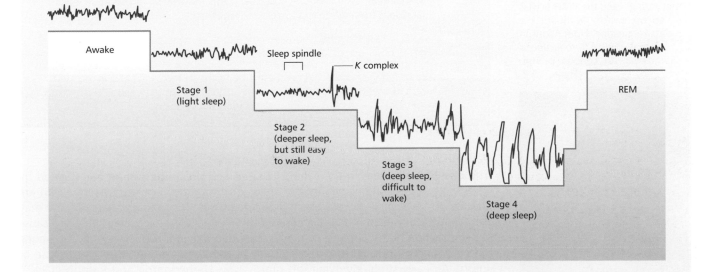

the physiological approach

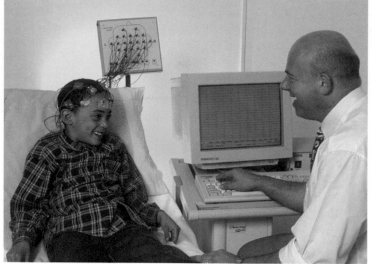

waves occur) and amplitude (how high the waves are) and is typical of a different activity. For example, small, fast *alpha waves* would be detected from waking adults with their eyes open whereas someone deeply asleep would have large, slow *delta waves*. *Theta waves* are associated with mental concentration and *beta waves* increase in response to change, such as opening the eyes. The exact 'meaning' of the different wave patterns is unknown but, because they tend to be consistent across individuals and situations they are a useful tool for investigating brain function. For example, in an experiment testing memory for words, Klimesch et al. (1997) found that theta patterns were greatest during accurate recall, and Martin (1998) showed that, in response to the smell of different foods, theta waves reduced more with chocolate than the other foods tested (including baked beans, rotting pork and coffee!).

figure 7.7
An electroencephalograph (EEG) measures the electrical current between electrodes on the scalp, which provides an indication of brain activity

electro-oculogram recording

One of the major applications of electrical techniques such as EEG has been in recording patterns of brainwaves in sleep. The Electro-OculoGram (EOG) is also used to study sleep, taking advantage of the fact that our eyeballs move when we dream. The EOG records the electrical potential across the eyeball (rather than muscular activity) which changes as the eyeballs rotate. The movements of our eyes tend to be synchronised, but it is usual to record from both eyes. The EOG is used to detect the rapid eye movement (REM) associated with dream sleep but identifies only changes in movement, not the direction. The movement of the eyeballs under the lids can be seen readily, so the direction of eye movements can be observed directly or via video.

figure 7.8
Lesioning of the lateral hypothalamus (LH) causes rats to become anorexic – they lose their appetites and do not eat enough whereas lesioning of the ventromedial hypothalamus (VMH) causes them to overeat and they become obese. These findings suggest that the LH serves as an 'on' switch for feeding – destroying it stopped the animals from eating – and the VMH acts as an 'off' switch – without it the rats kept eating. From Atkinson et al. (1990) *Introduction to Psychology*, HBJ, London, p. 368, Figure 10.2.

for+against

electrical recording techniques

+ Measuring brain activity using EEGs has allowed us to distinguish between different states of consciousness and stages of sleep, and given us reliable information on the relative levels of brain activity in these different states.

+ International standards for electrode placing and wave interpretation ensure that results from different sources are comparable.

– An EEG using scalp electrodes is a crude tool telling us only about the electrical activity of groups of neurones, rather than specific, individual ones.

– We do not yet know what precisely is being measured by an EEG in terms of brain function. Interpretation is based on correlations between EEG patterns and behaviour, so we can only infer activity in the brain.

lesioning

The role of brain areas in the control of sleep and dreaming can be investigated by observing changes in behaviour when parts of the central nervous system (CNS) are destroyed. *Lesioning* is the process of destroying tissue; for example, neural tissue may be damaged by suction, heat (cauterisation) or surgery. A *lesion* may therefore cause the destruction of a brain area or may cut through a neural tract or region, separating one brain area from another. Lesions may also occur naturally, through disease or injury. An early study involving this process was Hetherington and Ranson (1942),

lesioning

+ Lesioning can be carried out on live animals (*vivisection*) to observe their effects on the sleep/wake cycle so it can be used to investigate specific behavioural changes.

+ Lesioning enables us to identify the regions of the brain responsible for different aspects of sleep control as lesions of different brain areas will have differing effects on behaviour.

— The control of sleep in animals may not be identical to that of humans so they may not be appropriate models for understanding our physiology or behaviour.

— The sleep state is in part a subjective experience, which animals cannot report.

— Vivisection is invasive and causes suffering to the animal subjects so may not be justifiable in some investigations.

who lesioned part of the hypothalamus of a rat and observed that it ate until it had trebled its body weight.

Clearly there are good reasons why we cannot use lesioning in human participants. It causes irreparable damage! This type of study is always carried out on animals. However, sometimes lesions occur as a result of strokes or injury and neuropsychologists can study the effects of lesions in particular parts of the brain.

One case study that has baffled psychologists is that of YH, a war veteran who has a piece of shrapnel lodged in an area of his brain called the pons (Lavie, 1996). This area is known to play a role in the control of REM sleep. He typically sleeps little (4 to 5.5 hours a night) and, during investigations in a sleep laboratory, he showed no evidence of REM sleep at all on most nights. Very occasionally he experienced just a few minutes of REM, amounting to 2% to 5% of his total sleep time, compared 20% to 25% for most adults.

scanning techniques

A variety of techniques now exist that produce images of sections of the human body. Such techniques have many medical applications but they have become best known for brain scanning. There are two broad categories of brain scan, *structural* and *functional*.

figure 7.9
CAT scanner

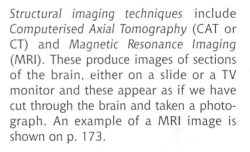

Structural imaging techniques include *Computerised Axial Tomography* (CAT or CT) and *Magnetic Resonance Imaging* (MRI). These produce images of sections of the brain, either on a slide or a TV monitor and these appear as if we have cut through the brain and taken a photograph. An example of a MRI image is shown on p. 173.

CAT and MRI work in quite different ways: CAT scans take x-ray photographs from several angles and these 'slices' are then assembled by computer into a single image; MRI scanning uses a powerful magnetic field instead of X-rays to produce a series of images that are likewise assembled by computer into one image. Magnetic resonance imaging is capable of producing much clearer images than CAT. These techniques are of some value to psychologists because they allow us to compare the structure of brains that are functioning normally and abnormally and hence help to establish whether a physical abnormality is responsible for a symptom. For example, physical damage to the brain damage resulting from a stroke or the presence of a tumour could be detected using such scans.

figure 7.10
PET scan

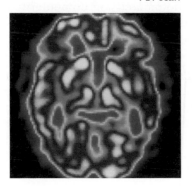

Functional imaging techniques are often more useful to psychologists because they allow us to visualise events that are actually happening in the brain. *Positron Emission Tomography* (PET) scanning involves injecting a radioactive isotope into the blood. This ceases to be radioactive quickly and so does not harm the participant. However, by measuring the radiation levels in different parts of the brain we can determine where the most blood is flowing to and hence which parts are most active. If the participant is scanned when inactive, as a baseline, and then performing a particular task, the difference between the two scans tells us which parts of the brain are involved in the activity.

This technique has enabled researchers to investigate active brain areas involved in tasks such as recognising different stimuli; for example, different brain areas are active when viewing famous faces and famous buildings (Gorno Tempini and Price, 2001). Maguire et al. (1997) investigated memory in London taxi drivers using PET scans (see also p. 175). They found that different brain areas were activated during recall of familiar routes than recall of familiar film sequences. When the taxi drivers were describing journeys from one location to another, the hippocampus, a brain area known to be involved in spatial memory, was activated.

media watch

brain scans show art and science in their true colours

Maev Kennedy, *Guardian*, 13 March 2002

An internationally renowned contemporary artist and a professor of neuropsychology peered into their own brains yesterday to see if they could identify what made them different.

Richard Wentworth, the artist, and Richard Gregory, emeritus professor of neuropsychology at Bristol University, discovered they had more in common than their first names. As boys they took carpentry classes on Saturdays; but if this was influenced by any part of their brains, neither could spot it, until yesterday.

No one had compared the brains of scientists and artists until then. Research has suggested differences in the brains of musicians and mathematicians, and one study found changes in brain function in taxi driv-

ers before and after they did the Knowledge – suggesting that sections of the brain work like muscles, and can grow.

Both men volunteered to go through a CAT scanner in a London hospital, as part of Head On, a science week opening at the Science Museum in London on Friday, which looks at the links between art, science and the brain.

'They're jolly different, aren't they?' said Professor Gregory. Mark Lythgoe, of Great Ormond Street Hospital, who did the scans, believes significant differences will be discovered between the ways the brains of scientists and artists work, but warned that no deductions were possible on a sample of the two.

questions

1 What factors other than brain structure might affect someone's decision to become an artist or scientist?

2 Why should we be cautious about basing conclusions about scientific and artistic brains on a small sample of two people?

A difficulty with PET scanning is that many tasks cannot be performed whilst in a scanner. One way around this is to use SPECT (Single Photon Emission Computerised Tomography). This also involves a radioactive isotope entering the blood but the difference is that once this type of isotope enters brain tissue it becomes trapped for some time. We can thus give someone a task in a suitable environment and scan that individual later, thus capturing activity at a single moment in time.

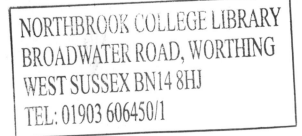

scanning techniques

➕ Scanning is a non-invasive technique so does not cause pain and can be conducted on live human participants as well as animals.

➕ Structural scans can be used to identify abnormalities in the brain, such as those resulting from a stroke or tumour, and to link particular brain abnormalities with particular psychological problems, such as language difficulties being associated with damage to the left side of the brain.

➕ Functional scans such as PET, unlike purely structural scans such as CAT, can give us some idea of how the brain functions as they allow a comparison between baseline (non-active) and active recordings. This enables researchers to identify brain regions associated with particular cognitive activities such as the role of the hippocampus in spatial tasks using human participants. Unlike animal studies using lesioning, this provides a more direct means to examine the role of different brain areas on behaviour.

➖ Most functional scans restrict the range of activities that a participant can perform whilst being scanned, thus limiting their usefulness to static activities.

➖ Currently scanning techniques are not sufficiently refined to tell us as precisely as we would like what is going on in the brain. We cannot for example track a thought through the brain.

➖ Many scanners rely on radioactivity (radioactive tracers or X-rays) so participants' exposure to the procedure needs to be limited.

where to now?

The following are good sources of further information regarding techniques for studying the brain:

▶ **Martin, G. N.** (2003) *Essential Biological Psychology*. Hodder Arnold, London. Although most of this text is beyond the needs of an A-level reader, there are interesting sections on methods and their applications to a range of areas of psychology including learning and memory.

▶ **Stirling, J.** (1999) *Cortical Functions*. Routledge. London. A clear and simple account of all the methods described here for studying the brain.

▶ **Carlson, N.** (1997) *The Physiology of Behaviour*. Allyn & Bacon, New York. An advanced undergraduate text that covers the major methods of studying the brain in great detail.

biological rhythms

We tend to get up in the morning and go to bed at night. Even when we're on holiday, we usually get up and go to bed each day. Why do we follow this pattern? Why, during the holidays, do we tend to lie in? And why, if we travel to our holiday destination by air, do we suffer sleep disruption? These are some of the questions we will try to answer in this section. Many physiological and behavioural responses of animals, including ourselves, are controlled by a regular cycle of bodily changes. These bodily rhythms may be *endogenous*, dictated by internal events or *exogenous*, controlled by external events. More commonly, control is exerted by interaction of the two factors.

Cyclical changes occurring more often than daily are described as *ultradian* rhythms (*ultra* means more, *dies* means day, so *ultradian* means more often than once per day). Our heartbeat, for instance, is an ultradian rhythm and like other functions it is affected both intrinsically, by the pacemaker, and by external factors, such as air quality. Similar rhythmicity can be seen in psychological functions, such as appetite and awareness. Cyclical changes occurring over the course of periods longer than one day are called *infradian* rhythms (*infra* means less than, and *dies* means a day, so *infradian* means less than once per day). In this chapter we are most concerned with *circadian* rhythms, those that last about one day.

circadian rhythms

Our most familiar behavioural rhythm is the sleep–wake cycle – the repetitive programme that insists that we go to sleep each night and wake up the next day. Whilst we can 'lie in', we can't keep ourselves asleep indefinitely, nor can we stay endlessly awake. Our patterned sleeping and waking runs on a circadian rhythm, one which lasts *circa dies* – about a day (hence *circadian*).

Tied to our 24-hour sleep–wake cycle is a rhythmical variation in awareness. When our body clock expects us to be asleep, our cognitive processing reaches a trough. Between 1 a.m. and 6 a.m. our sensitivity to pain, manual dexterity and reaction time bottom out, regardless of whether we are sleep deprived. So 4 a.m. might seem an ideal time to visit your dentist (because your sensitivity to pain is lower), but, given cyclical changes in dexterity, will it be safe? Some important consequences of our reduced task performance during the small hours relate to safety – on the road and in the work place. These applications are considered on p. 192. Other circadian rhythms are exhibited in behaviours such as eating and drinking, as well as our emotions such as cheerfulness, and physiological processes such as the metabolism of alcohol.

Our circadian rhythms regulate behaviours such as sleeping and waking. By affecting the activity of neurones in particular brain areas (including the hypothalamus and the suprachiasmatic nuclei) and neurotransmitters (such as acetylcholine, noradrenaline and serotonin) in a cyclical way, the daily pattern of sleeping and waking is precisely regulated. In the typical day, sleep onset coincides with the absence of daylight but even without this external cue the desire to sleep arises regularly. What happens to this cycle without exposure to daylight? Studies have been conducted with participants isolated from natural light–dark schedules in caves or in more comfortable experimental rooms (where they have exposure to light on demand, are able to request food or old newspapers at any time of day and can sleep whenever they like). One such case was reported by Folkard (1996). A university student was housed in a laboratory for 25 days with no access to cues about time of day. To indicate her perception of the passage of time, she was asked to play *Amazing Grace* on the bagpipes twice a day at what she believed was the same time on each occasion. The times she played became later over the study period. She began to sleep for longer – up to 16 hours at a time – and her sleep–wake cycle extended to 30 hours. Findings from such experiments suggest that the human biological clock maintains rhythmical activity but that the apparent day length extends (Czeisler et al., 1989).

Experimental evidence with rats confirms this shift in circadian cycle. Groblewski et al. (1980) found that rats' circadian clocks advanced an hour a day if they were isolated from daylight schedules. In such isolation experiments with humans, participants maintain 'daily' activities but, as with rats, these began to *free run*, that is, the biological clock extends the length of its cycle to a rhythm with a periodicity of about 25 to 30 hours instead of the normal 24. Daily exposure to bright light or to regular social cues such as a telephone call at the same time each day is sufficient to keep the human clock in time (Empson, 1993). Environmental factors other than light can also *entrain* (that is 'set') the clocks of animals such as hamsters. They will maintain a 24-hour sleep–wake cycle without light cues in response to regular feeding (Jilge, 1991), exercise (Mistlberger, 1991) or social interaction (Mrosovsky, 1988).

control of circadian rhythms

What controls a circadian rhythm such that it assumes a 24-hour cycle? Both internal and external factors seem to be involved. The most obvious cue to set the cycle, the *zeitgeber* (German for 'time-giver'), is day length – the sun rises and sets every 24 hours. How do we process this external cue so that it can affect our behaviour? Information about light levels is detected in the eyes and passed on to an area of the brain called the suprachiasmatic nucleus (SCN). This then connects to the pineal gland, part of the endocrine (hormonal) system, that is located beside the brain. Evidence suggests that these structures are responsible for the control of circadian rhythms.

detecting changing light levels

In humans, information about ambient light levels is detected in the retina, and passed on to retinal ganglion cells, which also contain a light-sensitive pigment (Provencio et al., 2000). These cells, when active, release a neurotransmitter (called acetylcholine) and have several effects. They activate the neurones that cause REM sleep and, in addition, a small percentage of these cells connect to the *suprachiasmatic nucleus* (a clump of cells in the hypothalamus). Although responsiveness to light is essential, rods and cones may not be. Berson et al. (2002) removed the rods and cones from rats' eyes and found that the retinal ganglion cells (RGC) deep inside the suprachiasmatic nucleus still responded to changes in light level. It is possible therefore that the RGCs, rather than the rods and cones, detect light levels and supply the SCN with information about cyclical changes in light levels.

the role of the suprachiasmatic nucleus

Rats that have been blinded lose their cyclical behaviour. They sleep for the same amount of time in total but they no longer have a clearly defined sleep phase. This confirms that visual information 'sets' the pattern but it would appear that once the cycle is established, it is self-perpetuating. Rats are nocturnal so, given an activity wheel, will run at night. This activity can be automatically recorded providing continuous data about periodic behaviour. Groblewski et al. (1980) kept rats under artificial illumination. Initially the lights were on for 12 hours during the day and the rats ran at night. When the lighting schedule was shifted so that the 12-hour light phase occurred 6 hours later in the day, the rats began to run later, stabilising their 'nocturnal' activity 6 hours later than previously. Finally, the rats were exposed to continuous light, but their patterned activity persisted. When allowed to free run in this manner, however, their clocks ran a little slow, extending their day to 25 hours instead of the customary 24.

Miles et al. (1977) reported a case study of a young man who was blind from birth and had a circadian rhythm of 24.9 hours. He experienced considerable difficulties trying to keep in step with a 24-hour schedule, even with continual use of stimulants (in the morning) and sedatives (at night). This evidence, and that of Groblewski et al., suggests that, whilst light 'sets the clock', i.e. acts as a zeitgeber, it is not essential for the maintenance of the cycle. So what internal mechanism maintains the endogenous rhythm once it is established?

the physiological approach

Lesions of the SCN in animals abolish regularity in various behaviours such as drinking and activity (Stephan and Zucker, 1972) as well as in their sleep patterns. Ralph et al. (1990) confirmed the role of the SCN in the sleep–wake cycle by transplanting the SCN between hamsters with different 'free-running' clocks. First they transplanted the SCN from foetuses of a mutant strain of hamsters with clocks that free ran at 20 hours, into the brains of normal adult hamsters whose cycles had been disrupted by lesions. Instead of reverting to their old 25-hour rhythm, the adult recipients assumed a new 20-hour 'day'. Likewise a second transplant, of SCN from adults free running at 25 hours into animals of the mutant strain, produced individuals with a new cycle of 25 hours. It would appear that the circadian rhythm is intrinsic to the SCN. Interestingly, the '20 hour' hamsters had experienced a mutation of a single gene (called *tau*), providing another example of the way in which genetics can directly affect behaviour (see p. 166).

The process by which the SCN generates its rhythm is, as yet, unclear. The assumptions that cycles result from interactions between neurones is opposed by the finding that circadian rhythms can be maintained by individual neurones. Michel et al. (1993) discovered that even isolated neurones from the eye of a marine mollusc (*Bulla gouldiana*) could display circadian changes in biochemical activity. This implies that endogenous rhythms may arise from cellular processes, rather than from neural interactions. This would be unsurprising given the endogenous rhythms demonstrated by cells within cardiac muscle that are myogenic – they generate their own rhythmic contraction.

the role of the pineal gland and melatonin release

The SCN responds to day length by sending neural messages to the *pineal gland* (Arendt, 1985). This small gland is part of the endocrine (hormonal) system but is tucked up inside the brain behind the hypothalamus and is insensitive to light. The cells of the pineal gland do, however, share characteristics with the rod-shaped photoreceptors of the retina, suggesting that its original role was as a light sensitive organ (as it is in some animals where it lies closer to the surface of the head). Darkness causes the pineal gland to secrete the hormone *melatonin*, whilst daylight inhibits its production. As day length shortens towards winter, night-time excretion of melatonin increases, thus acting as an annual as well as a circadian clock. Surprisingly, the absence of light does not prevent cycling. Even in uninterrupted light or darkness melatonin levels continue to rise and fall daily. The absence of light as a zeitgeber does, however, cause the rhythm to 'free run' (usually at a slightly longer day length). Destruction of the SCN, in contrast, does prevent cycling. Melatonin is important in regulating the sleep–wake cycle. It also plays a role in determining our mood. We shall return to the latter issue later in this chapter when we look at seasonal affective disorder.

research
now
studies in
detail

going out and lying in

Vinha, D., Cavalcante, J. A. and Andrade, M. M. M. (2002) Sleep–wake patterns of student workers and non-workers. *Biological Rhythm Research*, **33**(4), 417–426.

Aim: to investigate the effects of part-time employment on the sleep patterns of students. Adolescents often have irregular sleep patterns, sleeping late and reporting daytime sleepiness. Is this exacerbated in working students who have less time to catch up on their sleep?

Procedure: 31 students who had jobs and 48 who did not (mean age 17.4 years) were compared. They kept a sleep log over 16 days, reporting when, and for how long, they slept each day.

Findings: the non-working students reported longer nocturnal sleep and longer sleep time in total (during the day and night combined). Working students went to sleep and rose earlier but both groups exhibited delayed sleep onset and waking times at the weekend. The working students used the weekend to catch up on their sleep whereas non-working students did so on Mondays and Tuesdays.

Conclusion: the social life of students influences their weekend sleep times and, where they have work commitments, this can further affect sleep schedules. In either situation total sleep time is extended when possible by sleeping earlier or delaying wake up time.

⊘ discussion

The control of our circadian rhythm is clearly complex and new processes are still being identified. It is controlled both by external (exogenous) factors such as light and endogenous (internal) factors. Detection of light may, at a cellular level, involve more than one system (the rods and cones and the retinal ganglion cells) and two or more structures may act as 'pacemakers', being capable of maintaining the rhythm (the suprachiasmatic nucleus and the pineal gland). There are likely to be other clock sites, for example daily fluctuations in body temperature (that are normally synchronised with the sleep–wake cycle) may be controlled by a separate mechanism, as destruction of the SCN does not entirely eradicate this rhythm (Thompson, 2000). Although the most important *zeitgeber* is light, many other rhythmic stimuli may act to entrain the biological clock, a factor that may be of use in assisting people whose daily lives are not diurnal, such as those working shifts.

media watch

Any ideas to help me get to sleep at night? Look out for Slumber Bedtime Milk, a new organic milk that contains higher levels of melatonin, a substance that regulates your body clock and helps you sleep. The increase is achieved naturally by milking the cows at night when the melatonin in their system is at its peak.

figure 7.11 What physiological explanation would you give to account for the proposed effectiveness of Slumber milk?

sleep and dreaming

Sleep can be defined as a necessary state of altered consciousness experienced by animals with a central nervous system. It is characterised by rhythmical occurrence, limited sensitivity and reduced mobility. By its very nature, sleep is therefore difficult to study. How can we find out about a state that is distinguished by a lack of awareness of and interaction with our surroundings? After centuries of guesswork, psychologists can now use increasingly powerful techniques to investigate some of the biological aspects of sleep.

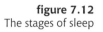
the physiological approach

rhythms in sleep

A night's sleep is a well-orchestrated sequence of psychological and physical changes. In general, we sleep once during each 24-hour period, a circadian rhythm. This is not, however, a single homogenous phase. Our sleep is broken into shorter, repeated rhythms during the night, called ultradian rhythms. This patterned activity has been traced using the methods previously described (see p. 173).

Asterinsky and Kleitman (1953) recorded the EEGs of sleeping participants and found that they sometimes consisted of *alpha* waves, resembling wakefulness. During these times the

figure 7.12
The stages of sleep

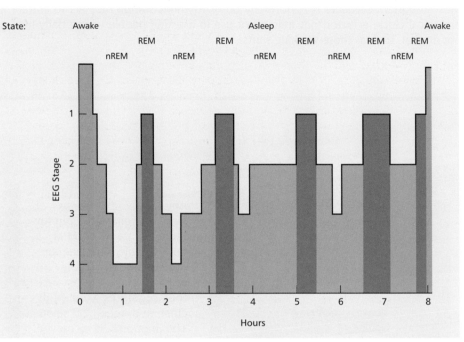

EOG was active, as it is when we are awake. Participants in this condition were hard to awaken but when roused they tended to report dreams. This 'paradoxical' stage, which shares characteristics both with very deep sleep and with wakefulness, was identified as a separate stage of sleep by Dement and Kleitman (1957). It has been variously described as *paradoxical sleep*, *dream sleep* or *REM sleep*, after the characteristic *Rapid Eye Movements* (40–60 movements per minute) which occur throughout the stage. Rapid eye movement sleep is also identifiable by the loss of muscle tone, measured with an electromyography (EMG). So while the EOG is active during REM sleep the EMG is inactive; our bodies are effectively paralysed.

Most of the night is spent in 'orthodox' or non-REM (nREM) sleep. Even this, however, is not a homogeneous phase, but consists of four stages:

◆ *Stage 1*: light sleep, where the sleeper is easily roused, has a slow heart rate and an irregular EEG, with little alpha activity.

◆ *Stage 2*: deeper sleep, where the sleeper is still fairly easy to wake. The EEG is interrupted by occasional *spindles* (high frequency low amplitude waves) and *K complexes* (occasional high amplitude waves).

◆ *Stage 3*: deep sleep, where the sleeper is unresponsive, has a slow pulse, low blood pressure and a lowered body temperature. The EEG contains some slow waves (low frequency delta waves).

◆ *Stage 4*: deep sleep, where the EEG consists mainly of high amplitude, low frequency *delta waves*.

Figure 7.12, which shows the stages of sleep, illustrates how we move from relaxed wakefulness into sleep and then through deeper sleep stages before returning through shallower nREM to reach our first REM phase. We then alternate between REM and nREM during the night. Several patterns can be seen in recordings from sleeping participants:

◆ the deepest sleep occurs early in the night;

◆ REM phases increase in length during the night;

◆ natural waking tends to occur during REM;

◆ each 'cycle' from stage 1 back to stage 1 or REM takes about 90 minutes (an ultradian rhythm).

the nature of dream sleep

Paradoxical sleep is readily identifiable by changes in the EEG (to alpha waves) and the EOG (REMs), paralysis and a number of other changes. During REM sleep our pulse, respiration and blood pressure become irregular and we are more likely to grind our teeth! The most psychologically interesting aspect of this stage of sleep, however, is our experience of dreams. Everyone has dreams, but we only recall them if we happen to wake up, even briefly, during REM. People who 'don't dream' simply always wake up in nREM and may have poor visual memories (Cory et al., 1975). On average, sleepers recall just over one dream a night, but this can vary between one every six months and three a night (Koulack and Goodenough, 1976).

To study dream content, participants may either be asked to keep a dream diary or to sleep overnight in a sleep laboratory. Here, a room within a psychology department is fitted with a bed and equipment to monitor the sleeping participant. They may be videoed or watched and may be interrupted during the night to test responses to stimuli and to answer questions. Dement (1978) woke participants when they were either in REM or in nREM sleep. Those in REM reported dreams on 80% of occasions, those in nREM, on only 15% of the wakings. Dream reports from participants woken during nREM sleep were less visual and vivid and were described as 'thinking' rather than as active 'dreams'. The differences described between REM and nREM dreams are believed by Beaumont (1988) to be due to the additional time it takes people to awaken from nREM sleep. When participants are slower to wake up they may forget more dream details.

An interesting question concerns why we remember so little about our dreams. Freud (1900), as we will see later, believed that we actively forget our dreams in order to protect ourselves from their content; this is the *repression hypothesis*. However, Reinsel et al. (1984) suggest that we actually recall emotional dreams better because they make more impact upon us. This enhanced memory for emotional dreams is called the *salience hypothesis*, suggesting that we forget dreams with unemotional content. Alternatively, we may fail to recall dreams because events that occur as we wake up provide a source of interference. This *interference hypothesis* is supported by the observation that sudden awakening produces better dream recall than gradual awakening.

interactive
angles

Ask someone to shut his or her eyes and pretend to be an umpire watching a tennis match. You should be able to see the person's eyes moving from side to side. In a classic study Dement and Kleitman (1957) observed sleeping participants' REMs and woke them to ask about their dream content.

classic research studies in detail

do eye movements tell us about dream content?

Dement, W. and Kleitman, N. (1957) The relation of eye movements during sleep to dream activity: an objective method for the study of dreaming. *Journal of Experimental Psychology*, **53**(5), 339–346.

Aim: to investigate the relationship of dream content and REMs and to establish whether dreams take place in real time, or whether they are condensed into a shorter period, as is popularly thought.

Procedure: participants arrived at the sleep laboratory shortly before their bedtime, having avoided consuming alcohol or coffee (as these reduce REM sleep). Each participant then went to bed in a dark, quiet room with an EEG and EOG running throughout the night. Intermittently, the participant was awakened by a bell, from both REM and nREM sleep (without being told which) and described their most recent dream then returned to sleep. To determine the correspondence between REMs and dream content, participants were woken following distinctive eye movements.

Findings: many more dreams were reported when participants were woken from REM sleep than nREM

sleep and the length of REM periods correlated with the length of the participants' dreams reports. Participants were also fairly accurate in estimating the length of their dreams. Distinctive eye movements were associated with dream content, for example one participant had a minute of very little eye movement followed by several large movements to the left. Their dream was of driving down the street and being crashed into by a car coming from the left. Another had been seen to have only vertical movements and their dream was of climbing up and down ladders.

Conclusion: the results showed that dreams are much more frequent and vivid in REM sleep than in nREM sleep. In addition, people dream in real-time (because their time-estimates were accurate) and REMs are closely related to dream content.

the physiological approach

Oswald (1980) compared the dreams and REMs of six men, three of whom had been blind from birth and three of whom had been blind for 3, 10 and 15 years respectively. The previously sighted participants all 'saw' things in their dreams and had REMs. Those blind from birth had non-visual dreams but did have very slight REMs. This could suggest that REM is not related to dream content, because there could be no match to visual content.

⊘ discussion

The nature of sleep is difficult to study precisely because of the participants' lowered level of consciousness. Perhaps unsurprisingly therefore, much evidence about the sleep experience is contradictory. Dreams occur predominantly in REM sleep, but can be reported by nREM sleepers; some evidence suggests that eye movements are related to dream content, other evidence suggests not. Our bodies are paralysed during REM sleep but our eye muscles are not, furthermore, many people (and animals – try watching for movement in a dog during REM sleep) experience arm and leg twitching during dreaming. Any effective explanation of sleep needs to account for these apparent contradictions.

theories of the function of sleep

Empson (1993) suggests that a sleepless alien would (quite reasonably) conclude from the household space, furniture, rituals and time we devote to sleep, that for earthlings this particular form of inactivity was a central preoccupation! Natural selection would only result in the evolution of a behaviour carrying the costs associated with sleeping if these were outweighed by its benefits. The costs associated with sleeping are considerable: we spend time asleep when we could be eating or reproducing and, because of our lowered level of sensitivity, we are at greater risk from the weather, competitors or predators. So what are the potential benefits which have made sleeping an evolutionarily worthwhile investment?

ecological theory

Meddis (1977) argued that sleep is an instinctive behaviour that has evolved to keep animals 'out of trouble'. For humans, being out in the dark is dangerous, so we sleep at night. Cats and owls, on the other hand, have better night vision than us and can gain an advantage over their prey in the cover of darkness. They sleep during the day when their chances of successful hunting are lower. It is beneficial for small desert mammals to avoid the intense heat so they sleep during the day. In each case sleep occurs when the animal is least effective. Empson (1993) has described this as the 'waste of time' theory; animals are simply biding their time until the environment is more suitable – in other words, the function of sleep is to 'waste time'!

figure 7.13
Small mammals are at risk from predators during the daytime so tend to sleep during daylight and be active at night. In the daytime, sleeping keeps them quiet and safe from predators and still so that they use little energy

The absence of motor activity during sleep can be accounted for by the ecological theory. Whilst 'keeping still' could explain the advantage of saving energy, being utterly inactive is even better: a motionless animal is less likely to attract the attention of predators. This can be extended to explain the reduction in sensitivity. For animals that rely on camouflage or concealment for protection, keeping completely motionless even when a predator is very near will lower the chances of detection. Being asleep ensures that the animal won't respond and blow its cover. It could even be argued that the reduction in brain activity ensures that the hiding animal is not motivated to seek out sources of stimulation.

If we wish to explain the existence of sleep through evolutionary adaptation, we need to be able to demonstrate that it has a long and common evolutionary history. Reptiles, believed to be the ancestors of modern birds and mammals, show various sleep characteristics. Lizards display unequivocal signs of nREM and REM sleep, with loss of muscle tone and rapid eye movements (Tauber et al., 1968), whereas in other reptiles REM sleep alone is seen. This observation may help to explain

ecological theory

+ Ecological theory can explain why different species sleep at different times of day because they stay awake at times for which they are better adapted, for example to hunt or avoid being hunted (such as owls and mice).

+ Ecological theory can account for the reduction of movement and sensitivity during sleep, since it views sleep as serving to keep animals still and quiet, thus reducing the risk of predation.

– Ecological theory cannot account for the absolute necessity to sleep, even when this is apparently maladaptive. The porpoise, for instance, sleeps with each brain hemisphere alternately (Mukhametov et al., 1977) suggesting that sleep has some purpose beyond keeping the animal out of trouble.

+ Ecological theory can explain the reduction in cognitive activity during sleep; a thinking animal would be more likely to respond to stimuli and put itself at risk.

– Ecological theory cannot explain other observations about sleep such as the cyclical nature of sleep or the existence and content of dreams.

the appearance of REM sleep before nREM sleep in the human foetus. In embryological development, characteristics generally appear in phylogenetic (ancestral) sequence. Birds and mammals, which maintain a warm body temperature, have very similar nREM and REM sleep (Empson, 1993).

restorational theory

figure 7.14
Athletes tend to sleep for longer following vigorous exercise

Restorational theory, proposed by Oswald (1969), suggests that we need to sleep in order to conduct growth and repair functions. The processes of restoration and activity are mutually exclusive; we cannot 'recharge our batteries' whilst we are still running off them. Oswald (1980) reports that high levels of ATP, the energy currency of the cell, are only found during sleep because during wakefulness we are constantly using up the ATP. This is especially so for the brain; it represents only 5% of our body weight but uses 20% of our energy. This suggests that a special state of enforced quiescence may be needed to allow brain cells to recuperate from daytime activity. Inactivity and insensitivity during sleep reduce the energy demands of the brain making ATP available for restoration. The same cannot be achieved simply by resting; the energy cost of sleeping is only about two-thirds of that at rest.

Bodily inactivity during REM sleep may be important for restoration of muscles. Adam (1977) and Shapiro et al. (1986) found a positive correlation between the weight of participants and the time they spent in REM sleep; heavier people spent longer in REM sleep. This is perhaps because heavier participants would expend more energy maintaining posture and moving during the day, so would need more time to restore their muscles at night. Zepelin and Rechtschaffen (1974) found a similar relationship between the activity levels of different animal species and the time they spent asleep.

sleep deprivation and restoration

One way to test the restorational function of sleep directly is to deprive people of sleep and observe the effects. Systematic sleep deprivation experiments suggest that humans begin to suffer after relatively short periods of sleep deprivation. Dement (1960) deprived young volunteers of REM or nREM sleep on five successive nights. The REM sleep-deprived participants became irritable, nervous, unable to concentrate and some reported hallucinations. When allowed uninterrupted sleep these individuals fell straight into REM sleep and spent up to 60% more time in REM sleep; this is called a

figure 7.15

The apparatus used by Rechtschaffen et al. (1983) to deprive one rat, but not its 'yolked' partner, of sleep. Whenever the deprived rat began to fall asleep, it was prevented from doing so by rotating the platform, keeping it awake (by making it walk to avoid falling in the water) for at least 6 seconds. In between these times the non-deprived animal could take undisturbed sleep

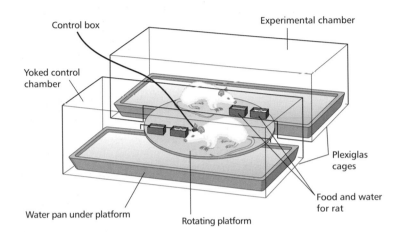

Control box

Experimental chamber

Yoked control chamber

Plexiglas cages

Food and water for rat

Water pan under platform

Rotating platform

REM rebound effect. Similar effects have been reported during total sleep deprivation such as experienced by Peter Tripp, a disc jockey who kept himself awake for 200 hours during a charity broadcast. Luce and Segal (1966) describe the decline in his cognitive ability and emotional stability, including his experiences of hallucinations and extreme paranoia. His extreme responses have, however, been attributed to his drug misuse.

Robert McDonald found his way into *The Guinness Book of Records* for the 'longest time without sleep' by staying awake for over 453 hours in a rocking chair marathon in 1988. He could, however, have slept momentarily without being noticed. A previous holder, 17-year-old Randy Gardener, was closely observed by Gulevich et al. (1966). He showed none of the problems exhibited by other sleep-deprived participants other than sleepiness and he successfully beat William Dement at 100 straight games on a baseball machine on his first sleepless night! Following his 264-hour sleep deprivation, he slept for 15 hours and awoke feeling quite normal.

Dement (1965) concluded that the severe effects of sleep deprivation reported in early research resulted from *experimenter effects*; the participants were expected to suffer bizarre sensations and these were duly reported. When warned of potential side effects and offered a round-the-clock psychiatrist, to whom unusual sensations could be reported, demand characteristics alone could have accounted for the hallucinations and paranoia experienced. More recent research suggests that even prolonged sleep deprivation, whilst reducing efficiency and concentration, has no more serious effects than to make the participants sleepy (Webb and Cartright, 1978).

media watch

how sleep can save your life

Anthony Browne, *Observer*, 29 October 2000

Ten million Britons are not getting enough time in bed, sleeping. They run the risks of strokes, obesity, depression and even cancer.

Did you get an extra hour's sleep last night after the clocks went back? As the nights draw in, will you try to curl up in bed a bit earlier? If so you might gain more than being more alert at work. You could save your life.

The link between regularly sleeping too little and mental disorders is well established. More recent studies, however, show that poor sleeping habits may also lead to colds, depression, obesity, diabetes, strokes, heart disease and cancer.

'One of the greatest public health challenges is sleep. Good sleep is a very important component of a healthy lifestyle,' said Professor Colin Espie, head of the Department of Psychological Medicine at the University of Glasgow. 'It's of the same magnitude as nutritional problems. It's a huge issue that hasn't been recognised.'

It used to be believed that the effects [of sleep deprivation] are just short-term; get a good night's sleep and you're back to normal. But there is mounting evidence that the effects of sleep deprivation build up over time and can seriously damage your health.

questions

1 What implications do the opinions expressed in this article have for restorational theory?

2 Does all the evidence support this conclusion?

restorational theory

+ Growth hormone is released at night but only if we enter deep sleep. It increases the level of protein synthesis and cell division. For children with stunted growth, growth hormone is more effective if injected at night rather than in the morning.

+ Restorational theory accounts for the cyclical nature of sleep as we cannot keep going without regular opportunities for growth and repair.

+ Athletes spend more time in deep sleep following intensive exercise suggesting that sleep is required for them to redress the balance of energy used whilst exercising.

+ Drug overdoses, withdrawal, brain damage or intensive ECT increase the time in REM sleep during which damaged brain tissue could be repaired.

— Restorational theory cannot account for our preference for sleeping at night as replacement or repair that happens during sleep could be conducted as effectively if we slept during the day.

— Restorational theory cannot explain the presence or content of dreams during sleep; in fact, such apparently 'unnecessary' use of energy is in direct competition with the efforts of restoration.

Sleep deprivation in animals can be maintained for much longer periods and the physical effects are much more severe. Early experiments were hindered by the confounding variable of forced exercise; it is necessary to keep the animal moving in order to keep it awake. Rechtschaffen et al. (1983) overcame this difficulty by designing a piece of apparatus in which pairs of animals could be housed and would experience identical exercise demands. One of the animals would be sleep deprived, the other not, so providing a well-matched control. The sleep deprived animals became very sick and some had to be put down.

Some recent research has revived the interest in the negative effects of sleep deprivation. Maquet et al. (1997) studied the blood flow to different regions of the brain during sleep (using PET) as an indicator of which areas were most active. They found that the areas which were least active were the orbitofrontal cortex and the cingulate cortex, two regions involved in emotional behaviour, thus implying there may be some physiological basis for the effects of sleep deprivation on emotional stability. Studying the emotional responses of participants in experimental settings is, however, confounded by the novelty of the setting. This study can be criticised further because of its exclusive use of male participants.

theories of dreaming

'To sleep, perchance to dream', wrote Shakespeare. Perhaps the role of sleep is to allow dreams, to provide a theatre for the mind. Certainly evidence from deprivation experiments suggest that REM sleep is essential. Participants deprived of sleep show a REM rebound. In chapter 5 we looked at Freud's psychological theory of dreaming (see p. 138). In this chapter we are concerned with physiological explanations.

reorganisational theory: the reverse learning mechanism

Reorganisational theories offer to the brain what restorational theories offer to the body – a chance to recuperate from the past day's activities and to prepare for the next. Crick and Mitchison (1983) proposed a neurobiological theory of reorganisation.

They suggested that dreams are the result of the random firing of neural networks (groups of neurones connected by synapses) which hold memories. These memories can be elicited by activating any part of the network (rather in the way that a spider can detect prey caught on any part of its web). This is because information is *distributed* (spread over many synapses) and *superimposed* (one synapse may be involved in many items of information). The random activation serves to *debug* the networks, removing unwanted connections that arise as a result of growth or experience. 'Nonsense' in a network could obscure or interfere with essential information so removing waste would increase the clarity of remaining memories. Specifically, Crick and Mitchison propose three detrimental effects that could arise if networks were allowed to continue to expand and become overloaded with too many simultaneous or overlapping memories. These are:

◆ *fantasies*: far-fetched or bizarre associations could arise;

◆ *obsession*: the same or a small number of states could arise whatever the input;

◆ *hallucination*: some networks may respond to inappropriate signals that would not normally generate a response.

The process of unlearning by the networks is described as *reverse learning*; storage of important information is enhanced by the removal of 'cognitive debris'. This is particularly important when neural nets become overloaded because concepts that share a single feature are likely to become conflated – linked together by mistake. Debugging weakens such 'parasitic associations'. In order to achieve this, Crick and Mitchison observe that the memory system would need to be isolated from inputs and outputs and given successive random activations from an internal source to determine and damp down the 'parasitic' connections.

The purpose of Crick and Mitchison's debugging is to increase efficiency of brain function so it would be expected that failure to debug would impair learning. This prediction is supported by studies of sleep, and particularly REM, deprivation. Rideout (1979) tested the maze-learning ability of sleep-deprived mice. Three deprivation conditions (total sleep, REM or nREM deprivation) were compared to non-sleep-deprived mice. Mice deprived of REM sleep, either selectively or by total sleep deprivation, were equally bad at maze learning when compared with nREM or non-deprived animals. Conversely, Horne and Minard (1985) found that, for humans experiencing mentally stimulating days, the following night's sleep contained more slow-wave (stage 4) sleep than usual.

Smith (1995, 1996) has conducted a series of experiments with rats and human participants investigating the effects of learning on REM sleep requirements. Rats that learned to respond to a light and avoid an electric shock spent more time than usual in REM sleep. If they were deprived of REM sleep for 4 hours immediately after training, they only remembered the response half as well as those that slept normally. If the sleep deprivation was delayed for more than 20 hours after training, the rats showed no reduction in learning. They seemed to need the REM sleep to consolidate their memories. The reverse learning theory would predict that extreme REM deprivation in people would result in hallucinations. However, as we have seen (p. 186), such effects do not seem to arise in well-controlled studies. Crick and Mitchison argued that such findings occur simply because we have, so far, failed to deprive people of sufficient sleep to demonstrate the effect.

In research with students, Smith found that in the week after revising for examinations, requirement for REM sleep increased. In tests on REM sleep deprivation, memory for cognitive-procedural tasks was particularly affected. For instance learning of logical puzzles, where symbols had to be manipulated according to arbitrary rules, was impaired by REM deprivation but memorising of paired lists of words was not.

A real-life investigation into the effects of sleep deprivation on learning is afforded by observations of junior doctors expected to work long hospital shifts without sleep. In casualty, doctors are required to listen to patients (who may be incoherent), extract medically relevant facts and memorise them in order to make accurate diagnoses.

Deary and Tait (1987) studied medical house doctors who obtained an average of 1.5 hours sleep per night whilst on emergency admissions. When tested on memory tasks designed to measure the skills required for effective work, doctors on duty performed significantly worse than those off duty.

Experimental investigation with human participants also suggests that REM sleep is essential for learning. Herman and Roffwarg (1983) generated a novel task by asking participants to wear inverting goggles (which cause the world to appear upside down). Following this experience, the participants spent more time than usual in REM sleep. Tilley and Empson (1978) asked participants to memorise a ghost story before going to sleep. By detecting each participant's sleep stage with an EEG and waking them up when they entered the chosen stage, some participants were deprived of REM sleep and others of stage 4 sleep. The participants deprived of REM sleep had far poorer recall for the story in the morning.

for+against

reorganisational theory

+ Studies have confirmed that cognitive functioning is impaired when people are deprived of REM sleep suggesting that REM sleep does play a role in preserving memories.

+ Studies have also supported the need for extra REM sleep following learning or novel experiences, deprivation and stress. This could be explained if dreaming was important following problem solving to remove or organise extra cognitive debris.

+ The random nature of the debugging process could account for both the existence of cognitive activity during REM sleep, as memories are being reorganised, and the bizarre nature of dreams, as the activation of networks for debugging is random.

– Crick and Mitchison's theory does not explain why dreams are such an intense subjective experience or why they hold more personal meaning for dreamers than simple recollection.

– Crick and Mitchison explained recurrent dreams as those that tend to awaken the dreamer causing them to recall the content and switch from reverse learning to enhancing the network, so reinforcing the memory for the dream content. Although this could explain how recurrent dreams arise and why we recall them, it is speculative and very difficult to test.

– Reorganisational theory would suggest that recalling one's dreams was unwise as it could reinstate unwanted connections that had been selectively destroyed. This practice is, however, important in some therapies which are beneficial, such as psychoanalysis (see p. 161).

activation-synthesis model

This model attempts to explain the physiological events that cause dreaming to occur and the psychological processes that account for our subjective experience of dreams. Hobson and McCarley (1977) suggested that dreams arise through a process of 'auto-activation' of the brain – that is, instead of brain activity being initiated by external stimuli, it is, in this case, the result of an internal trigger. Their physiological studies had demonstrated that this basic biological step began when giant nerve cells in the pontine reticular formation (PRF, part of the brain stem) became active. These cells produced rapid volleys of activity that precede dreaming and rapid eye movements. This biological process is the activation part of the model and accounts for the physical, brain events of dreaming – that is, how it occurs.

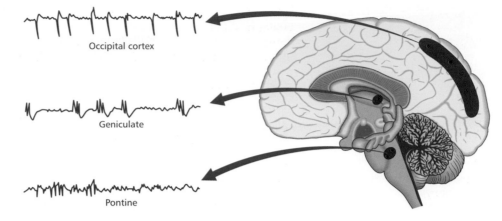

figure 7.16
Brain structures

Hobson and McCarley's theory also accounts for our subjective experience of dreaming – that is our attempts to make sense of the resultant activation. This process, called *synthesis*, occurs in the forebrain, especially in the areas associated with memory. According to Hobson (1988), these processes account for why dreams are coherent yet strange. Auto-activation can lead to unrelated images or sensations of movement being initiated, hence dreams are strange. Our tendency to organise any subjective experience (such as watching a film) into a narrative-scenario results in a 'best-fit' of the activated information into a coherent sequence.

This is possible because the brain is:

◆ *activated* (by the giant cells of the PRF) and this activation spreads through the *Pontine Geniculate Occipital* (PGO) waves, that is, from the PRF to the lateral geniculate nucleus, to the occipital or 'visual' area of the cortex;

◆ *isolated* by a sensory-input blockade resulting from both the *inhibition* of sensory circuits in the brain and *occlusion*, that is, the brain circuits associated with sensory stimuli are so busy processing auto-activated information that any incoming sensory data are either ignored or incorporated into the ongoing dream scenario as if they were internally generated;

◆ *movement-inhibited* by a motor-output blockade. This is essential to stop enactment of the dream scenario and is achieved by inhibiting the motor command neurones of the spinal cord and brain stem.

figure 7.17
A schematic representation of the brain processes underlying dreaming, based on Hobson (1988)

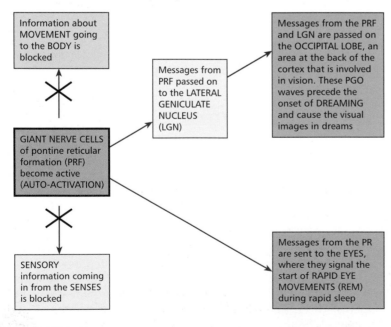

During synthesis, the brain interprets the internally generated signals as if they had originated externally, resulting in the dream scenario. Thus auto-activation of:

◆ *movement* areas would result in us dreaming about being physically active (although we would be prevented from acting this out by the motor blockade);

◆ *visual* areas would cause us to experience visual images in our dreams;

◆ *auditory* areas would lead to dreams containing sounds.

Each of these sources of internally generated information would be randomly activated from existing memories, hence dream content is often familiar and, indeed, may relate to recent or even anticipated events – as we could recall having *imagined* what might happen in the

interactive angles

If you recall your dreams (and remember, not everyone does) try to record what you can about your dreams as soon as you awaken. When you are fully awake, try to identify what kinds of memories (visual, auditory or motor) have contributed to the dream and whether you can recall the source of the original memories that were activated – are they recent or from a long time ago?

future. Dream content might appear unfamiliar either because the memories are not recent or because the process of synthesis has assembled a random collection of activated memories in an unfamiliar way and organised them into a story-like sequence. This accounts for the bizarre but apparently plausible content of dreams.

discussion

As both our relationship to the external world and our self-awareness are suspended during dreaming, the brain lacks cues to commit the 'experience' to memory, hence, unless we awaken and trigger such processes, dream content will be forgotten. The activation-synthesis model can therefore account for the physiological causation of dreaming, the subjective experience and content of dreams and our failure to recall them on waking.

Finally, although the activation-synthesis model does not suggest that dreaming has a particular function (in the way that, say, Freudian theory does – see p. 138), such a process could be beneficial. Hobson (1988) observes that it is highly implausible that evolution would allow so much wasted time and potential risk to accrue if sleep were not functional. He suggests that sleep and dreaming have many purposes (such as those of restoration and reorganisation addressed above). He also tentatively suggests that REM sleep may serve as:

◆ an 'active maintenance program' for the brain that tests circuits and activates little-used systems to ensure they don't decay through disuse – a system rather like the cleaning routine printers chug through when they haven't been used for a while;

◆ a way to practise the behavioural repertoire without risk;

◆ a creative mechanism that allows the brain to fabricate novel ideas and solutions and to test them in imaginary scenarios and by so doing may provide entertainment and better self-understanding.

These functions are, however, purely speculative.

for+against

the activation-synthesis model

+ Physiological evidence supports the idea of auto-activation, the role of the giant cells of the pontine reticular formation and the spread of PGO waves that ultimately trigger both cortical stimulation and eye movements.

+ Physiological evidence also supports inhibition of sensory and motor systems.

− More recent evidence suggests that there are many more brain areas and processes involved than originally envisaged by Hobson and McCarley.

+ Activation synthesis accounts for the bizarre yet sometimes familiar and story-like nature of dreams and for the appearance of sights, sounds and movements in dreams.

− However, if auto-activation were truly random, dreams about recent events would not be so common, nor should the same dreams reoccur.

+ Activation-synthesis can account for the lack of dreams about smells and tastes, as these areas of the brain are not stimulated during auto-activation.

+ Activation-synthesis can account for our failure to recall dreams, as the systems that form memories are deactivated.

+ New ideas for possible functions of sleep and dreams have arisen from the activation-synthesis model, providing further hypotheses for research.

where to
now ?

The following are good sources of further information about bodily rhythms, sleep and dreams:

▶ **Bentley, E.** (1999) *Awareness*. Routledge, London. A clear and comprehensible introductory text, covering all the above areas in detail.

▶ **Lavie, P.** (1996) *The Enchanted World of Sleep*. Yale University Press, New Haven. This book explores many interesting aspects of sleep in a readable way. Unusually for such an accessible text it is also well referenced.

▶ **Hobson, J. A.** (1988) *The Dreaming Brain*. Penguin, London. This small book provides a detailed account of the evolution of the activation-synthesis model and the physiological research that led to its development.

real lives
key application

the effects of shift work and jet lag

shift work

When we are working 'out of phase' with our biological clocks our performance is reduced, we are less attentive and are slower to respond regardless of whether we have slept (Mitler, 1988). Moore-Ede (1993) reports that prior to the ill-fated decision to fly the *Challenger*, NASA officials had been awake for 20 hours after only 2 or 3 hours' sleep the night before. Fatigue is a possible contributory factor in many disasters; consider those listed in Table 7.3, and the time of day when they occurred.

Lorry drivers, like doctors, the police and many employees, have to work shifts. Two independent problems arise with shift work, the need to maintain a 24-hour cycle which is out-of-sync with the world and the demands of changing shift pattern. People working shifts are often deprived of sleep simply because it is difficult to sleep well when it is light and noisy outside. The social constraints of being awake when nobody else is may tempt night shift workers to get up early or stay up late for company or facilities, depriving themselves of sleep. For example, Seo et al. (2000) found that older workers on night shifts, but not other shifts, had reduced total sleep times as they woke up early. To solve the problem of being woken up by daylight, shift workers

place	disaster	time disaster occurred
Bhopal	chemical plant explosion	12.40 a.m.
Chernobyl	nuclear reactor disaster	1.23 a.m.
Three mile island	nuclear reactor disaster	4.00 a.m.
Mexico City	Western airlines crash	3.30 a.m.

table 7.3 Some examples of disasters caused by human error by shiftworkers

figure 7.18 Assembly line production often runs 24 hours a day so employees work shifts. When they change shift, their body clocks are affected

are recommended to use thick curtains or blackout blinds. These also help to solve the second problem of circadian disruption.

In order to work shifts, people have to reset their biological clocks, so that they are awake during the late evening and/or early morning and sleep during the day. Unless workers succeed in resetting their biological clocks, they experience sleepiness at work and insomnia when they go home. This is particularly severe if shifts change often, or if they move 'against' the body clock. After a shift change people take a week or more to adapt to the new regime, during which time they are less effective at work as they are operating during their body's 'night' and restless when they should be sleeping.

Many workers on night shift are performing passive tasks such as monitoring and are often provided with warm, dimly lit environments. According to Czeisler et al. (1990) this is counterproductive with regard to keeping them alert. They compared the rate of adaptation of two groups of participants to an imposed 'shift change' by asking them to report to the laboratory during the night and sleep at home during the day. The control group worked during the night in ordinary indoor lighting of about 150 lux. The experimental group worked under bright illumination of 7000–12 000 lux, equivalent to early morning light. Members of the experimental group were asked to stay in complete darkness from 9 a.m. to 5 p.m., whilst the controls were given no specific instructions. The resetting of the participants' biological clocks was monitored by measuring body temperature, which varies rhythmically. After six days the experimental group had all shifted the low point of the circadian temperature rhythm by 10 hours, while the controls had moved by only one hour. A similar pattern was observed in task performance. Bright lighting in the work environment seems to be vital for ensuring that workers adapt to new shifts so that they sleep well during the day and are alert during the night. Even in this situation adaptation can take up to 4 days, so people who change shift every week would spend most of their time desynchronised from their environment.

Recent research has investigated the role that melatonin can play in helping shift workers to adjust to a new rhythm. Sharkey et al. (2001) found that orally administered melatonin could help shift workers to sleep during the afternoon (as they have to when shifts change), but only on the first day of use. It did not reduce alertness or performance during the subsequent simulated 'night shift'. Sharkey and Eastman (2002) went on to investigate whether melatonin, compared to a placebo, would help shift workers to adjust their circadian rhythm. The change in circadian rhythm (indicated by the body temperature cycle and the natural release of melatonin) was greater in participants taking oral melatonin than in those taking placebos, and this effect was greater at a dose of 3 mg than at 0.5 mg. Again, this suggests that melatonin can be used to move the phase of the circadian rhythm.

the physiological approach

jet lag

Air travel has introduced another problem for our internal clocks resulting in fatigue, gastrointestinal complaints and shortened attention span which cannot be explained by sleep loss alone. When we cross time zones we have to reset our biological clock to the local zeitgeber – sunrise and sunset. As with shift changes that extend the day, travelling east to west produces fewer problems, as we 'gain' time. The return journey however presents problems. Pilots can be severely affected by changing time zones repeatedly, due to frequent and erratic exposure to the bright light of sunrise. This causes them to sleep poorly when they can rest, resulting in tiredness when flying.

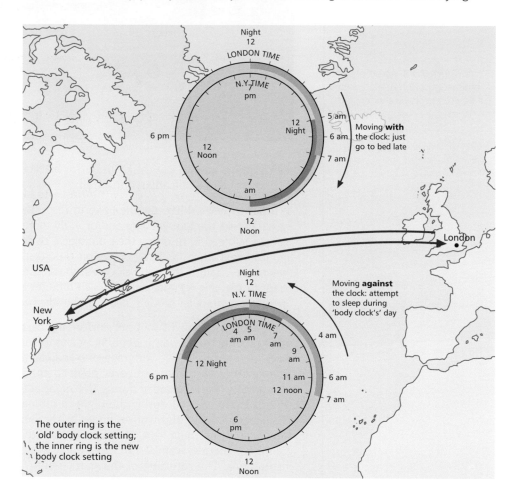

figure 7.19
Body clock settings

Harma et al. (1994a,b) and Suvanto et al. (1993) examined the effects of a 4-day flight, which crossed 10 time zones, on the sleep, attentiveness, body temperature and salivary melatonin levels of flight attendants. Forty female participants logged their subjective sleepiness and sleep quality each day. Their alertness, visual task performance, melatonin level and body temperature were monitored every 2 hours. They found that the participants became increasingly sleepy over the 4 days and had poorer sleep quality, but pre-flight patterns resumed quickly after their return. Measures of attention indicated that their cognitive skills were also controlled by an endogenous rhythm, although these responses shifted rapidly to new time zones. The rhythm of melatonin secretion and body temperature was delayed by almost 4 hours after the westward flight out but after 4 days of

figure 7.20
Pilots cross many time zones, putting them at risk from jet lag

travelling these two measures had desynchronised. Body temperature resynchronised more quickly than the melatonin secretion rhythm.

Recent research has explored the effectiveness of taking oral melatonin to combat the effects of jet lag. Herxheimer and Petrie (2001) reviewed the results of 10 studies and found that in nine of them participants reported experiencing decreased jet lag (from flights crossing at least five time zones) when taking melatonin compared to those given placebos. When taken at a time approaching the 'bedtime' of the destination time zone melatonin in doses up to 5 mg was more effective at inducing sleep whereas slow-release capsules were ineffective. This suggests that single daily doses of melatonin acted to assist in the resetting of the circadian rhythm.

media watch

Britain is losing too much sleep

Robin McKie, *Observer*, 7 April 2002

Once thought to be the ultimate restorative, and hailed by writers from Shakespeare to John Lennon, sleep is becoming a dirty word for the British. More and more of us are abandoning its soothing influence for round-the-clock hedonism as we go clubbing, shopping in supermarkets, watching videos, surfing the Web and clocking in to work at all times.

Scientists estimate we now take about two hours less sleep each day than our grandparents, damaging wakefulness in a way that poses serious health risks. Cases like Gary Hart – who fell asleep and crashed his car in front of a train at Selby last year, killing 10 people – are going to become increasingly common, they say.

Research by Dr Claudio Stampi, of the Chronobiology Research Institute in Boston, who worked with lone yachtswoman Ellen MacArthur, has shown that it is possible to survive on just four hours sleep a day. 'Ellen never had a single bout of sleep that was longer than two hours – and that worked because the first bit of sleep a person takes is the most recuperative' [said Dr Stampi].

Dr Stampi believes that 'polyphasic' sleep schedules will become increasingly useful as more people opt for 24-hour jobs and lifestyles. 'Consider a broker in Tokyo or London. He or she may have to monitor share or commodity prices round the clock as world markets open and close. Adopting a sleep schedule like Ellen's [MacArthur] may be the only way to keep ahead in the future.'

However, there is a limit to how much adjustment a person can make to sleep disruption. 'It used to be thought that people could adapt quite easily to shift work patterns that changed every week' said Dr Philip Tucker of Nottingham Trent University. 'But that doesn't seem to be the case. People spend most of their time adjusting. They never get a chance to settle into one pattern. Their performances always suffer.'

questions

1 Comment on this article using your knowledge of restorational theory of sleep (p. 185).

2 What negative effects on work performance and health can you see as a result of disruption to normal sleep patterns?

Some evidence suggests that light may not be the most important zeitgeber in adjustment to new time zones. Amir and Stewart (1996) have shown that rats who receive a breeze before their light phase can reset their clocks by a change in the time of the breeze alone. For people there may be many contingent signals that help to maintain our circadian rhythm that are absent when we travel abroad: the sound of birds in the morning, the time we eat, or television programmes. Whereas light schedules exist everywhere, other aspects of our regulated lives are harder to transport, particularly if we are on holiday. These factors may contribute to the slow rate at which we adapt to new time zones. The simplest way to combat the effects of a long-haul eastbound flight is to start going to bed and getting up progressively earlier before you travel.

We all experience a minor version of jet lag each time the clocks change between Greenwich Mean Time (GMT) and British Summer Time (BST). In the spring the clocks are put forward to BST and we lose an hour. In the autumn (or 'fall') we gain an hour when the clocks are put back an hour to return to GMT (remember: spring forward, fall back). We find the spring change easy because we gain an hour, simply allowing our body clocks to free run for a day. In the autumn the change produces poor sleep because we are trying to go to sleep early (Monk and Aplin, 1980).

where to now?

The following are good sources of further information on shift work and jet lag:

▶ **Bentley, E.** (1999) *Awareness*. London, Routledge. Very useful for this part of the topic as well as for sleep, dreaming and bodily rhythms.

▶ **Ayensa, E. S. and Whitfield, P.** (1981) *The Rhythms of Life*. Marshall, London. An excellent book on bodily rhythms and practical applications such as understanding jet lag.

talking
point
Contemporary issues

lucid dreaming

To most people, the dream experience seems real until they wake up. In a *lucid dream*, however, the individual is aware that his or her experience is a dream while it is happening. This awareness may arise spontaneously or it can be learned. Once lucid dreaming has been achieved, it may be possible for dreamers to control their dream content. How do we know that dreamers are *really* aware that they are dreaming, rather than just dreaming that they are aware? Hearne (1978) in England and La Berge et al. (1981) in the US developed similar techniques to test the lucidity of a dreamer. In both cases the participants were required to respond with a set pattern of muscle movements (eyes and/or hands) to a signal from the experimenter indicating that they had begun a lucid dream.

sleep signals, designer dreams

La Berge, S. P., Nagel, L. E., Dement, W. C. and Zarcone, V. P. (1981) Lucid dreaming verified by volitional communication during REM sleep. *Perceptual and Motor Skills*, **52**, 727–732.

Aim: to demonstrate communication by lucid dreamers.

Procedure: five participants, all suspected lucid dreamers, were taught a sequence of eye movements and hand clenches to be used to indicate the onset of lucid dreaming. They slept in a sleep laboratory with ongoing EOG, EMG and EEG recordings as well as direct observations.

Findings: signalling was recorded indicating 30 lucid dreams. All of these occurred during REM sleep and could not be mistaken for any other eye or bodily movements as they were complex signals such as an up-down eye movement (uncommon in dreams) followed by left-left-left left-right-left-left hand clenches.

Conclusion: lucid dreamers are aware of their dream state and can indicate this awareness to others.

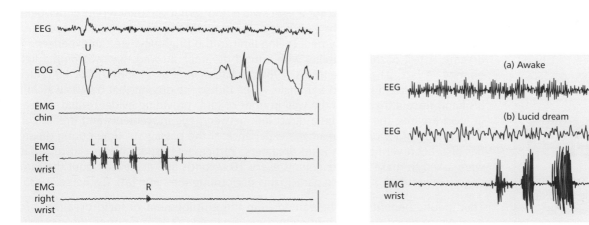

figure 7.21

Physiological readings from a lucid dreamer, SL. The EOG shows SL's up-down eye movement (one which, unlike the left-right movements – indicating REM sleep – that occur later in the trace, produce a characteristic pattern in the EEG); the EEG is typical of REM sleep; the chin EMG indicates paralysis and the left and right hand EMGs show the pattern of small movements used to indicate awareness by SL (they are the Morse code sequence for his initials); 20 seconds after this recording was taken, the participant awoke and reported recognising that he was dreaming and performing the signal

applying the physiological approach to understanding lucid dreaming

restorational theory

If sleep serves a restorational function, then the sleep state should be one of relaxation and reduced activity. Lucid dreaming seems to conflict with this aim. Green and McCreery (1994) observe that lucid dreams, being a higher state of arousal, could interrupt the restorative function of sleep by placing physiological demands on the brain. In fact, lucid dreamers report feeling well rested and positive after their experiences.

reorganisational theory

A further potential risk with lucid dreaming relates one proposed function of REM sleep. If Crick and Mitchison's reorganisational theory (see p. 187) is correct, then dreaming serves to remove unwanted memories. Directing the content of a dream could, therefore, have the capacity either to remove vital memories or disrupt the elimination of unwanted ones. As a consequence, memory efficiency could be adversely affected.

activation-synthesis

Recent research has investigated the personality of lucid compared to non-lucid dreamers. Since lucid dreaming gives the dreamer both awareness of and control over the events or content of the dream, it is possible that lucid dreamers differ in their need for control. Blagrove and Hartnell (2000) tested participants using the Locus of Control (LoC) scale (Rotter, 1966) which measures the extent to which an individual perceives themselves to be in control of events in their own life or accepts that control is 'external', that is, down to luck or the power of others for example. Blagrove and Hartnell found that lucid dreamers had a higher internal LoC (and other, related, measures of need for control) than non-lucid dreamers. Their findings indicate a continuity of cognitive style between waking and dreaming. These results parallel findings that in everyday dreams there is a continuity of content between waking and dreaming. This evidence supports the idea that the role of the brain during both waking and dreaming is one of synthesis and interpretation.

thinking critically

Lucid dreaming has useful applications because it provides researchers with a new gateway for investigating and verifying events during dreaming. For example, some individuals report dreams that occur in dimly lit surroundings and even when given a pre-sleep instruction to 'look for a light switch and turn it on' they report either being unable to find or operate the switch or only being able to do so with their eyes shut. This suggests that there may be a ceiling limit to the brightness we can experience in dreams. A test of this possibility with a lucid dreamer showed that switching a light on may, in fact, be possible (Moss, 1989). Schatzman et al. (1988) instructed a lucid dreamer to move his eyes in a triangle. As he did so, he dreamt that he was watching his hand trace a triangle on the wall in front of him, providing evidence that, at least in lucid dreams, there can be a direct link between eye movements and dream content. The accuracy of the dreamer's experience of the passage of time during dreams has also been verified with lucid dreamers. Participants experiencing a lucid dream were asked to make eye movements every 10 seconds and achieved about the same degree of accuracy as waking participants performing the same task (La Berge, 1985).

Therapeutic benefits may be gained from the employment of lucid dreaming, for example to divert the course of nightmares. Brylowski (1990) reported the successful use of lucid dreaming to avert nightmares by a woman with a personality disorder and major depression. Green and McCreery (1994) suggest that lucid dreaming may have many other therapeutic applications, such as offering sexual fulfilment to people unable to gain satisfaction in waking life through disability or feeling trapped inside a body of the wrong gender.

angling with the net

Use the Internet to find out about how people can teach themselves to have lucid dreams and try to explain the benefits that are claimed for the techniques.

where to now?

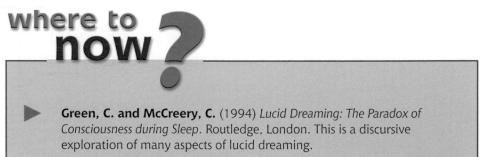

▶   **Green, C. and McCreery, C.** (1994) *Lucid Dreaming: The Paradox of Consciousness during Sleep.* Routledge, London. This is a discursive exploration of many aspects of lucid dreaming.

seasonal affective disorder

Winter depression or *seasonal affective disorder* (SAD) is a condition experienced in the short days of winter by as much as 10% of the population (Ferenczi, 1997). The symptoms of SAD include severe depression, craving for high carbohydrate foods and sleepiness. The prevalence of SAD among people in latitudes where winter nights are very long suggests that it may be related to day length. In Shetland, for instance, the shortest day lasts just 5 hours 53 minutes between sunrise and sunset, with no guarantee of any sunshine in between, with December promising just 15 hours of sunshine all month. In the lighter, longer days of spring and early summer the symptoms of SAD disappear.

applying the physiological approach to understanding SAD

As light acts as a zeitgeber in the control of the sleep–wake cycle, and one symptom of SAD is sleep disruption, one possible explanation for SAD is that processes of detecting or responding to light levels may be different in people with SAD.

the role of melatonin

During long winter nights secretion of melatonin reaches its peak then lowers as summer approaches. This pattern has tempted psychologists to search for a relationship between low exposure to light, high melatonin and SAD. This relationship is supported by the effectiveness of light therapy. SAD sufferers exposed to intense artificial lighting (1000 lux or more) during the winter generally find relief from their depression. Even as little as half an hour a day is effective, lifting depression within a week. How this exposure to light affects mood is, however, unclear. Ferenczi (1997) has suggested that it may either reset the circadian cycle or increase the secretion of serotonin, which is also implicated in mood disorders. Light therapy is not effective in all cases, although failure may be attributable to misdiagnosis rather than ineffectual treatment. The timing of light sessions has been the subject of much research and certainly simulated 'early dawn' is effective but brightness and total exposure, rather than timing, appear to be the key factors.

SAD patients wake up to sunshine

Avery, D. H., Kouri, M. E., Monaghan. K., Bolte, M. A., Hellekson, C. and Eder, D. (2002) Is dawn simulation effective in ameliorating the difficulty awakening in seasonal affective disorder associated with hypersomnia? *Journal of Affective Disorders*, **69**(1–3), 231–236.

Aim: to investigate whether dawn simulation, which is effective in treating SAD, affects difficulty of awakening in the morning.

Procedure: 50 SAD patients suffering hypersomnia (excessive sleepiness) received either one week of dawn simulation (250 lux) or exposure to a dim light (0.2–2 lux) placebo. Participants judged their drowsiness on awakening during a baseline week and the treatment week using the Stanford Sleepiness Scale (SSS). A psychiatrist also rated difficulty of awakening.

Findings: dawn simulation lowered both difficulty of awakening and the SSS score compared to the control (placebo dawn).

Conclusion: dawn simulation seems to be effective in decreasing morning drowsiness and difficulty awakening. This symptom could be explained by a delayed circadian rhythm in people suffering from SAD.

light sensitivity

An alternative explanation for the cause of SAD is insensitivity to light; SAD patients may be less responsive to the *zeitgeber* that should entrain their circadian rhythm so become 'phase-delayed'. Drake (2002) investigated this with SAD and non-seasonally depressed patients. He conducted depression ratings before and after participants were exposed to 1000 lux (bright) light from 11 p.m. to 12.30 a.m. (to induce phase delay – that is, change the circadian rhythm) and measured their body temperature (as an indicator of circadian rhythm change). Although no overall differences were found between SAD and non-SAD patients in temperature response, those individuals with a reduced thermoregulatory response to the bright light also had higher depression scores, suggesting that reduced sensitivity to light may make people vulnerable to depressive symptoms during the winter.

thinking critically

If light therapy raised mood by affecting the pineal gland, reduced levels of melatonin would be expected following treatment. Illnerova et al. (1993) have demonstrated a shifting of the melatonin cycle using bright lights to extend the day. Non-SAD participants were exposed to 3 hours of bright light each morning and evening for 5 consecutive days during the winter. Their circadian clocks advanced by 1 to 3 hours and the new rhythm persisted for 3 days after the light schedule was returned to normal. This suggests that, for SAD sufferers, exposure to bright light may affecti melatonin levels.

Koorengevel et al. (2002) attempted to find out whether patients with SAD were slower to adapt their circadian rhythm to changes in zeitgebers. They exposed SAD patients and control participants to artificial clock changes for 6 days (reducing day length to 20 hours), both during the summer and during the winter. The SAD patients did not differ from the controls in the speed at which they shifted their natural melatonin release cycle or their temperature rhythm but they did show lower amplitudes of daily variation – that is, the difference between daytime and night-time release of melatonin and body temperature was much smaller in the SAD patients. Koorengevel et al. concluded that the physiological variable of body temperature rhythm (which differs in SAD sufferers during the winter months) may be dependent on their smaller circadian melatonin variation.

Using a similar experimental protocol to the study described above, Koorengevel et al. (2003) investigated whether the enforced desynchrony of circadian pacemaker and environmental cues caused changes in mood. They compared SAD patients in summer and during the winter both when depressed and after recovery following light therapy to non-depressed controls. Although they found variations in mood relating to the circadian pacemaker and sleep-wake cycles over the short experimental period, these were not significantly different between conditions. So, although mood in SAD patients is related to their circadian rhythm, this is also true for non-depressed people.

angling with the net

There is a great deal of information available on the Internet about SAD. Find some that is directed at a non-scientific audience and prepare accompanying notes that explain the physiology behind the information given. Key words you might use to search include: SAD with seasonal depression, winter depression, winter blues or light therapy.

Light therapy only seems to be effective in SAD characterised by sleepiness, carbohydrate craving and worsening of symptoms in the evening. For sufferers who are suicidal, insomniac and experience more severe symptoms in the morning, light therapy is ineffective (Terman et al.,1997).

After reading this many of you might feel that you have SAD, feeling miserable and hungry through the winter and losing weight in summer. This wider experience, a mild form of winter depression called *seasonality*, is experienced by a much larger percentage of people. Ennis (1997) has identified a correlation between seasonality and premenstrual syndrome. This relationship might imply a tendency for some people to respond more strongly in terms of emotions to cyclical changes in hormone levels.

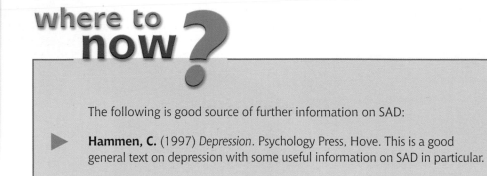

where to now?

The following is good source of further information on SAD:

▶ **Hammen, C.** (1997) *Depression*. Psychology Press, Hove. This is a good general text on depression with some useful information on SAD in particular.

conclusions

The physiological approach to psychology looks at the ways in which biology can be applied to helping us to understand human psychology. One area of study that is of growing importance in psychology is genetics, the study of inheritance. We have looked here at how genes are believed to affect individual characteristics such as personality and susceptibility to mental disorder. We have also looked briefly at the ways the human brain can be studied, and have gone on to look in some detail at the ways in which one aspect of physiological functioning – bodily rhythms – affects our psychological functioning.

One particularly important rhythm is the sleep–wake cycle, and we have examined the nature of sleep and dreams and some theoretical explanations for sleep and dreaming. Our understanding of the importance of bodily rhythms has several practical applications, for example in understanding the effects of shift work and jet lag. We have also looked here at two further contemporary issues: the nature and uses of lucid dreaming (a state of dream awareness), and our understanding and treatment of seasonal affective disorder (a form of depression associated with lack of daylight).

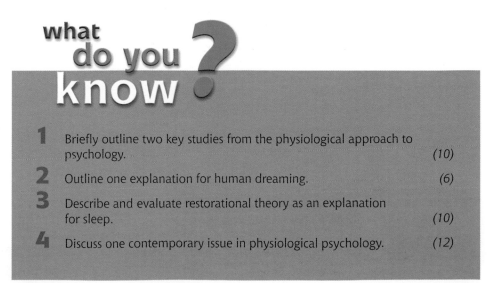

what do you know?

1 Briefly outline two key studies from the physiological approach to psychology. *(10)*

2 Outline one explanation for human dreaming. *(6)*

3 Describe and evaluate restorational theory as an explanation for sleep. *(10)*

4 Discuss one contemporary issue in physiological psychology. *(12)*

what's ahead?

T his chapter aims to help you through each stage of the coursework required for Unit 3 of your AS examination, from formulating an idea to presentation of the final document. References to other chapters will provide the details of the different research methods you could use but this chapter is devoted to the practical steps involved in planning, carrying out and writing up your own research. Throughout this chapter coursework *write-up wizard* boxes give you brief guidelines about writing up each step as you go along. If you can keep to a schedule and produce draft sections along the way you are more likely to complete your coursework by the deadline. Remember that not only does your coursework have to be handed in before the summer examinations but also that this one single piece of work is worth one-third of the marks at AS so it is important to try to gain as good a grade as you can.

write-up wizard: 1

general guidelines

follow these general pointers from the start of your write-up:

★ title (make it informative but not too long);

★ format (use the required section headings);

★ record the approval log number (unless you have used a title suggested by the examination board);

★ word process your report (and keep a copy on disk);

★ spelling and grammar check your work and read it through carefully for errors;

★ letter codes (put them in brackets after each heading and keep each section separate);

★ your final report should resemble a scientific journal article and should contain enough information for a psychologist to understand and replicate your study with no further input from you;

★ word limit (keep within the word limit or you will be penalised).

getting started

Your examination board has a list of coursework ideas that you can use. Alternatively, you might be expected to produce an idea of your own. Note that, if this is the case, it will need to be approved by the examination board as well as your coursework supervisor. The topic can be taken from any area of psychology except research using animals. You might find it useful to select a coursework idea that relates to part of your AS course to help you with your unit examinations, although this is not essential.

When asked to think up an idea to research most people find that their mind goes blank. Any ideas they can generate are either impractical or unethical! How can you find an interesting topic that is not too difficult to research?

There are two ways to go about it. You could think about daily life; what's interesting about the things that people do? Maybe when you look around you, you can see differences that catch your eye: do men and women use different techniques for taking off their jumpers? Do people who bite their nails also bite the ends of their pens? Which is easier, reading text presented to you upside down or reading with your head upside down but the text the right way up? Who would make more mistakes in reproducing Web addresses, young people or older people? Is it OK to do your revision listening to music?

Alternatively, you could start by reading about the research conducted by other psychologists. You might be able to think up related studies or different ways to tackle the same problem. For instance, Stroop (1935) investigated the effect of using coloured ink on response time for lists of colour names (such as *blue* written in blue or green ink). He found that people were slower to name the colour of ink that the words were written in when the words themselves were the names of colours and slower still if the colour ink and colour word did not match (were non-congruent). Similar effects have been demonstrated for time taken to read lists of colour-related words (such as *sky* or *grass*) in coloured ink and for other non-congruent stimuli.

figure 8.1

figure 8.2 Some psychological research is based on understanding everyday events

the Stroop effect

The first two columns are congruent words and colours; the second pair of columns show non-congruent stimuli. Try timing how long it takes people to read the words or name the colours in each list.

red	blue	green	purple
brown	green	red	brown
blue	purple	brown	blue
green	red	purple	red
purple	brown	blue	green

variations on the Stroop effect

A project could investigate other possibilities. Making the shapes of numerals out of matching or different numbers, making the outlines of animals such as a fish, snail, cat or mouse out of smaller illustrations or using geometric shapes could all lead to a Stroop effect.

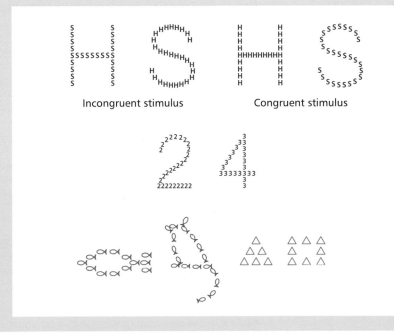

Incongruent stimulus   Congruent stimulus

figure 8.3

Although Stroop's original work was conducted many decades ago, the principle is still in use today (for instance to investigate schizophrenia and eating disorders). Current research may also offer interesting starting points for research. The obvious place to begin looking for ideas is in textbooks. Throughout the *Angles* series, particularly in *Angles on Psychological Research*, there are examples of recent studies. Many of these have been included because they are interesting ideas (see Table 8.1). Bear in mind that not all of these would be ethically acceptable for AS level students to replicate. Apart from textbooks, the Internet can be used as a source of information.

Any project idea you suggest will need to have ethical approval from the person supervising you and from your examination board. Before you start researching ideas, find out from your teacher whether your coursework needs to relate to a specific area of psychology. Remember – don't go too far with an idea before you are certain that it

text and page number	study
Angles on Psychological Research	
30	are we aware of being stared at?
35	talk about dogs
44	dogs as social catalysts
55	are alligators cute?
73	watch what you eat
76	sexuality examined by content analysis
79	eyewitnesses v. earwitnesses
87	sorted – student rubbish
115	do pets make older adults happy?
117	music and exercise
200	hearing when a pint of beer is full
Angles on Applied Psychology	
105	scary stories
110	leading questions
188	how to spoil a game of pool
313	personal space
347	crowded space and crabby shoppers
424	fast music costs lives
443	mobile madness
444	gender differences in emails
445	eyewitness testimony

table 8.1 Examples of interesting studies on which you might base coursework

is acceptable. Ethical guidelines are described in detail on pp. 223–225. They exist to protect the rights, privacy, safety and mental health of both participants and others. They give guidance to psychologists about how research should be conducted and, in tandem with examination board requirements, they govern what topics are suitable for your coursework and what methods are appropriate for students to use in different contexts. It is useful to consider the following questions when deciding whether a potential coursework idea is ethical:

1 Does the procedure involve deceiving participants?

2 Will the participants be safe?

3 Will participants, after participating, be in the same psychological state as before? If they might be embarrassed, confused, less happy or otherwise detrimentally affected the study shouldn't be done.

4 Is the study likely to generate questions from participants that you are not qualified to answer (for example, 'is it safe for me to . . .', 'will I be more successful if . . .' or 'does my result mean . . .').

5 What are the participants likely to tell others about the study and is this a fair representation of the purpose? If the participants may misconstrue your intentions or findings, the study shouldn't be done.

6 Could any participants or potential participants be discriminated against?

interactive
angles

Read the questions above relating to ethical issues in coursework. Which of these reasons would explain why each of the following coursework ideas might be ethically dubious? (More than one issue might apply.)

1 A study investigating the effect of punishment on smoking in which the experimenter snapped elastic bands on participants' wrists each time they wanted a cigarette.

2 An investigation into psychodynamic explanations of sexual fears in which students were attached to a heart rate monitor and were exposed without warning to the sight of a snake in a tank.

3 An experiment on memory in which participants learned a list of words and read out their scores in front of the group.

4 A questionnaire on promoting positive attitudes to homosexuality asking participants to rate their belief in positive and negative statements about people who are gay.

5 A computerised task intended to resemble concentrating on driving that can be performed while using a mobile phone, which shows attention is not impaired.

6 An observational study on the effects of invasion of personal space by neat or scruffy-looking individuals.

the introduction

finding information

If you are limited to conducting research within an area of psychology that you have been taught your starting point will be your textbook and other resources from your library. You will probably know what studies or theories are related to your research topic and will be able to look up key words with which you are already familiar. Look the idea up in several different texts – each will present the same information slightly differently and include some different evidence. If, however, you have chosen a new topic to research, it might be more difficult to make a start. Note that you do not need to locate a study that is exactly the same as you are planning to conduct (it might not exist) but you do have to find some fairly closely related material. It is vital that you can find some appropriate evidence because it's worth so many marks. If you can't, then choose another research area.

Whether you intend to conduct a familiar study, or are embarking on a new idea, the information you find that relates to your own study will become the basis of your introduction, a short piece of text at the beginning of your write-up that sets the scene for the investigation and explains the reasoning behind your hypothesis. The evidence you describe may be provided either by similar studies (ones about related topics or that use the same method to investigate another question) or theories that allow you to predict and explain the possible outcome of your study. Remember, you cannot embark on a study unless you can find information for your introduction – you must include background research.

For example, in the case of Stroop-type research with animal shapes, Stroop's original work with colour names would provide some of the basic evidence for a hypothesis that suggested we would be slower to name animals if their shapes were made up of conflicting stimuli – that is, different animals.

write-up wizard: 2

background research

for the 'background research' part of your *introduction* you will need to find out about three or four studies in the same area as your own and, if appropriate, a relevant theory. Your write-up of these needs to be:

★ concise (keep detail to a minimum);

★ selective (don't include too many studies – use only those that are directly relevant);

★ accurate;

★ approximately one typed side of A4 paper.

To decide on the order in which you will present the background studies you have found, use the *funnel technique*. This means that you are starting with the studies or theory in the broad area you are researching, then coming steadily closer to your own study. The final study in the introduction should be the most similar to your own.

Reference all citations fully (and keep a record of the source and page number for each one – you will need them for the references section and it's much harder to go back and look for them afterwards).

Do not quote without referencing; this is plagiarism and constitutes cheating. Do not copy other students' work.

When you are searching for information you can use both terms from the topic and any names of psychologists who have conducted related investigations. Begin by deciding on one or more areas of psychology that you hope to investigate. Think of a range of terms that could be used to look this topic up (for example, if it's about colour vision, you could use colour, vision, perception and cognitive psychology as well as the names of any psychologist you know to have done research in the area). Use general textbooks first, then try more specific texts (for example, textbooks on cognitive psychology or perception for information on colour vision). Look in your school or college library, your town or city library and, if you can access a university library, go there too.

Take each relevant text and look through both the *index* and *contents* pages, and beware, some books may have an *author index* in addition to a *subject index*. When you find useful information, remember to record a full *reference* for its location, you will need the author, date of publication, title of the book or journal and article, and the page numbers (also the name of the publishers and place of publication for a book, and volume number for a journal article) – see p. 240.

Look up the following studies in this text and decide what area of psychology they fall into and what key words you would use to explore the research area further. You might find it helpful to remind yourself of the names of the approaches covered by the specifications, and what topics fall into each one.

page	reference	title/topic
180	Vinha et al. (2002)	sleeping in working students
141	Koehler et al. (2002)	threatening words
21	Ellis and Fox (2001)	sexual orientation and helping behaviour
52	Godden and Baddeley (1975)	like a diver out of water!
85	Prior and Welling (2001)	reading aloud and children's understanding

table 8.2

You can also use the Internet as a resource, although searching may generate no matches at all or several thousand that are mainly irrelevant or incomprehensible. The tips below will help to improve the success of your Internet searches and *interactive angles* activities throughout this book will give you further ideas.

angling
with the net

◆ Compile a list of search terms before you log on.

◆ If you can, start from a psychology-based Web site, use a search engine that allows you to select 'education', 'science' or 'social science' (such as Yahoo!) or navigate through links on the *New Scientist*, British Psychological Society (BPS) or American Psychological Association (APA) Web sites.

◆ Pubmed (**www.ncbi.nml.nih.gov**) is a free site that allows you to search for summaries (abstracts) of psychology journal articles. Other similar sites, but that require a subscription, include BIDS and Infotrac.

◆ Use selection techniques such as '+' and put exact search terms in quotation marks.

◆ If the search engine produces a long list that looks irrelevant, remove the summaries so that you can page through the titles more quickly.

◆ Some journals are available online. Go straight to their Web site if you can.

◆ Remember to record the exact Web address for your references and the date and time you accessed the site.

planning and carrying out your research

aims

interactive
angles

Look back through this
book at some of the
research now and *classic
research* boxes and decide
what general format is
used for presenting the
aims of a study.

Having researched your chosen area you will have an idea about what you want to find out – that is, what particular question your investigation will try to answer. Answering this question is your *aim*. It is likely to explore the nature of the relationship between two variables. For example, the aim of Stroop's original research was to find out how letter colour affected reading and colour naming. Stroop was investigating the effect of variables he could control (the congruence of the words and ink colours) and the task type (reading or colour naming), on another variable that he could record (reading or naming speed). Therefore, his research clearly needed to use the experimental method. By devising an experiment that compared people's processing time in different conditions, whilst controlling other factors, he could assess the effect of congruent and non-congruent lists.

Ideally the aim should dictate the research method used to test it but, in reality, you might find that practical and ethical constraints mean that you have to alter your aims to fit what it is possible for you to do. As a consequence, you may find that decisions about your aim, hypothesis, variables and design are taken together, hence they are discussed together in the next section.

write-up wizard: 3

aims

for the 'aims' part of your *introduction* you will need to say:

★ what you are trying to find out;

★ whether your study is a replication or, if not, why it is different from previous studies.

One sentence may be sufficient.

As well as an aim, your introduction also requires a *rationale*. The rationale explains why you have chosen your particular approach to investigating your aims. It serves to indicate how your aim, hypotheses and method have arisen out of the research area. Draft your rationale before you plan your study then, when you are confident that you know how you are going to conduct your research, you can return to this section and finalise the rationale.

write-up wizard: 4

rationale

for the 'rationale' part of your *introduction* you will need to say:

★ what other researchers have found about the area;

★ what you are doing – include your method (for example, experiment, correlation, observation);

★ how what you are doing relates to the previous research you have described – how it is similar or different;

★ why this has led to a one- or two-tailed hypothesis;

Make this section brief – as little as one sentence for each of the above points may be sufficient.

choosing a research method

Once you have decided on your aim, ask yourself these questions:

◆ What *research method* would be best to tackle my aim?

◆ What *procedure* should I use?

◆ Is this procedure *ethical*?

◆ Is this procedure *practical*?

You may decide to conduct an observation, experiment, questionnaire, interview or any of the other methods described earlier in the text (chapters 2 to 7). Sometimes, you can see that the ideal way to investigate something might be to use a particular approach but for ethical or practical reasons you might need to settle for a less preferred technique. For example, if you were looking at cognitive development between 6 and 8 years you might wish to follow up the same children for 2 years to see how they develop. However, if you did this, your course would be finished before you found any results! You would have to settle therefore for comparing 6 and 8 year olds.

---

which research method should I use?

When you have a coursework idea, look through these questions to help you to decide how best to tackle it.

◆ If you are looking for differences (for example between males and females, adolescents and adults, ability on a task before and after a procedure) then you should do an *experiment*. Ask yourself which variables you are going to manipulate and what changes you expect as a consequence, and whether you can achieve this without deceiving your participants.

◆ If you want to know about attitudes, beliefs, opinions or emotions, you could use a *questionnaire* or *interview*. These may offer a way to collect data for an experiment. Ask yourself whether people have access to such information about themselves and whether it is fair to ask them to divulge it.

◆ If you are interested in people's behaviour in naturalistic environments you may need to conduct an *observation*. Ask yourself whether you can record the necessary information accurately and if you will be invading privacy by doing so.

◆ If you think there may be a relationship or link between two variables that cannot be manipulated you could conduct a *correlational study*. Ask yourself whether the variables can be measured effectively in every participant.

◆ If you want to look at the meanings behind the content of visual or written media, *content analysis* may be a suitable technique. Ask yourself whether the material and the meanings you are searching for are appropriate and whether there is enough material available.

As well as making an appropriate choice of research method and designing an investigation that is ethical, your study needs to be practical – it must be possible for you to collect data. Consider the following points when you design your procedure:

◆ Do you have access to sufficient participants?

◆ Do you have access to participants from particular groups if needed?

◆ Do you have or can you make the necessary materials or equipment?

◆ Can you find an appropriate space in which to conduct the study?

◆ Do you have enough time?

◆ Can you achieve and operationalise any manipulations of variables you are planning?

◆ Can you employ appropriate controls?

Student projects tend to be experimental (because you need to collect quantitative, numerical data) so we will focus on the process of conducting and writing up this method, but where relevant we will tell you how to do things differently if you are using a different method, such as a questionnaire or observation. You will need to justify your choice of method, so keep a record of the reasoning that allowed you to make this decision. Having selected a method you then need to plan how you will conduct the investigation.

hypotheses

You are now in a position to develop your *alternative hypotheses* (also called an *experimental hypothesis* in an experimental study). This is a testable statement that expresses the relationship that you believe to exist, for example, a difference between conditions in an experiment. Any hypothesis has to be testable, so you need to consider how you will collect data to support it – this is your design. In order to word an experimental hypothesis correctly, you must know what variables will be manipulated and measured, that is, operational definitions of your independent and dependent variables.

the alternative hypothesis

An alternative hypothesis in an experiment states that there is a difference between levels of the independent variable (or conditions), indicated by differences in the dependent variable. An alternative hypothesis (or H_1) therefore takes the general form 'There is a difference in (*the dependent variable*) between (*the levels of the independent variable*).' This is only a generalised formula and it will not apply exactly in every case. In Stroop's study, one H_1 might have been 'There is a difference in reading speed between lists of congruent and non-congruent colour words.'

directional and non-directional hypotheses

In the examples above, the hypotheses are *non-directional*, that is, they do not state the nature or 'direction' of the difference between levels of the IV, simply that there will be one. Sometimes it is better to use non-directional or *two-tailed hypotheses* because we cannot predict the nature of the expected difference reliably. For example, we might be confident that there will be a difference between the ability of children and adults in a skipping game, but not know which group will be better – perhaps adults as they are stronger, or children, because they are more familiar with the task.

directional and non-directional hypotheses

This is a two-tailed hypothofish . . . can you tell which way it will go?

This is a one-tailed hypothofish . . . can you tell which way it will go?

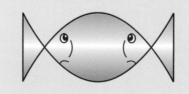 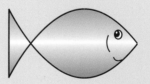

figure 8.4 In a one-tailed hypothesis, like a one-tailed hypothofish, the tail has a *directional* effect

interactive angles

For each of the aims stated below, write two versions of an alternative hypothesis, a directional one and a non-directional one.

1 To find out if males or females eat more chocolate.

2 To test whether younger or older children are better at judging the number of sweets in a jar.

3 To see whether recall of words can be affected by the use of verbal cues.

4 To investigate the likelihood of people sleeping for longer when they have been exercising.

In your background research for your study you may find good evidence that suggests a directional effect so you can confidently predict that one level of the IV will produce a particular change in the DV. For example, presenting participants with non-congruent stimuli in a Stroop task is likely to make their performance worse rather than better. In instances like this we may choose to use a *directional* or *one-tailed hypothesis*.

The alternative hypotheses for studies using methods such as observations, questionnaires and interviews are likely to be similar to those described above as, in the context of an AS investigation, these methods are best used as a means to collect data for the DV in an experiment. So, although you might have designed a questionnaire, your aim is likely to be to be an experimental one, comparing two groups or looking for differences in responses to two slightly different forms of a questionnaire.

In correlational designs, however, the format of your hypothesis would be slightly different as a correlation proposes a link between two variables rather than a difference between conditions. A non-directional or two-tailed hypothesis for a correlation takes the form 'There is a relationship ("link" or correlation) between variable A and variable B'. Directional or one-tailed hypotheses indicate the nature of the relationship between the two variables, taking the form 'There is a positive (or negative) correlation between variable A and variable B'. For example, two variables that increase 'together', such as vocabulary size and age, are positively correlated so a hypothesis might read 'There is a positive correlation between age and vocabulary size'. The corresponding null hypothesis takes the form 'Any relationship ("link" or correlation) between variable A and variable B is due to chance'. For more about the correlational method, see p. 168.

the null hypothesis

The alternative hypothesis is the statement that you will accept at the end of the study if your results suggest that the measures of the dependent variable are sufficiently different between levels of the IV to be attributed to the IV itself, rather than to random fluctuations or errors. Of course, the results of studies do not always support the H_1, so we need a conclusion in these instances. This is the function of the *null hypothesis*, a statement that says, in general form, that 'Any difference in (*the dependent variable*) between (*the levels of the independent variable*) is due to chance'. In other words, the null hypothesis (or H_0) suggests that differences arising between conditions, if there are any, are not due to the IV but due to chance factors such as uncontrolled variables. The null hypothesis is important for two reasons. It gives us a conclusion if the results of the study do not support our original prediction

interactive angles

Read the questions below and write an alternative and null hypothesis for each situation.

1 Are younger people more likely to be helpful than older people?

2 Are scientists less likely to hold religious beliefs than non-scientists?

3 Do dogs learn tricks faster than cats?

4 Do boys and girls differ in their ability at spatial tasks?

5 Are children more likely to imitate their parents than other adults?

6 Does emotional state affect memory?

and, in studies that go on to use statistics, it provides a statement that can be more readily disproved than the H$_1$ – it is easier to demonstrate that something is certainly incorrect than that it is certainly correct. The corresponding H$_0$ for Stroop might have been 'any difference between reading speed for congruent and non-congruent colour words is due to chance'.

Now write your null and alternative hypotheses. Once you have developed your research method fully and have started to collect data you should not change your hypotheses, regardless of your findings. Remember, if you are at all unsure about the effect one variable may have on another you can use a non-directional hypothesis.

write-up wizard: 5

the hypothesis

for the 'hypothesis' part of your *introduction* you will need to:

★ state your alternative hypothesis (H$_1$);

★ state your null hypothesis (H$_0$);

★ make sure that these are concise, testable and operationalised.

the method

variables

Variables are factors that can change. In research these factors may be manipulated, measured or held constant (that is, controlled) deliberately. Your aim and the research method you chose will determine the variables that are important in your investigation. In an experiment, the independent variable (IV) is the factor that you manipulate to create different levels or conditions. In the case of Stroop (1935) one independent variable was the nature of the stimulus lists:

◆ colour names – either congruent (same colour ink as meaning of word) or non-congruent (different colour ink than meaning of word);

◆ letter-like coloured shapes;

◆ coloured blocks.

It is the independent variable that you are predicting will cause a change in the behaviour or responses of participants in your study. This effect, the difference in the way people behave or respond, is the measure of your *dependent variable*. Stroop (1935) used time taken to read each list as one measure of the dependent variable (DV).

In order for you to be sure that any differences you observe between levels of the IV are indeed due to your experimental manipulation, any extraneous variables – other factors that could affect the dependent variable – are held constant. These are called *controlled variables* (see also p. 221). Experiments, particularly those conducted in laboratory conditions, rely on the rigorous control of variables in order to generate valid and reliable data. Controls employed by Stroop (1935) included having lists the same length, balancing out the frequency with which each colour name and colour of ink appeared in the lists and the amount of 'white' in the non-letter shape (for example, if you used Ξ it would cover much more of the page, so would present more colour than ∩). He also used each list in reverse order, seated every participant near a window, allowed participants time to adapt to the lighting conditions before starting the experiment and tested all the participants for colour blindness.

In order to plan your research, you will need to know what variables you are going to record and, if appropriate, those that you are going to manipulate and control as well. Table 8.3 outlines what variables are important in each research method.

research method	variable or recording unit	description
Experiment	Independent variable (IV)	This is the variable that you predict will have an effect on individuals. You will need to construct or find situations or people in two or more different 'levels' of this variable (that is, different ' conditions') in order to compare them
	Dependent variable (DV)	This is the variable that you predict will change; you will need to find a way to measure its value
	Controlled variables	These are factors that could influence the DV that are kept consistent across the levels of the IV
Observation	Coding schemes	You could measure the duration (time) and/or frequency of each behaviour you intend to record
Correlation	Measured variables	You will need to obtain two scores from each participant
Questionnaire	Choice of answer or response	Each question that contributes to the aim will need a scoring system – exclude any used to allocate participants to groups, describe the sample (such as the gender ratio) or to reduce demand characteristics by disguising the true purpose (for example in investigations on leading questions). Some responses may need to be 'reversed', for example on Likert scales
Interview	Answer or response	To generate sufficient quantitative data from interviews, they are likely to be structured, in which case the same points as raised about questionnaires above apply
Case study	Any of above	It is unlikely that you will be able to generate sufficient numerical data using this method. However, if you do, you are likely to use the methods of observation or interview (see above) to do so
Content analysis	Recording units	The criteria you will use to record data (such as individual words or images)
	Categories	Recording units are grouped into classes or categories for analysis (such as 'food related' and 'non-food related')

table 8.3 Variables in different types of study

So, in designing an experiment, you must consider how you will create different levels of your IV. This may be done by setting up different experimental tasks, situations or stimuli, for example comparing people's accuracy on a listening task with or without competing visual stimuli. Although such an approach is commonly associated with laboratory experiments, field experiments may also be designed using experimental manipulations.

Alternatively, the variable may already exist in the population, such as with different ages, genders or life experiences (for example, 'people who have been to boarding school'). In this case, you are not strictly 'manipulating' the IV but selecting and grouping participants (or the data from them) to create different levels. Having decided on the levels of your IV, you will need to operationalise the variables. This literally means producing a description that will allow you to put the variable into operation – make it useable. An operational definition of your IV should indicate how it has been manipulated.

Similarly, you will need to decide how, exactly, you will measure and record the dependent variable. Your operational definition here must state how the variable will be observed or measured. It might include the range of possible responses or any scale or units used to measure the response.

write-up wizard: 6

variables

for the 'variables' part of your *method* you will need to do the following. For an experiment:

★ give an operational definition for your independent variable;

★ give an operational definition for each level of your independent variable;

★ give an operational definition for your dependent variable and include any scales or units used.

For a correlation state the two measured variables, giving operational variables for each.

For other approaches describe any variables being measured, for instance the operational definitions being used with the coding scheme in an observation or the recording units in a content analysis.

design

Having operationalised your variables, you have decided in principle how to collect your data, so next you will need to create or obtain all the necessary resources to conduct the study. This might involve producing stimuli such as pictures, lists of words, recorded sounds or videos; structured questions for interviewing; questionnaires; or coding schemes for observations. This is also the time to consider the factors you will need to control in order to be certain that any effects that you find are due to your IV and not any extraneous variables (see p. 214 in this chapter).

validity and reliability

When you plan your study, for example in selecting materials for an experiment or preparing questions for a questionnaire or interview, you need to consider whether they are a valid test of the hypothesis. *Validity* is a measure of the extent to which a technique achieves the purpose for which it was designed. So a valid experimental task would test the independent variable it claimed to test. Imagine a Stroop test in which the colours were cyan, sienna, scarlet, magenta, mauve and maroon rather than the colours illustrated on p. 205. Would the reading test be a good measure of the influence of colour on reading? What other factor would be likely to affect reading speed? This is an extreme example to illustrate the point but, nevertheless, uncontrolled aspects of experimental situations can invalidate results so controls are necessary.

If you were testing the ability of different groups of participants (such as young/old or male/female) to recall real Web addresses how confident would you be that they had all had equal exposure to them? What simple change could be made to the design of this study so that you could be sure that the test was a valid measure of ability to learn new addresses rather than familiarity with old ones?

Another factor to consider in planning your materials is *reliability*; whether an exact repeat (*replication*) of your study would generate the same results – if so, it would be described as reliable. For example, if you are likely to test participants at different times of day, are you sure that their levels of alertness or hunger will not affect your measures of the DV?

Imagine a study in which students were measuring anxiety under two experimental conditions using a device that recorded how tightly a participant clenched their jaw. The first week a participant drives through rush-hour traffic and experiences road-rage on the way to the laboratory; the second week the participant walks to the lab through the park instead. How will this affect the reliability of this individual's measured anxiety level in the two experimental conditions? The control of variables is considered in more depth on pp. 221–222.

participant design

The *participant design* of an experiment is the way in which participants are allocated to perform in different levels of the independent variable. You will need to decide which of these designs is most appropriate if you are conducting an experiment. Remember to record the reasons for your choice so that you can justify the design in your coursework report. The possible designs are repeated measures, independent groups and matched pairs, although you are unlikely to use the latter.

In a *repeated measures design* all individuals participate in every level of the IV, hence the levels of the IV are compared by the participants each repeating their performance under different conditions. This design has the advantage that differences between levels of the IV are unlikely to be due to participant variables as the participants each act as their own control. However, participants can grow bored or tired (a *fatigue effect*) or learn the task when they repeat it (a *practice effect*). These two potential problems are called *order effects*. In addition, participants in a repeated measures design may also be more likely to respond to *demand characteristics* – features about the experimental setting or procedure that inform them about the aim and influence their behaviour independently of the experimental objectives. This is problematic because, in a repeated measures design, participants have greater exposure to the experimental setting.

In an *independent groups design* separate groups of participants perform in each of the levels of the IV so that the data sets relating to each condition or level are independent of each other. Each participant experiences the experimental setting only once so order effects cannot obscure the effects of the IV and participants are less likely to respond to demand characteristics.

write-up wizard: 7

design

for the 'design' part of your *method* you will need to:

★ state your choice of research method (experiment, correlation, case study and so forth);

★ justify your choice in relation to your aim;

★ relate the advantages of the chosen method to your study;

★ state your choice of participant design (in an experiment: repeated measures, matched pairs or independent groups);

★ justify the choice of participant design in relation to your study (consider such factors as participant and situational variables, order effects and demand characteristics).

apparatus

When selecting or producing your apparatus and materials you need to consider the issues of validity and reliability (see pp. 236–238). Think carefully about your choice of stimulus material, questions or equipment. You should ensure that:

◆ all tasks are equivalent across levels of the IV (for example, consider word frequency and length in word lists, familiarity, size and colourfulness in visual stimuli);

◆ tasks are not discriminatory (they should be equally accessible to all participants, such as those of different ages, genders or ethnic groups);

◆ you can justify your reason for choosing particular materials or apparatus rather than alternatives.

You should also bear in mind issues of ethics (see p. 223) including your responsibility to preserve the participants' safety and confidentiality. Make sure that any apparatus you use is safe (for example, have electrical equipment checked by your centre's health and safety officer) and do not put a space for the participant's name on any questionnaires or response sheets. It is important to check your proposed materials on a small sample of people who will not eventually be participants. This is a *pilot study*, and helps to identify and resolve any problems with the design, apparatus or procedure.

In order that your study can be replicated (repeated exactly) any important items should be clearly identified. For example, if you played participants recorded music then state the title and artist in your apparatus section. If you designed any apparatus or materials yourself (such as mazes or questionnaires) it is important that the reader can understand what they were like. Put a blank copy of any questionnaire used into an appendix (and refer to its location in the apparatus section). Also include answers or solutions where relevant, such as for puzzles or anagrams. If you have designed or used complex apparatus such as a maze, a diagram of the equipment can be useful.

write-up wizard: 8

apparatus

for the 'apparatus' part of your *method* you will need to:

★ list or describe the apparatus and materials used;

★ justify your selection of these;

★ refer to examples (for example, word lists, a blank questionnaire) in an appendix.

participants

The *target population* is all the members of the group from which the individuals selected to participate in your study are drawn and to which the results of the study are intended to relate. The population is specified by the shared characteristics of the group and includes all of the members of that group. A population might be defined by occupation – students (or staff) in a college, by geographical location – residents in a local area or by some common feature such as 'people who wear glasses'. In practice, the populations available to you will be limited by your access to them.

The process by which individuals are selected from the population to participate in the study is called the *sampling method*. It is likely that you will use an *opportunity sample* of your chosen population – that is, you will select individuals to participate on the basis of their availability. However, this sampling method is unrepresentative as there is no guarantee that the full range of diversity within the population will be obtained in the sample. Significantly, those individuals who are unavailable may share some important characteristic. Such a sampling error could result in biased findings that cannot be generalised back to the target population. If you do use opportunity sampling, there may be steps you can take to gain as wide a representation as possible. Could you sample at different times of day, at different locations or on different days? Alternatively, you could use a different sampling method that is likely to produce a more representative sample; however, these are more difficult and time consuming (see Table 8.4).

sampling method	description	advantages	disadvantages
Opportunity sampling	Sample is obtained on the basis of availability of individuals	◆ It is easy to obtain participants, so a large sample can be found quickly	◆ Non-representative ◆ Results may not generalise back to the target population
Random sampling	Each individual in the population has an equal chance of being selected. Sample taken from whole population in a truly random way – for example, by allocating each individual a number and using a random number generator or table	◆ It is representative so the results should generalise back to the target population	◆ Must have information on the *whole* population ◆ It may be difficult to access the whole population ◆ Selection technique must be truly random
Systematic sampling	Every *n*th person in the population is selected. The size of the sample is dictated by the basis of sampling – for example, in a population of 1000, taking every 20th person will produce a sample of 50 (1000/20)	◆ The whole population is considered the sample so it is more representative than in opportunity sampling	◆ The sample is not necessarily representative because there may also be systematic patterns in the population ◆ Planning and executing the sampling is time consuming
Quota sampling	The population is divided into strata or representative groups from which *quotas* – opportunity samples of the subgroup in the population – are taken in proportion to their appearance in the target population	◆ Representative, because each subgroup appears in the sample ◆ Results should generalise back to the target population	◆ Time consuming to sample each subgroup ◆ Sampling within each subgroup may not be representative ◆ It may be difficult to decide which criteria to use for subgrouping ◆ It may be difficult to obtain details about subgroups
Volunteer sampling	This is a description of a sample rather than a technique. Any sample in which individuals are aware that they are being selected requires them to be volunteers – to give their informed consent to participate	◆ Overcomes some ethical issues of deception ◆ Volunteers may be more likely to maintain an interest in a study so may be more likely to participate in multiple-phase investigations	◆ The absence on non-volunteers from a sample is a source of bias – they may share other important characteristics in addition to their disinclination to participate in a study ◆ The findings may therefore not generalise to the target population

table 8.4 Sampling methods and their advantages and disadvantages

Sampling in other research methods generally presents the same issues as experiments. However, in content analysis, the nature of the sample is very different. The sampling strategy is dictated by the aim and the recording units being studied.

The nature of your sample will depend on several factors, so consider the following questions to help you to decide:

◆ Does your research question dictate a particular population (such as children, females, or people who own pets)?

◆ What sampling procedure would be ideal (for example, random, quota, systematic)?

◆ Are you able to employ the ideal sampling method?

◆ How are you going to recruit your sample (face-to-face, by advertising, by telephone)?

◆ Is it practical and ethical to use your chosen sample?

Once you have decided on your population and how you will select your sample, you have some of the information needed for the *participants* section of your method. You will also need to add information about your actual sample when you have completed your data collection, such as the number of participants, the *gender ratio* (the relative number of males and females) and the *age range*. There may be other information about individuals that is relevant to particular studies, such as the importance of colour blindness in Stroop's experiment. In a study that requires participants to return for a second test or to submit a questionnaire, it is unlikely that all will do so. The proportion who do not, and so who have to be excluded from the study, is the *attrition rate* and is calculated in the following way:

$$\frac{\text{Total initial number of participants} - \text{Remaining number of participants}}{\text{Total initial number of participants}} \times 100$$

The attrition rate should also be included in the participants section if appropriate.

write-up wizard: 9

participants

For the 'participants' part of your *method* section you will need to:

★ state the target population;

★ state the sampling method;

★ justify the choice of sampling method;

★ state details of the sample (including the number of participants and other details where relevant, such as the gender ratio, age range, attrition rate);

★ in a matched pairs design, the criteria for matching should be given;

★ remember to refer to the people in your study as participants, not subjects.

procedure

In order to conduct your study you will need to plan exactly how you will go about collecting your data. In an experiment this means how you will introduce your participants to the study (your *brief*), how you will tell them what is required (your *standardised instructions*) and what you will say to them afterwards (your *debrief*). In addition, and very importantly, you need to plan what you, and the participants, should be doing throughout the study, this is the *protocol*. If your study is not an experiment, your procedure is equally important, Table 8.5 indicates some key issues for other research methods.

research method	important issues for the procedure
Experiment	◆ brief and debrief ◆ standardised instructions – they should differ only in respect of the IV ◆ protocol
Observation	◆ brief and debrief unless participants are in a truly public place and would expect to be seen ◆ observational strategy: – *checklist* (record each incidence of chosen behaviours) – *time sampling* (record the occurrence of chosen behaviours either during or at the end of fixed time intervals) – *event sampling* (record the frequency, duration and order of all behaviours being scored) ◆ may include techniques used to improve inter-observer reliability
Correlation	◆ brief and debrief ◆ standardised instructions for collecting data on the two measured variables ◆ protocol
Questionnaire	◆ brief and debrief (may be on the questionnaire) ◆ standardised instructions (may be on the questionnaire) ◆ protocol (may include distribution and collection of questionnaires, the time participants have to complete the questions, and so forth)
Interview	◆ brief and debrief ◆ protocol (may include sequencing of questions in a structured or semi-structured interview)
Case study	◆ brief and debrief ◆ protocol (will include any aspects of methods being utilised such as observations or interviews)
Content analysis	◆ may include techniques used to improve reliability between scorers

table 8.5 Key issues for the procedure in different research methods

write-up wizard: 10

procedure

for the 'procedure' part of your *method* you will need to:

★ state the brief and debrief;

★ refer to any standardised instructions (in an appendix);

★ describe the setting;

★ describe the protocol (what any one participant would go through in the study);

Your procedure needs to be: clear and replicable.

controls

When conducting an experiment, it is essential to keep any factors that could affect the DV constant across the levels of the independent variable – in other words, to *control* them. Controlling extraneous variables ensures that any difference in the DV is the result of the IV and is not due to other, chance, variations. Control measures that you might implement in your research will include any steps you take to ensure that the experimental conditions are identical in every way except the IV. Some ideas would include matching of materials, tasks or apparatus for variation in factors such as content, familiarity, complexity, colour, clarity, size or shape. These might apply, for example, to word lists, visual images or puzzles. Auditory stimuli, such as music, could be controlled for pitch, volume, familiarity, tempo and style. As well as controlling aspects of your materials, it is also important to control each participant's experience, by using standardised instructions and maintaining the same environment.

> ### standardised instructions
> Your report should quote the instructions you gave to participants, indicating whether they were presented visually or verbally and whether the participants asked questions (they should be allowed to do so). The instructions may be the same for all participants or, in experiments, there may be two almost identical versions for different conditions. If so, indicate how they were the same and different (for example, by providing a copy of each and underlining where the differences occur). A copy of the standardised instructions should appear in your appendix and should be referred to in the procedure section of your method.

In an experiment using a repeated measures design you should also attempt to counteract order effects. This can be done either using *counterbalancing*, so that equal numbers of participants perform the experimental conditions in each possible order or by randomisation of the conditions, so that, on average, each possible order of the conditions is used equally often. To employ counterbalancing you will need to subdivide the participants into groups, each of which performs the conditions in each of the possible orders. Taking a Stroop word reading task that is performed on a congruent (C) and a non-congruent (N) list, there are two possible orders, CN or NC, so the participants would be split into two subgroups.

Another feature that it is important to control for is the presence of *demand characteristics*, that is, the cues in an experimental setting that inform – or misinform – the participants about the purpose of the study and may, therefore, affect their behaviour. If participants know, or believe they know, the objectives of an investigation this may affect their responses. Such responses by participants may be deliberate or unconscious, for instance in the case of making more 'socially desirable' replies to questions. In order to avoid such effects you need to minimise the amount the participants are told or can deduce about the purpose of the experiment without deceiving them or denying them the chance to make an informed decision to participate. You will need to balance ethics against scientific rigour.

One way to identify uncontrolled variables is by looking at the sources of variation. Apart from your materials and procedure, the participants and the experimental setting itself may vary. Sources of error caused by random variation between individuals are called *participant variables*. We have considered some issues, such as the effects of hunger, level of arousal or stress. You may need to implement controls to attempt to overcome such variability. *Situational variables* are confounding variables that arise from the influence of the environment on participants' behaviour. For example, brightness may determine the difficulty participants experience with the Stroop task, the ambient noise level will affect how easily participants can understand and therefore recall a spoken word list, and temperature could affect people's mood and, consequently, the way they answer a questionnaire. You may not be able to control the absolute level of such factors in the environment directly, but you can ensure that your data are reliable by testing all participants in similar conditions.

Controls are also important in non-experimental designs. In observations you may need to identify why the use of more than one observer is potentially problematic. The use of procedures to improve inter-observer reliability is a control measure. In questionnaire and interview studies control measures may, for example, be employed by predetermining the order of questions, or the way in which they are asked, or by introducing distracter questions to reduce the influence of demand characteristics.

ethics

You need to be certain that the procedures you are planning to use conform to ethical guidelines. You are likely to need to brief your participants about the nature of the study to ensure that they are able to give their *informed consent* to participate. This means that they must have enough knowledge about the study to decide whether they want to be involved. Your dilemma is to provide sufficient details for them to judge, without risking invalidating your study by telling them too much. The brief may be printed for participants to read or you might say it to them (if so, you need to be sure that your tone does not oblige them to participate). If you are reading the brief (or standardised instructions) out loud, it is worth putting it on a card so that you remember what to say and so that you can be certain that each participant receives the same information.

BPS Code of conduct, ethical principles and guidelines (1998)

◆ *Competence* – work within your limit and strive to maintain and develop your skills.

◆ *Consent* – ensure that you have provided sufficient information for your participants or clients to make an informed choice about their commitment:
   (a) *deception* – do not mislead participants unless it is unavoidable, justifiable and accepted by appropriate authorities;
   (b) *debriefing* – after completion of your study, participants must be informed fully of the purpose and expected outcomes;
   (c) *right to withdraw* – participants must be reminded that they are free to leave a study at any time or to remove their results at the end, regardless of any payment they have received.

◆ *Confidentiality* – ensure that you have disguised participants' identities and stored their data securely.

◆ *Conduct* – be responsible. Treat participants or clients safely and without discrimination or exploitation.

If you are taking an opportunity sample, consider whether you are treating people equally, are you likely to offend anyone by failing to ask them to participate or by excluding them? During your study you must ensure that the participants are aware of their right to withdraw and that this is respected, even if it is expressed indirectly (such as when a child refuses to return to the test room).

---

the brief and debrief

Brief: Give enough information for the participants to give their informed consent – they must have a good idea about what they will be expected to do but try to avoid saying things you don't need to say about the purpose of the experiment and what you expect to happen. They must be informed of their right to withdraw and assured about confidentiality.

Debrief: This is usually read out to the participants after they have completed the study. It functions to thank the participants, to explain the purposes of the study and to reassure them.

At the end of the study you must fully debrief your participants. They must be thanked, offered a full explanation of the purpose of the study, reminded of their right to withdraw their results and reassured. They may ask about the findings of the study so far. Remember the guidelines about *competence* (you must not make claims you cannot substantiate) and *confidentiality* (do not use other participants' results as examples).

You are now ready to draft the *procedure* section of your report. When you have done so, you will need to check with your supervisor that your approach is ethically sound. Once this has been agreed you should not change your procedure without further consultation.

write-up wizard: 11

controls

for the 'controls' part of your *method* section you will need to:

★ describe clearly two controls that you implemented; or

★ state clearly two ethical issues to which you responded, indicating the guidelines that you followed.

In either case, the issues must be specifically related to your study.

recap

At this stage you should be able to:

◆ write an introduction with references to similar studies and relevant theories that back up your predictions. State your aims. State the rationale for your research. State an alternative and a null hypothesis;

◆ draft a method section with six subsections;

◆ write a design subsection that states the control measures including counter-balancing if appropriate;

◆ write a variables subsection operationally defining your IV and DV;

◆ draft a participants subsection that states the population and sampling method and will later contain the gender ratio and other relevant details about the sample;

◆ write an apparatus subsection that details all the items and materials you have used;

◆ write a procedure subsection that describes in detail the activities of the researchers and participants – the protocol. It should refer to the standardised instructions and include the brief and debrief but should not simply consist of these;

◆ write a controls subsection which describes either your implementation of controls or the ethical issues with which you have dealt.

Before you go out and collect data, you might find it helpful to work through the following checklist:

◆ Are you certain that you have permission to conduct your research?

◆ Where are you going to conduct the study?

◆ What is the target population and how will you contact them?

◆ Do you have the necessary equipment or materials to measure the variable(s)?

◆ If you need to manipulate any variables can you do so?

◆ Have you decided what to call the levels of the independent variable? (Give them meaningful labels and be consistent to avoid confusion later.)

◆ If you are using a repeated measures design have you decided how you will counterbalance or randomise the presentation of conditions to participants?

- What controls do you need to employ and how will you do so?

- Is the study you are planning achievable in the given time?

- Is the study you are planning ethical?

Good luck with your data collection!

the results

analysing your findings: descriptive statistics

The purpose of a results section is to inform the reader about the key findings of your research – that is, the important, general features of the data. This can be done numerically, by presenting measures of central tendency and dispersion in tables, or visually, using graphs. There are three measures of *central tendency* or 'average', which summarise a data set to a single index (a number or group) that represents a typical score. Measures of *dispersion* or 'spread' indicate the way that data points vary around the average, that is, how similar or different they are in general. Each technique can only be used on some types of data; this is determined by the level of measurement.

levels of measurement

The data generated by your study may be classified into one of four types: nominal, ordinal, interval or ratio. These *levels of measurement* describe the type of scale against which a variable is assessed. The level of measurement you are using to assess the dependent variable (or other measured variable) in your study matters as it determines which descriptive statistics (averages, measures of dispersion and graphs) you can use. In making this decision it is not important to be able to distinguish between 'interval' and 'ratio' data, so they will be combined and described as 'equal interval' scales.

nominal data

The simplest type of data a study can produce are *nominal data* – responses from participants that fall into discrete, named categories. Examples would be favourite food (cheese, carrots, cake) or 'Can you pat your head and rub your chest at the same time?' (yes, no) and are commonly found in studies using questionnaires consisting of closed, forced choice questions. Nominal data are the least informative as the categories do not lie on a scale so are not related to one another, each category simply generates a total or frequency.

ordinal data

Levels of measurement other than nominal are all *scales* consisting of data points that relate to each other in a linear way; scores are 'bigger' or 'smaller' relative to adjacent points. On an *ordinal scale* these points are only in rank order; they are 'smaller' or 'larger' than neighbouring points but the gaps between points may not be equal. For example, when participants rate their experience of a fairground ride as (1) *pointless*, (2) *okay*, (3) *great fun* or (4) *exhilarating* the *order* is clear; consecutive points increase in magnitude. However, there is no assurance that the intervals between each point are equivalent; is *exhilarating* exactly twice as exciting as *okay*?

Ordinal scales provide more information than nominal data because the scores are assigned *values*. We could ask how much people liked cheese, carrots or cake rather than just knowing which was their favourite. As with nominal data, questionnaires frequently generate ordinal scores.

equal interval data

Like ordinal data, *interval* and *ratio data* (*equal interval data*) are generated from a scale with points of increasing magnitude. In this instance the gaps between one point and the next are equivalent, hence 'interval' data. This is the case because each individual item on the scale is of *equal* value. Equal interval scales are commonly used in psychology to measure physiological variables such as heart rate and blood pressure. In addition, any scale for which the researcher can be confident that the gap between each point is 'worth the same amount' is also an equal interval scale, such as a list measuring recall in which each item is equally memorable (for example three-letter nonsense syllables of the form consonant-vowel-consonant).

interactive
angles

Read the following examples of possible ways to test psychological variables. Decide which level of measurement is being used in each case and justify your answer.

1 *Visual characteristics are more important than spoken ones for in-group identification* – football supporters were asked to identify songs, chants, names of players, scarves, emblems and shirts that were associated with different clubs. This produced totals for each of the six identifying features.

2 *Frequent shift changes cause disrupted sleep patterns* – uninterrupted sleep was measured to the nearest minute in employees on steady night shift and rotating shift patterns.

3 *Early childhood memories are better recalled when in the primary school environment* – participants were asked to rate their ability to remember the names of all the people in their first school class on a scale of 'all', 'most', 'some' or 'none' either when at home or when they visited their primary school on an open day.

You will need to identify the level of measurement you have used in your investigation before you can begin to analyse your findings for your results section. This list should help you:

◆ If you have two or more named categories and each participant selects one or more then the level of measurement is probably *nominal*.

◆ If your scores are rated – for example, opinions, attitudes or emotions – or if you cannot be sure that every point on your scale is the same, even if you've assigned them numbers, then assume it is *ordinal*.

◆ You are relatively unlikely to have equal interval data. Are you sure that the points are equivalent? Do the intervals between the points really remain constant over the range you are using? If so, it could be an *equal interval* scale. However, if the scale gets 'harder' as you go up then it's probably ordinal.

measures of central tendency

The *measure of central tendency* for a data set indicates the 'typical' score – how an 'average' participant is likely to have responded. As a measure of central tendency can be calculated to provide a summary of any data set we can use this to compare groups – for example levels of the IV in an experiment. We can then make generalisations about one group compared with another. The results in the two levels of the IV may be very similar, or participants in one group may outperform those in the other by a small or large margin. If the results in the two conditions are similar and both lie close to the top or bottom of the possible range of scores this may indicate a flaw in the design of the study.

the mode

The mode is the simplest measure of central tendency and can be used with any data. However, it is the least informative measure, so is only usually used with nominal data. The *mode* is the most common score in the data set, that is, the value that occurs the greatest number of times (hint: think *mode* = *most*). If two scores are equally represented then the distribution of scores is *bi-modal*. If there are three 'modes' it is *tri-modal* and so on. The best way to calculate the mode is to draw up a frequency table and see which score has the highest frequency, for example:

A student asked 25 people about the most vivid dream they could remember from the previous night, recording whether the participants thought they had dreamt in colour or 'black and white'.

type of dream	colour	'black and white'	no dream recalled
Tally of number of people	ⅢꞋ ⅢⅠ	ⅢꞋ ⅢꞋ Ⅲ	Ⅲ
Frequency	9	13	3

table 8.6 Types of dream recalled

From the frequency row we can see that the modal dream type for this data set is 'black and white' with a frequency of 13.

the median

The *median* is the measure of central tendency indicated by the middle score. That is, when a data set is ranked from the smallest number to the largest number (including every repetition of a score) it is the score that lies in the middle of the data set (hint: think *med*ian = *mid*dle). To calculate a median, follow these steps:

1   Rank the data from the smallest to the largest number.

2   Eliminate pairs of scores, one from each end of the ranked data.

3   Continue until either one or two scores are left. In a data set with an odd number of scores there should be one number left (this is the median).

4   In a data set with an even number of scores there should be two numbers left. In this case add up the two remaining numbers and divide the total by 2 to give you the median.

calculating the median

The student studying dream recall decided to improve on her technique and asked another group of people to count the number of nights in a week that they dreamt in colour, so each person could have a maximum score of 7.

She obtained the following scores:

1 4 7 2 6 6 4 3 2 7 5 7 2 3 2 1 3 5 2 5 5 4 2 1 4

In rank order the set looks like this:

1 1 1 2 2 2 2 2 2 3 3 3 4 4 4 4 5 5 5 5 6 6 7 7 7

Find the middle score in the ranked list – the middle, or median, value is 4.

Now, recalculate with a 26th participant (who reported 2 dreams in colour):

1 1 1 2 2 2 2 2 2 2 3 3 3 4 4 4 4 5 5 5 5 6 6 7 7 7

The two middle numbers are 3 and 4. If we now execute step 4, we get:

3 + 4 = 7, we then divide this by 2 to get 7/2 = 3.5. The median score is 3.5.

interactive
angles

Collect the following data:

◆ the time it takes people to open and eat a chocolate bar;

◆ people's favourite type of chocolate: dark, milk, white, none;

◆ get people to rate themselves on a scale of 1–10 on their current 'need for chocolate'.

From the scores, calculate an appropriate measure of average. You may wish to split it into male and female averages.

the mean

The *mean* is the measure of central tendency usually called the 'average'. To calculate this complete the following procedure:

1 Add up all of the scores in the data set.

2 Divide this total by the number of scores in the data set (including zero scores).

We timed how long each of a group of 10 people took to read a Stroop type list and the results were as follows (in seconds):

   45 63 51 65 54 48 60 44 49 48

So, firstly we add up all of the scores:

   $45 + 63 + 51 + 65 + 54 + 48 + 60 + 44 + 49 + 48$

Next, we divide the total score by the number of scores, which is 10:

   $527/10 = 52.7$

Therefore the mean time is 52.7 seconds.

measures of dispersion

Measures of dispersion indicate how spread out or clustered the data set is around the measure of central tendency. It is possible to have roughly equal averages but vastly differing dispersion figures for different groups so a measure of dispersion helps us to understand how variable the data set is. For example, in an experiment in which there is virtually no difference between the average scores for the two levels of the IV, the data from one level may vary greatly (have a wide dispersion) whereas the results for the other level of the IV may vary by only a few points. This could be an interesting pattern in the data.

the variation ratio

The *variation* ratio calculates the percentage of responses that are not in the modal category. It is the only measure of dispersion that can be used on nominal data, although it can also be applied to continuous data. It is used in conjunction with the mode and if we look back to the example on p. 227 we can see how it is applied to a data set. The equation for the variation ratio is:

$$\frac{\text{number of responses } not \text{ in the modal category}}{\text{total number of responses}} \times 100$$

To apply this formula work through the following steps:

1 Calculate the modal response category.

2 Add up the total number of responses.

3 Calculate *how many are not the modal response* (that is, take the frequency of the modal response away from the total number of responses).

4 Divide the figure from step 3 by the total number of responses.

5 Multiply this figure by 100 to express it as a percentage.

For the first dreaming example on p. 227, the variation ratio would be calculated as follows:

1 The modal dream type is *black and white* with a frequency of 13

2 The total number of responses is $9 + 13 + 3 = 25$

3 The number of responses that are *not* the modal response is *colour + no dream recalled*, which is $9 + 3 = 12$

4 $12/25 = 0.48$

5 $0.48 \times 100 = 48$, so the variation ratio is 48%.

This tells us that 48% of the sample tested did not fall into the modal category of dreaming in 'black and white'.

the range

The simplest measure of dispersion is the *range*, which gives a numerical value to the extent of the outermost data points in the set. This measure of dispersion can be used with any continuous data, that is, data with an ordinal or equal interval level of measurement. It is calculated in the following way:

1 Rank the data from the lowest to the highest number (as for calculating the median).

2 Subtract the smallest number from the largest then add 1. This is the range.

Look back at p. 228 to the data for Stroop task times. The range is calculated as follows:

1 The smallest was 44 and the largest 65

2 Largest – smallest: $65 - 44 = 21$

Difference + 1: $21 + 1 = 22$

so the range is 22.

This tells us that the extreme data points, the slowest and fastest participants, were 22 seconds apart.

the interquartile range

This measure of dispersion cannot be used with nominal data, but can be used with ordinal or equal interval data and is more informative than the variation ratio or the range. Unlike the range, it is not affected by very large or vary small 'outlying' scores. The *interquartile range* indicates the spread of the middle 50% of the scores in the data set and is used in conjunction with the median. It literally means 'between the quarter points'. If most of the data set is bunched around the median, the interquartile range will have a smaller value than if the scores are widely spread between the extremes of the range. The interquartile range is worked out in the following way:

1 Rank the data from the smallest to the largest number (as for calculating the median).

2 Divide the ranked list into two halves L (the lower half) and U (the upper half). If the data set has an even number of scores the median will not fall into either set. If the data set has an odd number, leave the median out altogether.

3 Find the middle score of each half, L and U; these are the 'quarter points'. Do this in exactly in the same way as you would find a median. The middle score of set L is the lower quartile and the middle score of set U is the upper quartile.

4 Subtract the lower quartile from the upper quartile and add one. This is the interquartile range.

Using the example from p. 227 again the interquartile range is calculated as follows:

1 The data set: 45 63 51 65 54 48 60 44 49 48
becomes 44 45 48 48 49 51 54 60 63 65.

2 Half L is 44 45 48 48 49.
Half U is 51 54 60 63 65. As it is a data set with an even number of scores the median of 50 does not fall into either set, so it is ignored.

3 The middle score for L is 48, this is the lower quartile. The middle score for U is 60; this is the upper quartile.

4 $60 - 48 + 1 = 13$, so the interquartile range is 13.

Try calculating the median for the first set of data on dreaming on p. 227. There is an odd number of scores so you will find that the median is one of the initial data set. You will have to calculate the quartiles by taking the two mid-point scores and averaging them.

summarising data: tables

Your descriptive statistics – measures of central tendency and dispersion – should be tabulated (put into tables). Work these out for each set of data (such as for levels of the independent variable or each item or group of items on a questionnaire or coding scheme). Tabulate these summary results using clear *row* and *column headings* (as we mentioned earlier, you need to use the actual headings of your conditions – the levels of the IV). Do not simply call them conditions 1 and 2. If you do, you run the risk of becoming confused and will lose marks. Remember also to give each table a clear, concise heading and indicate the units used at the top of each column.

	reading congruent colour words (e.g. RED)	reading non-congruent colour words (e.g. RED)
median		
interquartile range		

table 8.7 Time taken to complete a Stroop list (seconds)

write-up wizard: 12

tables

for the 'tables' in your *results* section you need to make sure that you:

★ give each table a clear title;

★ include column and row headings that are informative (for instance are the levels of the IV clear and not just labelled 'conditions 1 and 2');

★ include measures of central tendency and dispersion where appropriate;

★ write the units of measurement only once, in the column or row heading.

summarising data: graphs

Having calculated the appropriate measures of central tendency and spread for your data and having tabulated them, you also need to illustrate this summary information graphically. You should present your graphs with clear titles and axis headings, making sure that hand-drawn graphs (on plain or graph paper) are tidy and accurate and that computer-generated graphs are sensibly scaled and correctly plotted.

There are four main ways to plot data: bar charts (including bar and whiskers charts), histograms, scattergraphs and frequency polygons. These are used to represent data from studies using different research designs and for data with different levels of measurement.

write-up wizard: 13

descriptive statistics

for the 'descriptive statistics' in your *results* section, your choice of tables and graphs for your coursework depends primarily on your level of measurement – whether your results have been measured on a nominal, ordinal or equal interval scale. On this basis, the tables and graphs you need are as follows.

In an experiment use the following:

For nominal data:

★ table of totals and variation ratio for each group;

★ bar chart of each group total.

For ordinal data:

★ table of medians and interquartile ranges;

★ box and whiskers chart.

For equal interval data:

★ table of means and either the range or interquartile range;

★ bar chart of means or a bar and whiskers chart.

You may also find it helpful to include additional descriptive statistics, such as a line graph, but ensure that the technique that you are using is relevant and appropriate for the data that you have collected.

correlations

In a correlation you will need a table summarising the data and a scattergraph plotting the relationship between the two measured variables.

other methods

If you have conducted an observation, or used a questionnaire or another method, decide whether you have used that technique to collect data (for example, as a measure of the dependent variable) and, if so, whether your research method is really an experiment or correlation. If it is, follow the points above. If not, then compile a table of totals or averages in each response or behavioural category (choose a measure of central tendency appropriate to the level of measurement). You may also be able to include a measure of spread (such as the range). The data may be presented graphically using bar charts. Lay out your columns sensibly to achieve easy comparisons, for example, by putting opposing pairs next to one another to illustrate contrasts. Resist the urge to draw stacked bar charts or pie charts. If you use a computer to draw the graphs make sure the axes are appropriately scaled and labelled.

figure 8.5
Bar chart to show the mean time taken to read a Stroop word list

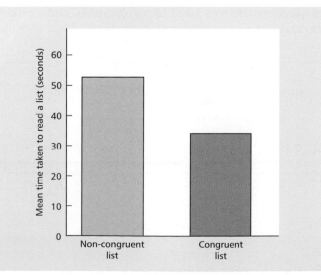

bar charts

These are used for representing totals of nominal data or for plotting measures of central tendency derived from ordinal or equal interval data. Put the categories of data (or independent variable) on the x-axis (horizontal axis) and the frequency of occurrences or average values (of the dependent variable) on the y-axis (vertical axis).

	non-congruent word list	congruent word list
mean time taken to read list (seconds)	52.7	34.1

bar and whiskers chart

This type of bar chart is used to display the median and interquartile range. A bar chart of the medians is drawn and labelled as above (although the bars should not be filled with a solid, dark colour). The interquartile range is the added to each bar as a 'whisker'. A straight line is drawn running vertically through the centre of the bar, beginning at the point of the upper quartile, topped with a short horizontal line and ending at the lower quartile, again with a short horizontal line. This should be clearly visible against the background of both the chart and the bar. If an interquartile happens to have the same value as the median, it is simply drawn along the top of the bar as part of the same line. This technique is a useful way to illustrate visually the spread of the data and is helpful in making comparisons between the spread of different groups such as levels of the independent variable.

figure 8.6 Bar and whiskers chart to show the number of nights per week that participants experienced dreams in colour or 'black and white'

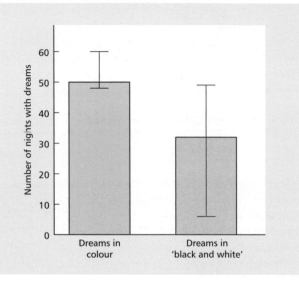

| | number of nights with dreams in: | |
	colour	'black and white'
median	50	32
lower quartile	48	6
upper quartile	60	49

histograms

These show the distribution of scores measured on a continuous (numerical) scale (ordinal or equal interval data) by plotting them on the x-axis (horizontal axis). The y-axis (vertical axis) should always be used for the frequency of occurrences.

Time taken to read a list is one way to measure the effect of interference on a Stroop task. The table below shows the time taken by a group of 60 participants on the reading of 26-item word list.

time taken to read word list (seconds)	40–44	45–49	50–54	55–59	60–64	65–69	70–74
frequency	2	3	16	19	10	6	4

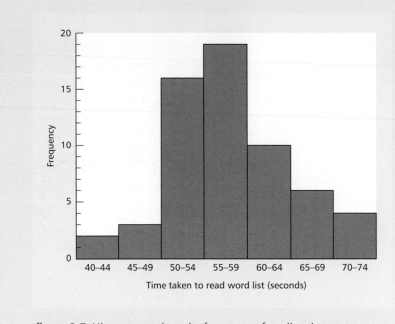

figure 8.7 Histogram to show the frequency of reading times on a Stroop task

scattergraphs

Scattergraphs (also called scatterplots or scattergrams) are used for plotting correlations. From a scattergraph it is clear whether a correlation exists or whether the distribution is random and, if the variables are related, whether the correlation is positive or negative. The x-axis (horizontal axis) should represent one of the numerical measures and the y-axis (vertical axis) the other (it doesn't matter which way round they go).

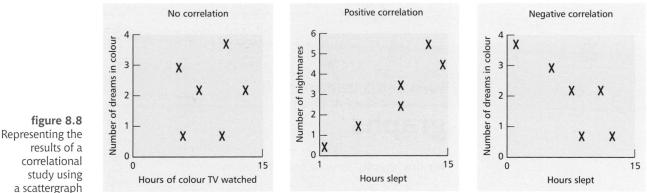

figure 8.8 Representing the results of a correlational study using a scattergraph

frequency polygons

Frequency polygons are also referred to as line graphs. They are used with two sets of data that can be compared on one graph. An example would be plotting the distribution of scores for males and females on a questionnaire measuring attitudes towards safe sex. The x-axis (horizontal axis) should have the scores on the task while the y-axis (vertical axis) represents the frequency of occurrences of the possible scores.

Time taken to read a list is one way to measure the effect of interference on a Stroop task. Another measure is to count the number of errors participants make. The table below shows errors made by a group of 60 participants on the reading of a 26-item word list.

errors made		0–2	3–5	6–8	9–11	12–14	15–17	18–20	21–23	24–26
number of participants	non-congruent list	3	8	6	15	20	7	1	0	0
	congruent	38	17	3	1	0	1	0	0	0

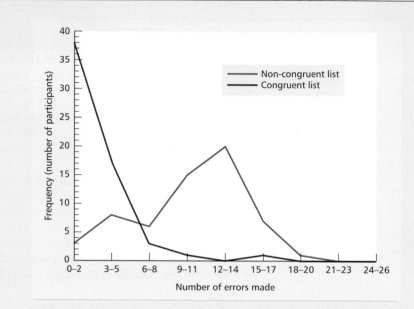

figure 8.9 Frequency polygon to show the frequency of errors made on a Stroop task

write-up wizard: 14

graphs

for the 'graphs' in your *results* section:

★ Select a technique for graphical representation that is appropriate to your data.

★ In general, it is better to steer clear of three-dimensional plots, pie charts and cumulative frequency graphs, and resist the urge to plot every single participant's results unless you have conducted a correlation and are drawing a scattergraph.

★ Use graph or plain paper for hand-drawn graphs.

★ Check the axes and accuracy of computer-generated graphs.

★ Give each graph a title that explains what it shows.

★ Make sure that you have clearly labelled each axis with both the variable and the units of measurement if appropriate.

In the remainder of your results section you need to provide a commentary on your findings. You do this by describing your conclusions from the summaries you have produced in tabular and graphical form. This aspect of your write-up is discussed further below. Finally, you need to conclude from your data whether you can accept your alternative hypothesis. This aspect of writing up your coursework is dealt with on p. 236. This is followed by a detailed description of how to tackle the writing up of your discussion. This is an important section that earns many of the marks – don't run the risk of leaving yourself too little time to finish it!

commentary on tables and graphs

Following tables and graphs, either in one section or two, you need to provide a commentary on your data. Each should consist of two or more detailed points and there must be at least four different ideas in total.

When describing your tabulated data, make sure that you do refer to the table, either to quote figures or to draw contrasts, with exceptional scores for example.

You can describe features such as whether there are differences between the measures of central tendency for different conditions, whether this is reflected in the dispersion of the groups – are they also different or do they overlap? The measures of dispersion will also indicate whether the scores in all conditions are similarly spread or whether some are more clustered. If you have used several conditions in an experiment, or done a correlational study, you may be able to see general trends in the data. Describe such observations but do not try to explain them yet.

write-up wizard: 15

commentary on table and graphs

for the 'summary table' commentary section of your *results* you need to describe at least two features of your data in relation to the table. For example:

★ What do the averages show?

★ What do the dispersions indicate about your data?

★ Are there any trends or patterns?

For the descriptive statistics commentary section of your results you need to describe at least two different features of your data in relation to the graphs, for example:

★ What do the averages show?

★ What do the dispersions indicate about your data?

★ Are there any trends or patterns?

If you are making the same points as in the previous section, make sure that there are at least four separate, detailed points in total.

relationship of results to hypotheses

End your results section by identifying whether your tables and graphs suggest that you have found a significant difference, correlation or pattern. Go on to use this to accept the appropriate hypothesis. If your results have supported your aims (and you have phrased you hypotheses correctly) then you should be able to reject your null hypothesis and accept your alternative hypothesis. If you predicted a directional (one-tailed) alternative hypothesis make sure that the difference you have identified is in the direction predicted. If a difference has arisen but it is in the opposite direction, then you must accept the null hypothesis. If your results have not supported your aims then you must accept the null hypothesis and reject the alternative hypothesis. If so, don't panic! There are no marks awarded for your actual findings, only the way in which you have written up these findings. Whichever conclusion you come to, make sure that you justify your decision by referring to your own data – use your averages, dispersions or graphs to back up your comments.

write-up wizard: 16

relationship of results to hypothesis

for the 'relationship of results to hypotheses' section of your *results* you need to:

★ decide whether to accept or reject your H_0, which determines whether you accept or reject your H_1;

★ justify your decision *based on your data* (using averages/dispersions/graphs).

the discussion

This section of your coursework has the greatest number of marks available, so make sure that you tackle each section well.

implications of study

Relate your findings to previous research – the theories and studies you mentioned in the introduction. Be specific; explain how your findings support the work of other psychologists that you have described (if you found a significant effect) or how it contradicts previous findings otherwise. Discuss how the models or theories discussed in the introduction can explain your results or consider flaws in the models if they cannot explain what you have found. You should not need to introduce new material in the discussion (except possibly if they have accepted your null hypothesis and can find other ways of explaining the effect).

write-up wizard: 17

implications

for the 'implications of study' section of your *discussion* you need a discussion of your findings in relation to the background research (in your introduction). This should:

★ be detailed;

★ indicate how your findings support or conflict with the findings of each previous study;

★ suggest whether (and, if appropriate, how) your results can be explained by any theories you described;

★ explain why you believe this in each case.

validity

The purpose of this section is to discuss whether your materials, measurements or tasks were a valid test of your hypothesis – that is whether the techniques used achieved the purpose for which they were designed. For example, when you were conducting your study, did the tasks you used appear to be testing the variable you were trying to measure or was performance actually affected by some other factor? In finding or constructing materials to create different conditions, did you succeed in generating situations that were sufficiently different and were they a valid test of your independent variable? Did the setting of your study create any additional, unwanted variation that could have affected validity? Could any aspects of your procedure have affected the validity?

measures of internal validity

The validity of the test items themselves in relation to the objective.

◆ **Face validity** is whether the measure appears (at face value) to test what it claims to. It is the least sophisticated measure of validity but is more worthwhile if an expert opinion is obtained.

◆ **Concurrent validity** compares a new test to other tests of the same phenomenon to see if they produce similar results. If the tests agree, they have concurrent validity.

◆ **Construct validity** is demonstrated by showing that the phenomenon being measured actually exists. So, the construct validity of a test of intelligence, for example, is dependent on a model or theory for intelligence.

◆ **Predictive validity** indicates that the measure is valid because it can accurately forecast performance on the measure under scrutiny. If an intelligence test has predictive validity it should be able to estimate participants' future success on tasks such as examinations.

measures of external validity

◆ **Ecological validity** is the extent to which a test measures a real-world phenomenon.

◆ **Population validity** is the extent to which a real, universal effect has been identified that is equally relevant to different populations. This has been an issue because many studies are conducted on students (and, for many years, predominantly white, Western male ones).

Try to avoid criticisms that should never have arisen in the first place, such as distractions from conducting the study in a noisy place (you should have gone elsewhere unless this was an essential part of the investigation). Aim to focus on comments that relate specifically to your method rather than general issues that might arise in any study, such as limited populations or sampling errors. Possible issues might include ceiling or floor effects (where the task is too easy or too hard, so all the participants scores are clustered at the top or bottom of the range); fatigue or practice effects (see p. 217), demand characteristics (see p. 222), participant or situational variables (see p. 222) or any other sources of confounding variable. Where subsequent problems may arise as a result of the possible solutions (such as ethical dilemmas) discuss these too.

write-up wizard: 18

validity

for the 'validity' section of your *discussion* you need to:

★ reconsider the validity of the operationalisation of your variables;

★ consider the influence that factors such as the setting and the method may have had on validity.

Make sure that your discussion:

★ is concise;

★ makes at least four relevant, separate points;

★ links the points you make to your study;

★ considers the validity of the IV in an experimental study;

★ considers the validity of the DV in an experimental study.

improving validity

The aim here is to offer solutions to the problems that you identified in the previous section, that is, the modifications you could make. You need to make specific suggestions for improving validity for each of at least two of the problems you have described. These improvements must be clearly linked to your study. In each case describe the possible effect this change might have of the results if it were implemented.

write-up wizard: 19

improving validity

for the 'improving validity' section of your *discussion* you need to:

★ suggest an idea for improving validity that relates directly to your study;

★ describe the possible effect of this suggestion on the results;

★ suggest a second idea for improving validity that relates directly to your study;

★ describe the possible effect of this second suggestion on the results.

reliability

This section is intended to allow you to assess the reliability of the measures you used in your study, that is, whether a replication of your investigation would produce similar results. If you were part of a group and several researchers were involved in data collection, you may have employed special measures to improve the reliability of your recording, for instance in observations or content analyses. However, even if this were not the case, there could still be factors that would result in different findings if the study were repeated. For example, you could consider the method you used, your sampling method and aspects of your design, instructions to participants or materials. You need to discuss the possible effect of several of these factors.

write-up wizard: 20

reliability

for the 'reliability' section of your *discussion* you need to consider the effect of a range of issues on reliability (such as sampling, and aspects of your procedure or materials). You will also need to make sure that your discussion:

★ is concise;

★ relates to two or more issues;

★ links the points you make to your study.

improving reliability

The purpose of this section is to discuss ways to overcome the reliability issues that you described in the previous section – that is, to suggest alternative techniques you could have used that would have been more reliable. You need to make specific suggestions for improving reliability for each of at least two of the problems you have described. These alternatives must be applicable to your study. In each case describe the possible effect the change might have on the results if it were implemented.

write-up wizard: 21

improving reliability

for the 'improving reliability' section of your *discussion* you need to:

★ suggest an alternative technique that could improve reliability;

★ describe the possible effect of this suggestion on the results;

★ suggest a second alternative technique that could improve reliability;

★ describe the possible effect of this second suggestion on the results;

★ make sure that these points relate directly to your study;

★ relate to the issues you suggested in the previous section.

generalisation of findings

In your study you will only have tested a sample from your target population. If this sample was representative it would allow you to generalise from your results – to apply the implications of the findings from the sample to the whole population. The purpose of this section is to explore whether you can justify the generalisation of your findings. Sampling is only one factor that affects the value of the results of a study, reliability and validity also affect generalisability.

write-up wizard: 22

generalisation of findings

for the generalisation of findings section of your discussion you need to consider the effect of factors such as sampling, validity and reliability on the generalisability of your findings. Make sure that your discussion:

★ is concise (two sentences may be sufficient);

★ relates to at least two issues.

application of the study to everyday life

You can then consider the value of your findings. Firstly, consider what implications they have for real life. These may be obvious if you have explored an applied area of psychology. If not, then could the findings be applied to areas such as education, advertising or road safety? How? Be specific and make suggestions about what might be done giving examples of your applications.

write-up wizard: 23

application to everyday life

for the 'application to everyday life' section of your *discussion* you need to:

★ provide a detailed description of how your study relates to real life;

★ make sure that your discussion is specific about the links between your study and everyday life and that it is not too long – as little as two sentences may be sufficient.

presentation

references

The purpose of the references section is to allow other people to find the resources that you have referred to. It is appropriate to indicate both the original source of a piece of research (the primary source) and the location in which you read it. So, if you have described a study that you read about in a book (a secondary source), you need to provide both the reference for the book you used and the article in which the research was originally published. There are several different conventions for referencing.

write-up wizard: 24

references

give the source (book, journal or Web site) of every citation you have made and list them alphabetically by author in a references section using the following layout:

★ **Book**: Author; Initials. (date) *Title*, Publisher, Place of publication (followed by a list of citations from that book with a page numbers if you are using it as a secondary source).

★ **Journal article**: Author; Initials. (date) Title of article, **journal**, **volume** (part number): pages.

★ **Web site**: state the whole web address and underline it. Add the date you accessed the site.

Some examples of this system in use would be:

★ Jarvis, M. and Russell, J. (2004) *Angles on Psychology*. Nelson Thornes, Cheltenham.

★ Stroop, J. R. (1935) Studies of interference in serial verbal reactions. *Journal of Experimental Psychology*, **XVIII**(6): 643–662.

★ http://faculty.washington.edu/chudler/java/ready.html [accessed on 8 August 2003].

appendices

The purpose of an appendix is to hold vital information that does not need to be presented in the body of the report. This should include any standardised instructions that you used and might also include interview questions, examples of stimuli and raw data tables. It should not contain every participant's copy of the answer sheet or questionnaire. Remember that participants should not be identifiable from their results.

conclusions

Working through this chapter should have helped you to plan, conduct and write up your coursework from finding information for your introduction, through designing your method to analysing your results and writing the final document. Remember two things; firstly, it doesn't matter what you find, only how you write it up and it is the process of doing the study, not whether you accept your alternative hypothesis, that will give you the experience you need to produce a piece of coursework that will earn high marks. Secondly, although the references are at the end of the report, keep a clear and thorough record of your sources from the beginning!

where to now?

▶ **Fisher, D. and Hanstock, T.** (1998) *Citing References*. Blackwell, Oxford. This small booklet provides a thorough and understandable account of the need to reference well and how to do it.

▶ **MacLeod, C. M.** (1991) Half a century of research on the Stroop effect: an integrative review. *Psychological Bulletin*, **109**(2), 163–203. This thorough article describes in brief the huge range of investigations that have arisen out of Stroop's original work.

▶ **Russell, J. and Roberts, C.** (2001) *Angles on Psychological Research*. Nelson Thornes, Cheltenham. This text provides a thorough explanation of each of the research methods you could use, including some of the more unusual ones, such as content analysis. It provides detailed explanations of questionnaire and interview design and contains many examples of recent research that could provide the foundation for coursework.

9 examination advice and guidance

what's ahead?

As the title suggests, this chapter is intended to provide advice and guidance on the Edexcel AS level examinations. This chapter will deal with a series of questions relating to the requirements of the exams, what is meant by certain types of questions, real examples of students' answers to some of those questions with comments and advice on how they should have been answered. Other areas covered will be practical advice on how to prepare for exams (revision and motivation) and how to cope with any issues that might arise in the exam room.

This chapter aims to bring together information to which you could gain access from a variety of other sources, combining teaching and examining experience, points made in examination reports and other tips and handy hints on revision.

how is my AS examined?

You will be required to sit two examination-based papers for units 1 and 2½ hours each), and produce one piece of coursework (approximately 2000 words) for unit 3.

Each unit has equal weighting.

unit 1 (72 marks)	unit 2 (72 marks)	unit 3 (72 marks)
Cognitive	Psychodynamic	You will be required to write a report (about 2000 words) of an investigation, based on a relevant topic from the specification.
Social	Learning	
Cognitive	Physiological	

what will the examiners be looking for?

The assessment objectives are outlined near the beginning of the specification document and you should discuss these with your teacher. However, a rough guide to the kind of skills each objective is looking for is shown below.

AO1 (Assessment Objective 1)

This will be assessed throughout the two examination papers and deals with your ability to show knowledge and understanding of the material covered in the content section of the specification.

Knowledge and understanding can usually be demonstrated by your ability to identify, name, define, outline, describe and explain some of the key information that you have learned in each unit (AO1 is worth 42/72 marks in each unit).

AO2 (Assessment Objective 2)

This will also be assessed throughout the two examination papers and is more concerned with your ability to analyse, criticise, evaluate, discuss and apply your knowledge and understanding of each approach (AO2 is worth 30/72 marks in each unit).

AO3 (Assessment Objective 3)

This is only assessed in the coursework section and is entirely concerned with your ability to plan, implement and analyse a modest piece of research on a relevant topic. This is shown through your knowledge of research skills and methods, as well as the research process itself (72 marks).

how will I know when to use AO1/AO2 skills?

In the unit 1 and 2 examinations you will be asked questions that reflect the type of skills set out above. For example, a typical AO1 question might ask you to 'outline *one* key assumption' from a particular approach. This question is looking for two things: 1. your knowledge of the key assumptions as set out in the content section of the specification; 2. Your understanding of the material you are outlining.

You can demonstrate 1. by showing that you can accurately recall the main points of one of the key assumptions you have learned. You can demonstrate 2. by showing that you can explain the point you are making clearly and in an appropriate amount of detail. Demonstrating 1. without 2. is unlikely to be sufficient to achieve high marks in any exam at this level.

For example, a typical AO2 question might ask you to 'evaluate *one* study/theory' from a particular approach. This question is looking for a number of things, but primarily it is assessing your ability to criticise and evaluate relevant material. Such critical evaluation can include both positive and negative points about the study or theory and helps to provide a thorough analysis of the information you have learned.

Some questions ask for both AO1 and AO2. This is often explicit, as in questions that say 'describe and evaluate *one* contemporary issue' from a particular approach, or another way of asking for the same thing is to replace 'describe and evaluate' with 'discuss'.

If you are faced with such a question it is worth knowing that if the total marks for the question are more than 10 then the marks for the question will be equally divided between AO1 and AO2. However, any such question will also carry within it marks for clarity and communication (AO1) and balance and breadth (AO2).

We will look at the use of these skills shortly, when we consider some sample examination questions and answers. However, it is worth noting a few of the common injunctions (words which indicate what you have to do) used in exam questions and what they are looking for before going any further.

how will I know what each question is asking me to do?

Below is a list of injunctions, some taken directly from the specification, some taken from questions asked in actual exams. It should not be considered an exhaustive list and other injunctions may appear:

◆ **identify** – to show knowledge of something by making it recognisable;

◆ **state** – to show an awareness of one specific point;

◆ **name** – to identify something by referring to the title or author/investigator;

◆ **define** – to explain what is meant by a particular term;

◆ **outline** – to briefly describe without explanation, identifying main points;

◆ **describe** – to give details without explanation;

◆ **explain** – to provide a clear account of a particular topic;

◆ **evaluate** – to comment on, giving advantages and disadvantages, or give a judgement;

◆ **assess** – to consider the quality of a particular topic or issue, by looking at its advantages and disadvantages;

◆ **discuss** – to give a considered or balanced, reasoned objective account of a particular topic;

◆ **distinguish** – to recognise comparable differences between two ideas or situations;

◆ **compare** – to identify similarities and differences between two sets of ideas;

◆ **apply** – to explain how a concept is significant when considering everyday issues or novel situations.

Most of these injunctions will appear in the sample questions and answers contained in the following pages. It is worth noting that all of these questions come from past exam papers but they are not meant to be a definitive guide to any future questions that might appear.

that's all well and good but how will I know what to write in the exam?

The sample answers that follow come from real candidates' responses and each one has a commentary written by the chief examiner that reflects the quality of the answer and the skills shown by the candidate in answering the question. The intention is to look at a particular question and have a good idea of how much you need to write and the sort of things you need to write about.

sample questions and answers

key assumptions

There are a few methods employed by examiners in asking questions about key assumptions. One is to ask very general questions from the specification, which may involve asking you to outline one or two key assumptions from a particular approach or to name the specific key assumption and then to explain what is meant by this. A very different approach is to provide you with a few alternative key assumptions from different approaches and then asking you to identify the correct ones for the named approach. The two examples that follow show these two ways clearly and the commentary on the answers provides ideas on how/how not to tackle such questions.

---

key assumptions, example 1: unit 1, May 2002

Outline **one** key assumption from the cognitive approach. (3 marks)

Our brains are like computers in the way they handle

information (✓) with an input (sensors, eyes, ears) then a

throughput (processing the information) then an output

(speaking) (✓).

2/3

---

comment:

This is a fairly standard question and the best way to approach it is on the basis that you will usually get one mark for correctly identifying **one** (placed in bold to emphasise the fact that you should outline only one and you will get no marks for outlining more than one) appropriate key assumption and two further marks for some appropriate elaboration (essentially explaining what the assumption means). This candidate has correctly identified an assumption from the specification and has provided some elaboration of what this means. Unfortunately, the candidate has fallen short of a full elaboration as it is still not very clear what the computer analogy means. A more clearly elaborated explanation, making a direct comparison between how our minds work and the working of a computer, would have helped. For example, computers have programs that influence the way in which information is processed; it is argued that we have schemas that do the same thing.

DO – use one of the key assumptions identified in the specification. With these you know you can't go wrong.

DON'T – try to create an assumption from one of the theories you have studied. Such assumptions are usually not general enough to cover the whole approach.

DO – provide an example to show that you really do understand what you are writing about.

DON'T – provide an example that has little or nothing to do with psychology.

DO – explain your assumption using at least as many different points as there are marks available for the question.

DON'T – merely identify the assumption and move on or, worse, leave a blank space.

---

key assumptions example 2: unit 1, January 2003

Identify the **two** correct statements in the table by placing a tick (✓) in the appropriate boxes. (2 marks)

The social approach is primarily concerned with the effects of early experience on personality.	☐
The social approach is concerned with the influence of groups on behaviour.	✓
The social approach is concerned with the development of abilities over time.	☐
The social approach is concerned with the effect of cultural norms on behaviour.	✓

2/2

comment:

This is obviously a lot more specific and seemingly a lot easier. All of the assumptions mentioned are taken from different parts of the specification; only the second and the fourth one are actually two assumptions from the social approach. The first one is taken from the psychodynamic approach and the third one from the cognitive developmental approach.

DO – read the instructions carefully and follow them so that you only use ticks in the boxes as you have been asked.

DON'T – use your own way of indicating: for example, crosses could be interpreted as indicating that you don't think it is that one.

DO – only tick two boxes. To avoid the problem of candidates guessing one mark is taken away from the number answered correctly for every extra incorrect box that is ticked.

DON'T – try to get smart and tick all the boxes as you will end up with no marks.

DON'T – tick randomly as this rarely gains any credit.

DO – have an educated guess if you're not sure.

research methods

Once again, there are different ways of asking questions on this topic. In general, they tend to fall into the same kind of categories mentioned above – general and specific. The added complication for research methods though, is that now you may be asked both AO1 and AO2 style questions. Typical general AO1 questions may simply ask you to identify a method or to outline/describe a method from a particular approach.

More specific AO1 questions may identify the method and ask you to describe its main features. General AO2 questions may ask you to outline strengths and weaknesses of the methods you have described, whereas specific questions may name the method and then ask you to evaluate that method. The two examples that follow show the difference in question style clearly and commentary is provided to explain how to answer such questions and how not to answer them.

---

research methods, example 1: unit 1, May 2002

(a) Name **one** research method commonly used in the cognitive-developmental approach. (1 mark)

1

Longitudinal study (✓)

....

(b) Evaluate the research method named in (a) in terms of **one** strength and **one** weakness. (4 marks)

We can assess how behaviour changes over a period of time (✓)

Strength

loss of participants often occurs during lengthy periods (✓)

Weakness

....

2/4

---

comment:

There is clearly no problem with part (a). This is one of the methods identified on the spec. for this approach and as such is a safe bet. Other possible methods would have been; observations (also identified on the specification), but also a few not identified on the specification but definitely creditworthy: clinical interviews, experiments and case studies. There may be others that are also applicable but don't make the mistake of thinking 'anything goes' because there are certainly some that are not appropriate, such as animal studies, analysis of symbols, surveys and most of the physiological methods.

Part (b) has gained one mark for the strength and one mark for the weakness.

Both answers are partially correct, really only identifying the potential strength/weakness without really explaining its effect.

There is no explanation of how the strength will prove beneficial to someone investigating cognitive development – such as 'this allows us to see if thinking changes qualitatively from childhood to adulthood'.

Similarly, there is no explanation of the effect of the weakness, such as 'this may mean that the participants remaining at the end are not representative'.

DO – name a method from the appropriate section of the specification. (It is better to be safe than sorry.)

DO – evaluate the method you have named, no marks can be gained for evaluating a different method, even if it is potentially correct.

DO – refer to one strength and one weakness. Even if you know lots of weaknesses, you can only get marked for one and not referring to a strength will definitely lose those marks.

DON'T – write down the first method that comes into your head. Even if you can't remember the correct one, you should at least be able to have an educated guess.

DON'T – change your mind halfway through without first changing the answer in (a).

DON'T – waste too much time doing more than one of each or worse leave a blank space.

research methods example 2: unit 2, January 2003

(a) Explain what is meant by the term lesioning. (2 marks)

Lesioning is a cut through a part of the brain (✓) which is

involved in brain activities. Disconnection between neurones

takes place (✓).

2/2

(b) Outline **one** advantage and **one** disadvantage of lesioning as a research method. (4 marks)

Advantage

It allows us to understand how the brain functions (✓) which can be very important because you may need to know how humans react to particular things (✓)

Disadvantage

It is mainly used on animals therefore it is not representative (✓) because animals and humans are qualitatively different in terms of brain structure (✓)

4/4

comment:

Part (a) of this question is somewhat different to the previous one as you are now being asked to outline a given method, rather than just name it. The candidate in this example has provided a very clear and accurate outline, which tells us enough about the method to achieve both marks. Crucially, this candidate has made two clearly separate points and it is easy to award a mark for each.

Part (b) in this case is broadly similar to the previous one except that strength and weakness have been replaced by advantage and disadvantage. This makes very little difference to the way it should be marked and on this occasion the candidate has provided more complete answers.

Both answers have a point followed by a 'because', followed by an appropriate elaboration. The elaboration, in both cases, provides enough detail to show that the candidate has indeed outlined one advantage and one disadvantage.

DO – try to make more than one clearly separate point when asked to outline a method.

DO – try to explain your point when elaborating (often helped by including the word because).

DON'T – provide an overly brief or rushed outline that only gives a vague idea of what the method is about.

DON'T – merely identify an advantage/disadvantage with no further elaboration.

in-depth areas of study

This is the theoretical part of the specification and, as such, contains the most diversity in terms of detailed areas of study, which is necessarily reflected in the range of question types that occur for this section (many more than for the previous two).

Questions here fall into similar categories as those mentioned above in that there are specific and general questions, AO1 and AO2.

The general AO1 questions provide the opportunity to demonstrate your knowledge and understanding of the theories/in-depth areas you have studied, by asking you to outline/describe them. Other questions may be much more specific about which parts of the theory you need to deal with.

General AO2 questions may ask you to provide some form of evaluation of the theory you have described or, in more specific cases, ask you to evaluate some named theory. Hopefully, the examples that follow will show the difference clearly and commentary is provided to explain how/how not to answer such questions.

---

in-depth area of study, example 1: unit 2, May 2002

Freud described several stages of psychosexual development in childhood.

Name the first three. (3 marks)

1 *Oral stage* (✓)

2 *Anal stage* (✓)

3 *Phallic stage* (✓)

3/3

comment:

This is a fairly straightforward question and shouldn't cause too many problems. Often students use mnemonics such as OAP (oral, anal, phallic) to remember such information.

However, such rote learning can be dangerous, something which can be seen by looking look at the next example.

---

in-depth area of study, example 2: unit 2, January 2003

Freud's theory of personality suggests that we pass through psychosexual stages during childhood. The table below gives adult behaviours associated with fixation. Name the psychosexual stage of development at which the fixation occurs. (3 marks)

adult behaviour associated with fixation	psychosexual stage of development
Very mean or generous with money very tidy or untidy	Oral stage ([**X**])
Cigarette smoking Very dependent or aggressive	Anal stage ([**X**])
Self-assured, vain or impulsive	Phallic stage ([✓])

1/3

comment:

Unfortunately, in this example the candidate has remembered the mnemonic, but has failed to read the question and consequently has fallen down quite badly on what should have been relatively easy marks.

DO – make sure you fill in all of the gaps in such questions.

DO – make sure that you read the question fully before continuing.

DO – use mnemonics to help you remember material.

DON'T – put more than one answer in each box: they will both be marked wrong.

DON'T – assume you know what the question will be before reading it.

DON'T – merely rote learn answers and try to use them regardless of the specific question.

in-depth area of study, examples 3, 4 and 5: unit 1, January 2003

The following examples all deal with definitions and highlight some of the issues involved in answering such questions.

What did Piaget mean by the term **schema**? (2 marks)

The way in which people learn and the stages in which they

learn

0/2

What did Piaget mean by the term **assimilation**? (2 marks)

Assimilation means that the input is changed ([✓]) to fit the existing schemas ([✓])

2/2

Explain what is meant by the term **prejudice**. (2 marks)

Prejudice is the attitude against an individual or group ([✓]) that could be because of culture or other groups of people

1/2

comment:

The three examples above show how you don't have to write much to get the most out of your answer.

◆ The first example shows that the candidate has some idea about the role of schemas in cognitive development, but is unsure about their exact role. This explanation/definition does not say anything specific about schemas, instead providing a general idea of the process of adaptation.

◆ The second example is right on the mark providing, as it does, a succinct definition of the term and managing to avoid confusion with other similar terms, for example accommodation.

◆ The third example lacks clarity and although the examiner might have a fair idea of what the candidate is getting at, it needs to be made clear in order to be credited with something more. There is just enough here to gain one mark for getting across the most fundamental points – an attitude that is in some way against an individual or group. However, it certainly is not clear enough to gain the extra mark that might come from saying that it involves forming an opinion without prior knowledge of the individual or group, or from referring to stereotyping, and so forth.

DO – read back through the answer you have given to ensure that it is at least clear to you, if it isn't then it probably will not be clear to the examiner either.

DO – try to ensure that you haven't got your terms confused (this is a particular problem with Piaget), possibly using some form of mnemonic.

DON'T – try to write as much as possible to cover everything; concise answers are often the best.

DON'T – leave them blank: a short and simple attempt at something you are not sure of is better than nothing.

in-depth area of study, example 6: unit 2, May 2003

(a) Match each type of learning with the appropriate description by drawing a line between them. (3 marks)

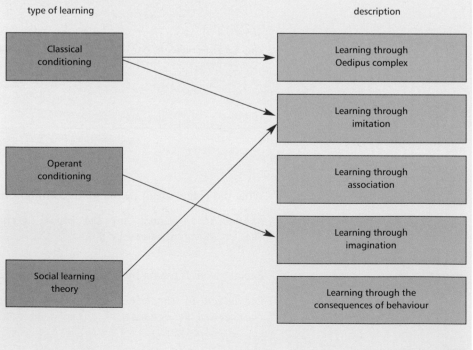

figure 9.1

(b) Evaluate social learning as an explanation of human behaviour. (4 marks)

The positive aspect of social learning is that it explains how children learn to speak, for example they watch their parents say and put together sounds and imitate it (✓), this would also explain accents, as the children imitate the sounds the parent makes.

The negative aspect of social learning theory is that other theories also explain the same ideas, for example a child learning to speak could also be explained through operant conditioning, when the child says something correctly they are praised (✓). It also doesn't explain the errors children make, e.g. 'sheepies' instead of sheep, as that wouldn't be imitated from a parent. (✓)

4/4

comment:

The first part of this question (a) is a fairly common type of question for identifying theories and provides an opportunity for more visual learners to use their ability. Unfortunately, it can sometimes lead to confusion, as is the case in the example shown above.

The candidate was only supposed to draw three lines, one from each type of learning on the left to its appropriate description on the right. This candidate became confused and thought that they should connect all of the boxes on the right with a box on the left.

In this situation, the examiner cannot second guess candidates and choose the right one on their behalf and so any box on the left with two lines coming from it is automatically disregarded and no marks awarded. This means that even though the candidate, despite clearly having the potential to gain three marks, only gained one.

The second part of this question (b) also illustrates quite a common approach to asking evaluation questions. In this case the candidate has chosen to make two main points and elaborate them. This has been done very successfully and the candidate has picked up a well-deserved four marks. The first two marks are for an application point that has been elaborated well with the point about accents.

The next two marks come from a comparison with other ways of learning and a very good example to show how social learning alone cannot explain all forms of behaviour.

It would have been just as acceptable to give four completely separate evaluative points to gain 4/4.

DO – read the instructions for the question carefully and make sure that you are doing what is asked, rather than what you think you have been asked.

DO – provide critical positive/negative evaluation points about the theory.

DO – provide relevant examples to show the application of the theory to real life. This does count as evaluation.

DON'T – rush into your answer. Even answers which simply involve drawing lines can go badly wrong.

DON'T – describe the theory when you have been asked to evaluate it. Saying it is good because it does what it says it does is very weak evaluation at best and description at worst.

DON'T – rely on 'glib'/one-line answers for your evaluation; they rarely gain any marks without explanation.

studies in detail

The specification mentions two studies for each approach and consequently any one examination paper could ask you to describe/evaluate two studies from a particular approach. General questions from the AO1 category might just ask you to describe a study from a particular approach, whereas specific AO1 questions might ask about a study from a particular area of that approach. AO2 questions tend to be quite similar in this area, often just asking you to evaluate a study, although on some occasions you may be given specific prompts to point you in the right direction, or to set the limits of the issues you are allowed to deal with, such as ethical or methodological aspects.

Once again, the examples that follow should show the difference between the types of question and provide commentary on how/how not to answer such questions.

---

studies in detail, example 1: unit 1, May 2002

Describe **one** study from the cognitive-developmental approach. (5 marks)

One study would be the three mountains study. (✔) This

would involve a child sat in front of three mountains, which

had a house, snow and a church on, respectively. (✔) A doll

was then placed at different positions around the set and the

child was asked what the doll could see. (✔)

3/5

Evaluate **one** study from the cognitive-developmental approach. (5 marks)

The 3 mountains study supports Piaget's theory of cognitive-

development, as the child can only centre on one aspect of a

conservation task. (✔) The study also has high ecological

validity, although the child may have felt pressurised by the

---

authoritarian figure such as a teacher who was conducting

the research.

comment:

The mark scheme for describing and evaluating studies has a standard formula that is used for all studies across both units.

For describing the study, candidates would need to cover the aim of the study or clearly identify the study (which they have done in the first line), the method/procedure involved (which this candidate has done twice, the results and the conclusion (neither of which this candidate has done). It is worth noting at this point that there are only two marks available for any one section, so there is no point writing a very long answer that only deals with the method.

For evaluating the study, the formula is less prescriptive and allows for many things to be used, but the mark scheme will still suggest the following:

◆ **Methodological limitations** – which this candidate has dealt with successfully once by looking at the effect of the authority figure, but the candidate has not done enough with validity to justify an extra mark. It would need explaining, although it would be hard to imagine how any amount of explanation could justify the point made above.

◆ **Ethical issues** – which have not been dealt with here but could have been.

◆ **Alternative findings** – from other studies that either support or refute this one (again this has not been dealt with here).

◆ **Social relevance** – how could the study be applied to real life? This was also not covered by this candidate.

In fact the only other point this candidate makes is a different, but nonetheless valid, point concerning support for Piaget's theory.

studies in detail, example 2: unit 2, January 2003

(a) Describe **one** study of classical conditioning in humans. (4 marks)

Little Albert was presented with a certain stimulus. ☑

A white rat, rabbit, a dog, masks with or without hair and

white cotton wool. He showed no fear. ☑ *However, to*

cause the fear, the banging of steel to hammer happened next to him. (✓) Then he was allowed to play with the rat and

the steel hammer banged. Albert became scared of the rat. It

was found that Albert associated the noise to the rat. (✓)

4/4

(b) Evaluate the study you described in (a). (4 marks)

Firstly, it was unethical because Albert is a human and the

fear could have stayed with him. (✓)

They did not give any time of removing the phobia in humans.

Straight after Albert left.

Natural responses were not caused because Albert did not show

fear when he sucked his thumb, but he was not allowed to suck

his thumb. (✓) However, we can see that fears can be

caused through association and got rid of the same way. (✓)

3/4

comment:

This candidate has managed to cover enough of the formula points for describing the study to achieve full marks. The study has been accurately identified, there are two method marks and one result/conclusion mark.

The evaluation is also a bit better this time around as we have a clear ethical point outlined, a methodological criticism concerning the conduct of the experiment and therefore its validity and an application to real life point. The only other point made in this answer didn't seem to make much sense.

DO – follow the formula for description and practise describing the four components.

DO – identify the study clearly, so that there is no need for the examiner to work out which study is being described.

DO – use a number of different ways of evaluating with clearly explained points.

DON'T – spend the whole time describing the method and obtain only two marks.

DON'T – provide an ambiguous description of a possible study; you may think you know what you mean but if it is not clear you will not get any marks.

DON'T – rely on methodological one liners, such as 'lacks ecological validity' without explanation.

key applications

The key *assumptions* were looking for material that showed what the approach was based on; the key *applications*, however, are looking for your ability to apply the concepts from each approach to certain issues that are important in attempts to use that approach in real life. Once again, there are many ways of asking such questions. Common ways may involve asking you to describe and evaluate the application for a particular approach in essay or structured questions form.

The examples that follow show the types of questions, and the commentary provides some evidence of how/how not to answer such questions.

---

key applications, example 1: unit 2, May 2003

Describe the effect of shift-work on circadian rhythms. (4 marks)

There will be a discrepancy between exogenous and

endogenous cues, (✔) meaning that our body will be telling

us we should be asleep when we need to be at work. (✔)

Industry needs people to be working all the time, but most

accidents occur during the night, examples are Bhopal and

three mile island, which both occurred between 1-4 am (✔)

Solutions are slowly rotating shifts to allow us to adjust our

body clocks. (✔)

4/4

---

comment:

This candidate has provided a clear example of how to use ideas and concepts from one of the approaches to explain a way that the approach can be applied to real life. The candidate has started by showing knowledge and understanding of some key terms that are particularly relevant to this application (exogenous and endogenous cues). The candidate has elaborated the point, showing clearly how two marks can be made from essentially one point.

The example of accidents which have occurred has been used well to show the effect and the potential solution is very important to the application of this approach.

key applications, example 2: unit 1, January 2001

Theories and studies in social psychology have been used to suggest ways in which prejudice can be reduced.

Discuss **two** ways of reducing prejudice that have been suggested in social psychology. (10 marks)

Prejudice is often caused by false negative stereotypes of other

groups of cultures. Often simple interaction between groups

can aid the break down of these stereotypes. (✓AO1) It is

also suggested that it allows groups to identify similarities

between them and to break down the homogeneity effect.

(✓AO1) Other investigations have revealed that simple

interactions are not enough to reduce prejudice. (✓AO2)

It is suggested that groups need to work together to achieve a

goal that is desired by both groups but cannot be achieved on

their own. This is termed superordinate goals. (✓AO1 MAX.)

Sherif proposed the realistic conflict theory to explain

prejudice, this suggests that people will only become prejudiced

against each other if they are competing for scarce resources.

AO1 = 3/3

AO2 = 1/3

Clarity and Communication = 2/2

Balance and Breadth = 2/2

Total = 8/10

comment:

This candidate has described the two ways very clearly and if there had been another mark available for description, the candidate would have been awarded it for the elaboration of the Sherif point. However, three AO1 marks was the maximum.

Unfortunately, the candidate's evaluation isn't quite so good and only one mark was awarded for a relatively weak point about one way not being good enough on its own.

The candidate needed to focus more on studies and research that supported either way or other 'real life' evidence to support or refute each way.

The essay contains some very appropriate psychological terminology and spelling and grammar are good, so two marks are awarded for clarity and communication.

The essay is slightly unbalanced if you consider AO1 and AO2, but given that the essay has covered ways of reducing prejudice in some depth and that the description was a little too detailed, two marks seems justified.

DO – read the question thoroughly first to make sure you are dealing with the right approach.

DO – ensure a good balance between description and evaluation points in order to maximise the potential for marks.

DON'T – ignore the specific demands of the question and cover three ways or even worse still only one way.

DON'T – provide evaluation in bullet points, as you may lose marks for the lack of explanation *and* lose marks for clarity and communication.

how are clarity and communication and balance and breadth marked?

clarity and communication:

0   Note form / unintelligible.

1   Essay format / some use of terms / some spelling mistakes (can be given even if content inappropriate).

2   Essay format / good use of terms / good spelling and grammar.

AO1 = 2

balance and breadth

0   Totally irrelevant response.

1   Adequate coverage of subject content / some irrelevancies. If only one explanation is addressed.

2   Good coverage of subject content and at least some evaluation.

A02 = 2

contemporary issues

This area of the specification encourages you to keep up-to-date with the subject and to be able to explain topical issues in relation to terms and concepts from one particular approach. General questions in this category may ask you to outline an issue that you are familiar with and explain it using concepts from the named approach. General questions may also come in the form of essays, which ask you to discuss a contemporary issue from a named approach.

More specific questions may come in the form of providing you with a stimulus/issue and then asking you to explain it using concepts/ideas from a particular approach. This means that you could be asked to apply what you know about an approach to an unfamiliar contemporary issue.

The examples that follow should clearly show the difference and provide commentary to show how/how not to answer such questions.

---

contemporary issues, example 1: unit 1, May 2002

(a) Outline **one** contemporary issue or debate that can be explained using the cognitive approach. (3 marks)

Accuracy of recovered memories. (✔) *Recovered memories*

are memories which have been forgotten or repressed during

childhood and have now (in psychoanalysis) been

recovered. (✔) *There is a debate over whether these are*

reliable or that the analyst may have simply given or

influenced an idea. (✔)

3/3

(b) Explain how the cognitive approach can help us to understand this issue or debate. (6 marks)

These memories may have been forgotten due to motivated

forgetting. (✔) This idea is that the memory was painful or

harmful and so it has been repressed. (✔) As we know from

Loftus and Palmer's work there may not be accuracy in this

memory. The therapist without realising could have asked a

leading question or given an idea. (✔) This has occurred

and the person has then accused a family member of rape

when they have not. This can be applied to reconstructive

memory and the interviewing because the information given

could be false. (✔) Also, the person wants to remove the

anxiety they are feeling which can be done by uncovering the

memory, this can mean they say yes to any suggestion (✔)

comment:

This is a fairly standard approach to dealing with contemporary issues, particularly in unit 1.

The first part is all AO1 and requires you to make clear what the issue is before you go on to explain the issue. One mark has been awarded to this candidate for identifying an appropriate issue. Two more marks have been awarded for clearly explaining what the actual problem is and why therefore it is an issue. It is very important to make sure that you do more than just identify the issue, to get three marks the issue needs to be elaborated twice.

The second part of the question is all AO2 and is asking you to use your knowledge of an approach and apply the terms and concepts from this to the issue. This candidate starts well with a reference to repression, which is obviously relevant to this issue, and then explains the causes of repression (two marks already). The reference to Loftus and Palmer is appropriate and the candidate gets another mark for clarifying how it relates to the issue. The next point is straying from the idea of using concepts/ideas from the cognitive approach and consequently doesn't get a mark. However, the references to reconstructive memory and suggestibility are both relevant and each achieves another mark.

contemporary issues, example 2: unit 2, January 2003

Use your understanding of the psychodynamic approach to describe and explain a contemporary issue in psychology. (12 marks)

Is psychoanalysis good and should people undergo it. ((✓)AO1)

Firstly, Freud himself has been criticised for his methods

because the methods he used were not good. However,

psychoanalysis is better than no therapy at all, this is because

it underlines to give you the causes of your disorder and not

cure. Many of Freud's patients themselves after the treatment

of psychoanalysis continued to show the same symptoms and

were not cured. ((✓)AO2). Therefore, is it a good form of

treatment? Today most of Freud's patients would have been

given physical treatment rather than psychoanalysis, because

what Freud interpreted as hysteria was in fact turned out to be

Something else and later one of his patients did show of other

symptoms which lead to their death.

Psychoanalysis is very expensive and time consuming ((✔)AO2)

It could have been that some methods used can bring about

slips of the tongue and made the patient distressed. The right

of withdrawal was allowed, however, patients would be

discouraged because of the accusation that maybe that can't

face up to their unconscience. Freud made people see their

fault which is good and to accept it they can move on.

Freud assumed of sexual stages or instincts in the

unconscience, it could have been that what he gave was not

right and wrong and instead of making people feel better he

made them feel worse.

A study shows that other techniques and analysis are better

and could be used. However, Freud looked in depth about the

person's life etc. and sometimes was very useful.

AO1 = 1/4

AO2 = 2/4

Clarity and communication = 1/2

Balance and breadth = 1/2

Total = 5/12

comment:

This is a different way of examining the contemporary issue (as an essay) and as such requires a slightly different set of rules. This time you need to work on the basis of equal numbers of descriptive and explanatory points and ensure clarity and balance at the same time. In this essay AO1 marks will come from describing the contemporary issue and AO2 marks from explaining it using ideas/concepts from the psychodynamic approach.

This candidate has a mixed start, gaining one mark initially for correctly identifying a relevant contemporary issue. However, the next section of the essay is less helpful. The next line states that Freud's methods were not good and we would certainly need some justification for this statement. The following line provides a potentially contradictory point about identifying causes not cure. (These are both classic examples where maybe examiners think they know what candidates mean but can't be sure that they really know what they mean – consequently, no marks.)

The next line though, *'psychoanalysis is very expensive and time consuming'*, is clearer and relevant to the issue and achieves an AO2 mark. Unfortunately, this is followed by another messy and unclear point about Freud's patients. The next mark comes from a fairly weak point about the methods being time consuming and therefore expensive, and then back to the rather confused points that mix a couple of ideas together so that neither of them is clear.

This candidate is an example of poor clarity and communication in an essay. Unfortunately for the candidate, the examiner can only go on what is written on the exam paper, not what the examiner thinks the candidate might have meant or what was going on in the candidate's head.

DO – make sure that even in the essay version of the contemporary issue you identify the issue clearly and spend some time explaining why it is an issue.

DO – ensure that you are making your points clearly; read back over them and follow the rule set out earlier – if your points are not clear to you, they will not be clear to the examiner either.

DON'T – launch into a tirade of criticism no matter how much you dislike the approach you are dealing with.

DON'T – rush through the essay, throwing in as much material as you can think of; the chances are that you will not make any of it clear enough and could end up with few or no marks.

conclusions

The samples of questions provided so far do not represent every possible question that could be asked in an examination. They are provided to give you ideas for ways to answer such questions and to help you look out for potential pitfalls.

The main aim is to give you a greater insight into the process of examination. This is not so that you can cheat or produced pre-planned answers (doing so would be counter-productive anyway) but so that when you are considering an answer you can stop and think: what is this question really asking me to do?

how can I write better essays?

Writing essays is a difficult skill and it therefore deserves an extra section of its own to deal with some of the things you need to consider when approaching an essay question. It is also a skill that you will need to demonstrate more at A2 and mastering it at this stage will be of great benefit to you in the future.

◆ The first thing to note is that any question on the exam which has 10 or more marks allocated to it will be marked using the essay marking scheme. This means that it will have an equal division of AO1 and AO2 marks, but will also be marked on the quality of the clarity and communication shown (two marks) and on the balance and breadth of the essay (two marks) as seen on p. 259.

◆ The next point to consider is what the question is actually asking you to do. It is very difficult to generalise about this as essays often ask for very different things. For this reason you need to make sure you have read the question thoroughly before you launch into an answer. The essay question in unit 1 January 2003 is a case in point: 'Theories from the social approach have provided explanations for both the formation and the reduction of prejudice. Discuss two explanations of prejudice according to the social approach.' Read it through and then consider what the question is asking of you and how you would answer it. If you decided that you would consider two ways of reducing prejudice, then perhaps you should read the question again. This question asks for explanations of prejudice and is therefore looking for theories of prejudice formation not reduction.

◆ Once you have decided what the essay should be about, it is worthwhile taking some time to plan what you are going to put into the essay. Hopefully it will be very clear from the process of reading and re-reading the essay title/question what you will need, and therefore your plan should be easy to do.

◆ Don't write an introduction, setting the scene for what is about to come, as it will not receive any marks and it will take up some of your valuable exam time. The first thing you should write about in your essay is your first AO1 point.

◆ Make sure that you have explained your AO1 points clearly and in enough detail for the examiner to award you a mark. This will require some re-reading on your part.

◆ Ensure that your AO2 points are not overly brief and avoid the use of 'glib' statements such as 'the method used to investigate this point was an experiment; these are bad due to the fact that they lack ecological validity'. This kind of point would be awarded no marks because you have provided no explanation to show that you have understood what it means.

◆ Try to make sure that you have fulfilled the requirement for the clarity and communication section of the essay by writing your work in sentences and paragraphs, rather than bullet points or notes, making sure that you have covered a fair range of psychological terms and that the spelling and grammar are reasonably good.

◆ Ensure that you have fulfilled the requirements for the balance and breadth section of the essay by covering a fair amount of detail, not just dealing with the basics, by making sure that you have covered both AO1 and AO2 in roughly equal measure and if you have been asked for *two* of anything that you have attempted to cover both in equal detail.

◆ Don't write a conclusion to your essay. This is not meant to be an English language essay and the conclusion would probably not gain any further marks as it would restate points already mentioned in the body of the essay.

◆ Read through the essay at least once when you have apparently finished. You will almost certainly find one sentence that doesn't make sense and needs changing to fulfil the criteria.

◆ Writing essays may well be an art rather than a science, but in this case a well-structured essay will gain higher marks.

how should I go about doing evaluation?

The most important thing to remember about evaluation is that it is done best if it involves you showing your ability to analyse and criticise material in the way asked for by the question. It is done worst, if it involves you trying to 'rote learn' a collection of points that you are attempting to use for any question that comes up on a particular topic, no matter what the questions asks for. A further guide to evaluation is provided in chapter 1.

how can I motivate myself to revise for the exam?

The best way to prepare for an exam is to start your revision weeks and even months before and to work at a steady pace. When approaching revision there are certain factors that you need to consider that may help or hinder your preparation, a major factor is motivation and as this is almost entirely a psychological factor, as such you are in an advantageous situation as a psychology student.

Some of the biggest influences on motivation include:

◆ your desire for success;

◆ your perceived level of control;

◆ your level of optimism;

◆ procrastination?

Your desire for success is linked to your need for achievement and your desire to avoid failure. According to Atkinson (1964), these two factors are the basis for many forms of behaviour and will hopefully be a big influence on your motivation prior to the exam. You should approach your exam with these things in mind and with an attitude that at least gives you the opportunity to succeed and that will influence your behaviour prior to the exam in terms of revision.

Your perceived level of control is also linked to psychological notions from the past. Rotter (1966) was interested in a person's locus of control – whether people believe that the outcome of their behaviour was in their control or not. In considering this we would need to consider who controls our destiny, who is responsible for our success and fail-ure, and whether there is anything we can do to change the future. Your answers will undoubtedly, once again, help to determine your behaviour prior to the exam.

Optimism is central to success in anything and it is no less important when looking for-ward to exams. A positive attitude may not help you answer a question that you don't know the answer to. However, it may well cause you to have a go at a question you are not sure about and provide you with one or two extra marks that might make the difference between one grade and another.

What the heck is procrastination I hear you cry? Well, maybe it is enough to know that in relation to exams procrastination is your enemy and should be avoided at all costs. Procrastination is the thing that stops you from doing your homework more than five minutes before it is due in and it is also the thing that may stop you from revising properly. Procrastination can be regarded as work avoidance; it is the little voice in your head convincing you that there must be something else you can do that is more important. It is procrastination that makes you decide that cleaning your room is sud-denly a really good idea or that it would be really helpful of you to do the ironing for the whole household. It may be procrastination that convinces you that you don't have enough time to do what is required and therefore there is no point. It is procras-tination that may encourage you to get all of your books out, spread them around yourself and then leave them there whilst you watch television, talk on the telephone or play a computer game. Revision by osmosis has never been known to work!

Procrastinators use all sorts of excuses to avoid doing the thing that they really need to do. Procrastination often occurs with large tasks such as revision that have no obvious end in sight, particularly when some of the other 'household' tasks have a clear begin-ning and end in sight and for that reason are more attractive.

practical tips for improving motivation

◆ Identify days and times that you can give over to revision.

◆ Spend time studying on each of these days so that you don't become too far behind with the work.

◆ As soon as you get the motivation to do some work, act on it.

◆ Make sure your study area and materials are organised. However, don't suddenly use cleaning as a means to procrastinate.

◆ Don't plan to revise for a number of hours at a time without a break.

◆ Break big tasks down into smaller tasks; make each of them achievable in a rea-sonable amount of time and keep a check on your achievements to show your progress.

◆ Every time you sit down to study, set a relatively small goal and achieve it.

◆ Allow yourself the opportunity to make mistakes and take the pressure off yourself to get it absolutely right first time; this way you will be less reluctant to start.

◆ Give yourself regular breaks in your revision, as long as it is not an excuse to pro-crastinate.

◆ Promise yourself small rewards after (not before) the study session. This could be anything from a cup of tea and a few biscuits to watching television for 15 min-utes.

◆ If you get stuck on something, don't spend hours worrying about it. Move on to something else and come back to it at a later time/date.

◆ Don't approach your revision with a negative attitude; use relaxation and focusing exercises to put yourself in a positive mood.

◆ Don't mope around thinking that your teachers or the exam board or anyone else aren't good enough and that they will cause you to fail come what may.

◆ Don't let what you can't do interfere with what you can do (John Wooden, basketball coach).

◆ Believe that the difference between success and failure is what you can do to help yourself now.

motivation questionnaire

Answer the following questions as honestly as you can to assess your current state of motivation.

This should provide you with an accurate assessment of whether you are on the right track or need to change a few things to improve your motivation.

	true	false
1. I usually get what I want in life.	☐	☐
2. If I do not succeed on a task, I tend to give up.	☐	☐
3. I work best at the last minute when the pressure is really on.	☐	☐
4. I like to get my room in order before starting a task.	☐	☐
5. The amount of work I do has no effect on my grades.	☐	☐
6. I never try anything that I am not sure of.	☐	☐
7. I know what I have to do but frequently find that I have done something else.	☐	☐
8. I carry my books/work around with me, but rarely open them.	☐	☐
9. I think that I could easily win the lottery.	☐	☐
10. I do not really believe that I can achieve all my goals.	☐	☐
11. I have been too tired, nervous or upset to carry out the difficult task that faces me.	☐	☐
12. I have often found that what is going to hapen will happen.	☐	☐
13. I don't think that I ever have enough time to study.	☐	☐
14. I can't do well in my exams because I don't have long-term career goals.	☐	☐
15. I don't think there is enough time between now and my exams to get enough revision done.	☐	☐
16. Most of the people in my group are cleverer than me, so I can never do as well as them.	☐	☐
17. I think there is too much material on the syllabus for me to cover.	☐	☐
18. I don't think there is any point in studying hard as I won't get anything out of it anyway.	☐	☐
19. My life seems like a series of random events.	☐	☐
20. The success I have is largely a matter of chance.	☐	☐

If you have answered 'True' to a lot of these questions, you may want to look back at the practical tips for improving motivation above, or refer to the some of the points made in chapter 1. Don't let anyone tell you that motivation isn't important!

what should I do just before the exam?

◆ Even if you have left your revision until the last minute, there is no point staying up late the night before the exam. You will benefit more from a good night's sleep, having plenty of energy for the task in hand the next day.

◆ Make sure that you have enough to eat before you go into the exam or your blood-sugar level will drop and you will find it hard to concentrate.

◆ Make sure you have plenty of water to drink, as once again, dehydration can make it hard to concentrate. However, don't drink too much water as you may spend the whole examination in the toilet!

◆ Make sure you arrive in plenty of time – at least 15 minutes before the exam is due to start. Rushing to get in at the last minute will make you overly anxious. On the other hand, don't arrive too early, as you will not be able to maintain your concentration for that long.

what should I do when I get into the examination room?

◆ When you go into the examination room check with the person in charge that you are in the right room and check the required seating arrangements at the same time.

◆ When you sit down at your table, make sure you have got everything you need ready to go. For most psychology exams this will only mean pens, but make sure you have a good supply just in case some do not work. Only ever use black or blue pens for examinations and no pencils unless they are asked for.

◆ When you are given the exam paper, make sure you read all of the instructions on the front of the paper carefully and follow them. You would not be the first student to answer too many questions, or not enough, or the wrong questions.

◆ Make a note of the time available and plan your answers accordingly. Remember, though, that some questions only require very short answers and will not need as much time as questions that need longer answers for a similar number of marks.

◆ Make sure your name appears on every separate sheet of paper you use.

◆ Read through the whole paper once and decide if there are any parts that are trickier than others; you may want to leave those until last.

◆ Read each question carefully to make sure that you understand what you have to do.

◆ Use extra sheets obtained from the person in charge of the examination to make notes if necessary.

◆ Write all of your answers on the examination paper provided and any extra sheets that are required.

◆ You should write on the lines provided on the paper and not try to subvert the process by writing two of your own lines for each line on the exam paper. If you run out of space, ask for additional sheets of paper and write the rest of your answer on them, clearly indicating the question you are answering.

◆ Read back through your answers to make sure that the points you are making are clear to you. If you cannot understand them the chances are the examiner will not be able to understand them either.

◆ If you find that you have made a mistake, it is not the end of the world. Simply cross out the incorrect part and write it again somewhere else, usually best to do it on one of those additional sheets of paper mentioned above. **Never, ever use Tippex.**

◆ After the examination it is usually best to avoid discussing the paper with fellow students or teachers. You will almost certainly worry yourself unnecessarily if you answered a question differently to them. You may have done it better! Put this examination behind you and concentrate on the next one.

and finally . . .

This chapter has been designed to give you the chance to prepare yourself a little better and have a greater knowledge of what to expect when you reach the examination room. It is not intended to provide a short-cut to success or to replace the real knowledge and understanding that you will gain from studying hard.

It is, however, an acknowledgement that the process of timed exams in controlled settings can be very daunting and sometimes quite artificial (psychologists know a thing or two about the validity of controlled tests). Hopefully, the points above will put you in a better position to cope with the demands of this process and help you to show off your true ability and achieve the grade that you deserve.

references

Abernathy, E. M. (1940) The effect of changed environmental conditions upon the results of college examinations. *Journal of Psychology,* **10,** 293–301.

Adam, K. (1977) Body weight correlates with REM sleep. *British Medical Journal,* **1**, 813.

Adams, H. E., Wright, L. W. and Lohr, B. A. (1996) Is homophobia associated with homosexual arousal? *Journal of Abnormal Psychology,* **105**(3), 440–445.

Adorno, T. W, Frenkel–Brunswick, E., Levinson, D. J. and Sanford, R. H. (1950) *The Authoritarian Personality*. Harper & Row, New York.

Aggleton, J. P. and Waskett, L (1999) The ability of odours to serve as state dependent cues for real–world memories: can Viking smells aid the recall of Viking experiences? *British Journal of Psychology,* **90**, 1–7.

Ainsworth, M. D. S. (1979) Attachment as related to mother–infant interaction. In: *Advances in the Study of Behaviour* (ed. Rosenblatt, J. O., Hinde, R. A., Beer, C. and Busnel, M.), Vol. 9. Academic Press, Orlando FL.

Ainsworth, P. B. and King, E. (1988) Witnesses' perceptions of identification parades. In: *Practical Aspects of Memory: Current Research and Issues* (ed. Oruneberg, M. M., Morris, P. E. and Sykes, R. N.), Vol. 1. Wiley, Chichester.

Alex, J. A. and Ritchie, M. R. (1992) School-aged children's interpretation of their experience with acute surgical pain. *Journal of Paediatric Nursing,* **7**(3), 171–80.

Allport, G. W (1947) *The Use of Personal Documents in Psychological Science.* Holt, Rhinehart & Winston, London.

Amir, S. and Stewart, J. (1996), quoted in 'Clocked off'. *New Scientist,* 8 November 1997, 29.

Andreani, O. D (1995) Knowledge and intrinsic motivation. *European Journal for High Ability,* **6**, 220–225.

Andrews, B., Morton, J., Beckerian, D. A., Brewin, C. R., Davies, O. M. and Mollon, P. (1995) The recovery of memories in clinical practice. *The Psychologist,* **8**, 209–14.

Anon (1994) Crime waves. 2600 *The Hacker Quarterly,* **11**(1), 4–5.

Aquiar, A. and Baillargeon, R. (1999) 2.5 month-old infants' reasoning about when objects should and should not be occluded. *Cognitive Psychology,* **39**, 116–157.

Arendt, J. (1985) The pineal: a gland that measures time? *New Scientist,* **1466**, 36–38.

Arnold, G. W. and Grassia, A. (1982) Ethogram of agonistic behaviour for thoroughbred horses. *Applied Animal Ethology,* **8**(1–2), 5–25.

Aronson, E. (1988) *The Social Animal,* 5th edn. Freeman, New York.

Aronson, E., Wilson, T. D. and Akert, R. M. (1994) *Social Psychology.* HarperCollins, New York.

Asterinsky, E., Lynch, J. A., Mack, M. E., Tzankoff, S. E. and Hum, E. (1985) Comparison of eye motion in wakefulness and REM sleep. *Psychophysiology,* **22**, 1–10.

Asterinsky, N. E. and Kleitman, N. (1955) Regularly occurring periods of eye motility and concommitant phenomena during sleep. *Science,* **118**, 273–274.

Astington, J. W. (1998) Theory of mind, Humpty Dumpty and the ice box. *Human Development* **41**, 30–39.

Atkinson, R. E. and Shiffrin, R. M. (1968) Human memory: a proposed system and its control processes. In: *The Psychology of Learning and Motivation* (ed. Spence, K. W and Spence, J. T.), Vol. 2. Academic Press, London.

Atkinson, R. C. and Shiffrin, R. M. (1971) The control of short-term memory. *Scientific American,* **224**, 82–90.

Avery, D. H., Kouri, M. E., Monaghan, K., Bolte, M. A., Hellekson, C. and Eder, D. (2002) Is dawn simulation effective in ameliorating the difficulty awakening in seasonal affective disorder associated with hypersomnia? *Journal of Affective Disorders,* **69**(1–3): 231–236.

Avis, J. and Harris, E. L. (1991) Belief-desire reasoning among Baka children: evidence for a universal conception of theory of mind. *Child Development,* **62**(3), 460–467.

Ayensu, E. S. and Whitfield, E. (eds) (1982) *The Rhythms of Life.* Book Club Associates, London.

Baddeley, A. D. (1995) *Your Memory: A User's Guide.* Penguin, Harmondsworth.

Baddeley, A. D. (1996) *Human Memory,* 2nd edn. Lawrence Erlbaum Associates Ltd, Hove.

Baddeley, A. D. and Warrington, E. H. (1970) Amnesia and the distinction between long- and short-term memory. *Journal of Verbal Learning and Verbal Behaviour,* **9**, 176–189.

Bagby, K. M., Schuller, D. R., Levitt, A.J., Joffe, R. T. and Harkness, K. L. (1996) Seasonal and non–seasonal depression and the five factor model of personality. *Journal of Affective Disorders,* **38**(2–3), 89–95.

Bai, Y. M., Lin, C. C. and Chen, J. Y. (2001) Internet addiction disorder among clients of a virtual clinic. *Psychiatric Services,* **52**(10), 1397.

Baillargeon, R. and DeVos, J. (1991) Object permanence in young infants: further evidence. *Child Development,* **62**, 1227–1246.

Bancroft, D. and Carr, R. (1995) *Influencing Children's Development.* Open University, Milton Keynes.

Bandura, A. (1977) *Social Learning Theory.* Prentice-Hall NJ, Englewood Cliffs.

Bandura, A., Ross, D. and Ross, S. A (1961) Transmission of aggression through imitation of aggressive models. *Journal of Abnormal and Social Psychology,* **63,** 575–582.

Banister, E., Burman, E., Parker, I., Taylor, M. and Tindall, E. (1994) *Qualitative Methods in Psychology: A Research Guide.* Open University Press, Buckingham.

Baron, R. A and Byrne, D. (1994) *Social Psychology: Understanding Human Interaction.* Allyn & Bacon, Boston.

Baron-Cohen, S. (1995) *Mindblindness: An Essay on Autism and Theory of Mind.* MIT Press, Cambridge MA.

Bateman, A. and Fonagy, P. (1999) Effectiveness of partial hospitalisation in the treatment of borderline personality disorder: a randomised control trial. *American Journal of Psychiatry,* **156**, 1563–1569.

Bateman, A. and Holmes, J. (1995) *Introduction to Psychoanalysis.* Routledge, London.

Baum, M. (1969) Extinction of an avoidance response following response prevention: some parametric investigations. *Canadian Journal of Psychology,* **23**, 1–10.

Baumrind, D. (1975) Metaethical and normative considerations governing the treatment of human subjects in the behavioural sciences. In: *Human Rights and Psychological Research: A Debate on Psychology and Ethics* (ed. Kennedy, E. C.). Thomas Y. Crowell, New York.

Beaumont, G. (1988) General practitioner prescribing for the driving patient. In: *Medicine and Road Safety* (Burley, D. and Silverstone, T.). CNS, London.

Bellezza, E. S. and Bower, G. H. (1981) Person stereotypes and memory for people. *Journal of Personality and Social Psychology*, **41**(5), 856–865.

Benjamin, J., Li, L., Patterson, C., Murphy, D. L. and Hamer, D. H. (1996) Population and familial association between the 04 receptor gene and measures of novelty seeking. *Nature Genetics*, **12**, 81–84.

Bentley, E. (1999) *Awareness*. Routledge, London.

Bergin, A. E. and Garfield, S. L. (eds) (1994) *Handbook of Psychotherapy and Behaviour Change*. Wiley, New York.

Bergin, A. E. and Lambert, M. J. (1971) The effectiveness of psychotherapy. In: Bergin, A. E. and Garfield, S. L. (eds) (1994) *Handbook of Psychotherapy and Behaviour Change*. Wiley, New York.

Berson, Y., Shamir, B., Avolio, B. J. and Popper, M. (2001) The relationship between vision strength, leadership style and context. *Leadership Quarterly* **12**, 53–73.

Berson, D. M., Dunn, F. A. and Takao, M. (2002) Phototransduction by retinal ganglion cells that set the circadian clock. *Science*, **295**, 1070–1073.

Bifulco, A., Brown, G. W. and Alder, Z. (1991) Early sexual abuse and clinical depression in later life. *British Journal of Psychiatry*, **159**, 115–122.

Blagrove, M. and Hartnell, S. J. (2000) Lucid dreaming: Associations with internal locus of control, need for cognition and creativity. *Personality and Individual Differences*, **28**(1), 41–47.

Blass, T. (1996a) Attribution of responsibility and trust in the Milgram obedience experiment. *Journal of Applied Social Psychology*, **26**, 1529–1535.

Boklage, C. E. (1977) Schizophrenia, brain asymmetry development and twinning; cellular relationship with etiological and possibly prognostic implications. *Biological Psychiatry*, **12**, 19–35.

Borich, G. D. and Tombari, M. L. (1997) *Educational Psychology: A Contemporary Approach*, Longman, New York..

Bornas, X. and Llabres, J. (2001) Helping students build knowledge: what computers should do. *Information Technology in Childhood Education Annual* **13**, 267–280.

Bowen, A. M. and Bourgeouis, M. J. (2001) Attitudes towards lesbian, gay and bisexual college students: the contribution of pluralistic ignorance, dynamic social impact and contact theories. *Journal of American College Health*, **50**, 91–96.

Bower, G. H. (1981) Mood and memory. *American Psychologist*, **36**, 129–148.

Bower, G. H. and Karlin, M. B. (1974) Depth of processing pictures of faces and recognition memory. *Journal of Experimental Psychology*, **103**, 751–757.

Bowlby, J. (1969) *Attachment*. Pimlico, London.

Bradmetz, J. (1999) Precursors of formal thought: a longitudinal study. *British Journal of Developmental Psychology*, **17**, 61–81.

Brenner, V. (1996) An initial report on the online assessment of Internet addiction: the first 30 days of the Internet usage. Marquette University Counselling Center and SUNY–Buffalo. http://www. ccsnet. com/prep/pap/pap8b/638b 12 p.txt.

Brigham, J. C and Malpass, R. S. (1985) The role of experience and contact in the recognition of faces of own and other-race persons. *Journal of Social Issues*, **41**, 139–155.

British Psychological Society (1978) Ethical principles for research with human subjects. Statement at Annual General Meeting, April 1978.

British Psychological Society (1985) A code of conduct for psychologists. *Bulletin of the BPS*, **38**, 41–43.

British Psychological Society (1990) *Ethical Principles for Conducting Research with Human Participants*. The British Psychological Society, Leicester.

Brown, D. and Redder, J. (1991) *Introduction to Psychotherapy*. Routledge, London.

Brown, G. W and Harris, T. (1978) *The Social Origins of Depression: A Study of Psychiatric Disorder in Women*. Tavistock, London.

Brown, N. R., Rips, L. and Shevell, S. K. (1985) The subjective dates of natural events in very long–term memory. *Cognitive Psychology*, **17**, 139–177.

Brown, R. and Kulik, J. (1977) Flashbulb memories. *Cognition*, **5**, 73–99.

Brown, R., Cazden, C. B. and Bellugi, U. (1969) The child's grammar from 1 to 3. In: Hall, J. P. (ed.) *Minnesota Symposium on Child Psychology*, Volume 2. University of Minnesota Press, Minneapolis.

Bruner, J. (1971) The course of cognitive growth. In: *Cognitive Development to Adolescence* (ed. Richardson, K. and Sheldon, S., 1985). Lawrence Erlbaum Associates Ltd, Hove.

Bruner, J. S. (1963) *The Process of Education*. Vintage Books, New York.

Bruner, J. S. (1966) *Towards a Theory of Instruction*. Norton, New York.

Bruner, J. S. and Kenney, H. (1966) *The Development of the Concepts of Order and Proportion in Children*. Wiley, New York.

Bryant, P. (1998) Cognitive development. In: *Psychology: An Integrated Approach* (ed. Eysenck, M. W.). Longman, Harlow.

Brylowski, A. (1990) Nightmares in crisis: clinical applications of lucid dreaming techniques. *Psychiatric Journal of the University of Ottowa*, **15**(2), 79–84.

Burns, A. (1998) 'Pop' psychology or 'Ken behaving badly'. *The Psychologist*, **11**(7), 360.

Burr, V. (1995) *An Introduction to Social Constructionism*. Routledge, London.

Bushman, B. J. (1988) The effects of apparel on compliance: a field experiment with a female authority figure. *Personality and Social Psychology Bulletin*, **14**, 459–467.

Carey, S. (1978) The child as a word learner. In: *Linguistic Theory and Psychological Reality* (ed. Halle, M., Bresnan, J. and Miller, G. A.). MIT Press, Cambridge MA.

Carli L. L. (1999) Cognitive reconstruction, hindsight and reactions to victims and perpetrators. *Personality and Social Psychology Bulletin*, **25**, 966–979.

Carlson, N. (1977) *The Physiology of Behaviour*. Allyn & Bacon, New York.

Cave, S. (1999) *Therapeutic Approaches*. Routledge, London.

Child, D. (1997) *Psychology and the Teacher*. Cassell, London.

Charlton, T., Gunter, B. and Hannan, A. (eds) (2000) *Broadcast Television Effects in a Remote Community*. Lawrence Erlbaum Associates, Mahway NJ.

Cherulnik, P. D., Donley, K. A., Wiewel, T. S. R. and Miller, S. (2001) Charisma is contagious: the effect of leaders' charisma on observers' affect. *Journal of Applied Social Psychology*, **31**, 2149–2159.

Chodorow, N. (1996) Reflections on the authority of the past in psychoanalytic thinking. *Psychoanalytic Quarterly*, **65**, 32–51.

Chorney, M. J., Chorney, K., Seese, N., Owen, M. J., Daniels, J., McGuffin, P., Thomson, L. A., Detterman, D. K., Benbow, C. P., Lubinski, D., Eley, T. C. and Plomin, R. (1998) A quantitative trait locus (QTL) associated with cognitive ability in children. *Psychological Science*, **9**, 159–166.

Clamp, A and Russell, J. (1998) *Comparative Psychology*. Hodder & Stoughton, London.

Cohen, G. (1991) *Memory in the Real World*. Lawrence Erlbaum Associates Ltd, Hove.

Cohen, N. J. and Squire, L. R. (1980) Preserved learning and retention of pattern-analysing skill in amnesia: dissociation of knowing how from knowing that. *Science*, **210,** 207–210.

Conway, M. A., Anderson, S. J., Larsen, S. F., Donnelly, C. M., McDaniel, M. A., McLelland, A. G. and Rawles, R. E. (1994) The formation of flashbulb memories. *Memory and Cognition*, **22**, 326–343.

Coolican, H. (1990) *Research Methods and Statistics in Psychology*. Hodder & Stoughton, London.

Coolican, H. (1996) *Introduction to Research Methods and Statistics in Psychology*, 2nd edn. Hodder & Stoughton, London.

Cory, T. L, Ormiston, N. W., Simmel, E. and Dainoff, M. (1975) Predicting the frequency of dream recall. *Journal of Abnormal Psychology*, **84**, 261–266.

Craik, F. I. M. (1979) Levels of processing: overview and closing comments. In: *Levels of Processing in Human Memory* (ed. Cermak, L. S. and Craik E. L. M.). Erlbaum, Hillsdale NJ, 447–461.

Craik, F. I. M. and Lockhart, R. S. (1972) Levels of processing: a framework for memory research. *Journal of Verbal Learning and Verbal Behaviour*, **11**, 671–684.

Craik, F. I. M. and Tulving, E. (1975) Depth of processing and retention of words in episodic memory. *Journal of Experimental Psychology: General*, **104**, 268–294.

Crick, F. I. and Mitchison, G. (1986) Sleep and neural nets. *Journal of Mind and Behavior*, **7**, 229–250.

Crisp, R. J. (2002) Social categorisation: blurring the boundaries. *The Psychologist*, **15**, 612–615.

Crook, C. (1994) *Computers and the Collaborative Experience of Learning*. Routledge, London.

Czeisler, C. A et al. (1990) *New England Journal of Medicine*, **1322**, 1253. Quoted in Taylor, S. (1990) Scientists make light work of night work. *New Scientist*, 2 June, 32.

Czeisler, C. A, Kronauer, R. E., Allan, J. S., Duffy, J. E, Jewett, M. E., Brown, E. N. and Ronda, J. M. (1989) Bright light induction of strong (type O) resetting of the human circadian pacemaker. *Science*, **244**, 1328–1333.

Dalenberg, C. (1996) The prediction of accurate memories of trauma. Paper presented at the NATO Advanced Study Institute of Recollections of Trauma, France, 15–25 June.

Davis, J. O., Phelps, J. A. and Bracha, H. S. (1995) Prenatal development of monozygotic twins and concordance for schizophrenia. *Schizophrenia Bulletin*, **21**, 357–366.

Deary, L. J. and Tait, R. (1987) Effects of sleep disruption on cognitive performance and mood in medical house officers. *British Medical Journal*, **295**, 1513–1516.

Delfabbro, P. H. and Winefield, A. H. (1999) Poker-machine gambling: an analysis of within session characteristics. *British Journal of Psychology*, **90**, 425–439.

Dement, W. C. and Kleitman, N. (1957) The relation of eye movements during sleep to dream activity: an objective method for the study of dreaming. *Journal of Experimental Psychology*, **53**, 339–346.

Dement, W. C. (1960) The effect of dream deprivation. *Science*, **15**, 1705–1707.

Dement, W. C. (1965) Studies on the function of rapid eye movement (paradoxical) sleep in human subjects. In: Jouvet, M. (ed.), *Aspects Anatomofonctionnels de la Physiologie du Sommeil*. Editions du Centre Nationale de la Recherche Scientifique, Paris.

Dement, W. C. (1978) *Some Must Watch While Others Must Sleep*. Norton, New York.

Deutsch, M. and Collins, M. E. (1951) *Interracial Housing*, University of Florida Press, Minneapolis.

Dion, K., Bersheid, E. and Walster, E. (1972) What is beautiful is good. *Journal of Personality and Social Psychology*, **24**, 285–290.

Dobbs, M. and Crano, W. D. (2001) Outgroup accountability in the minimal group paradigm: implications for aversive discrimination and social identity theory. *Personality and Social Psychology Bulletin*, **27**, 355–364.

Drake, C. L. (2002) Thermoregulatory response to light exposure: seasonal affective disorder. *Dissertation Abstracts International: Section B: The Sciences and Engineering*, **63**(1-B), 581.

Duck, J. M. (1990) Children's ideals: the role of real life versus media figures. *Australian Journal of Psychology*, **42**,19–29.

Duka, T., Weissenborn, R. and Dienes, Z. (2001) State-dependent effects of alcohol on recollective experience, familiarity and awareness on memories. *Psychopharmacology*, **153**, 295–306.

Duker, P. C. and Seys, D. M. (2000) A quasi-experimental study on the effect of electrical aversion treatment on imposed mechanical restraint for severe self-injurious behaviour. *Research in Developmental Disabilities*, **21,** 235–242.

Ebstein, R. P., Novick, O., Umansky, R., Priel, B., Osher, Y., Blaine, D., Bennett, E. R., Nemanov, L., Katz, M. and Belmaker, R. H. (1995) Dopamine D4 receptor (DRD4) exon III polymorphism associated with the human trait of novelty seeking. *Nature Genetics*, **12**, 78–80.

Eley, T. C. and Stevenson, J. (2000) Specific life-events and chronic experiences differentially associated with depression and anxiety in young twins. *Journal of Abnormal Child Psychology*, **28**, 383–394.

Elliott, D. M. (1995) Delayed recall of traumatic events: correlates and clinical implications. Paper presented at the annual meeting of the American Psychological Association, New York.

Ellis, J. and Fox, P. (2001) The effect of self-identified sexual orientation on helping behaviour in a British sample: are lesbians and gay men treated differently? *Journal of Applied Social Psychology*, **31**, 1238–1247.

Emmelkamp, P. and Kuipers, A. (1979) Agoraphobia: a follow–up study four years after treatment. *British Journal of Psychiatry*, **134**, 352–355.

Emmelkamp, P. M. (1994) Behaviour therapy with adults. In: *Handbook of Psychotherapy and Behaviour Change* (ed. Bergin, A. E. and Garfield, S. L.). Wiley, New York.

Empson, J. (1993) *Sleep and Dreaming*. Harvester Wheatsheaf, Hemel Hempstead.

Eng, L. (1995) Internet is becoming a very useful tool for campus radicals. *The Journal Star*, 22 January, 8.

Ennis, E. (1997) Seasonal variations in mood and behaviour and pre-menstrual syndrome. *Proceedings of the British Psychological Society*, **5**(1), 9.

Erikson, E. H. (1959) *Identity and the Lifecycle*. Norton, New York.

Eron, L. D., Huesmann, L. R., Leftowitz, M. M. and Walder, L. O. (1972) Does television violence cause aggression? *American Psychologist*, **27**, 253–263.

Eron, L. D. and Huesmann, L. R. (1986) The role of television in the development of antisocial and prosocial behavior. In: *Development of Antisocial and Prosocial Behaviour, Theories and Issues* (ed. Olweus, D., Block, J. and Radke-Yarrom, M.). Academic Press, New York.

Eron, L. D. (1995) Media violence: how it affects kids and what can be done about it. Invited address presented at the annual meeting of the American Psychological Association, New York.

Eysenck, H. J. (1952) The effects of psychotherapy: an evaluation. *Journal of Consulting Psychology*, **16**, 319–24.

Eysenck, M. (1993) *Principles of Cognitive Psychology*. Lawrence Erlbaum, Hove.

Eysenck, M. (1994) How many memory stores? *Psychology Review*, **1**, 1–4.

Eysenck, M. (1998) Memory. In: *Psychology: An Integrated Approach* (ed. Eysenk, M. W.). Longman, Harlow.

Eysenck, M. W. (ed.) (1998) *Psychology: An Integrated Approach*. Longman, Harlow.

Eysenck, M. W and Keane, M. T. (1997) *Cognitive Psychology: A Student's Handbook*. Psychology Press Ltd, Hove.

Ezell, H. K. and Justice, L. M. (2000) Increasing the print focus of adult-child shared book-reading through observational learning. *American Journal of Speech Language Pathology*, **9**(1), 36–47.

Fairbairn, W. R. D. (1952) *Psychoanalytic Studies of the Personality*. Routledge, London.

Fancher, R. (1995) *Cultures of Healing*. Freeman, New York.

Faulkner, D. (1995) Teaching and learning. In: *Influencing Children's Development* (ed. Bancroft, D. and Can, R.). Open University, Milton Keynes.

Faulkner, D., Littleton, K. and Woodhead, M. (1998) *Learning Relationships in the Classroom*. Routledge, London.

Fawcett, S. B. (1991) Some values guiding community research and action. *Journal of Applied Behaviour Analysis*, **24**, 621–636.

Ferenczi, M. (1997) Seasonal depression. http://nimnet51. nimr. mrc. ac. uk/mhe97/sad. htm.

Ferguson, E. and Cassidy, H. J. (1999) The Gulf War and illness by association. *British Journal of Psychology*, **90**, 459–475.

Festinger, L., Riecken, H. W. and Schachter, S. (1956) *When Prophecy Fails*. University of Minnesota Press, Minneapolis.

Field, M. and Duka, T. (2001) Smoking expectancy mediates the conditioned responses to arbitrary smoking cues. *Behavioural Pharmacology*, **12**(3), 183–194.

Fink, J. M., Willemsen, G. and Boomsma, D. I. (2003) The association of current smoking behavior with the smoking behavior of parents, siblings, friends and spouses. *Addiction*, **98**(7), 923–931.

Flanagan, C. (1996) A *Resource Pack for 'A' level Psychology*. Hartshill Press, Crewe.

Folkard, S. (1996) Bags of time to play. *Daily Express*, 28 September 1996.

Fonagy, P., Steele, M., Moran, G., Steele, H. and Higgitt A (1993) Measuring the ghost in the nursery: an empirical study of the relation between parents' mental representations of childhood experiences and their infants' security of attachment. *Journal of the American Psychoanalytic Association*, **41**, 957–989.

Foot, H., Morgan, M. and Shute, R. (eds) (1990) *Children Helping Children*. Chichester, Wiley.

Forde, E. M. E. and Humphreys, G. W. (2002) The role of semantic knowledge in short term memory. *Neurocase,* **8**, 13–27.

Foster, J. J. and Parker, I. (1995) *Carrying Out Investigations in Psychology: Methods and Statistics.* BPS Books, Leicester.

Fox, D. K., Hopkins, B. L. and Anger, W. K. (1987) The long-term effects of a token economy on safety performance in open pit mining. *Journal of Applied Behaviour Analysis,* **20**, 215–224.

Frankland, A. and Cohen, L. (1999) Working with recovered memories. *The Psychologist,* **12**, 82–83.

Freeling, N. R. and Shemberg, K. M. (1970) The alleviation of test anxiety by systematic desensitization. *Behavior Research and Therapy,* **8**, 293–239.

Freeman, N., Lloyd, S. and Sinha, C. (1980) Hide and seek is child's play. *New Scientist,* 304–305.

Freud, S. (1900) *The Interpretation of Dreams* (trans. A. A. Brill, 1913). George Allen & Unwin, London.

Freud, S. (1900) The *Interpretation of Dreams.* Hogarth, London.

Freud, S. (1905) *Three Essays* on *Sexuality.* Hogarth, London.

Freud, S. (1909) Analysis of a phobia in a five-year-old boy. *Collected Papers,* Volume III. Hogarth, London.

Freud, S. (1914) *Psychopathology of Everyday Life.* Benn, London.

Freud, S. (1917) Mourning and melancholia. *Collected Works,* Volume 14. Hogarth, London.

Freud, S. (1923) *The Ego and the Id.* Hogarth, London.

Freud, S. (1924) The dissolution of the Oedipus complex. *Collected Works,* Volume 19. Hogarth, London.

Freud, S. (1933) *New Introductory Lectures* on *Psychoanalysis.* Hogarth, London.

Frith, U. and Happe, E. (1994) Autism: beyond theory *of* mind. In: *Developmental Psychology: A Reader* (ed. Messer, D. and Dockrell, J., 1999). Arnold, London.

Gaertner, S. L, Mann, J. A, Dovidio, J. E, Murrell, A. and Pomare, M. (1990) How does cooperation reduce intergroup bias? *Journal of Personality and Social Psychology,* **59**, 692–704.

Gaertner, S. L, Mann, J. A, Murrell, A. J. and Dovidio, J. E. (1989) Reducing intergroup bias: the benefits of recategorisation. *Journal of Personality and Social Psychology,* **57**, 239–249.

Gaertner, S. L., Rust, M. C., Divisio, J. C., Bachman, B. A. and Anastasio, P. (1993) The contact hypothesis: the role of a common in-group identity on reducing intergroup bias. *Small Business Research.*

Garcia, J. and Koelling, R. A (1966) Relation *of* a cue to consequence in avoidance learning. *Psychonomic Science,* **4**, 123–124.

Garcia, J., Hankins, W. G. and Rusiniak, K. W (1974) Behavioral regulation of the milieu interne in man and rat. *Science,* **185**, 824–831.

Gardner, G. A. (1978) The effects of human subject regulations on data obtained in environmental stressor research. *Journal of Personality and Social Psychology,* **36**, 317–349.

Gay, P. (1989) *The Freud Reader.* Norton, New York.

Gelkopf, M. and Zakai, D. (1991) One more criticism of the multistore model of memory: an experiment on the first-in-first-out (FIFO) principle. *Journal of Psychology,* **125**, 497–499.

Geyer, A. L. J. and Speyrer, J. M. (1997) Transformational leadership and objective performance in banks. *Applied Psychology: An International Review,* **46**.

Gilboa, N. (1996) Elites, lamers, narcs and whores: exploring the computer underground. In: *Wired Women: Gender and New Realities in Cyberspace* (ed. Cherny, L. and Weise, E. R.). Seattle, Seal Press.

Gildea, J. H. and Quirk, T. R. (1977) Assessing the pain experience in children. *Nursing Clinics of North America,* **1**, 631–637.

Glanzer, M. and Cunitz, A. R. (1966) Two storage mechanisms in free recall. *Journal of Verbal Learning and Verbal Behaviour,* **5**, 351–360.

Godden, D. and Baddeley, A. D. (1975) Context dependent memory in two natural environments: On land and under water. *British Journal of Psychology,* **66**, 325–331.

Gomez, L. (1997) *An Introduction to Object Relations.* Free Association Books, London.

Goren, C. C., Sarty, M. and Wu, R. W. K. (1975) Visual following and pattern discrimination of face-like stimuli by newborn infants. *Paediatrics,* **56**, 544–549.

Gorno Tempini, M. L. and Price, C. J. (2001) Identification of famous faces and buildings: a functional neuroimaging study of semantically unique items. *Brain,* **124**, 2087–2097.

Goswami, U. (1998) *Cognition in Children.* Psychology Press, Hove.

Gottesman, I. (1991) *Schizophrenia Genesis: The Origins of Madness.* Freeman, New York.

Green, C. and McCreery, C. (1994) *Lucid Dreaming: The Paradox of Consciousness during Sleep.* Routledge, London.

Griffiths, M. (1999) Internet addiction: fact or fiction. *The Psychologist,* **12**, 246–250.

Groblewski, T. A., Nunez, A. and Gold, R. M. (1980). Quoted in Carlson, N. R. (1996) *Physiology of Behavior.* Allyn & Bacon, Boston.

Gross, R. (1996) *Psychology: The Science of Mind and Behaviour,* 3rd edn. Hodder & Stoughton, London.

Gross, R. (1998) *Key Studies in Psychology,* 3rd edn. Hodder & Stoughton, London.

Gross, R., Humphreys, P. and Petkova, B. (1997) *Challenges in Psychology.* Hodder & Stoughton, London.

Gulevich, G., Dement, W. C. and Johnson, L. (1966) Psychiatric and EEG observations on a case of prolonged (264 hours) wakefulness. *Archives of General Psychiatry,* **15**, 29–35.

Hagell, A. and Newbury, T. (1994) *Young Offenders and the Media.* Policy Studies Institute, London.

Hammen, C. (1997) *Depression.* Psychology Press, Hove.

Hansen, S. (2002) Excessive Internet usage or 'Internet Addiction'? The implications of diagnostic categories for student users. *Journal of Computer Assisted Learning,* **18**(2), 232–236.

Harlow, H. E. (1959) Love in infant rhesus monkeys. *Scientific American,* **200**, 68–74.

Harma, M., Laitinen, J., Partinen, M. and Suvanto, S. (1994a) The effect of four day round trip flights over 10 time zones on the circadian variation of salivary melatonin and cortisol in airline flight attendants. *Ergonomics,* **37**(9), 1479–1489.

Harma, M., Suvanto, S. and Partinen, M. (1994b) The effect of four-day round trip flights over 10 time zones on the sleep-wakefulness of airline flight attendants. *Ergonomics*, **37**(9), 1462–1478.

Harris, R. J. (1973) Answering questions containing marked and unmarked adjectives and adverbs. *Journal of Experimental Psychology*, **97**, 399–402.

Hardey, J. (1998) *Learning and Studying*. Routledge, London.

Hayes, N. (1998) *Foundations of Psychology*, 2nd edn. Nelson, Walton-on-Thames.

Hearne, K. M. T. (1978) *Lucid Dreams: An Electrophysical and Psychological Study*. Unpublished doctoral dissertation, University of Liverpool.

Hebb, D. O. (1949) *The Organization of Behaviour*. Wiley, New York. Henderson, J. (1999) *Remembering and Forgetting*. Routledge, London.

Herbert, M. J. and Harsh, C. M. (1944) Observational learning by cats. *Journal of Comparative Psychology*, **37**, 81–95.

Herman, J. and Roffwarg, H. (1983) Modifying oculomotor activity in awake subjects increases the amplitude of eye movement during REM sleep. *Science*, **220**, 1074–1076.

Herxheimer, A. and Petrie, K. J. (2001) Melatonin for preventing and treating jet lag. *Cochrane Database for Systematic Reviews*, **1**, CD001520.

Heston, L. L. (1966) Psychiatric disorders in foster home reared children of schizophrenic mothers. *British Journal of Psychiatry*, **112**, 819–825.

Hetherington, A. W. and Ranson, S. W. (1939) Experimental hypothalamohypophyseal obesity in the rat. *Proceedings of the Society for Experimental Biology and Medicine*, **41**, 465–466.

Hettema, J. M., Annas, P., Neale, M. C., Kendler, K. S. and Fredrikson, M. (2003) A twin study of the genetics of fear conditioning. *Archives of General Psychiatry*, **60**(7), 702–708.

Hobson, J. A. (1988) *The Dreaming Brain*. Penguin, London.

Hofling, K. C., Brotzman, E., Dalrymple, S., Graves, N. and Pierce, C. M. (1966) An experimental study in the nurse-physician relationship. *Journal of Nervous and Mental Disorders*, **143**, 171–180.

Hogan, R. A. (1968) The implosive technique. *Behavior Research and Theory*, **6**, 423–431.

Holliday, R. E. (2003) The effect of a prior cognitive interview on children's acceptance of misinformation. *Applied Cognitive Psychology*, **17**, 443–457.

Holm-Hadulla, R., Kiefer, L. and Sessar, W. (1997) Effectiveness of psychoanalytically founded brief and dynamic psychotherapy. *Psychotherapy and Psychosomatic Medicine*, **47**(8), 271–278.

Horne, J. A. and Minard, A. (1985) Sleep and sleepiness following a behaviourally 'active' day. *Ergonomics*, **28**, 567–575.

Horner, S. L. (2000) The effects of observational learning on pre-schoolers' book-related behaviors and alphabet knowledge. *Child Study Journal*, **31**, 1–11.

House, R. J., Spangler, W. D. and Woycke, J. (1991) Personality and charisma in the US presidency: a psychological theory of leader effectiveness. *Administrative Science Quarterly*, **36**, 364–396.

Hunter, C. E. and Ross, M. W. (1991) Determinants of health-care workers' attitudes towards people with AIDS. *Journal of Applied Social Psychology*, **21**, 947–956.

Hurley, A. and Whelan, E. G. (1988) Cognitive development and children's perception of pain. *Pediatric Nursing*, **14**(1), 21–24.

Huston, A. C. and Wright, J. C. (1998) Mass media and children's development. In: *Handbook of Child Psychology: Volume 4. Child Psychology in Practice* (ed. Damon W.). Wiley, New York.

Illnerova, H., Buresova, M., Nedvidkova, J. and Dvorakova, M. (1993) Maintenance of a circadian phase adjustment of the human melatonin rhythm following artificial long days. *Brain Research*, **626**(1–2), 322–326.

Inagaki, H., Meguro, K., Shimada, M., Ishizaki, J., Okuzumi, H. and Yamadori, A. (2002) Discrepancy between mental rotation and perspective–taking abilities in normal aging assessed by Piaget's three-mountain task. *Journal of Clinical and Experimental Neuropsychology*, **24**, 18–25.

Inhelder, B. and Piaget, J. (1958) *The Growth of Logical Thinking from Childhood to Adolescence*. Routledge & Kegan Paul, London.

Jacobs, M. (1992) *Sigmund Freud*. Sage, London.

James-Gordon, Y. and Bal, J. (2001) Learning style preferences of engineers in automotive design. *Journal of Workplace Learning*, **13**, 239–245.

Jarvis, C. (2001) School is Hell: gendered fears in teenage horror. *Educational Studies*, **27**, 257–267.

Jarvis, M. (2000) Teaching psychodynamic psychology: from discourse analysis towards a model of reflective practice. *Psychology Teaching*, **8**, 13–21.

Jarvis, M. (2003a) *Psychodynamic Psychology: Classic Theory and Contemporary Research*. Thomson, London.

Jarvis, M. (2003b) Buffy the vampire slayer and psychoanalysis. *Psychology Review*, **10**, 1–5.

Jilge, B. (1991) Restricted feeding: a nonphotic *zeitgeber* in the rabbit. *Physiology & Behavior*, **51**, 157–166.

Jones, E. (1951) *The Life and Works of Sigmund Freud*. Hogarth, London.

Jung, C. G. (1923) *Psychological Types*. Harcourt Brace & Co., New York.

Kagan, J., Kearsley, R. B. and Zelazo, P. R. (1978) *Infancy: Its Place in Human Development*. Harvard University Press, Cambridge MA.

Kahn, S., Zimmerman, G., Csikszentmihalyi, M. and Getzels, J. W. (1985) Relations between identity in young adulthood and intimacy at midlife. *Journal of Personality and Social Psychology*, **49**, 1316–1322.

Kassin, S. M. and Kiechel, K. L. (1996) The social psychology of false confessions: compliance, internalization, and confabulation. *Psychological Science*, **7**(3), 122–128.

Katz, J. (1997) The digital citizen. *Wired*, December, 68–82, 274–275.

Keel, M., Slaton, D. B. and Blackhurst, A. E. (2001) Acquisition of content area vocabulary for students with learning difficulties. *Education and Training of Children*, **24**, 46–71.

Kelly, C. and Breinlinger, S. (1996) *The Social Psychology of Collective Action: Identity, Injustice and Gender*. Taylor & Francis, London.

Kessler, R. C. and Magee, W. J. (1993) Childhood adversities and adult depression: basic patterns of association in a US national survey. *Psychological Medicine*, **23**, 679–690.

Kiesler, S., Siegel, J. and McGuire, T. W. (1984) Social-psychological aspects of computer-mediated interaction. *American Psychologist*, **39**, 1123–1134.

Kippin, T. E. (2000) Olfactory-conditioned ejaculatory preference in the male rat: implications for the role of learning in sexual partner preferences. *Dissertation Abstracts International: Section B: The Sciences and Engineering*, **61**(3–B), 1678.

Klimesch, W., Doppelmayr, M., Schimke, H. and Ripper, B. (1997) Theta synchronisation and alpha desynchronisation in a memory task. *Psychophysiology*, **34**, 169–176.

Koba, Y. and Tanida, H. (1999) How do miniature pigs discriminate between people? The effect of exchanging cues between a non–handler and their familiar handler on discrimination. *Applied–Animal–Behaviour–Science*, **61**(3), 239–252.

Koehler, T., Thiede, G. and Thoens, M. (2002) Long and short-term forgetting of word associations. An experimental study of the Freudian concepts of resistance and repression. *Zeitschrift fuer Klinische Psychologie, Psychiatrie und Psychotherapie*, **50**, 328–333.

Koenkhen, G., Milne, R., Memon, A. and Bull, R. (1999) The cognitive interview: a meta-analysis. *Psychology, Crime and Law*, **5**, 3–27.

Koorengevel, K. M., Beersma, D. G. M., Den Boer, J. A. and Van den Hoofdakker, R. H. (2002) A forced desynchrony study of circadian pacemaker characteristics in seasonal affective disorder. *Journal of Biological Rhythms*, **17**(5), 463–475.

Koorengevel, K. M., Beersma, D. G. M., Den Boer, J. A. and Van den Hoofdakker, R. H.(2003) Mood regulation in seasonal affective disorder patients and healthy controls studied in forced desynchrony. *Psychiatry Research*, **117**(1), 57–74.

Koulack, D. and Goodenough, D. R. (1976) Dream recall and dream failure. *Psychological Bulletin*, **83**, 975–984.

Krackow, A. and Blass, T. (1995) When nurses obey or defy inappropriate physician orders: atributional differences. *Journal of Social Behaviour & Personality*, **10**, 585–594.

Kramarski, B. and Mevarech, Z. R. (1997) Cognitive-metacognitive training within a problem-solving based Logo environment. *British Journal of Educational Psychology*, **67**(4), 425–446.

Krane, V. (1998) Lesbians in sport. *Proceedings of the BPS Annual Conference*, **6**(2), 109.

Kubinyi, E., Topal, J., Miklosi, A. and Csanyi, V. (2003) Dogs (*Canis familiaris*) learn from their owners' via observation in a manipulation task. *Journal of Comparative Psychology*, **117**(2), 156–165.

Kuczaj, S. (ed.) (1982) *Language Development: Volume 1, Syntax and Semantics.* Erlbaum, Hillsdale NJ.

La Berge, S. P., Nagel, L. E., Dement, W. C. and Zarcone, V. P. (1981) Lucid dreaming verified by volitional communication during REM sleep. *Perceptual and Motor Skills*, **52**, 727–732.

La Berge, S. (1985) *Lucid Dreaming.* Ballantine Books, New York.

Lacan, J. (1966) Function et champ de la parole et du language en psychoanalyse. *Ecrits*, Seuil, Paris.

Latane, B. and Bourgeois, M. J. (1996) Experimental evidence for dynamic social impact: the emergence of subcultures in electronic groups. *Journal of Communication*, **46**(4), 35–47.

Lavie, P. (1996) *The Enchanted World of Sleep.* Yale University Press, New Haven.

Lee, V. and Das Gupta, P. (1995) *Children's Cognitive and Language Development.* Blackwell, Oxford.

Lemma, A. (1996) *Introduction to Psychopathology.* Sage, London.

Lemma-Wright, A. (1995) *Invitation to Psychodynamic Psychology.* Whurr, London.

Leon, H. M. (2001) Why we love the monsters: how Anita Blake and Buffy the vampire slayer wound up dating the enemy. *Slayage: the Online Journal of Buffy Studies*, **1**, n.p.

Leslie, A. (1994) ToMM, ToBy and agency: core architecture and domain specificity. In: Hirschfield, L. and Gelman, S. (eds) *Mapping the Mind: Domain Specificity in Cognition and Culture.* Cambridge University Press, Cambridge.

Leslie, J. C. and O'Reilly, M. E. (1999) *Behaviour Analysis: Foundations and Applications to Psychology.* Harwood Academic Publishers, Amsterdam.

Li, C. N., Nuttall, R. L. and Zhao, S. (1999) A test of the Piagetian water-level task with Chinese students. *Journal of Genetic Psychology,* **160**, 369–380.

Lindsay, R. C. L., Lea, J. A., Nosworthy, G. J., Fulford, J. A., Hector, J., LeVan, V. and Seabrook, C. (1991) Biased lineups: sequential presentation reduces the problem. *Journal of Applied Psychology,* **76**, 741–745.

Linton, M. (1982) Transformations of memory in everyday life. In: Neisser, U. (ed.) *Memory Observed: Remembering in Natural Contexts.* W. H. Freeman & Co., San Francisco.

Littleton, K. (1995) Children and computers. In: *Influencing Children's Development* (eds Bancroft, D. and Carr, R.). Open University, Milton Keynes.

Loehlin, J. C. (1992) *Genes and Environment in Personality Development.* Sage, Newbury Park.

Loftus, E. E. (1979) *Eyewitness Testimony.* Harvard University Press, Cambridge MA.

Loftus, E. E. (1983) Whose shadow is crooked. *American Psychologist,* **38**, 576–577.

Loftus, E. E. (1986) Ten years in the life of an expert witness. *Law and Human Behaviour,* **10**, 241–263.

Loftus, E. E., Carry, M., Manning, C. O. and Sherman, S. (1996) Imagination inflation: imagining a childhood event inflates confidence that it occurred. *Psychonomic Bulletin and Review,* **3**(2), 208–214.

Loftus, E. E and Marburger, W. (1983) Since the eruption of Mount St Helens has anyone beaten you up? Improving the accuracy of retrospective reports with landmark events. *Memory and Cognition,* **11**, 114–120.

Loftus, E. E, Miller, D. G. and Burns, H. J. (1978) Semantic integration of verbal information into a visual memory. *Journal of Experimental Psychology: Human Learning and Memory,* **4**(1), 19–31.

Loftus, E. E. and Palmer, J. C. (1974) Reconstruction of automobile destruction: an example of the interaction between language and memory. *Journal of Verbal Learning and Verbal Behaviour,* **13**, 585–589.

Loftus, E. E. and Pickrell, J. E. (1995) The formation of false memories. *Psychiatric Annals,* **25**, 720–725.

Loftus, E. E. and Zaani, G. (1975) Eyewitness testimony: The influence of the wording of a question. *Bulletin of the Psychonomic Society,* **5**, 86–88.

Loftus, G. (1974) Reconstructing memory: the incredible eyewitness. *Psychology Today,* December, 116–119.

Lou, Y., Abrami, P. C. and D'Apollonia, S. (2001) Small group and individual learning with technology: a meta-analysis. *Review of Educational Research,* **71**, 449–521.

Luce, G. G. and Segal, J. (1966) *Sleep.* Coward-McCann, New York.

Luria, A. R. (1968) *The Mind of a Mnemonist.* Basic Books, New York.

Luria, A. R. and Yudovich, F. I. (1971) *Speech and the Development of Mental Processes in the Child.* Penguin, Harmondsworth.

Maguire, E. A., Frackowiak, R. S. J. and Frith, C. D. (1997) Recalling routes around London: activation of the right hippocampus in taxi drivers. *Journal of Neuroscience,* **17**, 7103.

Mahlios, M. C. (2001) matching teaching methods to learning styles. In: *Children and Stress* (eds Stanford, B. H. and Yamamoto, K.). Association for Childhood Education International, Olney.

Main, M. (1996) Introduction to the special section on attachment and psychopathology: 2. Overview of the field of attachment. *Journal of Counselling and Clinical Psychology*, **64**, 237–243.

Malan, D. (1995) *Individual Psychotherapy and the Science of Psychodynamics*. Butterworth-Heinemann, London.

Maltby, J. and Price, J. (1999) Conservatism and defence style. *Journal of Genetic Psychology*, **160**, 389–396.

Manstead, A. R. and McCulloch, C. (1981) Sex-role stereotyping in British television advertisements. *British Journal of Social Psychology*, **20**, 171–180.

Maquet, P. et al. (1997) from the *Journal of Neuroscience*, **17**, 2807. Reported in Motluk, A (1997) Emotions need forty winks. *New Scientist*, 10 May, 20.

Marcia, J. E. (1993) The relational roots of identity. In: Kroger, J. (ed.) *Discussions on Ego Identity*. Lawrence Erlbaum, Hillsdale NJ.

Marks, I. M. (1987) *Fears, Phobias and Rituals*. Oxford University Press, New York.

Marks, I. M. and Rachman, S. J. (1978) Interim report to the Medical Research Council.

Martin, G. N. (1998) Human electroencephalographic (EEG) response to olfactory stimulation: two experiments using the aroma of food. *International Journal of Psychophysiology*, **30**, 287–302.

Massie, H. and Szeinberg, N. (2002) The relationship between mothering in infancy, childhood experience and adult mental health. *International Journal of Psychoanalysis*, **83**, 35–55.

Masur, E. E. (1995) Infants' early verbal imitation and their later lexical development. *Merrill-Palmer Quarterly*, **41**, 286–306.

Matute, H. (1996) Illusion of control: detecting response–outcome independence in analytic but not in naturalistic conditions. *Psychological Science*, **7**, 289–293.

Mayer, J. D., Gayle, M., Meehan, M. E. and Haarman, A. (1990) Toward better specification of the mood-congruency effect in recall. *Journal of Experimental Social Psychology*, **26**, 465–480.

Mayo, E. (1933) *The Human Problems of an Industrial Civilisation*. Macmillan, New York.

McAdams, D. P., Diamond, A. and St Aubin, A. (1997) Stories of commitment: the psychosocial construction of generative lives. *Journal of Personality & Social Psychology*, **72**, 678–694.

McCafferey, M. (1972) *Nursing Management of the Patient with Pain*. Lippincott, Philadelphia.

McCarthy, G. (1999) Attachment style and adult love relationships and friendships: a study of a group of women at risk of experiencing relationship difficulties. *British Journal of Medical Psychology*, **72**, 305–321.

McGarrigle, J. and Donaldson, M. (1974) Conservation accidents. *Cognition*, **3**, 341–350.

McIlveen, R. and Gross, R. (1998) *Biopsychology*. Hodder & Stoughton, London.

McKenna, K. Y. A. and Bargh, J. A. (1998) Coming out in the age of the Internet: identity demarginalisation through virtual group participation. *Journal of Personality and Social Psychology*, **75**(3), 681–694.

McKnight, J. and Sutton, J. (1994) *Social Psychology*. Prentice-Hall, Sydney.

Meddis, R. (1977) *The Sleep Instinct.* Routledge & Kegan Paul, London.

McVey, C., McKechnie, K., Thomson, K. and Watt, S. (2003) Group dynamics: the effects of a bipartite selection on social interaction of castaways on a Scottish island. *Proceedings of the British Psychological Society,* **11**, 4.

Memon, A. (1998) Recovered memories: psychological issues and legal questions. In: *Psychology and Law, Truthfulness, Accuracy and Credibility* (ed. Memon, A. Vrij, A. and Bull, R). McGraw-Hill, London.

Memon, A., Vrij, A. and Bull, R. (eds) (1998) *Psychology and Law, Truthfulness, Accuracy and Credibility.* McGraw-Hill, London.

Memon, A. and Wright, D. B. (1999) Eyewitness testimony and the Oklahoma bombing. *The Psychologist,* **12**(6), 292–295.

Messer, D. and Millar, S. (eds) (1999) *Exploring Developmental Psychology.* Arnold, London.

Mevarech, Z., Silber, O. and Fine, D. (1991) Learning with computers in small groups: cognitive and affective outcomes. *Journal of Educational Computing Research,* **7**(2), 233–243.

Michel, S., Geusz, M. E., Zaritsky, J. J. and Block, G. D. (1993) Circadian rhythms in membrane conductance expressed in isolated neurons. *Science,* **259**, 239–241.

Mickelson, K. D. (1997) Seeking social support: parents in electronic support groups. In: Kiesler, S. (ed.), *Culture of the Internet.* Lawrence Erlbaum, Mahwah NJ.

Milavsky, J. R., Kessler, R. C., Stripp, H. and Rubens, W. S. (1982) *Television Aggression: A Panel Study.* Academic Press, New York.

Miles, L. E., Raynal, D. M. and Wilson, M. A (1977) Blind man living in normal society has circadian rhythm of 24. 9 hours. *Science,* **198**, 421–423.

Milgram, S. (1963) Behavioural study of obedience. *Journal of Abnormal and Social Psychology,* **67**, 371–378.

Milgram, S. (1974) *Obedience to Authority.* Harper & Row, New York.

Miller, G. A. (1956) The magical number seven, plus or minus two: some limits on our capacity for processing information. *Psychological Review,* **63**, 81–97.

Mineka, S. and Cook, M. (1988) Social learning and the acquisition of fear in monkeys. In: Zentall, T. R. and Galef, B. G., Jr (eds), *Social Learning Psychological and Biological Perspectives.* Lawrence Erlbaum, Hillsdale NJ.

Mistleberger, R. E. (1991) Scheduled daily exercise of feeding alters the phase of photic entrainment in Syrian hamsters. *Physiology & Behavior,* **50**, 1257–1260.

Mitler, M. (1988) Catastropes, sleep and public policy: consensus report. *Sleep,* **11**, 100–109.

Molnos, A. (1995) A *Question of Time.* Karnac, London.

Monk, T. H. and Aplin, L. C. (1980) Spring and autumn daylight saving time changes: studies of adjustment in sleep timings, mood and efficiency. *Ergonomics,* **23**, 167–178.

Moore-Ede, M. (1993) We have ways of keeping you awake. *New Scientist,* 13 November, 30–35.

Morris, P. E., Gruneberg, M. M., Sykes, R. N. and Merrick, A. (1981) Football knowledge and the acquisition of new results. *British Journal of Psychology,* **72**, 479–483.

Moss, K. (1989) Performing the light-switch task in lucid dreams: a case study. *Journal of Mental Imagery,* **13**, 135–137.

Mrosovsky, N. (1988) Phase response curves for social entrainment. *Journal of Comparative Physiology,* **162**, 35–46.

Mukhametov, L. M., Supin, A. Y. and Polyakova, L. G. (1977) Interhemispheric asymmetry of the encephalographic sleep patterns in dolphins. *Brain Research*, **134**, 581–584.

Muller, D. J., Harris, P. and Wattley, L. (1986) *Nursing Children: Psychology, Research and Practice*. Harper & Row, London.

Myers, L. B. and Brewin, C. R. (1994) Recall of early experience and the repressive coping style. *Journal of Abnormal Psychology*, **103**(2), 288–292.

Mystkowski, J. L., Mineka, S., Vernon, L. L. and Zinbarg, R. E. (2003) Changes in caffeine states enhance return of fear in spider phobia. *Journal of Consulting and Clinical Psychology*, **71**, 243–250.

Neisser, U. and Harsch, N. (1992) Phantom flashbulbs: false recollections of hearing the news about Challenger. In: *Affect and Accuracy in Recall: Studies of 'Flashbulb Memories'* (ed. Winograd, E. and Neisser, U.). Cambridge University Press, New York.

Nelson, K. (1973) Structure and strategy in learning to talk. *Monographs of the Society for Research in Child Development*, **38**(1–2, serial no. 149).

Nichols, J. D. (1996) Cooperative learning: a motivational tool to enhance student persistence, self–regulation, and efforts to please teachers and parents. *Educational Research and Evaluation*, **2**(3), 246–260.

Nicol, C. J. and Pope, S. J. (1999) The effects of demonstrator social status and prior foraging success on social learning in laying hens. *Animal Behaviour*, **57**, 163–171.

Nordhielm, C. L. (1994) A levels of processing model of advertising repetition effects. In: *Persuasive imagery: a consumer response perspective* (ed. Scott, L. M. and Batra, R.). Lawrence Erlbaum, Mahwah NJ.

Nyberg, L. (2002) Levels of processing: a view from functional brain imaging. *Memory*, **10**, 345–348.

Ohman, A., Fredrikson, M., Hugdahl, K. and Rimmo, P. (1976) The premise of equipotentiality in human classical conditioning: conditioned electrodermal responses to potentially phobic stimuli. *Journal of Experimental Psychology: General*, **105**, 313–317.

Oley, N. (2002) Extra credit and peer tutoring: impact on the quality of writing in introductory psychology in an open admissions college. In: *Handbook for Teaching Introductory Psychology*, Vol. 3 (ed. Griggs, R. A.). Lawrence Erlbaum, Mahwah NJ.

Olson, M. A. and Fazio, R. H. (2001) Implicit attitude formation through classical conditioning. *Psychological Science*, **12**(5), 413–417.

Olson, J. M., Vernon, P. A., Harris, J. A. and Jang, K. L. (2001) The heritability of attitudes: a study of twins. *Journal of Personality and Social Psychology*, **80**(6), 845–860.

O'Neill, R. M., Greenberg, R. P. and Fisher, S. (1992) Humour and anality. *Humour: International Journal of Humour Research*, **5**, 283–291.

Onyskiw, J. E. and Hayduk, L. A. (2001) Process underlying adjustment in families characterised by physical aggression. *Family Relations: Interdisciplinary Journal of Applied Family Studies*, **50**, 376–385.

Parker, I. (1999) Tracing therapeutic discourse in material culture. *British Journal of Medical Psychology*, **72**, 577–589.

Pawlak, C. (2002) Correlates of Internet use and addiction in adolescents. *Dissertation Abstracts International Section A: Humanities and Social Sciences*, **63**(5–A), 1727.

Perner, J., Stummer, S., Sprung, M. and Doherty, M. (2002) Theory of mind finds its Piagetian perspective: why alternative naming comes with understanding belief. *Cognitive Development*, **17**, 1451–1472.

Peters, K. and Richards, P. (1998) 'Why we fight': Voices of youth combatants in Sierra Leone. *Africa*, **68**, 183–210.

Pezdek, K. (2002) Memory for the terrorists' attack on New York 9/11/01. Paper delivered at the Tsukuba International Conference on Memory, March 2002.

Prior, S. M. and Welling, K. A. (2001) 'Read in your head.' A Vygotskian analysis of the transition from oral to silent reading. *Reading Psychology*, **22**, 1–15.

Provencio, I. et al (2000) A novel human ops in in the inner retina. *Journal of Neuroscience*, **20**, 600.

Reber, R., Perrig, W. J., Flammer, A. and Walter, D. (1994) Levels of processing and memory for emotional words. *Schweizerische Zeitschrift fuer Psychologie*, **53**, 78–85.

Riding, R. and Rayner, S. (1998) *Cognitive Styles and Learning Strategies*. Fulton, London.

Riniolo, T. C., Koledin, M., Drakulic, G. M. and Payne, R. A. (2003) An archival study of eyewitness memory of the Titanic's final plunge. *Journal of General Psychology*, **130**, 89–95.

Roazzi, A. and Bryant, P. (1998) The effect of symmetrical and asymmetrical social interaction on children as logical inference. *British Journal of Developmental Psychology*, **16**, 175–181.

Rotter, J. B. (1966) Generalized expectations for internal versus external control of reinforcement. *Physiological Monographs: General and Applied*, **80**(1), 1–28.

Rubinstein, G. (1995) Right-wing authoritarianism, political affiliation, religiosity and their relation to psychological androgyny. *Sex Roles*, **33**, 569–586.

Rybarczyk, P., Rushen, J. and De Passile, A. M. (2003) Recognition of people by dairy calves using colour of clothing. *Applied Animal Behaviour Science*, **81**(4), 307–319.

Salois, K. A. N. (1999) A comparative study of the Wechsler Intelligence Scale for children 3rd edition (WISC III) test performance: Northern Cheyenne and Blackfeet Reservation Indian children with the standardisation sample. *Dissertation Abstracts International* **60**, 1909.

Sandell, R. (1999) Long-term findings of the Stockholm Outcome of Psychotherapy and Psychoanalysis Project (STOPP). Paper presented at the Psychoanalytic long-term treatments: a challenge for clinical and empirical research in psychoanalysis meeting, Hamburg.

Schaie, K. W. and Willis, S. L. (1996) *Adult Development and Ageing*. HarperCollins, New York.

Schatzman, M., Worsely, A. and Fenwick, P. (1988) Correspondence during lucid dreams between dreamed and actual events. In: *Conscious Mind, Sleeping Brain: Perspectives on Lucid Dreaming* (ed. Gackenbach, J. I. and La Berge, S.). Plenum, New York.

Schlozman, S. C. (2000) Vampires and those who slay them: using the television programme Buffy the vampire slayer in adolescent therapy and psychodynamic education. *Academic Psychiatry*, **24**, 49–54.

Schmolck, H., Buffalo, E. A. and Squire, L. R. (2000) Memory distortions develop over time: recollections of the OJ Simpson train verdict after 15 and 32 months. *Psychological Science*, **11**, 39–45.

Schneidermann, N., Fuentes, I. and Gormezano, I. (1962) Acquisition and extinction of the classically conditioned eyelid response in the albino rabbit. *Science*, **136**, 650–652.

Schultz, N. V. (1971) How children perceive pain. *Nursing Outlook*, **3**(6), 670–673.

Searle, A. (1999) *Introducing Research and Data in Psychology*. Routledge, London.

Seitz, K. and Schumann-Hengsteler, R. (2000) Mental multiplication and working memory. *European Journal of Cognitive Psychology*, **12**, 552–570.

Seo, Y., Matsumoto, K., Park, Y., Shinkoda, H. and Noh, T. (2000) The relationship between sleep and shift system, age and chronotype in shift workers. *Biological Rhythm Research*, **31**(5) 559–579.

Shapiro, C. M., Catteral, J. R., Warren, P., Oswald, I., Trinder, J., Paxton, S. and East, B. W. (1986) Lean body mass and non-rapid eye movement sleep. *British Medical Bulletin*, **294**, 22.

Sharkey, K. M., Foggm, L. and Eastman, C. I. (2001) Effects of melatonin administration on daytime sleep after simulated night shift work. *Journal of Sleep Research*, **10**(3), 181–192.

Sharkey, K. M. and Eastman, C. I. (2002) Melatonin phase shifts human circadian rhythms in a placebo-simulated night-work study. *American Journal of Physiological Regulatory, Integrative and Comparative Physiology*, **282**(2), R454–63.

Sherman, L. W. (1992) The influence of criminology on criminal law: evaluating arrests for misdemeanour domestic violence. *Journal of Criminal Law and Criminology*, **83**, 1–45.

Skellington, R. (1995) *Race in Britain Today*, 2nd edn. Sage, London.

Skinner, B. E. (1938) *The Behavior of Organisms.* Appleton-Century Crofts, New York.

Skinner, B. E. (1948) Superstition in the pigeon. *Journal of Experimental Psychology*, **38**, 168–172.

Skinner, B. E. (1957) *Verbal Behavior.* Prentice-Hall, New York.

Smith, C. (1995) Sleep states and memory processes. *Behavioral and Brain Research*, **69**(1–2), 137–145.

Smith, C. (1996) Sleep states, memory processes and synaptic plasticity. *Behavioral and Brain Research*, **78**(1), 49–56.

Smith, P. K., Cowie, H. and Blades, M. (1998) *Understanding Children's Development.* Blackwell, London.

Smith, S. M. and Woody, P. C. (2000) Interactive effect of multimedia instruction and learning styles. *Teaching of Psychology*, **27**, 220–223.

Snyder, M. and Uranowitz, S. W. (1978) Reconstructing the past: some cognitive consequences of person perception. *Journal of Personality and Social Psychology*, **36**, 941–950.

Snyder, R. F. (2000) The relationship between learning styles/multiple intelligences and academic achievement of high-school students. *High School Journal*, **83**, 11–20.

Solms, M. (2000) Freudian dream theory today. *The Psychologist*, **13**, 618–619.

Steier, A. J. and Lehman, E. B. (2000) An observational measure of children's attachments to soft objects. *Child Study Journal*, **30**, 253–271.

Stephan, E. K. and Zucker, I. (1972) Circadian rhythms in drinking behaviour and locomotor activity in rats are eliminated by hypo thalamic lesion. *Proceedings of the National Academy of Science*, **69**, 1583–1586.

Sternberg, S. (1966) High speed scanning in human memory. *Science*, **153**, 652–654.

Stevens, R. (1983) *Freud and Psychoanalysis.* Open University Press, Milton Keynes.

Stiles, R. (1990) Is winter the saddest time of year? *New Scientist*, **1740**, 23.

Stirling, J. (1999) *Cortical Functions.* Routledge, London.

Straub, R. E., Maclean, C. J., O'Neil, F. A., Burke, J., Murphy, B., Duke, E., Shinkwin, R., Webb, R. T., Zhang, J., Walsh, D. and Kendler, K. S. (1995) A potential vulnerability locus for schizophrenia on chromosome 6p24–22: evidence for genetic heterogeneity. *Nature Genetics*, **11**, 28–93.

Stroop, J. R. (1935) Studies of interference in serial verbal reactions. *Journal of Experimental Psychology*, **18**(6), 643–662.

Subbotsky, E. (2000) Causal reasoning and behaviour in children and adults in a technologically advanced society: are we still prepared to believe in animism? In: *Children's Reasoning and the Mind* (ed. Mitchell, P. and Riggs, K. J.). Taylor & Francis, London.

Suler, J. (1996) Why is this thing eating my life? Computer and cyberspace addition at the 'Palace'. http://wwwl. rider. edu/–suler/psycyber/eatlife. html.

Suvanto, S., Harma, M., Ilmarinen, J. and Partinen, M. (1993) Effects of 10 hour time zones changes on female flight attendants' circadian rhythms of body temperature, alertness and visual search. *Ergonomics*, **36**(6), 613–625.

Symons, D. K. and Clark, S. E. (2000) A longitudinal study of mother-child relationships and theory of mind in the preschool period. *Social Development*, **9**, 3–23.

Tajfel, H. and Turner, J. C. (1979) An integrative theory of intergroup conflict. In: *The Social Psychology of Intergroup Relations* (ed. Austin, W. G. and Worchel, S. Cambridge University Press, Cambridge MA.

Tajfel, H. (1970) Experiments in intergroup discrimination. *Scientific American*, **223**, 96–102.

Tarnow, E. (2000) Self-destructive obedience in the airplane cockpit and the concept of obedience optimisation. In Blass, T. (ed.) *Obedience to Authority*. Lawrence Erlbaum, Mahwah.

Tauber, E. S., Rofas-Ramire, J. and Hernandez-Peon, R. (1968) Electrophysiological and behavioural correlates of wakefulness and sleep in the lizard Ctenosaura pectinata. *Electroencephalograpy and Clinical Neurophysiology*, **24**, 424–433.

Terman, M., Amira, L., Terman, J. S. and Ross, D. C. (1996) Predictors of response and nonresponse to light treatment for winter depression. *American Journal of Psychiatry*, **153**(11), 1423–1429.

Thompson, R. F. (2000) *The Brain: A Neuroscience Primer*. Worth, New York.

Thorndike, E. L. (1911) *Animal Intelligence: Experimental Studies*. Macmillan, New York.

Thorndike, E. L. and Lorge, I. (1944) *The Teacher's Word Book of 30,000 Words*. Teacher's College, Columbia University, New York.

Tienari, P. (1992) Implications of adoption studies on schizophrenia. *British Journal of Psychiatry*, **161**, 52–58.

Tilley, A. J. and Empson, J. A. C. (1978) REM sleep and memory consolidation. *Biological Psychology*, **6**, 293–300.

Torrey, E., Fuller, E., Edward, H., Bracha, H. and Bowler, A. E. (1994) Prenatal origins of schizophrenia in a subgroup of discordant monozygotic twins. *Schizophrenia Bulletin*, **20**, 423–432.

Totterdell, P. (1995) Effects of depressed affect on diurnal and ultradian variations in mood in a healthy sample. *Chronobiology International*, **12**(4), 278–289.

Troseth, G. L. (2003) Two-year-old children learn to use video as a source of information. *Developmental Psychology*, **39**(1), 140–150.

Tulving, E. (1972) Episodic and semantic memory. In: Tulving, E. and Donaldson, W (eds) *Organisation of Memory*. Academic Press, London.

Tulving, E. (1974) Cue-dependent forgetting. *American Scientist*, **62**, 74–82.

Tulving, E. (1983) *Elements of Episodic Memory*. Oxford University Press, Oxford.

Tulving, E. (1985) How many memory systems are there? *American Psychologist*, **40**, 385–398.

Tulving, E. and Pearlstone, Z. (1966) Availability versus accessibility of information in memory for words. *Journal of Verbal Learning and Verbal Behaviour,* **5**, 381–391.

Twycross, A. (1998) Children's cognitive level and perception of pain. *Professional Nurse,* **14**(1), 35–37.

Tylim, I. (1998) The vampire game. *Psychoanalytic Inquiry,* **18**, 281–290.

Vidal-Vazquez, M. A. and Clemente–Diaz, M. (2000) The attraction of media violence. *PSICO,* **31**(2), 49–80.

Vrij, A. (1998) Psychological factors in eyewitness testimony. In: *Psychology and Law, Truthfulness, Accuracy and Credibility* (ed. Memon, A., Vrij, A. and Bull, R.). McGraw-Hill, London.

Wagenaar, W. A. (1986) My memory: a study of autobiographical memory over six years. *Cognitive Psychology,* **18**, 225–252.

Walker, W. R., Vogl, R. J. and Thompson, C. P. (1997) Autobiographical memory: unpleasantness fades faster than pleasantness over time. *Applied Cognitive Psychology,* **11**, 399–413.

Wallace, P. (1999) *The Psychology of the Internet.* Cambridge University Press, Cambridge.

Walther, J. B. (1993) Impression development in computer-mediated interaction. *Western Journal of Communication,* **57**, 381–398.

Watson, J. B. (1924) *Behaviorism.* Norton, New York.

Watson, J. B. and Rayner, R. (1920) Conditioned emotional responses, *Journal of Experimental Psychology,* **3**(1), 1–14.

Waugh, N. C. and Norman, D. (1965) Primary memory. *Psychological Review,* **72**, 89–104.

Webb, W. B. and Cartwright, R. D. (1978) Sleep and dreams. *Annual Review of Psychology,* **29**, 223–252.

Weinrott, M. R., Riggan, M. and Frothingham, S. (1997) Reducing deviant arousal in juvenile sex offenders using vicarious sensitisation. *Journal of Interpersonal Violence,* **12**, 704–728.

Wells, G. L. (1993) What do we know about eyewitness identification? *American Psychologist,* **48**, 553–571.

Wertsch, J. Y. (1991) *Voices of the Mind: A Sociocultural Approach to Mediated Action.* Harvard University Press, Cambridge MA.

Wertsch, J. Y. and Tulviste, P. (1996) L. S. Vygotsky and contemporary developmental psychology. In: *Learning Relationships in the Classroom* (ed. Faulkner, D., Littleton, K. and Woodhead, M.). Routledge, London.

Wetherall, M. (1997) *Identities, Groups and Social Issues.* Open University, Milton Keynes.

Whitbourne, S. K., Zuschlag, M. K., Elliot, L. B. and Waterman, A. S. (1992) Psychosocial development in adulthood: a 22–year sequential study. *Journal of Personality and Social Psychology,* **63**, 260–271.

Whitley, B. E. and Lee, S. E. (2000) The relationship of authoritarianism and related constructs to attitudes toward homosexuality. *Journal of Applied Social Psychology,* **30**, 144–170.

Wilberg, S. (2002) Preschooler's cognitive representations of their homeland. *British Journal of Developmental Psychology,* **20**, 157–170.

Wimmer, H. and Perner, J. (1983) Beliefs about beliefs: representations and constraining function of wrong beliefs in young children's understanding of deception. *Cognition*, **13**, 103–128.

Winnicott, D. W. (1965) *The Family and Individual Development*. Tavistock Publications, London.

Wolpe, J. (1969) Basic principles and practices of behavior therapy of neuroses. *American Journal of Psychiatry*, **125**, 1242–1247.

Wood, D. (1991) *How Children Think and Learn*. Blackwell, Oxford.

Wortman, C. B. and Loftus, E. E. (1985) *Psychology,* 2nd edn. Knopf, New York.

Wright, D. B., Loftus, E. F. and Hall, M. (2001) Now you see it; now you don't: inhibiting recall and recognition of scenes. *Applied Cognitive Psychology*, **15**, 471–482.

Wright, D. B., Self, G. and Justice, C. (2000) Memory conformity: exploring misinformation effects when presented by another person. *British Journal of Psychology*, **91**, 189–202.

Wright, S., Taylor, D. and Moghadden, E. (1990) Responding to membership in a disadvantaged group: from acceptance to collective protest. *Journal of Personality and Social Psychology*, **58**, 994–1003.

Xuanhui, L. and Gonggu, Y. (2001) Internet addiction disorder, online behavior and personality. *Chinese Mental Health Journal*, **15**(4), 281–283.

Young, K. S. (1998) *Caught in the Net: How to Recognise the Signs of Internet Addiction and a Winning Strategy for Recovery*. John Wiley, New York.

Zepelin, H. and Rechtschaffen, A. (1974) Mammalian sleep, longevity and energy metabolism. *Brain, Behaviour and Evolution*, **10**, 425.

index